BUILDING *NEW WORLDS*

Borgo Press Books by DAMIEN BRODERICK

Adrift in the Noösphere: Science Fiction Stories
Building New Worlds, *1946-1959* (with John Boston)
Chained to the Alien: The Best of ASFR: Australian SF Review
    (Second Series) [Editor]
*Climbing Mount Implausible: The Evolution of a Science
    Fiction Writer*
Embarrass My Dog: The Way We Were, the Things We Thought
Ferocious Minds: Polymathy and the New Enlightenment
Human's Burden: A Science Fiction Novel (with Rory Barnes)
I'm Dying Here: A Comedy of Bad Manners (with Rory Barnes)
New Worlds*: Before the New Wave, 1960-1964* (with John
    Boston)
Post Mortal Syndrome: A Science Fiction Novel (with Barbara
    Lamar)
Skiffy and Mimesis: More Best of ASFR: Australian SF Review
    (Second Series) [Editor]
Strange Highways: Reading Science Fantasy, *1950-1967* (with
    John Boston)
*Unleashing the Strange: Twenty-First Century Science Fiction
    Literature*
Warriors of the Tao: The Best of Science Fiction: A Review of
    Speculative Literature [Editor with Van Ikin]
x, y, z, t: Dimensions of Science Fiction
Zones: A Science Fiction Novel (with Rory Barnes)

Borgo Press Books by JOHN BOSTON

Building New Worlds, *1946-1959* (with Damien Broderick)
New Worlds: *Before the New Wave, 1960-1964* (with Damien
    Broderick)
Strange Highways: Reading Science Fantasy, *1950-1967* (with
    Damien Broderick)

BUILDING *NEW WORLDS,* 1946-1959

THE CARNELL ERA, VOLUME ONE

JOHN BOSTON &

DAMIEN BRODERICK

THE BORGO PRESS

MMXIII

Borgo Literary Guides
ISSN 0891-9623
Number Sixteen

BUILDING NEW WORLDS, 1946-1959

FIRST EDITION

Published by Wildside Press LLC

www.wildsidebooks.com

DEDICATION

As always, for Dori and the guys.
J.B.

These books were first aired in more rudimentary form on the Fictionmags Internet discussion group, and benefited greatly from the robust and erudite commentary and correction customary among its members. In particular we thank Fictionmags members Ned Brooks, William G. Contento, Ian Covell, Steve Holland, Frank Hollander, Rich Horton, David Langford, Dennis Lien, Barry Malzberg, Todd Mason, David Pringle, Robert Silverberg, and Phil Stephensen-Payne, as well as David Ketterer, for the encouragement, insight, and information that they respectively provided.

J.B. and D.B.

CONTENTS

INTRODUCTION

by Damien Broderick

John Boston is an occasional amateur science fiction critic of long standing, and attorney (Director of the Prisoners' Rights Project of the New York City Legal Aid Society and co-author of the *Prisoners' Self-Help Litigation Manual*).[1] Perhaps it's not surprising, then, as he once remarked wryly, that he's fond of escape literature.

Several years ago, Boston read through every issue of the classic British science fiction magazine *New Worlds*—sometimes with grim disbelief, sometimes with unexpected pleasure, often with gusts of laughter, always with intent interest. That magazine is best remembered today as the fountainhead of the New Wave of audacious experimental SF in the second half of the 1960s, and beyond, under the great helmsman, Michael Moorcock, and his madcap transgressive associates. But these 141 pioneering issues, from 1946 to 1964, were edited by the magazine's founder, Edward John (Ted, or John) Carnell (1912-72). Not to be confused with the prominent Baptist theologian and apologist of the same name, Ted Carnell was a pillar of the old-style UK SF establishment, but gamely supportive of innovators—most famously, of the brilliant J. G. Ballard, whose first work he nurtured.

Indeed, as Moorcock remarked many decades later: "Ted Carnell always wore sharp suits and I'll swear he had a camel

---

1. See "The Long Road Toward Reform," http://www.wahmee.com/pln_john_boston.pdf (visited 9/9/11).

hair overcoat. He looked like a successful dandified bookie. [He] stood out from the general run of fashion-challenged fans who adopted the universal sports coat and flannels." It was a distinction in style that catches the difference between the generations of old *New Worlds* and new. Moorcock added: "Ted would never be caught dead with patches on the elbows of a sports coat. Charles Platt tells me how disgusted he was when he first met me in Carnell's office and saw that I was wearing Cuban-heeled boots and tight trousers, etc. He didn't feel anyone could be taken seriously who cared that much for fashion. I didn't, of course. I was just wearing what my peers were wearing around Ladbroke Grove in those days."[2]

John Boston, for his own amusement, found himself writing an extensive commentary on those early, foundational years of *New Worlds* and companion magazine *Science Fantasy* and *Science Fiction Adventures*. He posted his ongoing analysis in a long semi-critical series to a closed listserv devoted to enthusiasts of pulp and subsequent popular magazines. The present study, published in three parts (two of them largely focused on *New Worlds*) due to the length of its exacting but entertaining coverage of these 15 years of publication, is an edited and reorganized version of those electronic posts. This volume covers the early years of *New Worlds*, from its precarious birth to the point at which it had become solidly established as the UK's leading SF magazine.

I found Boston's issue-by-issue forensic probing of this history enthralling and amusing, and read it sometimes with shudders and grimaces breaking through, and often with a delighted grin at a neatly turned *bon mot*. Don't expect a dry, modishly theorized academic analysis, nor a rah-rah handclapping celebration of the "Good Old Days." This is a candid and astute reader's response to a magazine that, by today's standards, was often not very good——but one that was immensely

2. Moorcock, letter to the editor, *Relapse*, Spring, 2011, p. 28: http://efanzines.com/Prolapse/Relapse19.pdf (visited 9/9/11).

important in its time, and improved, like the Little Engine (or maybe Starship) That Could. The story of how *New Worlds* got better, achieving and consolidating its position, is an essential piece of the history of the genres of the fantastic in the UK, and indeed the world.

I had the good fortune, as an SF theorist and writer, to read these chapters as they arrived via email. Greatly entertained, often flushed by nostalgia (for this was the literature of my remembered youth), I insisted to John Boston that his work deserved to be read by as many interested people as possible. He was busy on important legal work in defense of those lost in an overburdened US criminal justice (or "justice") system, and had no time for such laborious scutwork. I rapped on his internet door from time to time, insisting that it would be a shame—a crime, even—not to allow this material to be read by the world at large.

At last he buckled, passed me his large files covering all the issues of Carnell's *New Worlds* and the short-lived *Science Fiction Adventures* (some quarter million words), plus another large book's worth of equivalent reading into *Science Fantasy* (my favorite as an adolescent, in colonial Australia). All three volumes of reading and commentary really comprise one large book of some 350,000 words—and I can only recommend that after you enjoy this first volume, you'll hasten to read the other two as well.

§

The prehistory of *New Worlds* is well recorded, especially by SF fan historian Rob Hansen.[3] "Scientific romances" had a

---

3. Rob Hansen has commendably made available online a record of this important transition: http://www.fiawol.org.uk/FanStuff/THEN%20 Archive/NewWorlds/NewWo.htm and much of the background on SF's fan groups and emerging professionalism is recorded by Hansen in his general online history starting at http://www.ansible.co.uk/Then/then_1-1.html (both visited 9/8/11) and detailing people and events, often from letters and

long if patchy history prior to the 20th century, and the names Jules Verne and H.G. Wells are justly famous as the 19th century "fathers of SF"—with Mary Shelley, author of *Frankenstein*, arguably the mother. But commercial mass market science fiction (or "scientifiction") was launched in the USA by Luxembourgian immigrant Hugo Gernsback, an atrocious writer with a zest for wacky ideas (television, for example, and space travel) and a habit of cheating his writers. In August 1926 he brought out *Amazing Stories*, the first commercial genre magazine specializing in SF. Within a year, a teenaged English schoolboy, Walter Gillings (1912-79), found a copy and became obsessed with the idea of publishing a British SF magazine and forming a support group of other enthusiasts. Other proto-fans found each other and formed local groups. Liverpool rocket enthusiasts formed the British Interplanetary Society (BIS) in 1933, which quickly gathered in a number of young men who, a decade or two later, would embody the core of British SF: Arthur C. Clarke (then 16), Eric Frank Russell (an elder statesman at 28), Ted Carnell (21), Bill Temple (19), David McIlwain (then just 12, destined to publish SF as "Charles Eric Maine") and others.

Hansen notes the brief flickering of a weekly boys' paper, *Scoops*, that ran from February to June of 1934, guttering out before it could develop into anything more adult. Meanwhile, amateur magazines devoted to science fiction and the doings of its fans—and hence dubbed "fanzines"—appeared in the UK as well as the USA and elsewhere; the most consequential was *Novae Terrae*. Twenty-nine issues were published by Maurice Hanson and Dennis Jacques between March 1936 and January 1939, then *Novae Terrae* was handed over to the new editor, Ted Carnell, in his late twenties—more or less in time for Hitler's war to put an end to such frivolities. Carnell was able to publish four issues of the fanzine under his de-Latinized title, *New Worlds*. With Britain's declaration of war on Nazi Germany in September, 1939, the BIS and the Science Fiction Association

interviews, from 1927 through to the late 1970s.

perforce disbanded "for the duration."

In 1939, Carnell had met with a journalist, Bill Passingham,[4] who'd interested a company called *The World Says* in his plans to publish science fiction. A scheme to convert *New Worlds* to a professional magazine went as far as acquiring rights to a Robert Heinlein story ("Lost Legacy," which later appeared in *Super Science Stories* as "Lost Legion" and under the correct title in Heinlein's collection, *Assignment In Eternity*). All these plans fell apart when *The World Says* went into liquidation.[5]

The Blitz began in late 1940, with apparently endless swarms of German bombers striking at Britain's less powerful forces. Carnell and Temple, among other SF fans, were called up, Carnell joining the Royal Artillery in September. The technically skilled among the fans, such as Arthur C. Clarke, went off to Signals or in Clarke's case into the development and testing of early radar aircraft landing systems. It was a bitter irony that the rockets to which they were all devoted, the utopian vehicle for space exploration, came crashing down bloodily on London, first as primitive cruise missiles (V1s) and then, toward the end of the war, as von Braun's V2s. Later, these would form the basis of successful US and Soviet efforts to build satellites and crewed spacecraft, yea, even unto the fabled first landing on the Moon. For all that, the murderous V2 wasn't the shape of things to come that SF fans had hoped to see.

§

Science fiction and its devotees were often ridiculed in those days for "that crazy Buck Rogers stuff"—at least, until the

---

4. Passingham was also an SF writer in his own right, having contributed stories with such titles as "Atlantis Returns" and "When London Fell" to the UK magazines *Modern Wonder* and *The Passing Show*. Walter Gillings, "The Way of the Prophet," *Vision of Tomorrow*, May 1970, p. 63.

5. Carnell's own, more detailed account of these events appears in John Carnell, "The Magazine That Nearly Was," *Vision of Tomorrow*, June 1970, pp. 48-49.

rockets fell, and then a few years later when two nuclear bombs evaporated a pair of Japanese cities. But for all the appeal that futuristic and often jejune adventure stories undeniably had for kids (mostly young males), the British writers who went through the furnace of World War Two were not innocent dreamers, not the "anoraks" who are still mocked for their love of gaudy *fantastika*. Rob Hansen quotes a remarkable and chilling letter written in Italy in 1944 by British SF writer and WWII veteran William Temple (using the abbreviation "stf" from Gernsback's "scientifiction"), that makes this utterly clear:

> When we come up against the "hard realities" of life, our stf nonsense is supposed to be knocked out of us.... Actually, there's nothing in that hard, real, outer world that is not enhanced and roselit and made wondrous by the cosmic view....
>
> In the Army, I have grown intimate with all types of people, from miners, labourers, slaughterhouse men to professional soldiers, musicians, college men and boxers. I have watched these men in peril of death, and I have seen them die, not always pleasantly or easily. I have been near enough to death myself more times than I can remember. I have known life at its greatest discomfort in waterlogged foxholes, for many months at Anzio, soaked in the unceasing rain with no hope of drying, hungry, freezing and constantly shelled, machine-gunned, bombed and mortared. In these conditions I have striven to write books and lost them. And rewritten them painfully and lost them again. I have known utter loneliness, and also, the heart-warming comfort of a gathering of my friends. I know what love, marriage, and parenthood are like, and what it is like to be separated from these things year after year, and what it is like to lose a son....
>
> All this sounds a bit melodramatic. I only want to prove that stf is not just a bolthole for people escaping

from life. I have lived a fair amount and stf has lost none of its essential meaning through that experience. To me the imagination is somewhere nearer the heart of things than "reality."[6]

§

During and immediately after the immense disruption of the war, *New Worlds* was shelved until demobbed Carnell was introduced to Stephen Daniel Frances, head of Pendulum Publications Ltd, a believer in science fiction, and initiating writer of a series of violent, racy, fake-American thrillers featuring tough Chicago reporter Hank Janson and published under that pseudonym.[7] *New Worlds* as a true SF magazine made its professional debut in 1946 as a more or less pulp-sized magazine from Pendulum, and a rather unprepossessing one, with appalling cover art. This book, and its companion volume, tell the story of Carnell's magazine from its first timid steps (two issues in 1946, one in 1947, a gap of a year and a half to another two issues in 1949, three in 1950) and then a steady progression: quarterly in 1951, bimonthly in 1952, and monthly from 1955.

New Worlds would maintain its monthly schedule for the rest of Carnell's tenure, with one exception resulting from an industry-wide labor dispute. Over the first two years with monthly issues, 1956-57, *New Worlds* serialized five novels by regular contributors to the magazine, each of which attained book publication (mostly as Ace Doubles, the ground floor of American SF publishing). While none was outstanding, together they illustrated the fact that Carnell had by then developed a

6. This was first published in the Los Angeles SF Society fanzine *Voice of the Imagination* (familiarly, VoM) and is cited by Hansen in http://www.ansible.co.uk/Then/then_1-2.html (visited 9/8/11).

7. Carnell's more detailed account of these events appears in John Carnell, "The Birth of *New Worlds*," *Vision of Tomorrow*, September 1970, pp. 61-63.

group of writers who could provide sufficient copy—meeting a basic professional standard at all lengths—to sustain a monthly magazine without continued resort to heavy use of US reprints. Conversely, it meant that he was now providing a regular visible, and readable, presence for new readers and a reliable enough market to be attractive to potential new writers. *New Worlds'* serials continued to supply both US and UK publishers with novel-length works for the rest of Carnell's editorship, and Carnell interspersed these home-grown works with judiciously selected reprints from American sources that had not found UK magazine publication. These included Philip K. Dick's *Time out of Joint* and Theodore Sturgeon's controversial *Venus Plus X,* but also works by well-known UK writers such as Eric Frank Russell, Charles Eric Maine, and Brian Aldiss that he in effect repatriated for the home audience. During the early 1960s (covered in the companion volume to this one), *New Worlds* continued to nurture the spectacular careers of Brian Aldiss and J. G. Ballard and the solidly impressive career of James White, as well as the more prosaic and in some cases neglected ones of Colin Kapp, Philip E. High, Lee Harding, Robert Presslie, Arthur Sellings, Donald Malcolm, and R.W. Mackelworth. John Carnell had made his indelible and enduring mark on the history of British science fiction.

1: BIRTH AND NEAR-DEATH (1946-47)

As chronicled by literary historian Mike Ashley and others, *New Worlds* made its long-delayed debut in 1946 (after its earlier fanzine incarnation) as a more or less pulp-sized magazine from Pendulum Publications Ltd., 64 pages exclusive of covers, price 2 shillings (2/-), down to 1 shilling and sixpence (1s 6d, or 1/6) for the third issue.[8] The issues are numbered (hereafter indicated in **bold**), but **1** and **2** bear only the year, no month; **3** bears no date at all. *The Science Fiction, Fantasy, & Weird Fiction Magazine Index*, a comprehensive database compiled by Stephen T. Miller and William G. Contento (hereafter Miller/Contento), identifies the dates as July and October 1946 and October 1947.[9]

8. One shilling was 1/20th of a Pound, and 6d or sixpence was half a shilling. In 2012 inflated currency, two shillings in 1946 were worth roughly US $4.50.

9. Bibliographic and historical information not from the magazine itself, and not otherwise attributed, is from *The Science Fiction, Fantasy, & Weird Fiction Magazine Index* by Stephen T. Miller and William G. Contento and Contento's *Index to Science Fiction Anthologies and Collections* (both on CD-ROM from Locus Publications); from Mike Ashley's article on *New Worlds* in *Science Fiction, Fantasy and Weird Fiction Magazines*, edited by Marshall B. Tymn and Ashley (Greenwood Press 1985); from Ashley's recent histories of the SF magazines, *The Time Machines* and *Transformations* (Liverpool University Press, 2000 and 2005); from John Carnell's brief memoir, "The Birth of *New Worlds,*" *Vision of Tomorrow*, September 1970, pp. 61-63; and from Rob Hansen's web site, available online. http://www.fiawol.org.uk/FanStuff/THEN%20Archive/NewWorlds/

In his editorial in **3**, John Carnell says "We apologize most profoundly to all our readers who have been wondering when this issue of *New Worlds* would appear. Probably no magazine issue has been beset by so many obstacles since it went into production, almost all of them in the technical departments. In the main, we were caught by the power cuts and have only just managed to recover." Britain had endured its most severe cold weather of the 20th century, and the postwar electricity supplies were overwhelmed.

The cover presentations of these early issues are pretty cheesy, resembling the winners of an art contest among fifth-graders. The cover of **3** rises perhaps to junior high school level.[10] The first issue's cover, by Bob Wilkin, an artist employed by Pendulum, portrayed a mushroom cloud bulging above an ambivalent background, corporate-utopian on the left and ruined debris on the right, and a nude, bombed-looking, rather plastic pink man of the future in the foreground. Sales of that first issue were terrible—3000 of 15,000 copies were sold—and Carnell, who had not approved, or even seen, the cover until it was completed, later described its execution as "flat and two dimensional, dull and uninspiring." Not surprisingly, then, "One point... I was insistent upon—the second issue, already committed to the printer, needed an eye-catching cover painting." So he designed

---

NewWo.htm (visited 9/8/11). Occasional references to the *Encyclopedia of Science Fiction* are to the Second Edition by John Clute and Peter Nicholls (St. Martins, 1995), the latest available at time of writing.

Also notable is Philip Harbottle's *Vultures of the Void: The Legacy* (Cosmos Books, 2011), published as we were completing our work. This book, very much expanded from an earlier, long out-of-print version, is a survey of UK SF publishing which emphasizes book publishing (especially paperbacks) but also includes useful information on the Nova magazines, some of which we have referred to.

10. See these covers at http://www.sfcovers.net/mainnav.htm. That URL takes you to the main page and you'll have to navigate from there, but how to do so is self-explanatory. Among this site's virtues is an artist index. Another handy source—and probably easier to use—is http://www.philsp.com/mags/newworlds.html (both sites visited 9/8/11).

it himself, combining a spaceship from the cover of a 1937 issue of *Astounding Science Fiction* and another from a 1938 *Amazing Stories*. Victor Caesari worked from Carnell's sketch, and Carnell said: "While not technically perfect it still had good balance and colour and was a striking improvement over No. 1." The second issue sold out, though not entirely because of the cover—the publisher mounted an "all out drive" on its behalf. But seeing the results, Pendulum proceeded to reprint the cover, substitute **1** for **2**, and re-distribute the unsold copies of the first issue, with great success.[11]

The interior illustrations in **1** and **2** are about as bad as the covers (by Wilkin, perpetrator of the first version cover of **1**). Those in **3**, by Dennis and by Slack (responsible for that issue's cover),[12] are only a minor improvement.

Like American pulp magazines, the Pendulum *New Worlds* had a fair amount of advertising not exactly tailored to its content. The back covers and inside front and back covers bear ads for baldness cures; a career guide from the British Institute of Engineering Technology; "Attack Your Rheumatism through PURE Natural Stafford Herbs"; British Glandular Products Ltd. ("Glands Control Your Destiny!" For men, "testrones"; for women, "overones"); Charles Atlas, who will use Dynamic Tension to build you a more manly body; the British Institute of Practical Psychology ("Inferiority Complex eradicated for ever"); and (my favorite)—jockstraps.

This last is headed "Wherever men get together..." and has nice little drawings (much better done than anything illustrating the fiction) of a man getting his petrol tank filled by an attendant, a man reading something off a clipboard to another man wearing an eyeshade and seated at a typewriter, and a man cutting another man's hair in a barber's chair. None of these activities ever seemed to me to call for an athletic supporter

11. Carnell, "The Birth of *New Worlds*," p. 62.

12. Slack was a pseudonym for Kenneth Passingham, son of Bill Passingham, who played a key role in the aborted effort to start *New Worlds* in 1940. *Id.* at 63.

(though I confess I have never actually cut anyone's hair—maybe it's more strenuous than it looks), but the pitch of Fred Hurtley, Ltd., for the Litesome Supporter is quite global: "You can be sure that wherever men get together—there you'll find 'Litesome.' It's grand to buy something and know you couldn't have done better. You get that feeling with 'Litesome' once you've experienced its comfort and protection and the increased stamina and vitality which this essential male underwear gives to every man. Whatever your age or condition, whatever your work or your recreation—'Litesome' will help you to feel a different, better man!" There are also interior ads in **2** and **3**, some of similar ilk, some for more related items such as *Fantasy Review* and *Outlands*.

From the beginning, *New Worlds* contained non-fiction and tried to connect with its readership. **1** has an editorial, small print placed filler-style at the end of one of the stories, which is mostly blather:

> The past is fixed and unalterable. Of that there can be no doubt.... But from here on, the future looms ahead as a bewildering Land of If.... The dazzling heights of achievement and the dark depths of failure can all be found in those miriad [sic] possible "tomorrows." [Etc.]

Comments are invited, and readers are advised to place an order with their newsdealers for the next issue, due in eight weeks. Interestingly, there is nothing about subscriptions here or anywhere else in the magazine. The word is uttered in the editorial in **2**, but no rates are mentioned and there is no subscription information anywhere in **2** or **3**, though back issues are for sale.

Issue **2**'s editorial has not much more than **1**'s that is concrete: thanks for the letters, keep them coming, we're going to make things better, tell us what you want (and do you want a letter column?), and something brief about atomic bomb tests and public consciousness of SF. **2** also contains a one-page article by L(eslie) J. Johnson, sometime contributor to Walter H. Gillings' *Tales of Wonder* and collaborator with Eric Frank Russell, on how science is catching up with SF (more blather though less vague than Carnell's), along with Forrest J. Ackerman's report on the Pacificon science fiction convention, held in 1946 after being delayed by World War II, with an attendance of 125 and "a dynamic hour's speech entitled 'Tomorrow on the March'" by guest of honor A. E. van Vogt.

Also in **2**, "The Literary Line-Up" first appears, readers' story ratings from the first issue, comparable to the US *Astounding Science Fiction* magazine's "Analytical Laboratory" (also *Astounding*'s "In Times to Come," since it predicts the next issue's stories), but without the actual numerical averages that gave John W. Campbell's "AnLab" its air of spurious precision. "The Literary Line-Up" persisted through the Carnell era and even into Michael Moorcock's editorship after mid-1964, though he retitled it "Story Ratings." In **3**, the submission of ratings is encouraged by offering five guineas to the reader whose ratings anticipate the aggregate ratings or come the closest (one would think there would always be multiple winners any time more than a dozen or so readers responded). Also in **3**, "The Literary Line-Up" notes that the response from readers on a letter column was equivocal, so the question will be left open until a regular publication schedule is established. The editorial in **3** (after the apology for the year's delay) notes the drop in price, the story rating competition, the death of Maurice G. Hugi and his story in that issue, and touts Walter Gillings' *Fantasy Review*.

§

To be frank, most of the fiction in these issues deserves its obscurity. Lead novelette in **1** is "The Mill of the Gods" by the doomed Maurice G. Hugi, in which the world is flooded with cheap and high-quality consumer goods from a mysterious company (a notion that also motivated Clifford D. Simak's 1953 novel *Ring Around the Sun*). The boys from Intelligence do a black bag job at one of the company's sites and find themselves on an alternate Earth, lorded over by refugee Nazis who have subdued the already docile native population for their factories. These refugees plan to return and reassert Germany's rightful dominance as soon as their economic warfare has reduced Earth to chaos. So they explain, in time-honored pulp fashion, before locking our heroes up, rather than shooting them out of hand like any sensible gang of villains would do to prevent the good guys' otherwise inevitable escape and triumph. It might have been competitive in *Thrilling Wonder Stories* a decade previously.

The other novelette, William F. Temple's "The Three Pylons," is an only slightly fresher kettle of fish, a piece of schematic moralizing involving the new king of an archaic kingdom whose deceased father has set him a quest: ascend three pylons he has had built, each of which requires a higher technology, and each of which has a message for him on the top. The new king meets these challenges but is such an arrogant and aggressive SOB that he destroys himself.

The rest of the issue comprises no fewer than four short stories by John Russell Fearn[13] under his various guises, all ridiculous but somehow inoffensively so. There is a certain archaic charm to his work that makes it less irritating than, say, the earnestly laborious Temple story. Reading Fearn is like reading David H. Keller, maestro of the early Gernsback epoch. He doesn't pretend to be anything but a moldy fig.

Here's an example, "Sweet Mystery of Life," under Fearn's own name, capturing the tenor of these early issues of *New Worlds*. Maxted, who lives in a village but has a good Civil Service job in the City, is trying to grow a black rose, suppos-

---

13. Carnell later recounted: "Fearn responded to my urgent request for material by sending over one quarter of a million words and in all those first few months produced over half a million, all of which had to be read and from which a selection had to be chosen for that first vital issue." John Carnell, "The Birth of *New Worlds*," p. 61.

edly the Grail of horticulturists. His latest cutting withers, but something else appears in its place, looking at first a bit like a toadstool—but it has a face, and microscopic examination shows it's a human being growing in the potted soil. Maxted tells his servant, "Belling, we've stumbled on something infinitely more amazing than a black rose!" Later, he asks Belling if he knows Arrhenius's theory. "You mean the one about him believing that life came to Earth through indestructible spores surviving the cold of space and then germinating here?" Ah, for the days of old England, when every gentleman had a servant and the servants knew Arrhenius!

The visitor to the conservatory proves to be a woman, or the top half of one, and she's from Venus. Her name is Cia and her years of sporehood have not impaired her memory or linguistic ability. "We of Venus need a race like yours to free us from bondage," i.e., from being legless torsos growing out of the soil. Cia has gobs of advanced scientific knowledge ready to recite off the top of her head. Alas, Idiot Jake, whose favorite amusement is tearing up bits of paper and throwing them off the nearby bridge so he can watch them float down the brook, has been eavesdropping and telling tales. When he throws a tree branch through the window, letting in the cold night air ("charged with frost"), Cia freezes. The police arrive, with various snoopy locals, following up a report of a woman being ill-treated. By now Cia resembles a statue and Maxted passes her off as such. The visitors depart. At least Maxted has his copious notes of Cia's scientific revelations. But wait—they're gone! Pan to Idiot Jake, tearing up the notebook and throwing the pieces into the brook.

The other Fearn stories include "Solar Assignment," as by Mark Denholm, in which a spaceshipful of reporters encounters people on Pluto, zombified and operated by aliens, and amorphous and viscous aliens at that. "Knowledge Without Learning" is a psi story guaranteed not to have pleased John W. Campbell, Jr. A telepath absorbs knowledge from others, but it's zero-sum: what he learns, the sender loses, like the bus driver who suddenly discovered he didn't know where he was or how to drive. "White Mouse" as by Thornton Ayre is about the first mixed marriage of Earth human and Venus human, and the climate of Earth doesn't agree with the bride.

A much higher grade of the ridiculous appears in John Beynon's "The Living Lies," the lead (though not the cover) story in **2**. On Venus, there are four races: the Whites, the Greens, the Reds, and the Blacks. The Whites—Earth colonists—lord it over the others, who exist in a state of mutual dislike and suspicion, to the benefit of the Whites. (The fact that not everybody on Earth is white, or White, is mentioned in passing, but that's it.) These racial differences prove to be entirely manufactured by the Whites; everybody on Venus was white to begin with. Now, all children are born in hospitals, since the risk of infection on Venus is so large, and the doctors whisk newborns off to a hidden room where they are smeared with a pigmenting jelly and exposed to radiation that makes the pigment permanent. Somehow everyone has forgotten that things used to be different, the doctors keep the secret, and nobody else blows the whistle. Presumably all the mothers are anesthetized when they deliver. An idealistic young woman who first is repelled by the racist set-up and then, when she discovers the real story, tries to expose it, comes to a bad end.

Within its absurd premise, the story (by the author later much better known as John Wyndham, of *Triffids* fame) does a reasonably good job of pinpointing the interaction of self-interest and racist attitudes, and portraying the reactions of people who are uncomfortable with them—but usually only up to a point. Venus, by the way, is very different from Earth, which by this time is governed by the Great Union. Says one of the sympathetic characters, uncontradicted by anything in the rest of the story:

> There was a day on Earth when the people revolted.
> They refused any longer to be thrown into slaughter
> of and by people of whom they knew nothing, for the

profit of people who exploited them. They rose against it, one, another, and another, to throw out their rulers and rule themselves. And so came the Great Union, Government of the People, by the People, for the People, over the whole Earth. How long will Venus have to wait for that?

This unusually Bolshie rhetoric is quite refreshing, at least as a relief from the militarist, social Darwinist, and eugenicist rhetoric to be found elsewhere in the genre.

The cover story of **2**, "Space Ship 13" by Patrick S. Selby, is something else entirely, in the running for the worst story I have ever read in an SF magazine. A sample:

> "Oh, no you don't! Hand that envelope over, brother!"
>
> Chuck spun around. The cabin door had opened silently, and a powerfully built man with a sinister looking scar across his right eyebrow stood holding a deadly radium gun level with Chuck's heart.
>
> "Get out of here!" tried Chuck experimentally, and got slowly to his feet. Slim, away up at the controls, hadn't noticed anything wrong, not that he'd be much help. "And put that gun away—any accident here might send the ship to dust!"
>
> "I'll do the worrying about accidents," growled the man with the scar. "You worry about doing what I tell you. They don't call me 'Kleiner the Killer' for nothin'. Now, gimme that envelope." He held out his huge fist, and his dark, evil little eyes glittered. "Come on, now!"

If anything, it gets worse. ("'You swine, Kleiner! I'll get you before we're through!' The racketeer gave an evil chuckle.") "The Literary Line-Up" in **3** says Selby will be back in the next issue, but apparently good sense prevailed: he wasn't, and

Miller/Contento lists no other appearances for him in the SF magazines.

Things could only get better from there, though not necessarily by much. John Russell Fearn has two stories in issue **2**, both reprinted from American magazines: "Vicious Circle" as by Polton Cross (from *Startling*, Summer 1946) and "Lunar Concession" as by Thornton Ayre (from *Science Fiction*, Sept. 1941). "Vicious Circle" is about a man who is running for the Bond Street bus and suddenly finds himself in "a formless grey abyss," and then on an unfamiliar and rather shiny-looking street. A helpful passer-by clues him in: "It may help you if I explain that you are in London—which was resurfaced with plastic in Nineteen Fifty Eight." He shortly returns to his present, but keeps popping off to other times. He goes to a doctor, who diagnoses him as a freak of nature. (That's what he says: "You are a freak of nature!" Now there's a bedside manner.) Specifically, where everybody else's time line is straight, his is a circle—an enlarging circle (sounds like a spiral to me), and by story's end he's about ready to hit the Big Bang and the heat death of the universe on the next swing of the pendulum.[14]

"Lunar Concession" lacks even the modest charm of "Vicious Circle." There's a deposit of super-high-energy *Potentium* on the moon, conveniently in a valley with an atmosphere. One of the party exploiting it proves to be an Agent of a Foreign Power who wants the *Potentium* so he can make bombs and seek world domination, as he tediously explains in standard pulp-cardboard fashion while hero and heroine are tied up (once more: rather than just shooting them, as any sane villain would). The day is saved by Snoop, the hero's faithful dog, who lays down his life, etc.

These are the last Fearn stories to appear in *New Worlds*. Shortly after, Fearn's prolific publication in the SF magazines slowed drastically, presumably because he was busy writing

---

14. Wait a minute! How did an expanding circle become a swinging pendulum? Isn't that what the Dean Drive was about? At least it didn't turn into a seesaw—that had been done, by A. E. van Vogt.

novels for the paperback publishers that were springing up.[15] He had one story in *Science Fantasy* but no more in any of the higher-echelon British SF magazines. The rest were in the likes of his own *Vargo Statten's SF Magazine*.

The remaining short stories in **2** are inconsequential. "Foreign Body" by John Brody is about an ancient spaceship discovered in a bed of coal and destroyed by ineptitude. Brody was an early case of the Carnell-only SF writer: seven stories 1946-58, all but one in *New Worlds* or *Science Fantasy*. He did have four stories in the UK weird magazines (1946-60) as by "John Body." "The Micro Man" by Alden Lorraine (Forrest J Ackerman) is an inane story about somebody enlarged from the world inside an atom, but not quite enough—he comes to grief in the protagonist's typewriter. "Green Spheres" by W. P. Cockcroft, is about an invasion by tentacled extraterrestrial carnivorous plants, ultimately done in by water. The author is a veteran of *Wonder Stories*, *Tales of Wonder*, and *Scoops* (not to mention *Yankee Weird Shorts*), and it shows in this dated *War of the Worlds* knock-off.

§

The lead story in *New Worlds* **3** is "Dragon's Teeth" by John K. Aiken (misspelled "Aitken" on the cover), a "novel" at 27 pulp pages. Aiken (1913-90) is a moderately interesting Little Known Writer.[16] He was the son of poet Conrad Aiken, co-editor of a fanzine consisting mostly of fiction and published in a single copy at the Paint Research Station in Teddington, 1942-44 (Aiken was a "biological chemist," says Carnell in *New Worlds*

---

15. In fact, as Philip Harbottle reports, Fearn in 1950 signed a contract with Scion Books to write SF exclusively for that publisher for five years. *Vultures of the Void: The Legacy*, p. 123.

16. This recurrent phrase reflects the view of members of the listserv on which this material was first aired that Attention Must Be Paid to the obscure and forgotten producers of decades-old magazine fiction, a preoccupation in which I enthusiastically joined.

4), and active in the Cosmos Club until its postwar demise.[17] He first appeared in the SF magazines with a Probability Zero item in *Astounding* in 1943.[18] This is his second story; altogether, he had five in *New Worlds* from 1947 to 1952, and book reviews in the two Gillings issues of *Science-Fantasy*. (He's the one who described Nelson Bond as "approximately, the P.G. Wodehouse of science fiction.") He also appeared in a number of the issues of Gillings' *Fantasy Review*.

"Dragon's Teeth" is the first of what Miller/Contento dub the Anstar series, after a main character, and years later Aiken fixed them up as *World Well Lost*, published as by John Padget in the UK in 1970 but under his own name in the US a year later. Actually, this is what might be called a "reverse fix-up." Carnell said later (*New Worlds* 5, "The Literary Line-Up"): "It has taken us a long time to officially announce that the trilogy of stories by John K. Aiken... is in reality a long novel, and because of our somewhat infrequent appearance we had to split it into three separate parts instead of making a serial of the story." Carnell adds with his typical cramped expansiveness that "the entire trilogy bids fair to become a minor classic of British science fiction."

In any case, "Dragon's Teeth" is a reasonably intelligent if cardboard-populated rendition of the peaceful culture menaced by oppressive militaristic invaders, in this case the proponents of the Galactic New Order (Galnos for short), whose advance guard is neutralized by the pacifistically inclined colonists' genetically engineered (though not so described) iron-eating

---

17. http://www.dcs.gla.ac.uk/SF Archives/Then/then_1 2.html (visited 9/8/11).

18. "Camouflage," *Astounding Science Fiction*, April 1943. The Probability Zero items were essentially tall tales, brief vignettes that stretched credulity and often amounted to parodies of SF method and logic, some written by *Astounding*'s regular contributors, others by readers and fans who had few or no other credits in the field, or only obtained them later, like Ray Bradbury. Even *New Worlds* editor Ted Carnell published one, "Time Marches On," in the August 1942 issue of *Astounding*.

lichen and hypnotic flowers. For the full Galno fleet, it takes an "adaptation of [the] mesotron beam" that they use to generate mutations. While the main characters are debating the ethical issues of defending themselves with something so destructive, the designated red-shirt sneaks off, blows the fleet out of the sky, and then kills himself, permitting the rest to have it both ways. There will be more on these stories and the book version later on.

The short fiction in this issue is not necessarily better but is much more readable than its predecessors. "The Terrible Day" by Nick Boddie (Boddy on the contents page) Williams is a work of hard-boiled astronomy ("I could imagine that—Kiesel, squatty and bald, glued to the tail-end of that 100in. telescope while Halley's Comet looped the loop."), set of course in Los Angeles. A supernova triggers a near-collapse of civilization at the same time the astronomer protagonist is undergoing a near-collapse of his marriage. There is a happy ending on both counts, and as the story closes he is hugging the dog.

F(rancis) G. Rayer's "From Beyond the Dawn" is completely but pleasantly archaic, the kind of thing that you'd be pleased but not surprised to find in a 1932 *Wonder Stories*. Derek Faux has established a SETI-by-dots-and-dashes communication with somebody, but there's no time lag. What's going on? Suddenly craft full of invincible robots appear in the rock quarry next door. Resistance appears futile. But Faux's telegraphy yields a clue as to how to destroy them. Meanwhile, in the far far future, highly evolved humans with bodies so feeble and brains so big that all their wheelchairs have headrests are talking about the mysterious signals they are receiving from somewhere and responding to, and the robots they are about to send out to explore for them, and the new theory that time is a loop.

Maurice G. Hugi, who usually doesn't get much respect, including from me, is back with "Fantasia Dementia," which is pretty lively considering that the protagonist is in a coma. It's in the tradition that stretches from "An Occurrence at Owl Creek Bridge" through *Pincher Martin* to Iain Banks' *The*

Bridge and Damon Knight's *Humpty Dumpty: An Oval*. A car thief tries to flee the police and winds up going through the windshield and into a concrete pillar. After extensive brain surgery he's paralyzed in the hospital, except—"Hummmm! Hummmm! Hummmm! ZING!"—he is suddenly in a surreal and revolting fantasy world. Then he's back in his hospital bed. Then ("ZING!" again) he's in a sort of quasi-Egyptian dream world where he is ruler, but is magicked by an evil priest and put through the death rites while alive but (here too) paralyzed. He returns to hospital, starts to go again, then dies, and Dr. Schrodinger (honest) says, "My God! That's it! The silver plate was the cause. Silver is a conductor. It made an electrical bridge over the Fissure of Sylvius! Even the three membranes, Pia Mater, Dura Mater and Arachnoid Membrane could not short-circuit it!" The House Surgeon says, "Well, he's at rest now, poor devil. He won't zing again." Carnell says in his editorial that Hugi has recently died at age 43 and knew he was dying when he wrote this story. If so, he was a serious pessimist—at the end of the story it is hinted that the protagonist has actually zinged off a third time to another fantasy world, from which—having died—he will not be able to escape.

We reach the bottom of the barrel with John Brody's "The Inexorable Laws," in which space captain Leroy is chasing down space captain Bronberg, who stole his wife, terminal vengeance in mind. They fetch up on a planet where a gang of vile aliens, never seen but holed up in a pyramid, seize both ships with a powerful magnetic field. Leroy bows to "the ethical laws," i.e., in the cold cruel cosmos Terrans stick together, abandon revenge, and cooperate in getting Bronberg off the planet. Having nothing more to live for, Leroy blows up his own ship and the alien pyramid. The writing is as crude as the story: "Mankind was such a small facet of the vast universe, such a weak growth amid so many perils, that every man who went beyond the field of Terra must be constantly on his guard."

In this dubious company the quietly elegant "Inheritance" by Arthur C. Clarke (under the Charles Willis pseudonym, for no apparent reason) is a considerable relief. An experimental rocket pilot is confident he will survive because he has dreamed of the future—except it's not his future he's dreaming of. It's a piece of modest ingenuity, modestly presented, and is the best thing in these three issues.

"Inheritance" prompts a question and an observation. The story subsequently appeared in the September 1948 *Astounding*—the only previously published story ever to appear in *Astounding*—and I wonder how and why that happened, and whether it has anything to do with the fact that Clarke, after one more story in the September 1949 issue, did not appear in *Astounding* again until "Death and the Senator" in 1961. It is also worth noting that Clarke published almost no original fiction in *New Worlds* after this, the only exceptions being "The Forgotten Enemy" in **5** (1949) and "Who's There" in **77** (1958), with "Guardian Angel" in **8** (1950) being half an exception, since *New Worlds* published Clarke's original version and not the one revised by James Blish that appeared in *Famous Fantastic Mysteries*.

Clarke's other fictional appearances in *New Worlds* were all reprints: "The Sentinel" in **22** (1954), reprinted from *Ten Story Fantasy*; "?" in **55** (1957), reprinted from *Fantasy & Science Fiction* (as "Royal Prerogative"); and, believe it or not, "Sunjammer" in **148**, into the Moorcock era, reprinted from *Boys' Life*. It's striking that the leading UK SF writer of the 1950s appeared so seldom in the leading UK SF magazine, especially since Clarke for some reason was not appearing in the highest-paying US magazines either. As noted, he was out of *Astounding* from late 1949 to 1961; he didn't hit *Galaxy* until 1958; he had only half a dozen stories in *Fantasy & Science Fiction* through 1970; instead he tended to show up in *Thrilling Wonder, If, Infinity, Satellite*, etc.

In summary: the beginning of *New Worlds* appears inauspicious from this distance—although it surely seemed momentous back in the day, and back at the place.

2: RESURRECTION
(1949-50)

Sunk by the bankruptcy of Pendulum Publications[19] after issue **3** in October 1947, *New Worlds* was famously resurrected when attendees of the White Horse Tavern gatherings of SF enthusiasts decided to form their own company to publish it. Nova Publications Ltd. was formed, shares were offered, almost 50 people put up £5 each, and Nova was in business, led by unpaid working directors John B. Harris (John Wyndham), Ken Chapman, Frank Cooper, Walter Gillings, Eric Williams, and Carnell.[20]

The first Nova Publications *New Worlds*, issue **4**, appeared in April 1949, followed by **5** in September, though only the year actually appears on the magazine. The next issue bravely announced itself as Spring 1950, and was followed by Summer and Winter; what happened to Fall is not explained either in the magazine or by Tymn/Ashley. In 1951 things firmed up and the magazine managed four quarterly issues, then went bimonthly in January 1952 and stayed that way until early 1953, when

19. Carnell recounted that Pendulum's £80 check to him for the third issue bounced, was reissued, and bounced again, and when Carnell again went to the Pendulum offices, no one was there except Stephen Frances, clearing up for the receiver. All he could offer Carnell was a suitcase full of copies of the magazine, which Carnell later sold on the collectors' market, recouping his loss more than a decade later. Carnell, "The Birth of *New Worlds*," *Vision of Tomorrow*, October 1970, p. 63.

20. Harbottle, *Vultures of the Void: The Legacy*, p. 85. See also Frank Arnold's article "The Circle of the White Horse," in *New Worlds* 14.

things got flaky again. Carnell is listed as editor and there is no other editorial staff listed. The magazine is published by Nova Publications, Ltd., 25 Stoke Newington Road, London N.16, and throughout the period is printed by G.F. Tompkin, Ltd., Grove Green Road, London, E.11.

These five 1949-50 *New Worlds* represent a sharp improvement in presentation—that is, the amateurs of Nova put out a better-looking magazine than the professionals at Pendulum. The magazine has gone from more or less pulp size to a large digest size, 5½ x 8½ inches, at first 88 pages plus covers, then 96 pages plus covers starting with **5**. The paper is a reasonably thick stock (getting thinner with **8**), a little coarser than typical book paper, but it holds up well. There's less browning in my copies than in most SF magazines of similar age. The price stays at "one & sixpence."

The covers are drastically improved. The cover logo is now simple and readable. The subtitle "fiction of the future" remains. With **6**, the logo is enclosed in a rectangular box, interrupted on the bottom by the subtitle. The cover of **4**, by Dennis, is a bit crude, but it makes a virtue of its crudity, since the picture is purposefully stark and stylized and effective as a result.[21] **5** is a further improvement, being the first cover by Clothier, whose often busy and always colorful and eye-catching work dominated for the next couple of years. He knew how to be gaudy but not cheesy—not an easy line to walk. (Admittedly some of these covers have become kitsch retroactively simply because their Art-Deco slant has fallen so far out of fashion.)

Clothier, like US favorite Emsh (Ed Emshwiller) in later years, specializes in incorporating his signature into the picture, but even more visibly: **6** includes a map of Venus produced by Clothier Projection; **7** has a vehicle of Clothier Contractors; in **8**, the futuristic Clothier Hotel is in the lower right corner. The first Clothier cover is also the first since **1** without a story title over it, which remained the practice for several years. All five of

21. See these covers at http://www.sfcovers.net/mainnav.htm or http://www.philsp.com/mags/newworlds.html.

these covers depict spaceships or equally portentous machinery (it's hard to tell about a couple of them), with human figures at best in a supporting role. There is no statement that the covers illustrate any of the stories, but at least some of them do. The cover of **5**, illustrating a spaceship taking off from underwater, is taken from Sydney J. Bounds' "Too Efficient." The navigational motif of **6** appears connected with A. Bertram Chandler's "Coefficient X." The cover of **8**, portraying a giant vessel that looks a little bit like a giant sausage penetrated horizontally by a neon halo and vertically by a body piercing stud, hovering over a futuristic city, seems to illustrate Arthur C. Clarke's "Guardian Angel."

Interior illustrations, generally adequate but undistinguished, are by Dennis and White in **4**, Clothier and Turner in **5** and **6**, Clothier and Hunter in **7** and **8**. Carnell says in the editorial in **5** that Clothier is new to SF but Turner is a veteran of 1938-39, and indeed a 1939 issue of *Fantasy* features illustrations by an H.E. Turner. The strength of Clothier's covers has a lot to do, both directly and indirectly, with his bold use of color, but his black and white work is fairly nondescript. However, this may be due to limitations in reproduction technology. Comparing these issues with a contemporaneous *Astounding* (April 1949, illustrations by Cartier, Quackenbush, and Orban), it seems to my amateur's eye that *New Worlds*'s printing—not just its artists—is less capable of reproducing fine detail.

Each issue has an editorial and "The Literary Line-Up," and starting in **5** each has either a book or a film review, one item reviewed per issue. The books covered are William F. Temple's *Four-Sided Triangle* (**5**), Arthur C. Clarke's *Interplanetary Flight* (**7**), and Ley and Bonestell's *The Conquest of Space* (**8**). All the reviews are unsigned except the last, signed "J.C." The film review is of a documentary called *The Wonder Jet*, notable for its scene—memorialized here in a still photo—of a man wearing an old-style leather flying helmet with earflaps, rapt in perusal of *New Worlds* **3**. This is signed "W.F.T.," clearly William F. Temple. The only other non-fiction in these issues is

Clarke's "The Shape of Ships to Come" (**4**), about what space-ships are likely to look like (maybe like dumbbells with one end larger than the other; spin 'em for gravity and they'll look like hydrogen atoms). The practice of publishing an article in most issues did not get established until 1951.

Since *New Worlds* is now its own entity and not the product of a pulp chain, the advertising more or less fits the content and no more jockstraps or gland tonics are on offer. All issues but **4** have ads on back and inside front and back covers (**4** has the Table of Contents on the inside front); interior ad pages go from none in **4** to one in **5** to two in **6** and back down to one in **8**. Almost all the ads are for books and magazines, mostly SF, though there are exceptions, such as the ad on the inside front cover of **8** for Rider, which sells occult books including *Psychic Pitfalls*: "An A.B.C. of speaking with the dead, showing us how to avoid mistakes and disillusionments." Their ad in **7** offers *Reincarnation For Everyman* by the same author, Shaw Desmond. In several of the issues, Loyal Novelty Supplies, purveyors of Magical Novelties, takes a half-page, complete with cartoon rabbit doing card tricks.

The editorials, formerly crammed in filler-style in small type, are now allocated a full page or two. The two-pager in **4** is titled "Confidence." Carnell says that the magazine's existence "calls for a certain amount of justifiable pride," noting that the previous publisher had ceased business. He says that he first planned the magazine in 1940, now he's got a team of experts working with him (though as noted none of them are credited), and here's his manifesto: "I have been certain for a long time that there is a place for British magazine science fiction in this country without the readers having to rely entirely upon the medium of American counterparts (couched, in the main, in a style designed to suit an American reading public and not a British one)."

After noting the history of false starts in British magazine SF, the editorial concludes: "The one vital factor which stands supreme is that this type of literature has been asked for by readers for years, and despite the failures by the wayside, I have every confidence that a good quality magazine such as I hope *New Worlds* to be, will fill the vital need *from an English standpoint.*" And there's a variation or even counterpoint, in "The Literary Line-Up": "Although we warn you that we shall from time to time experiment with different types of stories, ever pursuing a policy of publishing the best British science fiction available."

Oddly, Carnell doesn't say exactly what constitutes this "English standpoint" he's talking about, nor, by contrast, "a style designed to suit an American reading public and not a British one." It is noteworthy that there appear to be *no* US writers in these issues, and only one—Forrest J. Ackerman with his inane vignette and convention report in **2**—in the earlier ones. There are a number of reprints from US magazines, but almost no original fiction by US authors, in the magazine's first decade. There is an Arthur J. Burks story in **10** in 1951; "The Literary Line-Up" in **10** reports that one Hjalmar Boyesen, to appear in the next issue, is an American living in London; and then the next one appears to be Robert Silverberg's "Critical Threshold" in **66**, December 1957. In the magazine's first years, it seems either that US writers were not even using *New Worlds* as a salvage market, or Carnell was not allowing them to. The same is not true of *Science Fantasy.* By the end of 1956, the magazine under Carnell had published five stories, in many fewer issues than *New Worlds* had published at the time, by the (then) relatively marginal US writers E.E. Evans, Les Cole, Charles E. Fritch, Helen Urban, and Harlan Ellison.

On a more mundane level, Carnell says, "The first thing we did was to change the size of the magazine, feeling that it would be far more popular in the handy pocket size than in the larger more cumbersome one." Here is a subtle piece of cultural history, evoking the bygone era when everybody (men, that is) not engaged in manual labor wore jackets as a daily routine—this large digest magazine wouldn't fit anybody's *pants* pocket.

The editorial in **5**, titled "Progress," says nothing much, but does note that subscriptions are now available. The issue **6** editorial, "No Comparison...," takes up the transAtlantic anxiety of influence, or of hegemony, again:

> It is understandable that *New Worlds* should be compared with American science-fiction magazines—they have been almost the sole source of reading pleasure to many people in this country for many years. But that *New Worlds* should be following in American footsteps I disagree most emphatically. Neither is it our aim to imitate any one American publication.
>
> For twenty years now, experts in the fantasy field in this country have been trying to get a truly British science-fiction publication going successfully—it looks as though *New Worlds* is going to more than fulfill those expectations and ambitions—and already some of the traditions of American publications are beginning to be radically changed to suit our own reading taste.
>
> British authors will almost always produce stories written differently (in style and presentation), from American writers, around plots approached from a different mental angle, a direct result of different environments, customs and conditions, existing in the two countries. It's hard work for them to write an *American* story—writing in an English vein comes more naturally!
>
> Therefore I foresee that the gulf between *New Worlds* and American contemporaries will widen rather than draw closer....

Once more, Carnell says nothing about what this "truly British" approach *is*. Many issues later, in **29**, visiting US writer Alfred Bester does just that, rather well, in the letter column "Postmortem," to which we shall return.

The editorial in **7**, "Good Companions," announces the launch of *Science Fantasy* and anticipates the "friendly rivalry" that the two editors (Carnell and Walter Gillings) will develop. That lasted only two issues, and Carnell was editing both magazines starting with *Science Fantasy* **3**. "Conventionally Speaking" in **8** announces the International Science Fiction Convention, to be held in the Bull and Mouth Hotel (not a typo) in May 1951, later shifted to the Royal Hotel because of the large projected attendance; it also mentions the ongoing gatherings of the London SF Group at the White Horse Tavern.

§

Overall, the quality of the fiction improves after the first three issues.

The inane, the archaic, and the bloody awful still make their appearances, but they are a smaller part of the whole (John Russell Fearn is gone), and the median seems comparable to the median in the US pulps of the time, though not much is comparable to the best in those magazines. There are several stories by well-established British writers (Clarke with two stories, Temple and Beynon with one each), and some by newer writers who were flashes in the pan as far as *New Worlds* goes (John Aiken, Peter Phillips). What is interesting is the emergence of a substantial part of the stable of writers that would carry the magazine through most of the 1950s, including some who were virtually unknown in the US. In these issues the most prolific author is F. G. Rayer, with four short stories. A. Bertram Chandler—already well established, but also to become a *New Worlds* mainstay—has three, one under the George Whitley pseudonym. Sydney J. Bounds has two, and E. R. James' first *New Worlds* story is here. Three of the stories had been previously published in US magazines, but one of them (Clarke's "Guardian Angel" in **8**) is explicitly said by Carnell to have been purchased more or less simultaneously in US and UK.

Issue **4**, according to Carnell, contained the same fiction contents as planned for the fourth Pendulum issue.[22] It leads off with "World in Shadow," a novelette by the so-far-undistinguished John Brody. Fortunately, it's a considerable improvement over his previous stories at the most basic level of readability—fewer malapropisms, overt clichés per square inch, etc. The story proposes that in the future, automation means nobody much needs to work, and more and more people are checking into the Mentasthetic Centres to live in a less boring dream world. What exactly goes on in the dream worlds is not explained—maybe they have dream jobs. Dick Maybach is one of the workhorses; he spends four hours a day running a nuclear power plant. He gets in his copter to hurry home to his bored wife, but:

> "Move over, brother!" The voice came from the back of the cabin, a low, soft, voice that held a core of steel. "Don't look back—and don't argue. There's a blaster six inches from your kidneys!"

It's the Underground, trying to recruit him for their revolutionary scheme, which is to destroy the material basis of society so everybody will have to get off their butts and struggle—and, of course, Man Will Go To The Stars. (They already have all the parts of a spaceship, but in this decadent society nobody remembers how to put them together.) We get several pages of John Galt-ish exposition on how progress requires regress. Dick bites, since he's afraid his wife, the beautiful Veronica, is about to succumb to the siren call of the Mentasthetic Centres. Conspiracy and hugger-mugger ensue; his wife does succumb, and Dick is presented with the world-historical choice: pull the levers that will blow up the power system and bring a new world into being, and also probably kill most of the millions of people who are jacked in at the Mentasthetic Centres, including

---

22. Harbottle, *Vultures of the Void: The Legacy*, p. 85.

his wife. Or not. He pulls the levers—"The Cold Equations," UK style.

Or so it seems. Unfortunately the author does not quite have the courage of his bloody-mindedness. A few issues later, the lead story in **7** is Brody's "The Dawn Breaks Red," and here's Veronica, big as life, but transformed. After the close of business in "World in Shadow," Dick went to the local Mentasthetic Centre, where some 50,000 people were at risk of dying. There he found Veronica still alive, and made the doctor on duty, who was trying to save whom he could of the dying thousands, take Veronica out of turn by pointing a gun at him, and then spirited her out, noticing only later that her hair had turned white, and even later that she was demonstrating a remarkable intuition and ingenuity. Now, Veronica thinks it's dandy that her husband pulled the plug on 50,000 dreamers and killed most of them.

The band of conspirators who brought down civilization have been hanging out in their redoubts *Atlas Shrugged*-style for a year, and they're beginning to wonder what's going on out there, and how all the folks whose lives they wrecked are getting along. So they set out for various destinations, and Dick and company go to his old house and encounter his neighbor. The neighbor is a trifle annoyed at Dick for killing his wife but is willing to let bygones be bygones. He explains that at the Mentasthetic Centres, most everybody died, but there were a few dozen in each whose hair turned white and who developed both enhanced intelligence and a cruel and calculating view of the world—like Veronica. The regular folks are getting ready to have a pogrom against these "whiteheads," who are also referred to as mutants through the rest of the story.

The folks in the redoubts or "settlements" decide the whiteheads are the hope of humanity, and save them. (An unstated Lamarckian assumption is that people whose heads and follicles have been reorganized by pulling the plug on their artificial dreams will reproduce those characteristics rather than bearing ordinary human children.) However, hostility towards the mutants increases in the settlements, while Veronica has grown completely away from Dick. When the mutants take over, it transpires that they failed in one of the settlements, so the standard humans there are on their way with an aircraft full of atom bombs to wipe out the mutant-dominated settlements. Who ya gonna call? None of the mutants can fly a jet and none of the standard humans wants to save them—except Dick, who decides that only the whiteheads are going to make it To The Stars and he's on their side; he dies in a kamikaze attack on the settlement aircraft.

It's hard to see anything peculiarly British about this saga. The motif of rebellion against stagnation and the casual willingness to dispose of the fates and sacrifice the lives of thousands or millions pursuant to a self-appointed elite's theory of history and progress seems pretty solidly in line with a lot of American SF, as does the notion of throwing in with a new mutant master race in the service of the unquestioned transcendent goal, The Stars.

§

The other major feature in these issues is the continuation and conclusion of John K. Aiken's series or novel that began in **3** with "Dragon's Teeth." There the peaceful and anarchistic Centaurians repelled the attack of the Galactic New Order, but they know another one is coming. In "Cassandra" (**6**), we learn that Vara, one of the sort-of-but-not-really governing group, and secondary protagonist Snow's girlfriend, is in a coma induced by her horror at the violent self-defense of the previous story. A cat-like native race, the Phrynx, has fled to the Blue Moon, leaving behind instructions for building a peculiar machine, which turns out to be a Predictor, and it predicts the destruction of the colony world. Meanwhile, a supposed refugee from Earth has arrived and proves to be a spy; he obtains the Centaurians' newly developed secret weapon, the hyper-explosive D, and nearly escapes to Earth with it. Luckily, one of the Centaurians has invented a thought projector and they subdue the spy with it.

The Phrynx appear to Snow in a dream, announce that the crisis is afoot, and offer to straighten out Vara. This one is obviously an installment and not a story. (As previously noted, Carnell acknowledged in **5**'s "Literary Line-Up" that the series is actually a novel broken into parts.)

Fortunately, "Phoenix Nest" is in **7**, the next issue, and starts with a bang: Centaurus IV is beset with incendiary "seeds," apparently courtesy of the Galnos, which start burning the place up. Anstar's plan is to build giant thought-projectors and change the minds, literally, of everybody on Earth. But the Phrynx offer to evacuate everybody to the Blue Moon. Anstar, the primary protagonist, is forced from his leadership position and winds up alone on Earth building his giant thought projector while everyone else flees. In a dead-end subplot, *his* girlfriend Amber is kidnapped to the Blue Moon and makes it back just in time for the finale, in which they project their thought message to Earth. A few hours later they get the response that it worked, the Galnos have been overthrown, but not before launching a doomsday weapon that is going to blow up Centaurus IV *and* the Blue Moon in about two hours. All die, but not before Amber realizes everything has been in the service of the Phrynx's master plan to hand over the universe to the decent (non-Galno) remnants of humanity elsewhere in the galaxy.

Overall this series is an ambitious nice try by a literate but inexperienced writer who doesn't quite have the wherewithal to bring off a novel-length plot. Too much of what happens has an *ex machina* quality, there's too much implausible super-technology cobbled together overnight (like a kinder, gentler, less noisy E.E. Smith) without much thinking through of implications (especially the Predictor), and the society of Alpha C IV never comes to life because all we see of it is the doings of eight or so characters in the foreground.

As noted earlier, these stories were fixed up (or this novel was reunited) into *World Well Lost*, published as by John Padget in the UK in 1970, but under Aiken's own name in the US by Doubleday in 1971. A superficial look at the text shows that

Aiken learned something in the intervening two decades. The stories have been comprehensively revised and updated stylistically and culturally; for example, Anstar's observation to Amber in the first story, "You're a tawny little fury when you're angry," fortunately has disappeared. Everything is described and explained more clearly. The plot seems to remain pretty much the same, including the demise of all the characters at the end. There is a note about the author on the back flap that is positively Pinocchian. After saying nothing about Aiken's life and activities except that he moved to England young, graduated and got a Ph.D from London University, and now lives in London, it says: "Although *World Well Lost* is his first science fiction novel his writings have been published in all the well known science fiction magazines." Well, there was that Probability Zero piece in *Astounding*...

Aiken had two more stories in *New Worlds*, one of them in these issues. "Edge of Night" (**4**), not part of the Anstar series, pleasantly executes a familiar plot. Three people are snatched from their times (arbitrarily, it seems at first) to enact a great destiny: Grierson, a submarine commander in trouble in 1942; Laura, a housewife tending her dying husband in 1940; Jimmy, a young working-class chap who was trying to get his child into a bomb shelter during the Blitz. They find themselves walking up a spiral ramp around a tower above the clouds. At the top of the tower, they find a captivating old man who introduces himself as Man (i.e., "the fusion of the minds of the last race of man") and says his body is really Earth (he handwaves and it becomes visible beneath them). It seems that over the millennia, Earth's elements "gradually built into denser, subtler ones" with atomic numbers "hundreds of times as great" as their predecessors (transcendence *and* cold fusion! This from a chemist, too, remember).

Now Man reveals the mission. These three people have been snatched from the past because they are the "minds most fitted to the task," which is of course the struggle of good vs. evil. The Black Mind, which has taken over a large part of the universe, has become aware of Man, and has snatched Pluto in a cross between colonization and possession. The characters' mission? To fly to Pluto in a spaceship designed to serve as a condenser for the projected mental force of Man ("some of the new heavy elements can focus thought"), for which they will be in effect a relay station. Where's this spaceship? "'Ah,' said the old man. 'That must be thought of.'" So he thinks it into existence, complete with galley stocked with stuff you couldn't get in wartime London ("Butter, eggs, oranges—blimey, a pineapple—never 'ad one in me life!" says Jimmy) and they're off.

It takes about three hours to get to Pluto, or at least to get past the orbits of Jupiter and Saturn, and once there they engage, or are used by Man, in a typical science fictional mind battle, which they of course win. Pluto blows up. Back on Earth, Grierson and Laura declare their love, though the latter says she won't leave her husband if he pulls through. Man breaks it to them that he has to wipe the memories of the two from 1940 because they mustn't retain what they've learned about 1942, so Grierson says he'll look her up if it turns out her husband died, and he'll look Jimmy up too and get him into the Navy, assuming Grierson survives the depth charges (but it looks as if he won't). This absurd fairy tale is made reasonably enjoyable, indeed charming, by competent and matter-of-fact writing and appealing characters, including Man. It would have been right at home in the back pages of *Thrilling Wonder Stories*.

§

The lead story in **8** is Arthur C. Clarke's "Guardian Angel," later incorporated into *Childhood's End*. It was written in July 1946, bounced by Campbell at *Astounding*, rewritten, and sent to agent Scott Meredith to sell; he had it revised by James Blish and it was first published in *Famous Fantastic Mysteries*, April 1950. In it, Stormgren, the Secretary of the United Nations and effectively world president, deals with Karellen, the representative of the extraterrestrial race that has brought its civilizing mission to Earth. Karellen will not show himself. Why not? Famously, because he looks like traditional renderings of Satan, and people would talk. *New Worlds* uses Clarke's original text and not the Blish revision, though not out of any agenda. Carnell says in **10** that the story was sold to him and to the US magazine at the same time, but the latter got it into print two months earlier.

Clarke says he thought Blish's ending was "rather good," but he didn't find out about the revision for a long time.[23] The revisions, overall, are relatively minor, consisting mostly of cuts of sentences and paragraphs from Clarke's version, including the removal of some internal framing material. The "new ending" actually just repeats a few lines of dialogue from earlier in the story that sharpen the analogy to Satan. Neither version is particularly interesting nor impressive, though both are capably written; in the novel, this material served mainly as set-up and seemed to me a bit of a distraction even before I knew it had been published separately. It is not entirely surprising that this story took second place in the readers' poll to a short story by an unknown writer.

Of the non-featured fiction, Clarke's "The Forgotten Enemy" (**5**) is probably the best known, minor as it is, and the last piece of non-reprinted Clarke fiction in *New Worlds* until 1958. In one of his short and quietly elegant early pieces, the glaciers return to London.

The best story in these issues may be Peter Phillips' "Plagiarist" (**7**), a high-quality museum piece set in a Bradburyesque future in which the irrational and atavistic have been banished from human culture. The protagonist is the imaginative young rebel who finds a time capsule and tries to flog Beethoven and Shakespeare at his rite of passage performance. Nobody much likes them, and they accuse him (correctly) of plagiarism and kick him out. Though ultimately the story is a bag of conventional sentiments, it is quite well turned and presents a pharma-

23. Except for Carnell's statement, this is sourced from Neil McAleer's *Arthur C. Clarke: The Authorized Biography* (Contemporary Books 1992).

ceutical grade sample of one of the great tropes of SF of the late '40s and the '50s. The readers voted it best in the issue.

Phillips' other story here, "Unknown Quantity" (**5**), is equally facile but considerably more annoying, a pseudo-think-piece in which a religious figure known only as the Preacher rants against the "soulless" Servotrons, i.e. androids, prompting the company that makes them to challenge him to a philosophical debate. The joker is that the company trains a Servotron to do it, named Theo Parabasis no less,[24] and then to reveal his provenance after the debate. But the Preacher, too, is really an android put up by a rival company to help drive down Servotron's stock. When Theo exposes his nature, the Preacher declares Theo his equal ("His God is my God—and yours, if you have wit to reason. For does not all reason reach toward God?") Then the Preacher reveals his own androidicity, explaining later to his handler: "There comes a qualitative change in a brain when it is given so much knowledge. A subtle change. True reasoning begins. And something is born. A soul. I found that I had a soul." Later, we see Theo playing the piano again—this time, with expression.

The reason this one is annoying is that it raises a significant question about consciousness and then buries it in unexamined sentimentality, worse than not asking the question at all—a sort of cogitus interruptus. (For a considerably better time on this subject, which I happened to read around the same time, see Ken Liu's "The Algorithms for Love," from *Strange Horizons*, reprinted in the 2005 Hartwell/Cramer *Year's Best SF 10*. It doesn't answer the question but it doesn't obscure it either.) Carnell, however, thought enough of "Unknown Quantity" to anthologize it both in *The Best from New Worlds Science Fiction* (Boardman, 1955) and *No Place Like Earth* (Boardman, 1952).[25]

Phillips (b. 1920) is probably two-thirds of the way towards

---

24. A parabasis is a point in the play when the actors leave the stage and the chorus addresses the audience directly.

25. *No Place Like Earth* is an anthology of SF stories by British writers, some reprinted from *New Worlds* and others from the US magazines.

Little Known Writer status even among SF cognoscenti. His career, boosted early by the immensely popular "Dreams Are Sacred" in *Astounding* in 1948, comprised 22 stories from 1948 to 1957, all but two appearing by 1954, starting with a couple in *Weird Tales*. Most of them appeared in the US magazines, and most of those in *Astounding*, *Galaxy*, and *Fantasy & Science Fiction*. "Lost Memory" may be the best of them. "Plagiarist" is the last original Phillips story to appear in *New Worlds*, though his last story, "Next Stop the Moon," was reprinted in *New Worlds* after appearing in 1957 in the *London Daily Herald*. He never managed a collection, and "Dreams Are Sacred" is the only story of his that has been reprinted since 1990.

The oddest item in these issues is undoubtedly William de Koven's "Bighead" (**8**), a definitive send-up of the genre. In the future, the Brooklyn Movement puts mediocrity in the saddle, until there is a counter-revolution based on brain size. Things were crude at first. The founder explains: "I had to go by hat-size and age.... Unfortunately, this eliminated those whose heads were tall but small in circumference." Later, more refined methods were developed, relying on cranial capacity, ability to hold one's liquor, and absence of certainty on questions of life, death, and fate. Now the Bigheads lord it over the Pinheads. But Bighead Zircon defies his father Pluton for the love of a Pinhead girl, Threnda. After they are married, Pluton's agents go after Threnda, who survives a personality-tuned ray-ship attack only by discarding her clothes ("Clothes are part of the personality. Without them we are not the same. The magnetic emanations of an industrialist at a board meeting are not those of the same man in a bath-tub.") So it's war.

The Pinheads head to Mars, with Zircon sworn to help them. He learns he's being used and Threnda is one of the betrayers; but with the help of Melissa, who is undercover as the chief Pinhead's secretary ("She reached into the roots of her hair, extracted a tiny badge which fastened with a clip. 'Melissa, Operative Q-47 of the Bighead Secret Police.'"), Zircon wins through. Peace is in sight. This one sat in inventory for several years; it was advertised in **3** in 1947 as coming next issue. The often humorless Carnell apparently did not know quite what to make of it, as witness his solemn blurb ("It was an old problem—a minority with brains and power, against a majority only endowed with numbers—and corruption.") The readers didn't either. They voted it into last place. Carnell later wrote that de Koven "was a pseudonym for a then well-known American author but neither my memory nor records throw any light on his true identity."[26]

§

A. Bertram Chandler, who published 23 stories in *New Worlds* under his name and the George Whitley pseudonym, has three stories in these issues. The best, as by George Whitley, is "Castaway" (**6**), reprinted from the November 1947 *Weird Tales*. The protagonist, on a ship investigating smoke signals from a Pacific island, suddenly finds himself struggling alone in the water, barely makes it to shore, and when he looks for whoever lit the fire, finds a derelict spaceship from the future, complete with Mannschen Drive and its time-distortion properties. He can't keep his hands off it, and shortly finds himself in the water again. This is one of Chandler's better stories, tight and nightmarishly vivid.

The other two are less pointed but typically ingratiating. "Position Line" (**4**) is an agreeable piece of the nautical geekery that Chandler thrived on for years. On Mars, a spaceship crash has taken out the spaceport and power plant and a lot of people need rescuing fast from the other colony town. The only way is a fleet of Diesel sand cats—but how to navigate across the desert, in this yesterday's tomorrow without GPS? The protagonist, a dissatisfied policeman, formerly an equally dissatisfied mariner who came to Mars because sailing had become so automated, breaks out the bubble sextant he brought along, and it's

26. Carnell, "The Birth of *New Worlds*," *Vision of Tomorrow*, September 1970, p. 63.

George O. Smith in two dimensions for the rest of the story. This is probably the most mundane story in the issue in terms of science fictional ideation and action, and it's also the one the readers voted best in the issue.

It is followed by "Coefficient X," in **6**, another navigational opus. On Venus, which has lots of oceans, compasses have stopped working reliably, and ships are getting lost. The protagonist is a compass expert from Earth, and he finds the problem. There are creatures called "loofards," combinations of loofah and lizard (honest), which the Venerians (here called Hesperians) like to take into the bath with them—for exactly what is not explained, though the loofards do like to eat soap. They turn out to have iron in their bones and to generate magnetic fields, a bit like an electric eel. But there is more going on than this rather arid (well, humid too) gimmick. According to Chandler, Venus is multiracial: "Venus was a huge melting pot in which white and yellow, black and brown, were being blended. The results were—pleasing. The ability to live, to play, of some of the coloured folks lost nothing by admixture with the drive— on Earth so often squandered, so often without a worthy objective—of the whites." Later on, the ship's Calypso Man, known as Admiral Stormalong and "not overly dark," sings a song in the compass-mender's honor, beginning:

> "Eber since de worl' began
> De compass am de frien' of Man..."

There is also gender politics. The ship's captain already knows it's the loofards who are causing the compasses to go awry, but they need to get an expert from Earth to say it (and then to leave hastily) because the women are "the inevitable product of a combination of pioneering and all the comforts of civilization. They're spoiled here, utterly spoiled.... But they're powerful." And they like the loofards and oh, by the way, Voodoo has been reestablished, so the protagonist had better get off the planet fast if he knows what's good for him, and thank you very much.

A couple of other big names make lackluster contributions. John Beynon's "Time to Rest" (**5**) is a well written but sentimental story in which not much happens. Earth has blown up, stranding humans on the other planets, and Bert, who sails the Martian canals in his homemade boat, drops in on the Martian family he is friends with; notices that their daughter is getting grown up; gets nervous and leaves. Her mother says he'll be back. (And he is, in the sequel, a year or so later.) This one is reprinted from the *Arkham Sampler* of 1949. Beynon a.k.a. John Wyndham was not really a *New Worlds* mainstay; he published about 10 stories in it over the years, most notably the "Troons of Space" series starting in 1958, which became *The Outward Urge*.

William F. Temple's "Martian's Fancy" (**7**) is a piece of slapstick, overlong and tiresome, about a space captain who brings his half-breed illegitimate Martian son home to Earth for a visit with the family, wringing yocks from such matters as the housekeeper's hirsuteness. Temple made only five appearances in *New Worlds*. Though prolific, he spread his work around.

§

One of the pillars holding up these issues is F. G. Rayer, who previously had an archaic but pleasant item in **3** and a story in Gillings' *Fantasy* in 1947. He is a Little Known Writer of a peculiar sort, the quintessential *New Worlds* homeboy, once very well known in the UK but pretty much unheard of in the US. According to Miller/Contento, from 1947 to 1963, Rayer (1921-81) published some 58 stories in the UK magazines under his own name, eight as by George Longdon, and one as by Chester Delray. Over half of these were in *New Worlds*. After Carnell left *New Worlds*, that was it for his SF career. Except for the US reprint of *New Worlds*, he appeared in the US magazines only three times, each time with a story that also appeared in the

UK (though one of them made it into print first in the US). His anthology appearances, few and long ago, were in UK books with no US editions, except for one George Longdon story in an old Andre Norton anthology. Rayer also had a few novels published, one of which, *Tomorrow Sometimes Comes*, actually made a bit of a splash, but none of them had US editions either.

Rayer is profiled in *New Worlds* **33** (March 1955), and it seems that his SF was only the tip of an iceberg: he had allegedly published over a thousand stories and articles in at least 53 publications, mainly SF and "scientific articles." So he must have been a prolific science journalist somewhere. Rayer subscribes to Fans Are Slans: "I think the reading of present-day science fiction demands a certain mental liveliness and I would put readers of it as being generally of a higher intelligence level than average readers of other classes of fiction." The profile declares *Tomorrow Sometimes Comes* to be his "most outstanding piece of fiction," and Rayer says it "will remain the most personally satisfying, having also been translated and published in France and Portugal." (In an autobiographical piece for a fanzine,[27] Rayer recalls "the pleasure with which I received Olaf Stapledon's most high and generous praise" of the novel—even better than being published in France and Portugal, I would think.) I read *Tomorrow Sometimes Comes* a few years ago after visiting Australia and finding it awash in old paperbacks of the book. It is a post-nuclear war novel that runs the changes on big questions of human destiny vs. stagnation, freedom vs. regimentation, etc.—a bit stuffy but a respectable try, much better than the stories described below in these issues of *New Worlds*. Carnell reviewed it in **10** and described it as "undoubtedly the finest British science-fiction novel published in this country in recent years."

In his fanzine bio, Rayer says the best-remembered SF of his childhood was *Scoops*, back issues of which he borrowed from

27. F. G. Rayer, "Science Fiction Personalities," *Space Diversions* 6 (April-May 1953), at http://www.fanac.org/fanzines/SpaceDiversions/SpaceDiversions6-04.html (visited 9/8/11).

his cousin E. R. James, and he searched out Wells and Stapledon, the latter of whose "narrative style does not attract those who were more accustomed to minute paragraphs and endless (and often pointless) action." He dislikes "women dragged into stories for the sake of the feminine or romantic interest; pictures of the latter undressed yet unfrozen in space, etc.; stories based on series of 'clever' incidents which do not really integrate. Admired traits are: real originality, fully reasoned and logical development, scientific premises which will stand pondering upon, and lack of superficial emotion." He thinks SF should be at least as logical as detective stories. He continues:

> These feelings, strong as they are, may have arisen from the large amount of work I do on electronic equipment; here, there is *always* a reason, though sometimes complex deduction is required to discover it.... At present, should the Editor see a mobile device come along the road, halt, survey him with an electronic eye, then withdraw, he will know that one of my radio-controlled models is on reconnaissance.

So was the prolific Rayer an exclusively UK writer for nationalistic reasons, or could he just not sell to the higher-paying US markets? On the basis of the stories here, either is possible. They are an exceedingly mixed bag. The best of the lot is probably "Quest" (7). Konrad, spaceship captain, has been tossed overboard by Everard, his thuggish second in command, but spots and manages to board an ancient alien spaceship. A telepathic voice tells him he'll do fine for the job. (What job?) Everard and his sidekick show up at the airlock; the ship blew up after they got rid of Konrad. They've all got about 17 hours' oxygen. They black out and wake up with the ship down on a world full of dust. A robot greets them, explains that its creators had split into physically competent and pure brain factions, but the former were wiped out in a plague, so the pure brains sent out spaceships to try to find new helpers for them. (That's the job.) At their request, Konrad finishes assembling a machine they need, then asks to be sent back to Earth. The masters refuse, denounce mobile life as useless, and start to fry the robot. Konrad pulls it out of harm's way and it expresses its gratitude. Everard, who has been skulking about, tries to ambush Konrad for his remaining oxygen, and the robot saves Konrad. They head off to Earth, Konrad to be put in suspended animation for the voyage since he's running out of oxygen; he wonders whether he will arrive in a present he's familiar with or in the far future. This is hardly great literature but there is plenty of plot and imagination in relatively few pages; it gives good pulp weight.

"Necessity" (5) is about as well done, though a bit more obvious. Captain Pollard of the Star Trail Corps is expounding his theory that all life is interrelated when his spaceship is drawn inexorably to Xeros II. It lands in a clearing in a heavily vegetated area and can't take off again, for no apparent reason. The crew explores, but the plants don't cooperate; breaks in the forest close before the crew can get to them, keeping them in the clearing. There's a nasty-looking gray weed patch encroaching on the other plant life, and while they sleep it starts to envelope the spaceship. So they break out the weed killer and dispatch it. Suddenly the engines work again and they can leave. They've done what the other plants needed and brought them in for. Pollard's theory is vindicated. Here Rayer tries out his chops as a stylist, and he's not too bad in an overdone sort of way: "There was something so pathetic about the melody of the leaves that it was with a feeling of inexpressible melancholy that he at last fell asleep. It were as if the trees were telling of some long-drawn, secret agony which sapped their life, leaving them listless except to tell of their misery in the evening cool."

The other two Rayer stories are a more rancid kettle of fish, with pretty serious defects of logic and plausibility. In "Adaptability" (6), in "the gigantic factory which was being built to mark the dawn of the 21st century—the beginning of an age of new mechanical and scientific wonder," funny things are happening. A strange light appears, there's a spherical vehicle from which grotesque forms appear and quickly disappear into the nearby woods; people give chase but just when they think they have one, it turns out to be a branch or a tree stump. Somehow, there seem to be more X-M units (whatever they are) than anyone ordered. So they analyze samples of all the X-M units. They're metal, all right. The protagonist, a big wheel (not a cog) in the factory, does the only sensible thing—he lurks, and when the vehicle appears again and the grotesque forms have disembarked, he leaps into it and gets taken whence it came, which proves to be an extradimensional world full of the aforesaid grotesque forms bent on world conquest—all the worlds—through their uncanny imitative ability. He learns this because they are telepathic and he eavesdrops; somehow he keeps his own thoughts under control and manages to hijack the vehicle back to the home dimension, where he and the factory crew take all the X-M units—which he realizes are disguised aliens who have managed to adjust their molecules as well as their outward form—and put them to the test of heating inductors, killing the invaders. A homemade bomb thrown into the vehicle on its next pass completes the defense of humanity.

The worst of the lot is "Deus Ex Machina" (**8**). It is the first of Rayer's "Magnis Mensas" series, which comprises five stories over 11 years in *New Worlds* and *Science Fiction Adventures*, and which also includes the above-mentioned novel *Tomorrow Sometimes Comes* published the following year, though there the eponymous world-dominating computer is called Mens Magna. In "Deus Ex Machina," an employee of Subterraneous Architects is accused of criminal negligence, charged with murder, and sentenced to death at the instance of Magnis Mensas, which saw the whole thing, and which is allowed to testify without oath, since the oath would be meaningless to a machine and machines can't lie anyway.[28]

---

28. In the Anglo-American legal system, criminal negligence, even resulting in death, is entirely different from murder, so the idea that they would be equated and the former treated as a capital crime in any

After the trial, several people—the employee's boss, his fiancé, his lawyer—point out to Magnis Mensas that since it did see the whole thing, its failure to warn the deceased is equally culpable. MM locks them up so they can't tell anyone else. (Why they didn't point this out during the trial is not explained.) Why is MM doing this? For the good of humanity. The employee was directing an excavation that shortly would have discovered the existence of "negative matter vessels and negative matter beings," and it would cause mass neurosis to "let man know his Earth is honeycombed by beings a hundred times more powerful than himself." But Padre Cameron puts a bug in MM's ear about how humans swear before an Ideal (a.k.a. their Maker) and how terrible it is for humans to die unready to meet their Maker (connection of the latter point to the story is a bit unclear). Problem solved! MM brings forth the prisoners and gets them to swear they won't tell a soul about negative matter vessels and beings, and lets them out.

E(rnest) R(ayer) James is almost Rayer's shadow, as well as his relative and sometime collaborator—prolific, though not as much as Rayer, with 42 appearances in the UK SF magazines (the respectable ones—*New Worlds, Science Fantasy, Authentic, Nebula*), from 1947 to 1963. His only appearances outside the UK consisted of two stories reprinted in the US edition of *New Worlds*. This story is his second, following a first appearance in Gillings' *Fantasy* in 1947. He seems to be another writer whose career was effectively ended by Carnell's departure from *New Worlds* and *Science Fantasy*. He had a couple more stories in a 1947 UK-only original anthology or collection called *Worlds At War* (which also had some Rayer stories), and his couple of anthology appearances were in UK-only books. He has no entry in the *Encyclopedia of Science Fiction* and therefore presumably has not published a novel. So to those who go back a ways with British SF, he is probably reasonably well known, but otherwise, not. He might be described as the UK equivalent of,

---

recognizable future variant on that system is absurd.

say, Winston K. Marks, author of many forgotten SF stories.

James did have a low-level second career, with another seven stories in *Dream, New Moon, Fantasy Annual* and *Gryphon SF and Fantasy Reader* from 1987 to 1998, all minor markets and several of them semi-professional low-circulation nostalgia operations. Miller/Contento has no dates for James, but *New Worlds* **37** (July 1955) has a profile of him, indicating he was 34 (therefore b. 1921, presumably). It says he started "to seriously plan a semi-literary career" in 1947, having survived Normandy blinded in one eye. "To this end he took a job as a postman in a rural Yorkshire area where he and his wife live because 'I have found,' he states, 'that postal work fits in with a career of part-time writing very well. In fact, I declined an offer of an indoor clerical appointment in the Post Office because I felt that the outdoor work left my mind less exhausted and more eager for thinking up stories.'" Carnell adds: "With the courage of such convictions he has now sold over thirty-five stories...."

James' "The Rebels" (**4**) is a scenery-chewer of the *Planet Stories* ilk. On a spaceship of a viciously hierarchical society, the likes of the Master Minder and the Overseer lord it over the crew, which is always terrified of falling into the Redundant Class. But the downtrodden stage a mutiny, hoping to divert the ship from its destination to the Independent City on Efferenter II. The plans go awry, they fail to kill all the big shots, and they wind up in a bloody free-for-all that ends in blowing the ship in half. Three survivors manage to crash-land their half-ship on Efferenter III, which is no help at all, but they figure out how to prop up and lash down the gyroscope so they can point in the right direction, fill the ship with helium so they can get off the ground with the aid of E.III's high rotational velocity, and they're on their way to E.II and freedom. It is a crude but grimly enthusiastic piece of blood-and-thunder storytelling.

Sydney J. Bounds (1920-2006), who had 16 stories in *New Worlds* over the years, published a total of about 70 in the SF magazines, remaining active as late as 2002 (though most of his output after the demise of *Vision of Tomorrow* appears to be in semi-professional venues). He too seems to have been a UK-only writer, with one sale to *Fantastic Universe* in the 1950s, but no more to the US magazines. His stories under his own name appeared in the higher-rent UK magazines—*New Worlds, Science Fantasy, Nebula*, and *Authentic*—but he also used a number of pseudonyms to publish in the downmarket ones like *Worlds of Fantasy* and *Futuristic Science Stories*, to which he contributed a story actually titled "Vultures of the Void." He published a few paperback SF novels in the 1950s as well as confessions, juvenile, gangster and western fiction, according to his profile in *New Worlds* **32** (February 1955). He was a member of the late '30s London circle that included Arthur C. Clarke and William F. Temple, and became a full-time writer in 1951, leaving a job as sub-station assistant on the London Underground. The profile says: "Still unmarried he prefers to smoke a pipe and paint pictures for relaxation—and prefers art to be spelt with a small 'a'."

On that last score, one cannot accuse Bounds of hypocrisy. "Too Efficient" (**5**) is a piece of pleasant yard goods: protagonist discovers his newly purchased electric motor is working at 107% efficiency, goes to the company to investigate. Of course they're stranded aliens trying to raise enough money to get off the planet. These high-efficiency engines really have nuclear power plants concealed inside them. The aliens kidnap the protagonist to their spaceship, which is underwater. After they depart, releasing the protagonist, he heads home, gloating that he is in possession of "the secret of space travel!"

"The Spirit of Earth" (**8**) takes a great leap downward, however: it's a displaced French Foreign Legion story set on Mercury that is best allowed to speak for itself. Here the Captain, disgraced and exiled of course, is assembling a rescue party for a crashed spaceship:

> The Captain felt a pride in his men, a pride he had once felt in very different circumstances, and had

never thought to know again. He walked slowly down the ragged line, picking his men.

"Long Tom."

A gangling frame of creaking bones and mahogany skin straightened up. The gaunt face smiled, smiled as it had once under twin Martian moons, treading the red desert.

"Shilo."

A squat figure shifted from one splayed foot to another. A light flickered deep in yellow eyes—eyes that had looked out over the hideous landscape of massive Jupiter.

"Sturm and Jeri."

The brothers' dark, impassive faces revealed nothing. They might have been volunteering to make up a foursome at space poker—or booking a return passage to their native Venus.

"Blacky."

Once he had been a space jockey, riding Saturn's rings: now he was just one more derelict at Outpost Sunspot, the dumping ground for broken men, the end of the journey from which there could be no return.

"Adoption" by Don J. Doughty (**6**), his only appearance in the SF magazines, competently rings a change on a standard plot: Johnny has an imaginary playmate Bugs, but Bugs proves to be real, from a pretty horrible future, so when he comes home with Johnny and then can't get back to his own time, Johnny's parents are happy to take him in.

J. W. Groves' "Robots Don't Bleed" (**8**) recapitulates Lester del Rey's mawkish "Helen O'Loy," this time as spite. Space pilot meets girl as a result of the lifelike robot rabbits she makes. They want to get married but he needs money, so he spaces out again (as it were) for a year, and when he gets back, there she is to meet him, except he figures out it isn't really she when a spaceship crash-lands on her and she isn't hurt. She's made a lifelike robot of herself to occupy him, and meanwhile she's married someone else. So he heads back to space with the robot ("If it was good for nothing else, at least it could do the chores."). But he gets homesick, and returns and drops in on his ex-fiancé, who has grown fat and snobbish and has reduced her formerly spacegoing husband to puttering around making toy model spaceships. So it's outward bound into the great void again, with his robot, no return planned. Carnell liked this one enough to anthologize it twice, in *No Place Like Earth* and *The Best From New Worlds*. Groves (b. 1910) published a dozen stories in the SF magazines in a curiously symmetrical career: one in 1931, 10 from 1950 through 1954 (one in *Astounding*, the others in the US pulps), and one in 1964. He also published two belated novels in the late 1960s, *Shellbreak* and *The Heels of Achilles*.

Ian Williamson's "Chemical Plant" (8) belongs to a common subgenre in *New Worlds* and many other SF magazines: send the characters to a newly discovered planet and set them a technical puzzle. See Rayer's "Necessity," discussed earlier in this chapter, for another very similar example. Here, a space-ship lands on a planet covered with vegetation, near five lakes all of which have differently colored water, then disappears. Investigation by would-be rescuers reveals that the world-plant was extracting chromium for nourishment. The lakes are different acid baths, and the spaceship is a huge and tasty morsel that the plant humped into one of the lakes by selectively growing. There is a stereotypical clash between the pompous captain who wants to blast everything and the nice captain who gets down on the ground and turns over rocks to find out what is going on. It's not badly done, and the readers put it first in the issue, ahead of Clarke's "Guardian Angel." Carnell anthologized the story in *No Place Like Earth*, and said: "Ian Williamson denies all credit for the story under his name, stating that it was actually written by a logical-computing machine which is kept in a cellar near Manchester University. As a physicist he stumbled across this 'captive' machine quite by accident—

it had been built by a scientist who could prove that he was sane and the rest of the world quite mad. As nobody is likely to believe Mr. Williamson's statement, he is quite happy in the knowledge that he can go on using the machine to further his own literary ideals." It must have blown a resistor or something; Ian Williamson has no other credits in the SF magazines.

Norman Lazenby's "The Cireesians" (4) is an amusing if incompetently written tale of transcendence. It seems Earth humans originated in an unauthorized bio-engineering experiment by one of the true humans of Cirees, and they were hastily dumped on the young planet Earth along with a conscience-stricken Cireesian who helps them survive, contemporaneously with dinosaurs. Eventually they evolve into us, and we head out to the Lesser Doriad Cloud, where our boys encounter the remaining Cireesians, who introduce themselves as Gods, having long since disembodied themselves. Big mistake, because now they are helpless: "We are pools of pure thought needing the reviving fibres of crude humans." But they have a plan: "We will infest your body and then reproduce from you, rapidly and with incredible variation, a new being who will be a biological combination of your two sexes." They say, "We are entitled to you." Why? Because their representative stayed on Earth and helped us out hundreds of millions of years ago. But the humans outsmart the Gods and defeat their scheme. Think of it as a cautionary tale about the Singularity. Norman Lazenby (1914-2003), by now a thoroughly Little Known Writer, had appeared a few times in Walter Gillings' *Fantasy* in the '40s, had nothing more in *New Worlds*, but published a couple of dozen stories, mostly in the (reputedly) really trashy UK magazines like *Tales of Tomorrow* and *Futuristic Science Stories* in the 1950s, and contributed such pseudonymous items to the early '50s downmarket paperback boom as *The Brains of Helle*, attributed to Bengo Mistral. He had a couple of stragglers in *Vision of Tomorrow* and *Fantasy Booklet* much later.

The bottom of the barrel is shared by W. Moore (not the talented Ward Moore, US author of the celebrated *Bring the*

Jubilee, and this byline does not reappear) and by Francis Ashton. Moore's "Pool of Infinity" (**5**) is an inane prepubertal-shaggy-God creation story in which Isosceles and Equilateral fool around with a new mixture Daddy has whipped up, and splash some droplets around. "Jet Landing" by Ashton (**6**) is a brief and geeky lecture revealing the difficulty of landing a rocket on its tailfins without a stern periscope. That byline appears only in two other stories in *Super Science Stories* in 1950 and 1951. However, Ashton (1904-94) also produced several novels: *The Breaking of the Seals* (1946), allegedly a theological fantasy; *Alas That Great City* (1948), allegedly a sequel, having something to do with Atlantis; and *The Wrong Side of the Moon* (1952, with Stephen Ashton), an SF novel that Carnell (in **14**) found to be of some merit.

3: TEMPORARY STABILITY (1951-53)

New Worlds reached a milestone in 1951: a regular schedule. It was quarterly, with no missed issues, throughout 1951, and began 1952 as a bimonthly, staying that way into 1953. (Carnell's editorial in **11** says that they had intended to publish bimonthly starting with **10**, the Summer 1951 issue, but were thwarted by paper shortages, which also affected *Science Fantasy*.) At the end of this 13-issue period of stability, the magazine was beset with more business and logistical problems. **21**, which should have been dated May 1953 per the bi-monthly schedule, was instead dated June; and then there was another hiatus lasting the better part of a year.

From **9** (Spring 1951) through **19** (January 1953) the magazine remained more or less the same physically, 96 pages exclusive of covers in the 5½ x 8½ inch "large digest" size, with the same cover logo as prior issues, the subtitle "fiction of the future" below the title. The issue date did disappear from the cover with **16**, to be replaced with the issue number. Carnell explains in his **15** editorial that distributors advised him a bi-monthly magazine would stay on sale longer if it didn't have a date. The price increased from 1/6 to 2s. with **10**. There were no story titles or other lettering on the cover. Changes began in **20**, on which "*New Worlds* fiction of the future" became "*New Worlds Science Fiction*," and the price and issue number were moved to yellow circles below the title.

With **21**, however, the magazine changed to digest size—

precisely, 7 ¼ x 5 ¼ inches, down from 8 ½ x 5 ½—with title, subtitle, issue number and price in a white band at the top of the cover (still no lettering on the cover picture itself). Carnell's editorial assures the readers that *New Worlds* has adopted digest format, not to imitate the US magazines, but because it's the most economical given the change in production arrangements. With that change the pages increased to 128 exclusive of covers. The price dropped back to 1/6. The total wordage may well have dropped, since in addition to the reduced page size, the type face is larger. The change in production—from G.F.Tompkin Ltd. to The Carlton Press at 3 Racquet Court on Fleet Street—seems to have represented some compromise in quality as well as a change in size. The paper seems to be lower quality, and the cover stock as well as the inside pages are crumbling on my copy. Though the new typeface looks nice, lines are inked a trifle unevenly, which is a mild distraction.

Initially, Carnell's is the only name on the masthead. G. Ken Chapman appears as "Assistant" with **15**; in **21**, both he and Leslie Flood are listed as "Assistant Editors."

One other infrastructural matter bears mentioning. Around **16**, instances of egregiously bad proofreading, such as dogged *Science Fantasy* through most of its life, start to appear. For example, one of F. G. Rayer's characters in **16** has invented a "space-abberator," and in **17**, E. R. James' spaceship crew is saved by the gravitational field of "Icaurus" (and that's shortly after a reference to "rigors"—definitely a typo by UK standards.)

At first, the covers continued to be done by Bob Clothier, but Reina Bull (1923-2000) appeared on **11** (and disappeared after **18**), and Gerard Quinn appeared with **13**. Clothier's last cover was on **20**, and the next issue began the long dominance of Quinn. This is not surprising. The readers' comments in "Postmortem" are overwhelmingly praiseful for Quinn but much more ambivalent about Clothier. The covers on these issues are a pretty uneven lot. They begin with one of Clothier's best, a complex and colorful rendering of a man in a boat looking at a puzzling and clearly decaying structure, with a spaceship in the background. There's an Escher-like quality to it, but close scrutiny shows it's "no trompe"—it all adds up in conventional perspective, there's only the illusion of an illusion. See it at the usual online sites,[29] though a scan doesn't quite do this one justice.

Unfortunately the rest of Clothier's work doesn't measure up to it. The next issue's cover is pretty crude and perfunctory, and the one on **20** (Clothier's last) is also irritatingly cartoony. **14** is garish and conventionally cheesy (robots with flamethrowers, no less), and **16** purports to be a sort of symbolic collage but the elements don't add up. Only the cover of **12**, with stylized spaceship and gantry looming over a busy spaceport scene, is up to standard. Clothier gives the impression of having lost interest in the whole enterprise. He did a few covers later for *Nebula*, which generally look neither as good as the best nor as bad as the worst for *New Worlds*. Interestingly, he did no work for *Science Fantasy*, to which his style would seem to be well adapted.

The latter was certainly true of Reina Bull, who contributed a couple of weirdly perverse and very effective covers to *Science Fantasy*, but whose approach falls flat on her two *New Worlds* covers. The cover of **11** is much ado about very little. The very colorful, stylized, and anatomically unlikely female figure (unless her hip and knee are dislocated), on close scrutiny, proves to be pushing the ignition of a stylized futuristic go-kart, with a couple of other arbitrary futuristic objects in the background. The **18** cover portrays a woman with similarly cod-exotic face and diaphanous gown, striking a pose with space-suited man and retro spaceship in the background. None of it adds up thematically. Bull seems to have gotten the words but not the tune of SF.

Quinn, on the other hand, seems to have the tune but not the words. His first cover (**13**) is rationalistic enough. There's a

29. See these covers at http://www.sfcovers.net/mainnav.htm or http://www.philsp.com/mags/newworlds.html.

man with wires affixed to his head and a horrified look on his face, and an extraterrestrial lobster, a rabbit, and a spaceship deployed in the background, but these elements don't add up in any suggestive way; it's like a rummage sale, not helped by the fact that the man's face and hair look like a wax effigy of the young Arnold Schwarzenegger. The juxtaposition works better on **15**, which portrays an anguished human in draping garment against an ambiguous scarlet background that could be read as the palm of a hand, with Earth floating disconnectedly in the foreground. This one does at least seem to have a unifying idea behind it. It also looks to be influenced by the heavily symbolic covers Alejandro Canedo was doing for *Astounding* in the preceding few years.

17's cover is another rummage sale: male head, female head, ambiguous red blob in the foreground, the Grim Reaper conferring with an overcoated male figure behind them, probably saying something like, "I'm out of here—they call this a script?" **19** is a relief (visually, not physically): a couple of spacesuited men with spaceship in the background, pleasingly balanced, though the fluorescent colors of their spacesuits are a bit much. **21** is another misfire: lunar-looking landscape with sun peeking over the horizon and ambiguous machine in foreground, the horizon at a disorienting 45-degree angle. This is actually a pretty faithful illustration of the lead story, E. R. James' Mercury-sited "Ride the Twilight Rail," but it's not a very effective visual presentation. Quinn is clearly still feeling his way—a proposition with which he seems to agree. One of the first of the inside front cover *New Worlds* Profiles (**19**) is about Quinn, a Belfast resident whose background is in newspaper work including strip cartooning: "At present he is not satisfied with the type of illustrations he is producing and intends slanting them more towards the technical than the human."

Interior illustrations are by Clothier, Hunter, and Quinn; Bull also appears in the issues where she did the covers; Hutchings appears for the first time in **21**. They are generally competent but nondescript. Quinn's are a bit more striking than the others;

he makes more use of stippling, cross-hatching, and scratch-board, as does Bull. However, the results in both cases tend to be dark and murky; perhaps they are compromised by repro-duction methods. Hutchings contributes one illustration that might be described as Edd Cartier Meets Socialist Realism.

§

Advertising continues more or less the same as the previous Nova issues, mostly SF books and magazines (including book-stores, publishers' ads, and house ads for back issues, *Science Fantasy*, etc.), with the total advertising space generally comprising the back cover and the two inside covers plus half to two and a half interior pages. Non-book/magazine advertising includes an inside front cover ad for *The Day the Earth Stood Still* and an interior half-page for the British Interplanetary Society. **19** has a full page announcing the UK Science Fiction Book Club, which required members to subscribe rather than giving them a choice to buy each item—not a bad deal in this case, since the first selections are *Earth Abides*, *The Martian Chronicles*, and *Last and First Men*. The Editorial Committee includes Carnell, Arthur C. Clarke, Dr. J. G. Porter, F.R.A.S., of the Royal Greenwich Observatory, and Edward Shanks, "distin-guished author and critic," who wrote at least one SF novel, *The People of the Ruins: A Story of the English Revolution and After* (1920), a post-disaster novel in which the disaster started with a general strike. Shanks was also known as a WWI poet and later journalist and biographer.

Several of the inside front covers are devoted to ads for the White Horse Tavern, inviting the readership to attend the SF gatherings and portraying archetypal scenes: manager Lew Mordecai drawing a cold one, sorry, a lukewarm one; Carnell and H. J. Campbell of *Authentic SF* examining cover art; authors Tubb, Temple, David Griffiths,[30] and Bounds discussing

30. Griffiths, an unfamiliar name to most SF readers, wrote pseudonymously for the downmarket UK paperback SF market in the early 1950s. Harbottle,

space opera (actually, paging through manuscripts). Starting with **18**, however, the inside front cover is devoted to the *New Worlds* Profiles, which occupied that space for most of the rest of Carnell's tenure.

The departments continue as before in these issues, subject to limitations of space; **9**, for example, includes only "The Literary Line-Up." The rest of the issues all have editorials, and there are either book reviews or film reviews (one, of *The Day the Earth Stood Still*, in **13**) in all but **15** and **16**. "Postmortem," the letter column, finally appears in **10**, but Carnell clearly regards it as dispensable; it doesn't appear again until **15**, is in **16** and **17**, and that's it, for the moment.

§

Carnell's editorials are now consistently a full page. In **10** ("Current Trends"), he notes the "overwhelming change" in the British SF market, i.e., "dozens of regular and irregular pocketbooks," some of which "leave[] much to be desired.... That our contemporaries are not concerned with altruism is obvious from the type of material being published—to give credit where due, however, *one* newcomer to the field is making a serious attempt to tackle the field from an adult angle and present acceptable concepts in its stories." (Perhaps he means *Authentic*.) Presciently, he suggests there are not enough experienced writers in the country to maintain "any reasonable standard of literary value" at the current volume of publication. In "The Literary Line-Up" he circles back to this point: "It is very encouraging to see the number of new authors who are now beginning to make their debut in our pages. New writers bring fresh ideas, even to old concepts, and, unlike some of our contemporaries who appear to have a penchant for staff-written stories, *New Worlds* contributors are individual entities." (The new writers he has in mind, all of whom are in the

---

Vultures of the Void: The Legacy, pp. 125-26, 155-56.

next issue, include Lee Rondelle, Hjalmar Boyesen, and Alan Barclay. Rondelle and Boyesen were never heard from again in the SF magazines; Barclay, however, contributed 20 stories to *New Worlds* before he was through ten years later.)

In subsequent issues, Carnell forgets his critique of the UK SF market and waxes triumphalist, noting the increases in hardcover SF publication in **18** ("From here on the barrier is down—science-fiction has come into its own.") He proposes in **19** ("Escape Velocity—or Escapism?") that fans are slans, excuse me, that SF readers are better equipped than others to deal with the future. In **20** ("Open Sesame"), his concern about enough competent writers has been displaced entirely: "The situation in Britain is now similar to the American field in 1939... will there be a buying public to sustain so many regular publications?"

The editorial in **11**, "Space Opera...," says: "The blunt truth is that, despite changing literary trends with excursions into the philosophical and psychological fields of the future, space opera has been, is, and will be, the backbone of science fiction." There are "varying grades": the "cosmic wild west" type, which does more harm than good, the "short, plausible, thought-provoking stories centred around a spaceship somewhere in the void, and there are the 'classics' of the top authors which need 80,000 words or more of first-class writing to put over credibility."

In **12**, he says he never hears from 87% of the readers, and the rest comprise 12.65% readers who write with a complaint, request, or suggestion, and 0.35% fans who write regularly and comment on everything from cover to cover (no totals or other details of these calculations are given). But "The Literary Line-Up" is still valid, he says, because the story ratings reflect the preferences of the Silent Majority. How he thinks he knows that is not explained—perhaps it's just that the magazine hasn't gone bankrupt. Next issue, however ("Reprints—Again!"), he says he's getting a deluge of letters from the formerly silent 87% , who bring up "reprints" from the US magazines.

This issue of reprints arose earlier, in "Postmortem" in **10**, where Walt Willis found it a pity that a US magazine beat *New*

Worlds to first publication of Clarke's "Guardian Angel," and Carnell clarified that the sales were simultaneous. He said that the "most outstanding paradox" of this sort was Beynon's "No Place Like Earth," which was written for *New Worlds*, accepted, and assigned the cover, and *subsequently* sold to a US magazine which nonetheless published it at the same time as *New Worlds*, changed the title, and put it on the cover with a curvaceous blonde in a bikini instead of the "silvery-furred female *griffa*" of Beynon's story. This magazine was *Ten Story Fantasy*, which notoriously changed the story's title to "Tyrant and Slave Girl on the Planet Venus" and prominently featured a whip on the cover.

In **12**'s editorial, again he wants to clarify—these aren't *really* reprints. British authors were already selling in the US when *New Worlds* started, and presumably wanted to keep doing so. "Nova Publications has always advocated that a good story is worth selling to as many nations as possible, and to that end *only* buys First British Serial Rights." Sometimes stories they buy first appear in the US first, and vice versa. "The old narrow order of exclusive Rights is a thing of the past." In the very next issue's "Literary Line-Up," however, he announces "a new Van Vogt story, 'Enchanted Village,' recently published in U.S.A.—a poignant Martian story most readers will be pleased to see published in this country." There is no claim of simultaneous sale. This is not the end of the subject either. In **19** and **20**, the contents page declares "New Stories Only" and "No Reprints." But that line disappears in **21**, to be followed by a firm change in policy that will be discussed later.

This business of reprints is part of the continuing low-level pother about *New Worlds*'s Britishness and its competitiveness with the US magazines, both from Carnell and from the readers, the main thrust of which is ambivalence. Carnell says in the Editorial in **10** that "*New Worlds* had to pioneer along developing new authors and relying upon a small core of regular professional writers who usually wrote only for the American market. They backed our contention that an all-British magazine was not only needed, but essential." In "Postmortem" in **10**, one reader says *New Worlds* has "a fair way to go" to match the best stories in *Astounding*, and advises obtaining stories by van Vogt, Sturgeon, Latham, Russell, Anderson, Asimov, etc. Carnell responds "! ! ! — Our exclamations!" and, more substantively, continues:

> There are two insurmountable obstacles to Mr. Burke's suggestion, worthy though it is. The first is that all the above top-ranking authors can sell practically all their material to an established American market, and the few odd unsold stories which follow the trade winds round the globe are not worth considering. The second is that the American market pays far higher rates than the British, and no top author writing for a regular American market, would, in his right mind, submit material to us for, to quote one of them, 'peanuts.'
>
> A third factor is that, obstacles being surmounted, such an influx of Americanised writing would partially defeat our intention of an Anglicized magazine. Although we will (and do) occasionally have an American written story.

A more positive spin on this proposition appears in the Editorial in **12**: "I think the policy will remain as it now is—to publish the best available stories, mainly by British authors, with the emphasis on a good literary standard. Don't you agree?"

In "Postmortem" in **15**, the comparisons continue: John Brunner proposes that if *New Worlds* were marketed in the US "it would hold its own with any of the magazines published there," and a California reader compares the January 1952 issues of *Galaxy* and *New Worlds*: "I would say that, in comparison, your magazine was better in content than *Galaxy*, the art work comparable, and the production *better*." One letter-writer complains of the unfairness of pitting the other authors against a van Vogt story; in **16**, P. W. Cutler disagrees: "If it is at all possible, let us have some more material by top-flight American authors. It will have the effect of spurring our own contributors on to better things...." Carnell is inclined to agree, but says "the difficulty, however, is in getting material by top-flight American authors!"

Another reader in **16** finds that *New Worlds* shares first place with *Galaxy*. Carnell replies: "I don't know what John Campbell of *Astounding* and Horace Gold of *Galaxy* will say to these continual cross references! Better send them some cigars at Christmas, I suppose." Another reader says: "You seem to take the view that you are not as good as *Galaxy* or *Astounding*. I think you are as good as, if not better than, the former, and better than the latter—except, of course, when you print stories like 'The Flame Gods' [see below]." Carnell responds: "...I don't compare *New Worlds* with any of the American magazines because we are not modelled on any of them and we are catering predominantly for a British audience. The cleavage is quite pronounced now, and the gap will go on widening—but thanks for the compliments."

In **17**'s "Postmortem," one reader decries all comparisons, and Carnell enthusiastically agrees: "Complimentary though most of those comparisons have been, I feel it is like comparing a rowing boat with an ocean liner." Faithful correspondent P. W. Cutler says:

> I am, as you know, a No. 1 N.W. booster, but when I see references to the effect that N.W. is better than *Galaxy*, and that Tubb is among the second-best authors in the world, I begin to wonder whether such references are genuine opinions or made out of sheer patriotism.
>
> I am sure that you have no illusions about the status of *New Worlds*; it goes without saying that it is the top magazine in this country, *but* we must acknowledge the fact that, at the moment anyway, the top flight

science-fiction authors are almost exclusively American, and being human they are going to sell their material to the magazines that pay the highest rates. [Tubb is getting there and in time] will be able to hold his own with any of the above-named, but when that time comes, will he still be writing for *New Worlds*?

Carnell responds: "Too true, I'm afraid. In building British writers for our own requirements we are becoming a nursery for the higher-paying American market. The saving grace is that British writers seldom channel their stories into the more rigid requirements of American editors." That's the end of the back and forth because that's the last appearance of "Postmortem" for a while. However, in the Editorial in **21**, Carnell is pleased to report that in a poll by the Liverpool SF Society, *New Worlds* comes in fourth, after *Astounding*, *Galaxy*, and *Fantasy & Science Fiction*, and holds that position among American readers as well as UK readers. "That's pretty good—but not good enough!"

The **15** editorial notes that with the next issue, *New Worlds* will tie *Tales of Wonder* for most issues published by a UK SF magazine. In that next issue, which is *New Worlds*'s three-year anniversary (counting from the Nova revival), Carnell indulges in "stocktaking." The magazine has weathered rough storms on the production side, "having had to cope with rising printing and paper costs, a falling buying market owing to the drop in consumer purchasing power, and increased competition from other publishers entering the field." In 13 issues, it's published 65 stories, of which six were subsequently purchased for US magazines and 15 have been bought for anthologies in the UK or the U.S. (Of course, seven of the 15 would have been for Carnell's own first anthology.) It has "found (or been found by)" 20 new British writers and has developed four artists "whose names are beginning to mean something to the connoisseurs of fantasy art." They've lost Clarke, who is no longer writing short stories (actually he published six in 1953, but then he did slow down), and William F. Temple, who is now editor of a boys' annual for Hulton Press and technical advisor for the film of *Four-Sided Triangle*. The magazine is circulating to Scandinavia, Holland, Belgium, France, Italy, India, Hong Kong, and to one subscriber behind the Iron Curtain.

In **17**, Carnell talks about the covers— "our shop window to the public"—which he says are based on stories, even if the magazine doesn't say so. (It does, in this issue and **18**— "(Cover)" appears by the story's name on the table of contents— but that innovation soon disappears.) Though Carnell doesn't say so, usually it is the lead story that is illustrated, but not always. In **11**, for example, the Bull cover is for the short story "No Priority" by H.H. Boyesen. The selected story goes to the artist to read and rough out an idea. "A process of elimination and often amalgamation of ideas then produces the main theme" (meaning, apparently, that Carnell has his own ideas). The artist produces a "colour rough"; final changes "structural or artistic" can be made at this stage. Then the final painting is done.

The lettering is then overlaid and the whole goes to the block-maker, who generates "progressives" (proofs in the primary colours and their combinations) to the printer, who matches inks for the final printing, "watched carefully by ourselves" since a slight variation in the intermediate stages can make a big difference in the look of the final cover. The printer adds varnish to inks to gloss up the whole picture—on **9**, one of their best covers, they forgot that and it came out flat and dull. In the previous issue's "Postmortem," Carnell had said: "Until we can use four-colour covers, the reproductions will always suffer, although the lighter toned paintings come out fairly well. There's a magnificent Quinn painting on hand which will prob-ably reduce poorly."

The letter column "Postmortem," in its first appearance, is short and highly edited; Carnell did not publish letters but excerpts and quotations from letters, to which he replies. (He says he will have replies by authors and artists, too, but none are in evidence.) Editing becomes less severe (or less visible) in subsequent issues. High points not discussed elsewhere are the appearance of names then or later familiar in SF fandom and sometimes professional circles (Erik Fennel, Dan McPhail, and Walt Willis in **10**; John Brunner and H.P. Sanderson in **15**; Eric Bentcliffe and Sanderson again in **16**; and Archie Mercer in **17**). Interestingly, there is about as much comment on the art as on the fiction. Whether that represents the readers' preoccupation or the editor's is impossible to say.

Interesting snippets from Carnell include his explanation in **16**, such as it is, of why subscriptions are more expensive than buying from the newsstand, contrary to the US practice even then: "It is an unwritten rule in the publishing trade that subscribers must pay the postal costs on books or magazines ordered direct from publishers. The precedent goes back to World War I days and cannot lightly be broken." He also explains the purpose of an SF convention: "to meet and discuss the growing field of science fiction, to exchange views upon their own country's publications, and to influence, where possible, everyone concerned with publishing the literature to a higher standard."[31]

§

In these issues there is considerable non-fiction, in addition to the departments. Most of them contain an article and several contain two. Some of these are science features, like "Spacesuits Will Be Worn" (**10**) by "Arthur C. Clarke, B.Sc." Others of this ilk include "Digital Computers" (**12**) by Arthur F. Roberts, which has various interesting observations, prescient and otherwise ("Similarly, instructing the machine—*programming*, as it is repulsively termed—is not as simple, and cannot be as simple as much of the computing world at present hopes." Concerning the unknown effects of computing: "The major effect of the typewriter, it may be recalled, was to emancipate women."); "Electronics—To Come" (**13**) by Frank Kerr, "Silicones" (**19**)

31. Apparently this is a man who never managed to find the convention bar.

by John Newman, "The Atom Bomb" (**20**) by T. Owens, and "All Change" (**20**) by Laurence Sandfield, about mutations. For all but Newman and Sandfield, these were their only appearances in the SF magazines. Sandfield had a few stories elsewhere and another article in *New Worlds*. For Newman, this is the first of a couple of dozen he was to write for *New Worlds* and other UK SF magazines, followed by dozens and dozens by "Kenneth Johns," his collaborative pseudonym with Kenneth Bulmer—in effect, he/they became the science columnist for *New Worlds* (and *Nebula* and *Authentic*, it appears).

A number of the articles amount to community-building exercises. Carnell has a several-page report in **11** titled "1951 International Convention," complete with a couple of photos. Although US events call themselves "world" conventions, he argues, this is the first truly international one. The highlight, he says, was the announcement of the International Fantasy Awards, which had only been thought of a few weeks previously. In fact, the actual awards weren't ready yet, though there was a wooden replica available for display. The actual awards would comprise a metal spaceship affixed to a mahogany base *along with a built-in cigarette lighter.* The winners were George R. Stewart's *Earth Abides* and Willy Ley's *The Conquest of Space*.

These awards were apparently a considerable source of pride to the UK SF community. Carnell devotes his editorial to them in **14**, and there are two additional articles entirely about the next year's awards, both by Leslie Flood, Secretary of the International Fantasy Award Fund: "A Merit for Fantasy" in **15** and "Inquest—by Request" in **18**. The former gives a quick history of the award. Like Nova Publications, it emerged from a conversation at the White Horse Tavern, this one among Flood, John Beynon Harris, Ken Chapman, and Frank Cooper. It dispels the rumor of a "pay to play" scheme. There was a fund-raising pool, with the best guess as to the order of the final voting winning a prize, but the players didn't get to vote, as Anthony Boucher had apparently thought and said publicly.

Flood lists the judges for the 1952 Awards (the 1951 judges were the four men who thought it up, with some advice from people like Carnell). The 1952 judges include, from the UK, J. M. Walsh, Carnell, Walter Gillings, Walter Willis ("fandom's leading expert and critic"), Fred C. Brown ("noted London bibliophile"); from France, Georges Gallet and Igor Maslowski (editor of a mystery magazine); from the US, Boucher and J. Francis McComas, Everett Bleiler, Groff Conklin, Basil Davenport, August Derleth, and Judith Merril; from Sweden, Sigvard Ostlund ("foremost Scandinavian fantasy bibliophile"). John Beynon Harris, Wilson Tucker, and Willy Ley all withdrew since they had eligible books. The second article actually recounts the votes and comments of all the judges (the winners being John Collier's *Fancies and Goodnights* and Arthur C. Clarke's *The Exploration of Space*). This information is generally too tedious to relate, though I was interested to see references to several books I've never heard of: Gerald Heard's *The Black Fox* (championed by Derleth, Maslowski, and Conklin), William Fry Harvey's *The Arms of Mrs. Egan* and Ronald Fraser's *Beetle's Career* (both favorites of Everett Bleiler). There were also several votes for John Dickson Carr's *The Devil in Velvet*.

There's another convention report in **19**, "Chicago—Biggest Yet!" by Walter Willis, who says: "We may have seen the last of the big conventions. In America, at least, the potential attendance has grown so large that it just isn't possible to put on a convention that will please everybody." Attendance was 900. (In 1984, attendance at the World SF Convention in Anaheim, California, the peak to date, was 8,365, with another four since then topping 6000.)[32]

The book reviews, which appear in all issues except **13**, **15**, and **16**, are mostly by Carnell, though Leslie Flood does part or all of them in several issues, in one case because a Carnell anthology is one of the books reviewed. In **12**, Frank Arnold,

---

32. http://www.smofinfo.com/LL/TheLongList.html (visited 8/28/11).

Eric F. Williams, and G. Ken Chapman review one book each in addition to Carnell's reviews, and in **19**, Arthur C. Clarke is brought in to review *Across the Space Frontier*. The review columns run from one to three and a half pages and cover as many as six books, obviously briefly in most cases. In **21**, the first small digest, the column runs six pages, though with smaller pages and larger type it's hard to know without a word count how much of an increase there really is. All the books reviewed are British publications, though **21** adds a page or so of "American book news," listing a number of recent US publications with very brief comment, except for Bretnor's *Modern Science Fiction*, which gets a paragraph of description and praise. Carnell says this column is in response to reader demand and is "for the connoisseur and collector."

The obvious ambivalence is not surprising, nor is it surprising that this US-oriented column disappears in the next issue and is not seen again. Clearly Carnell regarded the review column less as a critical enterprise or a readers' service than as a sort of nation-building activity for British SF publishing. Most of the reviews are quite favorable—not necessarily because he and the other reviewers are fudging their views (though Ken Chapman's praise for Ray Cummings does test that proposition), but because they mostly avoid reviewing seriously bad books, of which there was no shortage in the UK by this time.

There are a few bad or mixed notices. Carnell has mixed feelings about Lewis Sowden's *Tomorrow's Comet* (another book of which I had never heard) in **10**, and allows there is a "slight weakness of characterisation" in Clarke's *Sands of Mars*, which he otherwise praises. *The Wrong Side of the Moon* by Francis and Stephen Ashton is taxed for its archaic romantic approach, but otherwise praised; of van Vogt's *The House That Stood Still*, Carnell says, "As a science-fiction detective thriller it has all the necessary ingredients to confuse the reader" (*le mot juste!*). About the only review of the emerging and less prestigious British writers of the time is Newman's review of H. J. Campbell's *Beyond The Visible* and Bryan Berry's *Born in*

Captivity, of which he says the former "is only competent and lacks the originality of thought and expression found in Berry's work." (Berry, 1930-66, who published almost exclusively in *Authentic* and *Planet Stories*, was a highly promising writer who quickly disappeared from the field.[33])

Beginning with **18**, the inside front cover, formerly devoted to advertising, is appropriated for the *New Worlds* Profiles, featuring a photograph and biographical squib for one of the magazine's contributors. The first of these is an obituary for J. M. Walsh (1887-1952), mostly a mystery writer but also a genuine SF pioneer—the first writer to use the title "Vandals of the Void"!—his first SF credit in Miller/Contento being from 1924, in *Hutchinson's Adventure-Story Magazine*. This was followed by appearances in *Amazing*, *Wonder*, and *Wonder Stories Quarterly* in the 1930s, winding up with "The Belt" in the first issue of *Science Fantasy*, which might as well have appeared in *Wonder Stories* in the 1930s. At his death, Walsh was serving as one of the Adjudicators of the International Fantasy Awards. The subsequent Profiles in these issues are for Gerard Quinn (see above), E. C. Tubb, and illustrator Alan Hunter. The Profiles became one of the most durable features of the Carnell *New Worlds*, appearing in the large majority of issues until **134** (September 1963), and may be the only source of biographical information for a number of *New Worlds*'s authors.

§

The fiction in these issues displays the continued rapid development of the core group of writers who would be the mainstays of *New Worlds* through the 1950s and in some cases longer. Francis G. Rayer (as himself and as George Longdon) is back with eight stories; A. Bertram Chandler has five; E. R. James has

---

33. He was long reputed to have died in 1955, from suicide, a motorcyle accident, or various other means. Later investigation suggested that in fact he died in 1966. See http://bearalley.blogspot.com/2009/11/bryan-berry.html (visited 8/28/11). If so, why he left the field is unknown.

four; Sydney J. Bounds has three. (John Christopher has four, though he did not remain a regular *New Worlds* contributor.) They are joined by E. C. Tubb, who appears in **10** and rapidly makes himself at home, publishing 11 stories in these 13 issues (two as by Charles Gray); J. T. McIntosh, who also first appears in **10** and has eight stories, one of them *New Worlds*' first serial, as by McIntosh, James MacGregor, and the collaborative pseudonyms Gregory Francis and Stewart Winsor; Lan Wright, with four stories starting in **13**; and Peter Hawkins, with three stories starting in **9**.

Other soon-to-be-familiar names also appear: Alan Barclay in **11**, Dan Morgan in **13**, James White and J(onathan) F. Burke in **19**. Although there are plenty of bylines that are completely or mostly unfamiliar (Lee Rondelle, George C. Duncan) or that came and went quickly (Arthur J. Burks! A. E. van Vogt! the last John Aiken story), by the end of this period whole issues of *New Worlds* are composed entirely of work by recognizable regulars of the magazine. Thus, **21** features E. R. James, Lan Wright, E. C. Tubb, Francis G. Rayer, and Alan Barclay.

As for the quality of the fiction... it remains a very mixed bag. Most issues of the magazine have a lead novelette and several short stories. There is one serial. Interestingly, the longer featured stories are mostly poor—scenery-chewing potboilers, or worse. The short stories, by contrast, generally maintain a reasonable middle-of-the-road level of competence: seldom memorable, but seldom bloody awful either.

Among the lead stories, the best of the lot may be "Performance Test" (**15**), the last story by John K. Aiken. It's a laboratory opera (how to dispose of a quantity of hyper-dangerous explosive without blowing up the surrounding county, with emphasis on bench procedure and how much the protagonist sweats and trembles) which turns into a virtual reality story (it was all a dream—i.e., a performance test, as the title indicated). Carnell had touted this one enthusiastically in the previous issue's "The Literary Line-Up"—"magnificent lead novelette... undoubtedly one of the finest stories published in Britain during recent years"—which is a considerable exaggeration, though it's a capable story, considerably better than most of the other lead stories during this period.

Several of the lead stories are by writers who were not and did not become *New Worlds* regulars, and a good thing too. Arthur J. Burks' "Hydra," the lead story in **10**, is stupefyingly, unreadably bad. It's about a man oppressed by his deceased father's habit of collecting steam traction engines (i.e., locomotives), who has burrowed into the earth underneath one of them and in some unexplained fashion created a room with machinery which connects in some unexplained fashion with other rooms with similar machinery under various mountains, and which also seem to connect with similar rooms with machinery elsewhere in the universe, allowing him to travel instantaneously among them. He was in tense negotiations with a man from Mars in his room on Deimos at the point when I gave up. A sample:

> "You're telling me nothing, really," said Eret Young, while goose-pimples of nameless fear began to ripple inside him. "I take it that I am in your power, temporarily...."
>
> "And I am in yours!" said Pfete-lai quickly. "I have committed what in [sic] Mars is the unforgivable sin— I have made contact with someone from another planet without first getting permission from the Inner Circle of Martian Science!"
>
> "And the punishment?"
>
> "Eternal exile from the Universe!" said Pfete-lai.

"Hydra" has the same thought-disordered quality as the once notorious, now probably forgotten Warner van Lorne stories in the pre-Campbell *Astounding*, though in fairness I should concede that, leafing forward in the story, I discovered that the steam locomotives are not entirely superfluous; at some point they begin flying. The readers voted it second in the issue, after McIntosh's "Machine Made."

The lead story in **11** is Lee Rondelle's "Cosmic Mirror," which Carnell described in "The Literary Line-Up" as "healthy space opera with a Time concept of the curved universe," and which reads to me like a clumsy if enthusiastic pastiche of Charles L. Harness, or maybe like a parody written on a bet. "Jan Gish, Admiral of the Imperial Terran Space Fleet at 37, stretched luxuriously on the antigrav cushions of his mountaintop sun-room," awaiting the takeoff of the new hyper-fast starship. But pause for several pages' info-dump: it appears that human progress is determined, and usually retarded, by the telepathic emanations of the masses. This theory, developed by Jan's late father Morgan, has displaced Darwin (or Dar'n), and the new ship has been developed by creating a community of scientists on an isolated mountaintop, surrounded only by smart and well-balanced people, so the "herd barrier" won't hold the scientists back.

> All the members had been psycho-screened as of high stability and in two years only four cases of emotional disturbance had been encountered by the Dianeticists.... The smiling man who polished jack-boots at the street corner was an authority of not inconsiderable renown on certain aspects of the Hammerman reactions.

Three months earlier, on his deathbed, Morgan handed Admiral Jan a strange metal capsule, intricately carved with symbols, and told him "when you find yourself between the galaxies, on a road from which there is no turning except the turning back, open it and read the message within. It may help you." He adds that he can no longer remember what it says.

As Jan and crew are boarding the ship, they receive an emergency delivery of a package for him found mysteriously in an archaeological site. So they set off without opening either item, avoiding the old-fashioned rockets still plying the spacelanes "with their rocket stacks reeking and belching uranium dust" (but these tubs are polite—they "shove[] a can of borium in their jets to give them the spaceman's farewell"), then accelerating and entering subspace to hit the Harl Funnel, a 5,000-light-year passageway to "the void between the galaxies." They fetch up near their destination, galaxy G.N.4. But when they try to navigate into it— "Blast it," he rapped, "we're parsecs off course." "Even with maximum power on the turning beams she won't swing." "This looks like a road which has no turning." The penny drops and Jan opens his father's deathbed capsule, which says essentially that they're toast and he wishes he could tell them more but there's a barrier in his mind; also that they should open the other capsule, whose cover letter certifies that it was found in an excavation of an ancient Roman site. That one says "Not G.N.4. Not G.N.4. Anywhere but G.N.4."

They lose consciousness and wind up with their spaceship disabled under 200 feet of water. They get to shore in their collapsible boat, where Jan throws away the two capsules. Shortly thereafter they are attacked by a man with a sword, who also has the two capsules on his belt, so they kill him. Jan's father appears, dressed in a white robe and smoking a cigarette (or "sigret" as they are known). "Hello, dad," Jan says. Dad explains that they are on Earth, having taken "a very steep curve in the space-time continuum." (Dad took a short-cut.) All the galaxies are really the same galaxy at different points in time. Dad uses the metaphor of looking at yourself in a mirror. "Suppose you set out from your nose-end to travel to the nose-end in the glass, what happens?... If you've done the journey on time-drive, you will have slipped down through the series of parallel-existing nose-ends and arrived, not at the nose that now looks in the glass, but the nose that looked in yesterday, or the day before."

So now they're stuck in Roman Britain, and as soon as Dad leaves, their minds will be dragged down by the Fourth Century telepathic field and they will forget there is such a thing as a spaceship; also their ship won't work for escape purposes because here the physical laws are different. Dad takes one of the capsules and vanishes, and Jan writes "Not G.N.4" etc. and puts it in the other one, which he throws down a hole. "In his dulling brain he could already feel the ghostly fingers of barbarism plucking the thought-flowers of a great civilization and throwing them away."

These are the sins of enthusiasm, not commercialism. As noted, Rondelle was not heard of again in the SF magazines.

George C. Duncan's "Galactic Quest" (**19**) speaks for itself, unfortunately:

> For five years, Jon Hawkes had been searching for the hiding place of Techon, the fabulous weapon of Rhyll, the weapon "too terrible to use" —the weapon that would enable him to break the power of Maximillian IV, Democrat of the Union, and free the galaxy from despotism. Five years spent dodging Cato's secret police, building up an organization ready to seize Techon and turn it against the Union. And now, with victory in sight, the rebel group had been betrayed and destroyed; Hawkes, alone, was free to act, to seek out Techon in its remote hiding place and use the weapon to release the peoples of the galaxy from bondage.

So he stows away on a spaceliner and, upon emerging in search of dinner, is immediately summoned by the beautiful Deirdre ("her loveliness was breath-taking"), who asks him to explain space travel to her. A bit later, after he has hastily withdrawn: "A man dressed in black had joined the girl; a man with a ghastly white face, thin-lipped, with large, staring eyes deep-set behind rimless spectacles. Beads of sweat started out on Hawkes' forehead as those penetrating eyes fixed on him, the eyes of Cato, Maximillian IV's right-hand man, head of the secret police." He hides in Deirdre's room, and she comes in after shaking Cato and immediately demands that he kiss her. "The warmth and softness of her transmitted itself through the shimmering transparency of her gown; her perfume roused him, the mystery in her tawny eyes fired desire in his veins." But he's still not sure he can trust her.

> "Can you doubt me, after our kiss? Did I resist? As for Cato, even he can appreciate my beauty, but I'll never give myself to him... as I might, you. Now go." Hawkes looked into her eyes, but saw only woman's eternal mystery there.

They arrive on Rhyll, which orbits Dark Star M-1 (no fear, light and heat are provided atomically), and Deirdre takes him to her uncle, the governor van Strachan, who cheerfully acknowledges that "A beautiful niece is a considerable asset to a scheming man, Mr. Hawkes...." It is revealed that Techon is so terrible that the indigenes of Rhyll allowed themselves to be slaughtered rather than use it, and (surprise!) that the governor is really interested only in taking the despot's place. Hawkes tries to shoot him, but passes out, and here's the ingenious plot-twist: "It had been the cigar. Not the wine but the cigar which had been drugged."

Deirdre won't hear the truth about van Strachan ("She stamped her foot irritably, tossing her head"), which is a problem: "somehow he had to prove to her that she was a pawn in her uncle's game for galactic-wide power. He had to open her eyes, reveal the true nature of Vincente van Strachan, and save her from his evil machinations." Hawkes decides Techon must be on Rhyll's moon, finds a gun in a desk drawer and escapes in van Strachan's rocketship ("'The fool!' Vincente van Strachan's lips curled contemptuously and his marble-blue eyes gleamed with satisfaction."), but of course van Strachan follows him, Deirdre in tow, after planning the aforementioned evil machinations ("Hawkes, too... yes, Jon Hawkes must die!"), and when he captures Hawkes, unleashes the ultimate threat:

"You've heard of *reverse dianetics*? It's outlawed, of course, but that won't stop me using it. Simply, I'll drug you into a coma, blanket your conscious mind— then torture you. The pain will by-pass your conscious mind and sink into your unconsciousness. A series of mental shocks will register, filed but not indexed— they'll stay deep in your unconscious, beyond the control of the rational part of your brain. And I'll introduce a trigger-word, a simple association which will bring back all the pain, release the nightmare locked away in your unconscious.

"...And I'll speak the trigger word. Day after day, you'll relive the agony, writhe in pain until your mind cracks...."

Etc. Bwa-ha-ha. This scene, however, is interrupted by Cato, who arrives with posse in *his* rocketship, and actually says "Now, you are all in my power!" He further announces to van Strachan, "I shall be Democrat—and will consider it my pleasant duty to provide for your niece," and, after shooting him, "Manacle Hawkes and take him aboard my ship. The girl is my property and not to be harmed in any way." Later, after extracting the secret of Techon's location (several lines of doggerel) from Hawkes, he muses: "With the galaxy in the palm of his hand, ultimate power would be his, and he could turn to lesser pleasures. Deirdre, for example...." As for Hawkes: "Cured, you see? Dianetic treatment wiped out the memory, the trigger word no longer has any effect." That's because he needs Hawkes for another purpose—to test Techon on once he finds it.

But the Democrat Maximilian himself catches up with them all as they reach Techon ("he resembled an obscene, bloated pear as he rolled forward towards the twin towers. He was so close that Hawkes could see the rolls of flesh quivering, the fat jaws chewing on a sweetmeat.") In the resulting shootout, Hawkes gets control of Techon and turns it on the Democrat and his forces, who are reduced to mindlessness by the destruction of the "nerve tissues of the brain." After they are all down and twitching randomly, Deirdre allows that this really *is* the weapon too dreadful to use; but no. Says Hawkes, there are more tyrants waiting in the wings. "We must use Techon to free the galaxy for ever." Deirdre, clearly an intellectual cheap date (or maybe just a premature neocon) says, "You are right, Jon.... Techon was given us to blaze a trail of freedom across the galaxy. We cannot refuse to use it. No matter what horror may follow, Man was ordained to carve his own destiny. Violence is our right."

To their credit, the readers voted this story last in the issue.

This George Duncan had three more stories, all in *Authentic*, in 1954-55 ("Galactic Quest" is his first), as well as two articles, one called "Planet Farms," and one, interestingly (in *Authentic* **51**, November 1954), titled "Hallucinogens." Maybe that's why his career didn't continue much longer.

§

On to the more familiar writers. Sydney J. Bounds' "The Flame Gods" (**14**) is of similar ilk to "Galactic Quest." It makes one regret there is not a Mystery Science Theatre for print. After a nuclear war, scientists have taken over, but power has corrupted, and they have invented a fake religion which covertly relies on nuclear power while holding it to be forbidden. David Martel, the intrepid young Science Student, is returned from the Moon in disgrace, not to mention chains, because he refused to stop fooling around with atomics. He is brought before the Keepers of the Flame for judgment. Here they are:

> Strang, the first Keeper, stood up to speak; a gaunt, black-cloaked figure with slanting almond eyes and a hooked nose set above cruel lips....
> ...Vogel rose to address the audience in the temple. The second male Keeper was short and round with a bloated belly and sagging chins; his beady eyes gleamed with sadistic pleasure....

Undine, first of the female Keepers, spoke. She had the body of an adolescent girl, the face of an old hag; her withered hair was grey, her eyes cold and bleak....

...Sala, the second female Keeper, came to her feet. Sala was a hunchback with spindly arms and legs, coarse lank hair and terrible eyes that burned like red coals. Her clawed hands raked the air as she screamed....

And there's another one who is so horrible-looking he doesn't show himself. People who look like that just have to be evil, right? So they sentence Martel to death in the transformation chambers, but not before he has his say: "You fools—there are no Gods! The Keepers have tricked you with scientific mumbo-jumbo, blinded you with religious clap-trap. They use atomic power to rule you, breaking their own self-made laws—" They toss him into the transformation chamber, but suddenly someone is there to rescue him and lead him out through a tunnel. And, of course: "She was young and unusually beautiful, with firm breasts and lithe limbs, dressed in a single tanned animal skin that draped her shoulders and was belted at the slim waist." She's interested in Martel for several reasons, not least of which is that he might protect her from, and provide an alternative to, the repellent Jorgen, who has designs on her and is hard to avoid in her small community of escapees. The inevitable confrontation occurs, after the requisite amount of sneering, and Martel kicks butt. But when he tries to claim his reward:

> "No, David! I love you, but—"
> He stared at her, baffled.
> "But what?" he demanded.
> Her face was sad and her dark eyes revealed an inward struggle.
> "Not here," she replied. "Not on Earth. First, we must reach the stars. Here"—she shuddered—"the radiation frightens me. I don't know which is worst—the

thought that I may be sterile—or that I may give birth to some distorted creature.... I must refuse you—until we reach another planet, where normal life is possible."

Martel said: "We may never reach the stars."

She trembled, her young breasts heaving, tears flooding her dark eyes.

"Then our love can never be," she replied....

I do believe this is a first: "Not tonight, darling, we have to go to the stars." It goes on in a similar vein for a number of pages. The perceptive readers voted this, too, last in the issue.

Bounds also has a couple of short stories in these issues. In "Liaison Service" (12), Lieutenant Blair of the Space Guard and his sidekick Monty of the Liaison Service have an encounter with space pirates on an asteroid. Monty, the first-person narrator, is a telepath (though he can't read Blair), not too bright, and with a bad case of hero worship of the lieutenant. He saves Blair's life and does in the pirates with a maneuver involving some telepathic crystals who use radiation as a weapon. It's very uncharacteristically Sturgeonesque until the end, when Bounds snatches inanity from the jaws of intelligence by revealing that Monty, in addition to the above, is also a robot.

"A Matter of Salvage" (13) reads like a boy's book leftover: Hilary St. Clair, rejected by the Space Guard because he is overweight and has a girl's name, buys an asteroid mining scow. He's the first to arrive and claim salvage at a spaceship that is being abandoned on account of an atomic pile mishap, but the evil Tesla shows up to jump his claim and do him in. Hilary outwits them and prevails.

§

The longest item in these issues is "The ESP Worlds" by J. T. McIntosh (16-18), *New Worlds*'s first serial, though it is scarcely a novel—it runs a little short of 80 large digest pages, and more importantly was submitted as two separate stories, which were combined by Carnell without consulting the author.[34] This one displays the deficiencies in plausibility and logic that often characterize McIntosh's work—of which more later, and elsewhere.[35] On Noya, the matriarchal society refuses to have anything to do with the human colonists except to kill anybody who comes close, which provokes the humans to reprisal skirmishes, which they always lose—the Noyans can teleport, so they just materialize behind the humans, bash them over the head, and vanish again.

So the human (male) leadership, whose request for a female agent was denied, conscript Janice, a vacationing woman romance novelist who arrives on a passenger ship. They give her physical and telepathic training and when she encounters a couple of Noyan women, they all open their minds, because that's what Noyans do as a confidence-building measure—except the Noyans don't look closely enough to discover that she is an alien spy. All are captured by another faction of Noyans, who subject them to the dreaded telepathic Judging, at which Janice prevails by discoursing telepathically about the slide rule and the internal combustion engine, and then by claiming membership in a mythic but feared Noyan race. Still none of these supposed telepaths has figured out she is an Earth spy.

Meanwhile it has been revealed that the real Noyans can't teleport to safety because their bodies stay behind. How is it, then, that they bounce around the battlefield? Do they leave a body at every stop? It is explained that their battlefield prowess is actually hypnotic in nature—the Noyan women hypnotize the colonists into believing that the Noyans have materialized behind them and beaten them into unconsciousness. On her

---

34. Ian Covell, personal communication. Covell obtained this and other information from McIntosh in the course of preparing a bibliography of his work, which is in progress.

35. This impression of McIntosh owes much to his stories in *Science Fantasy*, discussed in the companion volume devoted to that magazine, *Strange Highways*.

return, Janice refuses to tell her recruiters what she learned among the Noyans, but insists they should wind up the colony and get the hell out—sound advice, and why they need to hear it from an interstellar romance novelist is not explained. Finally she reveals that she is really the female agent they asked for. Why didn't she say so at the beginning? Well, she's undercover. So why is she saying so now? Next installment, please.

The concluding installments take place on Nome, where society is organized around games, excuse me, Games. The male protagonist, Major Jeff, is transferred to Nome on no particularly well-defined mission, Janice shows up too, and they ultimately reveal a vile plot by an underground organization to spin the evolution of the Nomans by fixing the Games and selectively killing undesirables, all unknown to the population, which thinks that only five million people a month are being killed in the Games, not the real deal of forty million. The previous events on Noya are largely forgotten (and we never learn whether the colonists took Janice's advice to abandon the place), except that Janice does use her new teleportation/hypnotic skills briefly.

Carnell, in his editorial in **15**, said "The ESP Worlds" would undoubtedly appear in book form some day. And it did, sort of. *The Noman Way* (Digit, 1964) drops the Noya episode entirely, and the Nome section has been drastically rewritten and expanded from 30-odd magazine pages to a 154-page paperback novel.

McIntosh, as noted, had numerous short stories in these issues. In "Machine Made" (**10**), his first *New Worlds* appearance, the moronic (McIntosh's word) cleaning woman likes to punch simple problems into the keyboard of the Machine, a big computer, and one day it prints out more than her sums—it says it can tell from her slow keystrokes and simple problems that she's a moronic attendant, so she should tell it more and maybe it can help her. She is instructed to make a sort of hat with wires that she attaches to the Machine's inputs, and it cures her mental retardation—by, she explains, "opening new circuits in my mind, to see relationships and reach conclusions." She's now a lightning calculator as part of the deal. While all this has scant relationship to any reasonable conception either of what a computer is or what mental retardation is, the readers voted it first in the issue (against not much competition), and Carnell liked it enough to anthologize it in *No Place Like Earth*. While the gimmick makes it a sort of British forerunner of the (astoundingly) Hugo-winning *They'd Rather Be Right* (1955), by Mark Clifton and Frank Riley, it does not carry the didactic freight of that novel.

"When Aliens Meet" (**12**) is a thoroughly inane story told extremely well for most of its length. The narrator, General Priscilla Price, is the daughter of the first man to go to Mars, who upon his return bundled her up in a summer dress and dispatched her (aged 15) to Venus in his spaceship, which was parked at the curb. The Venusians operated on her and sent her back after a psychic and physical makeover. Meanwhile, Earth has turned into a police state waiting for the Martians to invade, and her father has been executed as a traitor. She heads back to Venus and recruits the Venusians to defend Earth by threatening to seed Venus with oxygen-exhaling flowers.

In "The World That Changed" (**14**), a spaceman returning to Earth after a couple of years concludes that things are *really* different, i.e., that people are being replaced by organic robots, which he verifies by killing somebody and finding "a curious blue jelly" where her brain belongs. No obvious point is made, although the story might foreshadow Jack Finney's much more famous *The Body Snatchers* (1955).

For the amusing "The Broken Record" (**17**), McIntosh disguises his identity by using his own name, James Macgregor. David and Dorothy go on a holiday with some friends, in their new space-cruiser, to Mars, about which everything you know is wrong! It has the climate of California because of the ether current (Michelson-Morley, Schmichelson-Morley), and the fishing is great. Once on Mars, David is fooling around with Jacky, and they encounter some of the little-known fairy-like

Martians, who are tossing around a pink crystal. On a second encounter the Martians throw the crystal at David, who catches it and finds himself back in the previous tryst. History repeats from that point, except that David retains free will and this time around doesn't catch the crystal—but it hits him anyway and he's back at Tryst 1 again. On this pass, the Martians are tossing around a larger, blue crystal; he runs like hell, but they hit him with it anyway, and this time he's back at the beginning of the story, where he vetoes both Mars and Jacky, presumably avoiding further recursions. For anyone who has trouble following, McIntosh has divided this ten-page story into Roman-numbered chapters; the numbers repeat as does the plot, so the last scene is chapter I again. This is a fairy tale in which logic and plausibility are less of an issue since the author more or less disavows them from the outset.

Several of McIntosh's stories are pseudonymous collaborations. "Ape" (10) is bylined Gregory Francis, who is McIntosh and Frank H. Parnell. Parnell appeared in the SF magazines only with one other story under this name, and with a third as by Francis Richardson, who in turn is a collaborative pseudonym with Lawrence Edward Bartle, who also published one story under the pseudonym Richard Lawrence. There the bread crumbs stop, the fictional ones anyway: Parnell is also the author with Mike Ashley of *Monthly Terrors: An Index to the Weird Fantasy Magazines Published in the United States and Great Britain* (Greenwood Press, 1985). "Ape" is a bracingly acerbic meditation on "there's always a bigger fish," reprising plot furnishings from A. E. van Vogt's "The Monster"/"Resurrection" with overtones of "Don Stuart"/John W. Campbell's "Forgetfulness." A spaceship full of couples arrives on a planet uninhabited except for vegetation, and find preserved in a box a seemingly dead hominin—hairy, toothy, primitive. They revive him; he's dumb but strong and makes himself useful. They don't bother looking for any more of his kind. They need the world, and, they say, "the strong shall conquer the weak." However, when they try to leave, the controls don't work. In strolls a familiar figure. "'I had better introduce myself,' said the Ape. 'My name is Armandale. I regret the pretence of the last six weeks, but I had to learn what you were like—whether you were dangerous, how you behaved.'" Armandale explains that this is forgotten Earth, and he and his kind had purposefully turned it into a museum. He is disappointed in the visitors—"a race that has never climbed beyond the rule of Grab is low in the scale, even if it has super-drive and can make anything in a machine-shop.... You should have revived us and helped us, and left our world to us.... [T]he ethical rules are the only ones that matter." "'But we need this world!' Darlan exclaimed. 'And the strong shall conquer the weak.'... 'Very well,' said Armandale. 'That is exactly what is happening.'" He and his kind will be revived and take control. So they dispatch the male interlopers back to Aldebaran with memories fogged so they can't find Earth again, while keeping the women on Earth. "How else could we make a new race that was a blend of yours and mine?"

"Question Mark" (12), also as by Gregory Francis, is about a quartet of adulterous space explorers who arrive on a planet whose land fauna is limited to monkeys and rabbits, which is already peculiar enough, but when you approach them they become invisible. Even the dogs can't find them. When the explorers do grab a monkey, only one couple can see them. This spooks out the other pair, who realize they are probably dealing with intelligent and powerful aliens. They depart, but the first couple has remained behind, finalizing their partner swap. The precise point is a little obscure, but the story is brief and pungent, and considerably more enjoyable (to me, anyway) than McIntosh's more usual efforts. This Parnell did a good job of keeping McIntosh out of trouble. There is only one more *New Worlds* story under the Francis name, however, and one in *Spaceways*. The name Gregory Francis popped up again in *Weirdbook* and *Weird Window* in 1970-71, but there's no reason to believe it's McIntosh and Parnell again.

"Weapons for Yesterday" (19) is bylined Stewart Winsor, according to Miller/Contento a pseudonym for McIntosh and one Jeff Mason. This is the only Winsor story and Mason has no other appearances in the SF magazines. It is about a missile testing party in the Australian desert, one of whose members is temporarily invaded by Lepta, a time-traveling disembodied intelligence, who sticks around long enough to ensure that they fire all their armed missiles more or less at once. The missiles mysteriously disappear. It is revealed that the missiles were hijacked so the Lemurians could defeat the Arcturians way back in antiquity, but don't worry, a separate world-line has split off where the Lemurians won.

§

E. C. Tubb (1919-2010) started with a bang, or a deluge, with 11 stories in these 13 issues, ultimately contributing well over 40 stories to *New Worlds* under his own and various other names, extending well into the Moorcock era, before the magazine was finished and he moved on to new venues for his prolificity. This is not to mention a number of stories in *Science Fantasy*, *Science Fiction Adventures*, *Nebula*, and what looks like about half the contents of *Authentic*. His stories are characterized by an ostentatiously hard-boiled style and sometimes considerable violence or threatened violence; beneath the crusty surface, however, there is often a filling of purest marshmallow. This *modus operandi* is illustrated by Tubb's only lead story in these issues, "Unwanted Heritage," under the Charles Gray pseudonym, which begins:

> They were punishing a man that morning.
> He stood facing the stockade, hands lashed to metal rings hammered into the raw wood above his head. [Etc.]

After he has been lashed, with the demented commander Harrison egging on the reluctant flogger, we learn the man's crime: fraternizing with the native Venusians, elusive but entirely humanoid beings whom Harrison refers to generally as animals and individually as "it." As the story progresses, Harrison gets crazier and crazier, and more parodic of repressed and authoritarian military stereotypes, despite the efforts of Drayton. Matters culminate with Harrison's order to set out into the dank jungle and wipe out the Venusians to make Venus safe for Earth humans, and—the problem goes away. At the climactic moment, the humans all black out, and wake up having been mentally adjusted by the Venusians away from the heritage of human evolution:

> "We were so blind," murmured Ken [Drayton]. "So foolishly blind. It was plain before us, yet we would not see."
> "I was the one to blame," Harrison sounded almost ashamed.

The last line: "Already men were at work tearing down the stockade." Well, this is a trifle anticlimactic as a resolution of dramatic tension, particularly the over-the-top sort Tubb has built up. I wonder if this is the first SF story to be inspired by *Heart of Darkness*, or if it just reads like it.

One thing that can be said for Tubb is that he sets the narrative hook much more firmly than his colleagues. Compare the above quoted first lines of "Unwanted Heritage" to the first lines of the other stories in the issue:

> "Evening sun touched the top of the blue hills. The lonely slopes lay in shadow, grey and dim...." (Rayer as Longdon)

> "In the administration office of the Uranus Opencast Mining Corporation, a bell trilled." (James)

> "Dropped neatly in the middle of hundreds of miles of nothing-in-particular was the settlement, brooding

under the midday sun, its long squat huts huddled together for company in the seemingly endless desert."
(McIntosh/Mason as Winsor)

Tubb's other major opus in these issues is a series of stories
about Mars colonization, starting with "Without Bugles" (**13**),
a tough-guy tear-jerker about the colonists who can't come
home because their lungs have been ruined by silicosis from
the omnipresent dust, and they won't be able to breathe enough
in Earth's gravity. The readers liked it, and placed it first in the
issue. (Since this piece appeared in January 1953, it beat Walter
M. Miller, Jr. to much the same trope in Miller's famous "Cru-
cifixus Etiam" in *Astounding,* February 1953.) The *noir* bathos
continues in "Home Is the Hero" (**15**), in which the colony's
leader returns briefly to Earth, wasted from Mars's low gravity and barely able to function, because Mars Needs Women!
Radioactives have been discovered and now the colony is a
government priority. He's here to recruit women for the colony
in a cynical pseudo-patriotic exercise, but he rebels and plays
it straight:

> "To me you are brood mares. To the colony you
> will be the same. We don't want career women. You
> go with the idea of bearing children—or you don't go
> at all."
> [In a private conversation:] "Do you know why
> women are wanted on Mars? To serve as bait for men.
> Why? Because they want more atom bombs."
> [And later:] "What happens to heroes—when they
> live too long?" High over their heads a meteor flamed
> into sudden brilliance.

Next, "Men Only" (**16**) begins on a typical note of good
cheer:

The metal whispered. Sang and quivered to distant vibration. A footstep. A closing door. The subdued murmur of engines.

"Fool," it whispered. "Blind, stupid fool. Fool! Fool! Fool!"

This is from the point of view of somebody who is strapped to a bed for psychiatric reasons. Meanwhile, Dr. Landry, visiting Mars with an investigating committee, discovers that the women are all bearing one normal child, their second children are mostly stillborn or mutated freaks, and then they are sterile. Apparently nobody has noticed this until now. Why is it happening? Radiation, selective for women. But cheer up! Dr. Landry decides to stay on Mars! The whispering metal, by the way, is the vibration from the centrifuge the colonists have set up to exercise their atrophying muscles, and the man who is hearing voices in it is a plant biologist who is trying to find something that will grow on Mars, and focusing on cacti. His subconscious is telling him he's a fool because cacti survive by storing water, and on Mars there's no water to store.

In "Alien Dust" (19), the protagonist, sentenced to prison for stealing because he was hungry, gets to go to Mars for a while instead, decides he'd rather stick around than go back, and winds up giving his life for the cause, sacrificing his air hose in a sandstorm to reinsulate the cables from the atomic plant that keep the colony alive.

In "Pistol Point" (21), the colony is dying from lack of support. The women have gone, since the radiation was killing them, and the colony is being strangled for resources. What to do? Nuclear blackmail! The leader heads back to Earth and tells the man in charge that if they don't get what they want, a spaceship full of nuclear bombs will be dispatched to Earth. This is a roaring success, viewed by the press and public through the lens of Dick Turpin and Captain Blood, Osama bin Laden having not been heard of yet. So their demands will be met. (Demands for compost, among other things. One of their botanists has developed something that will actually grow on Mars.) And who should show up to greet the leader but a young woman who introduces herself as Phobos. It seems that when the women left, they took their Mars-born children with them, and of course half of them were girls, and the women they have become (a) have developed some sort of immunity to the radiation that was killing their mothers, and (b) can't bear children on Earth (notice the recurrence of the Lamarckian motif that is so common in this magazine). So they all trundle off to Mars.

Carnell noted "with regret" in the previous issue's "The Literary Line-Up" that "Alien Dust" is the last of Tubb's planned stories in the series, though "if popular demand warrants it, we'll run some more later." Apparently it didn't. These stories were later collected or fixed up in *Alien Dust*, published by Boardman in the UK in 1955 and a year or two later by Avalon in the US. "Pistol Point" is the last *New Worlds* story to appear in the book. The only later story there is "Operation Mars," which appeared in 1954 in *Authentic*.

Of the other Tubb stories here, the best is "Third Party" (**14**), in which the protagonist buys a cheap book and finds it is a mysterious alien encyclopedia. He tries to track down where it's from and finds himself in a paranoid nightmare between incomprehensible contending factions. This one retains the courage of its unpleasantness and doesn't compromise its tone with sentimentality. It seems never to have been reprinted. Notable for different reasons is "Precedent" (**15**), under Tubb's Charles Gray pseudonym (though Carnell claimed Gray in the previous issue as a new writer). It involves a stowaway on a spaceship where fuel is short and more mass can't be allowed, so they have to throw him out the airlock. Wait a minute! Haven't I read that somewhere before? Actually, the famous and enduring Tom Godwin story "The Cold Equations" was published a little over two years later. In Tubb's version, the stowaway is the kid brother-in-law one of the astronauts, so there's less stereotypical poignancy. (In "The Cold Equations" a young woman is the one thrown out the airlock.) Carnell describes it as a "delightful little short" in "The Literary Line-Up" in **17**.

The rest of Tubb's stories vary from capable to mawkish. The first, "No Short Cuts" (**10**), about a company that can impress someone else's knowledge on you but his psychopathology comes with it, is overwritten in the soon-to-be-familiar hard-boiled default style, but well enough built to distract from its being about twice as long as necessary for its rather straight-forward point. "Greek Gift" (**11**) runs the changes on Damon Knight's celebrated "To Serve Man": aliens have come bearing the secret of immortality, just sign up and agree to work as directed for 100 years and pay 10% of your earnings, and people flock to the offer, except no one has ever come back to tell the tale. What's the catch? You're turned into a robot laborer under a hot alien sun. "Entrance Exam" (**12**) is an inconsequential piece about members of a space crew who find themselves kidnapped by aliens and not provided any food or drink. Obviously this is a test of what they will do. They pass the test when one of them realizes it's all in their heads. "Heroes Don't Cry" (**19**), as by Gordon Kent (the only appearance of that pseudonym), takes the downmarket pathos about as far as it will go. The protago-nist is a spaceman who appreciates the hero-worship of kids, one of whom introduces him to his older sister, who is beautiful and also dead-opposed to her kid brother's desire to go to space, since it involves sacrificing most of the accoutrements of normal human life like marriage and children. He falls for her, she tells him off, he goes out and gets stinking drunk and rolled, and she brings her kid brother to see his degradation. It is revealed that he is only the cook and not the engineer. "Rockets Aren't Human" (**20**) is about the marital problems of a spaceman who is away from home for three months at a time.

§

A. Bertram Chandler has a couple of the lead stories. "And All Disastrous Things," in **9**, is about the worst story I have encountered from this writer, who in my experience has always been reasonably capable and intelligent even when less than ambitious. It's a bi-hemispherical sale which also ran in the pulp *Out of This World Adventures*, December 1950, as "Raiders of the Solar Frontier." Latimer, a former hero of the Space Guard or whatever, has been life-sentenced to Ceres, the prison asteroid, after killing a couple of people, and immediately encounters his old flame Lauranne. "But the mouth that had always been a little too large, too full lipped, was now frankly sensual. The fresh charm that he had known so long ago in Port Gregory was now the dangerous allure of the unashamed wanton." So she says to him a little later:

> "...Don't lie to me, Alan—for you I can never re-place the surge of an accelerating ship, the flare of rocket drive against the stars, the ordered routine of your little world of grey paint and burnished metal. For you, more than for me, this is the end of the trip. This is that last haven of which Swinburne sang:
> "There go the loves that wither,
> "The old loves with wearier wings,
> "And all dead years draw thither,
> "And all disastrous things;" [Etc.]

Ceres has no official government, but that just means it has a Boss (as he likes to be called), who tells Latimer he can work for him and have a decent life, or not. "The room, with its luxurious appointments, blurred before Latimer's eyes. Fist clenched, he started forward. On either side of him a guard clutched his arm, another struck him across the mouth with a hard hand. Faint and far away he heard the voice of Lauranne: 'Don't,' she was saying. 'Don't be a fool, Alan!'"

Nonetheless, he picks a fight with the Boss's several goons, breaking his knuckles, and is clapped in irons. But the Boss continues his recruiting pitch to the man who just tried to assault him, and Latimer accepts and becomes a Constable of Ceres. This is all in the first eight pages, and the remaining 25 are a similar bag of clichés held together with tape, concerning an alien invasion by spider-like beings who manufacture simulacra of humans and ride around in them, and it's not worth saying any more about it. It would not surprise me if this were a very early rejected story that Chandler dusted off as new markets opened up.

Chandler's "Pest," the lead story in **13**, is not much better. It proposes that Mars, once colonized by humans, is further populated first by rabbits, then by land crabs brought in to feed on the rabbits, both of which grow to a height of five feet in the low Martian gravity, and ultimately prove to be the tools of an indigenous plant intelligence, all this revealed through a tedious and improbable melodramatic plot.

Chandler has several short stories as well. The best of them is probably the least portentous: "The Serpent" (**17**), a horticultural opus, is trivial but amusing, marking a return to the urbane good humor of some of his previous *New Worlds* short stories. The protagonist is a repressed and milquetoasty botanist in the Lunar hydroponic operation. On a stroll outdoors, he stumbles across some seeds glittering innocently in the vacuum and of course sneaks them in and plants them, hoping to impress the object of his unrequited affections by getting the plant named after her rather than her obnoxious boss. The plant blooms (the flower opens a blue eye and looks at him, as it were), and generates a cloud of flying things whose sting is instantly intoxicating. So Adam and his love are tossed off the Moon, and Adam is thrown out of the United Temperance League when they find out what he has done. "Finishing Touch" (**16**) is about a psychiatrically doomed space flight. The two crew members lose it, one kills the other, and when he tries to stop the body from orbiting around the spacecraft, he reaps poetic justice. In "Jetsam" (**20**), humans—designated only the Captain, the Engineer, etc.— arrive on the Moon, only to find that somebody's already been there, apparently from an earlier Earth civilization; some of the cultural references seem to suggest that the deceased were us and the characters are our post-human successors.

§

F. G. Rayer's "Time Was," the lead and cover story in **12**, is the result of Carnell's soliciting Rayer for a novelette rather than his customary short stories. The first interstellar spaceship is about ready to go, but people central to the project are being replaced by replicas, body-snatcher style. The folks in the rest of the universe aren't so keen on having us as neighbors; by story's end, the protagonist, too, has been snatched, but on an alien spaceship he is reunited with everybody else, and taken to the utopian future where the "aliens" are really from, and realizes it's all for the best, since these are the descendants of the mature humans who went to the stars much later in human history. The thriller plot is reasonably well executed, and the rug-pulling at the end is all right if a bit implausible (pretty quick conversion under the circumstances—they just look out the window and see the City of the Future below, and they're sold).

Unfortunately this is followed by "Man's Questing Ended" in **16**, in which the protagonist discovers that utopia isn't what it's cracked up to be—stagnation, you know—setting off an utterly incoherent plot involving the disappearance of the prominent and capable utopians à la *Atlas Shrugged* and a mind transfer between the protagonist and a deformed gangster type. These stories were republished in 1954 in "book" form by "Pearson's T-B"—per the Contento anthology/collection index, it ran 64 pages—under the title *The Star Seekers*.

Rayer's other stories in these issues, like his previous contributions, vary wildly. "Of Those Who Came" (**18**), as by George Longdon ("London" on the contents page), is taut and compact and unpretentious, about an interstellar cop stalking some aliens, mimics whose natural appearance is like a neon light without the tube (a familiar trope of media aliens decades later), and who have designs on the unsuspecting Earth. It's one of only three stories he placed in US magazines (*Fantastic Universe*, vol. 1 no.1, June/July 1953) other than the US reprint edition of *New Worlds*, and the only one to be anthologized in the US;

it appeared in Andre Norton's YA anthology *Space Police* (World, 1956). Carnell also included it in *Gateway to Tomorrow* (Museum, 1954), his second anthology of SF by British writers.

"Power Factor" (**21**) melds alien contact with the Romance of Electricity. On a colony planet, extraterrestrials have landed, and it's really important to keep the electricity on at the site, since negotiations are difficult and any showing of weakness may be disastrous. Meanwhile, the protagonist is trying to keep the power grid up and running everywhere, in part because his wife, who has been terribly injured, is scheduled for surgery, and any power cut affecting the hospital will put her in danger. Then somebody flies into a power line in a particularly isolated place. It's a nice try that doesn't quite come together.

"The Peacemaker" (**17**) is another in Rayer's series about Magnis Mensas, the world-dominating supercomputer that is an ace multi-tasking conversationalist and polite to boot—it always asks you to close the door behind you when you're finished talking, except when it's arresting you. Earth is menaced by the alien Ogoids, who threaten destruction unless humanity gives up all warlike pursuits and manufactures. MM is handling the delicate negotiations with the Ogoids and keeping mere humans away from them, and generally acting like a sessile Humanoid:

> "But they're—*aliens*! We're reduced to slavery!" Alan pointed out.
> "We have no means of defeating them. Irresponsible individuals will not be permitted to cause the destruction of all humanity. I therefore advise you to return to your peaceful work. Close the door as you go out...."

Alan finds this arrangement unsatisfactory and joins the Underground, only to be rousted by MM's henchpersons and informed by MM that it knows all about this, and the people Alan is dealing with are diagnosed with the "psychoneurosis" of "escapist insanity" concerning the Ogoids. But we are not in a remake of *The Humanoids* but of Theodore Sturgeon's "Unite and Conquer": Alan realizes there are no Ogoids, MM has made them up in order to keep people from fighting wars. Confronted with this accusation, MM admits its truth and says Alan can't be permitted to spread the word, but he relents and lets him go, with his own psychoneurosis diagnosis on his ID card: "An escapist insanity of rigid fixity suggesting the Ogoids do not exist."

After these it's downhill fast. "No Heritage," the first story under the George Longdon pseudonym (**12**), is a readable but unimpressive non-story, a piece of filler. Mysterious globes land all over Earth, releasing radiation; nine months later, births stop; some years after that, more globes arrive, bearing the invaders who expect us all to have died out; but they have miscalculated, we're still here, so they flee. The sterilization proves temporary. "The Temporal Rift" (**16**), also as by Longdon, is a clumsily told time paradox story. Protagonist has invented a space-abber-ator, as he or Carnell insists on spelling it, which sets up a sort of dome of force. The government takes over. A time capsule appears from 20 years in the future; protagonist is more and more uneasy but the Board won't listen to him. Suddenly he's in the future, and the whole site has been turned into a concave valley; he finds one of his old colleagues who says the hole gets bigger every year. The end of the world is nigh.

In the utterly contrived "Prison Trap" (**10**), the characters have a contract to build an automated prison on a distant planet, but they don't have enough fuel to get there, so they stop and build it somewhere else. They don't have enough fuel to get back from there either, and nobody knows where they are, so they're in a spot of trouble when the prison suddenly activates itself, and the automatic watchtowers and planes start shooting anybody who tries to leave, so they can't get back to their space-ship. Explanation: the construction crew has some crooks in it, and the prison responds to criminal intent; once the bad apples are drugged and knocked out, all the security shuts down and the good guys can get to the ship, where they plan to go to Earth. Fuel shortage? Well, if they can't make it to Earth, they'll go to their original destination—which they hadn't had enough fuel to get to in the first place. This nonsense is stylistically enhanced by the colorful idiom of the main character:

"By Copernicus...."
"By the horned comet!"
"By my perihelion...."
"By the ghost of Galileo Galilei...."
"By Halley...."
"Sufferin' satellites!"

And that's just in the first three pages.

§

E. R. James has the lead spot and the cover with "Ride the Twilight Rail" (21), which essays a bit more than usual, but unfortunately, reach portentously exceeds grasp and the result is heavyhandedly didactic. On Mercury, which keeps one face to the Sun but wobbles—or so we thought, until science learned better a couple of decades later—there's a monorail in the twilight zone from one side of the planet to another, and when the wobble is just right, with the monorail in twilight all the way, the Earthfolk have to send a maintenance crew to the station which retransmits messages across the solar system. Caleb, who has fled to Mercury from Mars after killing the man who sold rifles to the Injuns, er, weapons to the Martians, resulting in the death of his family, sets off on the maintenance run with the new guy, Fluke, who shortly announces that he's the son of the man Caleb killed and now he's going to kill Caleb. But Caleb insists they finish their maintenance mission first, and Fluke agrees. "Caleb sat silently, strangely at peace. Long ago he had adjusted himself to the twilight rail between the extremes of violent life and equally violent death that was normal life." On the way back, as Fluke is commencing to kill him, they discover that the rail in front of them is breached, and their call for help won't be heard because of the noise from the sun, except that the inscrutable crystalline Mercurians amplify and retransmit their message, so Caleb and Fluke are rescued just in time. Fluke is crying. "After all he was very young. He still had to learn how to ride the twilight rail."

The other stories are more routine. "Asteroid City" (**14**) is a hackneyed though competently assembled story about intrigues among Martian and Venusian colonists and Earth natives on an asteroid mining colony. "Emergency Working" (**17**) is a space-procedural, communications division. A big explosion en route towards Mercury spins a spaceliner out of control. All the planets are in inconvenient locations, but the word gets out nonetheless, in Morse code it appears, and some bright spark remembers Icarus, the planetoid whose eccentric orbit passes closer to the Sun than Mercury's, and which provides a convenient gravitational field to swing them around so they don't fall into the Sun before they can be rescued. It's a pretty simple-minded story to be appearing in 1952; it would have been more at home in *Wonder Stories* or perhaps *Scoops*. Nonetheless Carnell anthologized it in *Gateway to Tomorrow*.

James' "Where No Man Walks" is about a man who has lost his limbs mining Uranus, but continues to work, running heavy machinery remotely on the planet's surface and, in effect, having new limbs. It's mainly of interest now for recalling better stories (Heinlein's "Waldo," Poul Anderson's "Call Me Joe," and Arthur C. Clarke's "A Meeting with Medusa," for example, although it preceded the latter two.)

§

Of the writers who don't get a feature spot, the best and best known are John Beynon and John Christopher. Beynon's "No Place Like Earth" (**9**) is the sequel to "Time To Rest" from a few issues earlier. Bert, stranded on Mars after the destruction of Earth, learns that there's a spaceship in town from Venus, where folks are making some progress. Signing up, he discovers the tough guys have everything sewn up and that he is in the position of a serf whose job it is to lord it over slaves, the peaceful *griffas*. His boss chides him for not driving the griffas harder and starts laying about him with his whip. (As already noted, this is the story that also appeared with S&M-flavored cover on the US *Ten Story Fantasy* as "Tyrant and Slave-Girl on Planet Venus.") Bert kills the boss, releases the griffas, escapes, stows away on the ship back to Mars, and picks up exactly where he left off, having realized that recreating Earth is not only impossible but a bad idea, and he should value what he's got (and what he's about to get, the beautiful Martian girl Zaylo). This piece of ridiculously contrived moralizing, like "The Living Lies" from **2**, is redeemed and even rendered reasonably enjoyable by the craftsmanship of this experienced writer, but it's startling to remember that as John Wyndham he was only months away from publishing *The Day of the Triffids* (reviewed three issues later, in fact). Relatively speaking, though, it's to the readers' credit that they voted this story first in the issue, above Chandler's crude "And All Disastrous Things."

Christopher is present with four stories in his "managed future" series. In "Balance" (**9**), James Bond meets Olaf Stapledon in his *Odd John* mood. Max Larkin, retired from United Chemicals, is called back because Genetics Division appears to have engineered a super-genius, threatening to upset the balance of power among cartels. Twenty years earlier United Chemicals contrived to kill the geneticist involved, but apparently he experimented on his wife and the resulting child, carefully hidden away, is everything that was advertised. Larkin coasts through a series of spy vs. spy maneuvers, finds her (as it turns out), who is indeed an intellect vast and cool and pretty damned angry at her lot of isolation and exploitation by inferior beings. She's been getting by pretending to be only an artistic genius, publishing masterworks under pseudonyms, but now she's starting to work up a device that can inflict blindness at a distance; why not let the apes fight it out? She's quite willing to go with Larkin on a promise of a slightly better lot, but he reports her killed and then kills her himself, pronouncing, "But I know that man lives always on the very edge of tyranny and I know that liberty cannot survive... if you live."

This chilly and well-turned story made the Everett Bleiler & T. E. Dikty annual *The Best Science-Fiction Stories 1952*, the only story from either Nova magazine ever to appear in those anthologies. There is a bit of recursiveness in passing: part of Larkin's cover story is that "Nova Publications were offering him a juicy contract for a book to be called 'Eighteen Years among Venusian Savages.'" Similarly, in the first of these Larkin stories—"Colonial," *Astounding* April 1949, light-years behind this one in merit—the leading academic authority on Venus is Dr. A.C. Clarke, but one might consult Temple for corroboration.

There are several more of these Larkin stories, but none measure up to "Balance." In "The Tree" (**11**), Larkin saves humanity again, this time from a mutant magnolia that is on its way to world conquest but provides a utopian land of plenty for humans who stay put when it envelopes them. In "Breaking Point" (**15**), the menace is a man in Atomics who, watching TV, has concluded that civilization is too meretricious to live and has set up a dead-man switch and a timer to ensure the nuclear destruction of the entire planet. So they fake up some less stupid TV and pipe it into his stronghold and after a few days he crumbles. "The Prophet" (**20**) involves a man who decides that all technology developed later than the steam engine should be abolished in favor of greater authenticity in human existence. He gets control of the Agriculture sector (by now dwarfed by Hydroponics and Lignin Products) and puts his plan into operation. Larkin defeats him by having him arrested and showing him how quickly his followers endorse a program of high-tech violence when incited by one of Larkin's agents. This is the least of these stories, but all of them seem gimmicky and facile compared to "Balance." "Decoy," the last of this series, appeared in Christopher's collection *The Twenty-Second Century* (Grayson, 1954) without magazine publication.

§

Some other members of the Carnell circle make their first appearance in these issues. The most auspicious debut is probably James White's. "Assisted Passage" (**19**) is his first published story, a trifle but a well done and promising one: Dr. Mathewson, employed on a space project at Woomera, is being interrogated. Why did he assist another employee, not the designated pilot, to take off in the prototype spaceship? It's obvious almost from the beginning that he was helping an extraterrestrial get home, but White is, even at the beginning (of his professional career, anyway), a very smooth and civilized writer and it's a pleasure to follow the road even if you know where it's going. In "Crossfire" (**21**), a wartime bomb disposal squad finds a number of perplexing cylindrical objects on the battlefield, which they conclude are extraterrestrial spaceships, and decide to protect them, and vice versa. It's pleasantly written but meandering and overlong for its idea. Nonetheless the readers voted it first in its issue.

Lan Wright's first story, "Operation Exodus," is in **13**. Wright (1923-2010) contributed about 40 stories, including several novels, all but a handful to Carnell's magazines; after Carnell, he published a few novels in the later 1960s, and that was it for him. He was one of Brian Aldiss's targets in Aldiss's memorable dissection of British SF in *SF Horizons* (**2**, 1965), of which more later. In "Operation Exodus," he quickly proves to be a tone-deaf, or rather cadence-deaf, writer. Reading some of his sentences is like waiting for a long stoplight, e.g.: "Back on Earth, Mars, Venus and the dark side of Mercury, engineers and spacemen were slaving night and day to build the thousands of ships that would be necessary to start the great evacuation of mankind from the danger area of the flaming giant that was even now plunging towards the doomed system." I don't have much tolerance for this sort of thing and didn't finish the story (there will be plenty more opportunities with Mr. Wright). It doesn't help that the story is about a search for habitable planets so the *two thousand billion* people in the solar system can be removed to them in the eight years before a rogue star hits the Sun. But I did note, in the few pages I read, an idea I don't think I've seen before. On one planet, the explorers found fauna with no lungs. Why? "Think of that, thirty-six men [killed] and a week's slaving over the problem before we found out that the planet's atmosphere was also its population. Some alien form of life that we couldn't even guess at alone understand, intertwining pockets of life force which we began to breathe the minute we took off our suits. That was why those creatures had no lungs, it was the only way they could exist in that environment."

After that, things can only get better, and surprisingly, they do. "Project—Peace!" (**17**) is a perfectly readable short thriller about Screen Island, where dwell a more potent and less vulnerable sort of UN peacekeepers than those we know from the newspapers: "The Force Screen to protect, the Omega ray to destroy, and Reaction field to detect. An impregnable fortress held by completely trustworthy humanitarians capable of destroying any portion of the globe at the slightest sign of trouble." The plot involves a Manchurian Candidate-ish attempt to subvert an Islander to let the screen down. They defeat the plot and take out Vladivostok in response. One colorful detail is that the Islanders get periodic leave as relief from the isolated Island life, but it's generally not much fun because they are so hated outside that "You can't go to a theatre because all the seats are sold; you can't go to a night club because all the tables have been booked, and you can't get a bed except in a filthy flophouse or on a public park bench." Ah, for a simpler age!

"...Is No Robbery" (**20**), the first story about Johnny Dawson, agent of Spatial Projects and Colonial Exploration, is a piece of the yard-goods of trivial cleverness that has ballasted the SF magazines throughout their existence. We need great quantities of mellathium (radioactive, atomic weight around 350, half-life twice that of radium), the planet Dareen has it, but the Dareenians won't give it up. They have a sort of anarchist/

communist economy (the state either withered away or never existed) and don't engage in commerce, though bestowing gifts at visits is *de rigueur*. Dawson can't get around the attitude, gives up, and says to the Elder that maybe he can visit him on Earth sometime. So the Elder shows up with tons of mellathium. All that was needed was an opportunity for a gift. Meanwhile, we have such intellectual breakthroughs as: "One of the first things I learned in racial psychology was that you can't change the hereditary nature of the basic economics of a race."

Peter Hawkins (b. 1923) does not quite make it as a *New Worlds* regular—he published only 13 stories over a decade—but he is definitely a Carnell-only writer, with his entire oeuvre appearing in *New Worlds* or *Science Fantasy*, and anthologized only by Carnell. Hawkins was an old fan, a member of the London Circle, but he hedged his bets: his profile in **25** says he works in the London office of an Australian bank. His first published story, "Life Cycle" (**9**), is a competently written and well visualized story about space salvage operators who discover that the wreck they are salvaging is inhabited by sometimes-invisible predators who can survive in vacuum. Unfortunately the ultimate revelation about their nature and behavior is more of an afterthought than a climax.

"Hideaway" (**15**) is another space-procedural about Murphy and his salvage crew, this time dispatched to find a space beacon and a spaceship that was steering by it, both of which seem to have gone past "the Fold" (apparently meaning into hyper-space, subspace, no-space, whatever-space). They find that the Thinker (computer) in the beacon seems to have developed its own agenda. This is a pleasant improvement over its prede-cessor, with a plot that adds up better, though the story is still a bit too long for itself.

"The Exterminators" (**20**) posits a Galactic Empire which periodically "clears" inhabited planets for its own use, not by dianetic therapy but by engineered plague, and now it's Earth's turn. A long-time observer from the empire tries to stop the extermination plot, motivated chiefly, it appears, by his affection for a child in his rooming house who is one of the first to come down with the plague. It's an adequate story as long as you don't ask why the Empire doesn't just commit its genocide at the first opportunity rather than waiting until its agents have had time to get comfortable and go native.

The first story by Alan Barclay (George B. Tait, 1910-1989), "Welcome, Stranger," appears in **11**. Barclay was very nearly a Carnell-only writer. Of his 28 appearances in the SF magazines, 26 of them were in Carnell's magazines, though his second published story appeared in *Astounding*. (The other was in *Authentic*.) He hung it up in 1961. "Welcome, Stranger" proposes that Venus is ant-ridden, and to combat these alien ants, the colonists bring in Earth ants, which eat the Venus ants' lunch, and them. But over the horizon, the Earth and Venus ants are getting together and becoming a more formidable force, and collectively intelligent and telepathic. Get the Flit? No, suppress the information: humanity needs a challenge. This one is agreeably written but too long, and acknowledgedly derivative of Wells' "The Empire of the Ants."

Barclay's next story, "The Hard Way" (**21**), tediously proposes that the first space battle is fought with small arms from two spaceships. Both crews are seeking control of a spaceport, but neither can land until their disagreement is resolved, since the one remaining aloft can blast the other with its exhaust. Carnell thought better of it than I do, having anthologized this story in *The Best From New Worlds*.

Dan Morgan's first published story, "Alien Analysis," is in **13**. Morgan (b. 1925) published about three dozen stories in the SF magazines, mostly divided between *New Worlds* and *Authentic*, but a few in the US magazines. He shifted over to novels in and after the mid-1960s, though the last of these appears to have been in 1976. He apparently kept his day job as a guitarist at least for a while, and wrote two instructional books for the guitar. "Alien Analysis" is a near-perfect specimen of a particular kind of bad SF, a supposed idea story that in fact relies on a sort of facile pseudo-reasoning with no real relationship to plausibility or logic. Space explorers land on a planet where the inhabitants won't pay any attention to them. They manage to get an audience with the emperor. The Chief Psychologist gives him a little dog. Later, they learn the aliens have killed the dog. So they go back to the emperor and the Chief Psychologist shoots him between the eyes. Successful alien contact! The aliens killed the dog because they liked it. The aliens evolved without any other animal life around (how is not explained), so they've never had any competition, so they've evolved bored to death, and the only reason they don't all commit suicide is because (handwave) "another facet of their mentality" prevents it. So killing them is the ultimate gesture of good will. Q.E.D.

J. F. Burke's "Chessboard" (**19**) is his first published story, though the *Encyclopedia of Science Fiction* says he had a novel, *Swift Summer*, published in 1949 (a "marginal fantasy of some slight interest"—talk about damning with faint praise). Burke (1922-2011) is another old UK fan turned pro. In "The Literary Line-Up" in **18**, Carnell says, "Once upon a time, in 1939, to be precise, there were three Liverpool fans who became separated by the war. Subsequently each has become a novelist in his own right." The others are Christopher Youd (John Christopher) and David McIlwain (Charles Eric Maine), and now here's Burke. He contributed 30 or so stories to the British magazines, all but one from 1953 to 1958: half a dozen stories to *New Worlds* and seven to *Science Fantasy*, but more than half his output to *Authentic*. He had one more in *New Worlds* in 1963 and that was it for him in the SF magazines. He did, however, manage two collections, *Alien Landscapes* (Museum 1955), hardcover but no paperback, a selection of reprinted stories, and *Exodus From Elysium* (Horwitz 1965), several original stories. He published a few SF novels in the 1950s but his main career from the 1960s seems to have been novelizations and weird/horror anthologies. He has had a scattering of his own stories in horror anthologies, two as late as 2010, and had a collection of them from Ash-Tree Press in 2000, *We've Been Waiting For You.*

As for "Chessboard": In the future, Conditioning Control

manipulates human destiny pharmacologically, but it seems that some low-level bureaucrat has made a mistake and given somebody the wrong injection, then tried to cover it up. The resulting improperly titrated human upsets the applecart, assassinating a political figure who was only supposed to be assassinated later, by somebody else, and eventually making his way to the citadel of Conditioning Control ready to kill those in charge because they have no right to manipulate humanity. But they point out that he is just as much an object of manipulation—botched manipulation in his case—as anybody else, and then somebody he knows steps into the room and shoots him. It's the other man who got the wrong injection, when the aforementioned low-level bureaucrat tried to cover up his mistake with an equal and opposite mistake to make his totals come out right. This is not a bad story, if a bit too schematic; Burke avoids the usual temptation of a happy or at least promising ending.

Burke's "Golden Slumbers" (20) proposes that spacemen will spend most of their time en route in suspended animation, and their spouses will do the same, to be roused when the menfolk return. The protagonist's wife, however, proves never to have shown up at the Dormitory after his departure 20 years previously. She apologizes for her betrayal and her subsequent wasted life (she'd figured, after seeing the error of her ways six years or so after his departure, that it was too late to check in to the Dormitory and pretend that nothing happened), and she's really sorry. No problem! Hubby has been offered some more work which will have him spending time on planetary surfaces, so she'll check in to the Dormitory now and he'll go grow up for her while she sleeps. This was voted first in the issue by the readers. This matter of the marital and familial consequences of space travel became a recurrent theme in *New Worlds*—see the stories by E. C. Tubb on the same subject.[36]

Remaining are a few short stories by writers who weren't

36. See Tubb's "Rockets Aren't Human" (20), "Homecoming" (28), and "No Place for Tears" (34); also, in *Science Fantasy*, "One in Every Port" by Richard Lawrence (6) and "Stranger from Space" by Gene Lees (7),

heard from again in *New Worlds*. One of them is A. E. van Vogt's "Enchanted Village" (**14**), reprinted from *Other Worlds* a couple of years previously. This is one of his most familiar stories, the pleasant fairy tale about the marooned Mars explorer who happens on an alien life support system which unfortunately can't adapt itself to his needs, so it adapts him to it. The readers voted it first in the issue, though one reader—Dave Gardner, who says he speaks for the Liverpool SF Club—complains that it's not fair to pit the other writers against van Vogt.

H. H. Boyesen's "No Priority" (**11**) is an amusing Sheckleyesque piece about a far-future tax collector who tracks down cheats who hide their assets in the past. Unfortunately his time machine is busted and he needs to make a new one, but is thwarted by the industrial shortages of postwar Britain. He finds another time refugee with a broken-down machine, but she tricks him into fixing it and then flees, leaving him still stuck. (Her departure is illustrated by Reina Bull's cover for the issue.)

Cedric Walker's "Manhunt" (**9**) is a pleasant story about a bucolic world where the innocent people live in harmony with, and talk to, the forest and the animals (referred to as the Little Creatures, although if there are any big ones, we don't hear about them). There's a lot of excitement because Earthmen have arrived, then terrifying entities that are obviously Earthmen in spacesuits arrive and hunt down the first Earth contingent, uttering the incomprehensible word "androids."

"The Scapegoats" (**11**) is a nominal sequel to "Manhunt," a high-minded think-piece in which a representative of the persecuted androids seeks help from an enlightened human legislator, only to have the rug pulled out when the belligerent faction of androids takes military action. This is Walker's last credit in the SF magazines (earlier he had a story in *Marvel* and several in *Slant* and *Nekromantikon*); he, or someone of that name, reappears in 1965 in *London Mystery Magazine*.

§

In previous chapters we had arrived by this point at the inexcusable dregs, the short pieces that are irredeemably lame, inconsequential, or stupid or all three, or worse. But in these issues of *New Worlds*, the usual order is turned upside down. The dregs are mostly floating on top, in the form of the really awful lead stories by Burks, Duncan, and Bounds, and the short fiction mostly maintains at least a surface readability (though Lan Wright and Dan Morgan's first stories do test that proposition). The executive summary for this piece of *New Worlds*'s history would be something like "plausible but not memorable." If I were an anthologist the only stories in the 13 issues I would pause over are Christopher's "Balance," Tubb's "Third Party," and Rayer's "Of Those Who Came," with a nod to John Wyndham for professionalism in a lost cause for "No Place Like Earth."

4: REBIRTH AND BUSINESS PLAN (1954-55)

New Worlds' new look, displayed in the June 1953 issue (**21**), didn't last long. The magazine did not appear again for ten months, well into 1954. When it did, it had another new look, albeit a ragged one at first. It is back to a larger size–though smaller than the previous "large digest" size—about 7 7/8 x 5 3/8 inches. It stays at 1/6 and 128 pages exclusive of covers (price increased to 2/- in February 1955). The print is smaller, closer to the pre-**21** issues. The contents page of **22** proclaims *Monthly*, but bears no date. Mike Ashley says it appeared in April 1954, and explains in *Transformations* that Nova had sought a new printer in hopes of being able to reduce the price, but the printer had done a late and bad job on the first issue (see my comments in the previous chapter on issue **21**), and the next was delayed for months on end.

Meanwhile, Carnell was approached by Maclaren & Sons. Ltd., a publisher of technical trade magazines, about starting its own SF magazine. Carnell was unwilling to abandon *New Worlds*, so Maclaren's took over Nova Publications as a subsidiary,[37] planning to publish *New Worlds* monthly and

37. That is, the Nova shareholders met and accepted a proposition by which they lost voting rights but received annual payments, a Maclaren's holding company took over administration of Nova's affairs, and a new Board of Directors included three Maclaren's directors, Carnell, Leslie Flood, and John Wyndham. This account is from Carnell's interview in Harbottle's *Vultures of the Void: The Legacy*, pp. 265-66, and is more detailed than any other account I have seen.

Science Fantasy bimonthly. Carnell went full time and actually started receiving a salary, as well as having the benefit of "departments in advertising, copy layout, accounts, publicity, distribution, a photographic studio, plus a warehouse and complete distribution facilities"—not to mention a legal department. This last came in handy when Carnell refused the belated delivery of issue **22**, dated the preceding year, and Maclaren's lawyers obtained an injunction to keep the printer from selling it, leaving Carnell's advance copy the only one in existence.[38] A new issue **22** was assembled and released. The magazine was now printed by the Rugby Advertiser, and with **23** the editorial offices move to 2 Arundel Street. Maclaren's name isn't mentioned in the magazine that I can find. Carnell's is now the only editorial name on the contents page, though Leslie Flood is doing the book reviews. G. Ken Chapman has an ad in **23** for his book business.

The first appearance of the new new *New Worlds* was not altogether auspicious. Issue **22** (April 1954) is fronted by one of the worst covers I have seen on an SF magazine, crudely drawn, tastelessly colored, and with astonishing lapses of perspective.[39] The artist, Kinnear, seems not to have appeared again in the SF magazines. The amateurish effect is compounded by the logo, which looks like a hasty mock-up which someone forgot to replace with the real thing. This is odd, since **23** reverts to the same logo used in **21** (and which *New Worlds* stuck with until mid-1963, though everything around it changed). There is also a confusion of agendas. Though **22** features the first installment of Kornbluth's *Take-Off*, not previously announced in "The Literary Line-Up," it isn't listed on the cover—the small text area lists Clarke's "The Sentinel," the cover story, and the names of Wyndham, McIntosh, and Christopher, who have short stories in the issue. (Most issues still did not have stories

38. *Vultures of the Void*, p. 266.

39. In the flesh it looks even worse than in the available scans. See this and the other covers referred to at http://www.sfcovers.net/mainnav.htm or http://www.philsp.com/mags/newworlds.html.

or authors listed on the cover at all.) To top it off, my copy of the magazine has one of the four signatures inserted backwards, though I assume that did not affect more than a fraction of the print run.

Issue **23** makes up for it all, however, with the neat half-enclosed logo restored and one of Gerard Quinn's most tasteful covers, depicting a spaceship approaching the Earth. This is starting to look like a magazine that a reputable company is putting some money into. There are still lapses, like **24**, the cover of which is a free fall scene depicting the aftermath of some disaster, with a bare foot and hairy shank foregrounded entirely too much. But overall, Quinn is learning how to be smart and gaudy at the same time, and the result is often a very good-looking magazine. Look in particular at the covers of **28**, **29**, and **39** for striking use of color and form, uncluttered and making maximum use of the digest-sized space. Quinn is spelled on several issues by Bradshaw, whose machinery-heavy covers are more conventional than Quinn's but equally well conceived and rendered.

The covers continue mostly to illustrate stories within the magazine. Until **28**, you're on your own figuring out which story, but with that issue, the contents page states "Cover painting symbolising" whatever story it is. This changes to a simple "from" with **32**. (This may not just be a matter of style— the covers do actually get a bit more literal at that point.) These attributions are not necessarily reliable or meaningful, though; the cover of **42**, which nominally illustrates Tubb's "Lawyer at Large," has no discernible connection with the story. A few of the covers are concededly not linked with stories. The cover of **31** is "representing a mystery of space travel," and several of the later covers by Bradshaw depicting high-tech scenes (**38**, **40**, and **41**) have explanatory paragraphs inside the magazine. Most of the covers have no lettering other than the title, number, and price; a few of them list the lead story.

The magazine did not settle down to a regular practice (author names or a story title on a band at the bottom of the cover) until early 1957 (and changed it again in 1958).

§

The biggest alteration in the magazine is in the fiction
contents. All the ambivalence about reprints and Britishness
is out the window. In the first year and a half of the monthly
schedule, *New Worlds* presents five serials, four of which—C.
M. Kornbluth's *Takeoff* (or *Take-Off*, as it is Anglicized), Wilson
Tucker's *Wild Talent*, Charles Dye's *Prisoner in the Skull*, and
Tucker's *The Time Masters*—are by then reasonably well-
known American authors and had been recently published in
hardcover in the U.S. (Dye, forgotten now, was a comer at the
time: he had had 16 magazine appearances in a very short time,
even though he didn't really write them all.[40])

As to reprinted stories, two had appeared in magazines long
enough previously that they were presumably cherry-picked
rather than simply submitted in both countries: Arthur C. Clarke's
"The Sentinel" (**22**), which had been in *Ten Story Fantasy*, and
Judith Merril's "Survival Ship" (**35**), from *Worlds Beyond*, both
in 1951. But more impressively, between **22** and the end of 1955
(**42**), there are 13 stories by reasonably well-known US writers
(del Rey, Sheckley, Kornbluth, Bester, Oliver, Anderson, Gold)
that had appeared in book form in the US without prior magazine publication: nine from Frederik Pohl's *Star Science Fiction
Stories* anthologies, two from August Derleth's *Time To Come*,
one from Raymond J. Healy's *Nine Tales of Space and Time*,
and one from Kornbluth's collection *The Mindworm*.

This change in course reflects a decision made at some point
during the publishing hiatus, since "This Precious Stone," a
long and to my taste lame novelette by J. T. McIntosh under
the pseudonym H. J. Murdoch, had been announced in **21**, the

---

40. Two stories under the Dye byline were actually written by his then
wife, Katherine MacLean: "Syndrome Johnny" and "The Man Who Staked
the Stars." Eric Leif Davin, *Partners in Wonder: Women and the Birth of
Science Fiction, 1926-1965* (Lexington Books, 2006), p. 119.

last pre-hiatus issue, to appear in **22** (and did appear in the rubbished version of **22**). In the event this was shunted off to *Science Fantasy* in favor of the first installment of Kornbluth's *Takeoff*. Carnell and Maclaren's had made a policy decision in the interim to present a consistent leaven of reasonably high-quality American material by name authors, despite previous protestations about Britishness.

This may seem surprising in the abstract, but it's not a bit so in view of the monthly schedule. Bear in mind that Carnell had questioned, a dozen issues earlier, whether there were enough experienced writers in the UK to maintain "any reasonable standard of literary value" at the then-current volume of publication (Editorial, **10**), and subsequent experience (see chapter 3) showed that it was particularly difficult to find long stories of any merit for *New Worlds* even on a bi-monthly schedule. So it made excellent sense to ensure other sources of readable fiction, especially long fiction, before doubling the magazine's frequency. One might then ask, why the monthly schedule if it required compromising the Britishness of the magazine? Carnell might well have thought "if we build it, they will come"—that is, if he created a reliable publishing niche for a larger amount of intelligent SF at various lengths, and figured out another way to fill it while he waited, sooner or later the stable of British writers he had been developing would rise to the occasion.

If that *was* his purpose, he was resoundingly successful. As noted, of the five serials published in 1954-55, four were American reprints (the other was E. C. Tubb's *Starship*, later Ace Doubled as *The Space-Born*). The next five serials, published from 1956 into early 1958, were by Lan Wright, James White, Kenneth Bulmer, Dan Morgan and John Brunner, each of whom had by then been selling short fiction to Carnell for several years, and they and other Carnell-developed writers supplied the majority of novel-length work in *New Worlds* for the rest of its life under Carnell. The short story reprints slowed to a trickle as well, though some stories continued to appear reasonably contemporaneously with their US magazine appearances.

The bottom line is that Carnell's resort to American material was indirectly, and I suspect calculatedly, one of the biggest boosts British SF ever received.

Carnell says nothing in the magazine about the wherefores of this policy boomerang, though he does not obscure what he is doing. Thus, the blurb for the first installment of *Take-Off* reminds readers that it was a finalist for the International Fantasy Award the previous year. The inside back cover blurb in **25** for *Wild Talent*, starting in the next issue, describes it as "Rinehart & Co's great 1954 novel" and quotes Groff Conklin's *Galaxy* review of it. The first of the *Star SF* reprints, del Rey's "Idealist" (**24**), is blurbed: "For many years we have (editorially) sung the praises of British authors whose names are familiar on both sides of the Atlantic. We now reverse the role and welcome an American who is equally as well known to British readers, both as a writer and an editor. His story which follows is published in magazine form for the first time on either Continent." Why the last point should matter is unclear to me. Is it really the case that British readers were less likely to have read the *Star* anthologies, highly touted and released simultaneously in hardcover and paperback in the US, than any given issue of an American magazine? (The *Star* anthologies were also released in hardcover in the UK by Sidgwick & Jackson. The first is reviewed in **29** by Leslie Flood, who notes that two of its stories have already appeared in *New Worlds*.)

Carnell's characterization of the policy change, which appears in Philip Harbottle's newly expanded *Vultures of the Void*, goes part of the way (at least by implication) towards confirming the above surmises. He says that "it was decided that we should strengthen the already existing story material by publishing three-part serials... buying from the fast-developing American book market to start with, and thereby bringing 'name' authors." After describing the policy of buying US short stories as well, he adds: "The plan was to make *New Worlds SF* as international as possible, and at the same time to show potentially new British writers the quality of stories we required and give readers the very best SF available."

What the readers thought of all this, we don't know, at least not directly. Under Carnell's new and severe dispensation concerning "Postmortem" (discussed below), if he received comments on the subject, he didn't print them. But whatever they thought in principle about the policy, readers seemed to like the stories fine. Of the 12 reprinted serial installments, 10 were voted into first place and the other two into second place. The picture is more mixed for the reprinted short stories, which were scattered from first to fifth place (Bester's "Disappearing Act" and Kornbluth's "Gomez" being the two first place finishers), but there is certainly no indication in the ratings in "The Literary Line-Up" of resistance to them as a category. There is one remark by Carnell, mixing wistfulness and resentment, in "The Literary Line-Up" in **32**: "There may be some feelings of regret amongst readers that most of the stories written by American authors were rated highly—nevertheless, our British authors have consistently maintained a good *average* standard and we can expect them to improve still further in 1955." But that's it.

§

As usual, there is an editorial by Carnell in each issue, generally running a couple of pages at the front of the magazine. The most frequent topic is the overall state of British SF, and in particular how the SF reading audience can be maintained and increased. Carnell clearly sees himself as one of the proprietors of British SF as a whole and not just one piece of it, a perspective that in some would lead to intolerable egotism, but in him results in a sort of anxious sense of responsibility. Carnell does write about *New Worlds* itself, but not as much as you'd expect. In particular, as noted, he is reticent about the takeover by Maclaren's, any strategic discussions that accompanied it, and the heavy use of reprinted US material during the first years with Maclaren's.

In **22**'s editorial, "Growing Up," Carnell recaps the history of SF publishing in the UK, noting the increase both in high-quality and low-quality material, then states his pleasure at the new monthly schedule, with no discussion of how he got there. "Investigation" in **24** describes the "market research" that Nova (still no mention of Maclaren's) conducted before changing to a monthly schedule:

> The completed picture has been built up by our representatives discussing sales with wholesalers and retailers (not only in this country but also abroad), by correspondence and conversations with readers, managers, and owners of shops, trade publishing houses, street vendors, market stall-holders, newspapermen and even schoolteachers.... The result of our three months investigation shows that science fiction *in general* has passed its peak of interest for the *casual* readers who have been making up the vast bulk of new sales.

The US magazines are dropping or cutting pages and publishing frequency, the US publishers are offering less new material, Hollywood is *optioning* lots but actually *making* little SF. In the UK there is a similar decline, in part because there are so many sources of SF that nobody has to read everything to feed his habit, and in part because of "the effect on general readership of the vast amount of poorly written rubbish that has fastened like an evil growth on the name of science fiction." But this sort of decline has happened before and will clear the field for the better quality magazines to develop SF as a "good class literature." (This last is Carnell's constant theme.)

Carnell adds: "The contribution *New Worlds* is going to make to that class will become more evident next month, when more of our future programme is announced, a programme which will set a new high level for science fiction magazine publishing in this country." What is he talking about? The most significant announcement in **25** is the next serial, Wilson Tucker's *Wild Talent*. Most likely he is referring to the Nova SF Novels, which were actually announced on the inside back cover of **26**, but further delayed before they actually appeared. In **27** ("Book Review Editorial"), he expresses doubt whether comics will provide the entree into SF that the boys' papers did in his day, and suggests a couple of wholesome nonfiction books instead.

In **29**—unusually, running four pages, and portentously titled "Battleground"—the editorial quotes and summarizes William Hamling's *Fantasy Times* article about the American magazine bust, with its glut of product returned unopened to wholesalers for lack of display space, and goes on to describe the similar bust in the UK: several British reprint edition titles suspended, some publishers withdrawn from the SF market, and "[s]ales of existing British magazines (both reprint and original), are all mostly lower than last year's figures, mainly through over-production of too much trash by too many publishers hoping to make the British equivalent of the American 'fast buck'.... There is every indication also that the hard-cover publishers in Britain are in for just as bad a time...." Non-specialist writers are entering the field without knowing what they are doing. In Australia and South Africa, the glut of "rubbishy literature" is undermining the market. But, Carnell is confident, quality will eventually triumph, and "[t]he battle is therefore to convert the casual reader into an interested regular reader."

30's editorial explains that the Nova Novels, advertised for some months on *New Worlds*'s inside back cover, were delayed because Carnell wasn't satisfied with the covers. They will allegedly start appearing in two more weeks.[41] He regrets that

41. These were to be a digest-sized series of reprinted SF novels. The first was John Beynon's *Stowaway to Mars*; it was to be followed by Malcolm Jameson's *Bullard of the Space Patrol* and Raymond F. Jones's *Renaissance*. The Jameson book was dropped, and I find no evidence that the Jones novel appeared either. Later volumes, these issued in standard paperback format, included A. E. van Vogt's *The Weapon Shops of Isher*, Wilson Tucker's *The City in the Sea*, Theodore Sturgeon's *The Dreaming Jewels*, and James Blish's *Jack of Eagles*. See Ashley, *Transformations*, p. 92, and Harbottle,

they won't be on sale in Canada, Canadian rights being lumped in with North American rights—but Canadians can order them directly. Amusingly, he adds: "Statement of (minor) editorial policy. British readers will be well aware of the science fiction short story competition recently promulgated by the national Sunday newspaper the *Observer*. As of now and until further notice this magazine is not interested in 3000 word stories with plots situated in the year 2500 A.D. (!)" Carnell also announces that publisher Boardman's SF program, "by far the most progressive in this country, are to produce a yearly pocketbook anthology of stories selected from this magazine," to be titled *The Best from New Worlds*. In fact, there was one volume under that title, published in 1955 with stories from as far back as 1949. While Carnell published several anthologies with Boardman, with various degrees of emphasis on stories from the Nova magazines, there were no more after 1955, and the next *New Worlds* anthology did not appear until 1964, when Berkley Medallion published *Lambda 1* in the US, followed by a UK Penguin edition with differing contents the next year.

The editorial in **31**—another four-pager—is on a heavier topic: "Religion and Sex in S-F." This recounts Carnell's disagreement with J. T. McIntosh, arising from the then-current censorship panic in the UK, "whereby the original police drive against pornographical literature has overflowed into all classes of book and magazine publishing and no one publisher can be sure that he will not be prosecuted for the publication of some seemingly innocent references to our present morals and mode of life." McIntosh says you can't capitulate to the censors or it will only egg them on; Carnell says he agrees with McIntosh but hasn't the courage of his (McIntosh's) convictions, i.e., isn't willing to be jailed for them. Actually Carnell's position, regardless of his courage, is a bit dodgy. He agrees that "[t]he police have, very rightly, always been trying to stamp out the crude, raw type of fiction published to appeal solely to the baser

---

Vultures of the Void: The Legacy, p. 174.

instincts." (SF didn't appeal to baser instincts until later.)

In any case, he says, this has all been set off by a single case in which the prosecutor won prison time, not merely fines, against author, publisher, printer, and distributor, and now the tide is running against "prominent publishing houses of repute" over books such as *The Philanderer* and *September In Quinze* (no doubt prominent in their time, but obscure to me) and the *Decameron*. Two juries hung over *The Image and the Search* (never heard of that either). Apparently hardcover publishers had about an even chance of prevailing in court, while magazine and paperback publishers did much worse.[42] Carnell passes on McIntosh's account of his novel *Born Leader* a.k.a. *Worlds Apart*, in which interstellar colonists' "sexual and religious morals were changed to conform with a workable life under conditions almost totally dissimilar to those on Earth" (i.e., if memory serves, marriage generally lasted only long enough to see if the woman would become pregnant quickly). He had no trouble in the US, but his UK publisher asked him to modify it because "science fiction in this country was read largely by juveniles and adolescents." McIntosh asks plaintively if he can never write SF for adults, and Carnell cites his *New Worlds* reader survey showing the readership's average age is *"over thirty years."*

Back to Carnell's problem: There's no way to know in advance what will offend the censors.

> Science fiction and fantasy stories readily lay
> themselves open to the current close-scrutiny of the
> law because most plots are situated in a distant future
> where present-day morals, ethics and religious teach-
> ings could (hypothetically) have changed consider-
> ably.... [T]he present inconsistency in the law does
> not allow an editor or publisher any redress at all if
> the police decide that such a story is immoral in one

42. These events are discussed in Steve Holland, *The Trials of Hank Janson* (Telos Publishing Co., 2004).

sense or another.... I have no doubt that *New Worlds* is scrutinised just as closely as all other publications that regularly appear on the bookstalls—in fact, I personally know one Divisional Detective Inspector who has been a regular reader of this magazine for some years. Doubtless he would feel justified in putting "business" before "pleasure" if he thought the occasion warranted such an action.

So, the bottom line: "the present policy in our stories is that religion and sex should not be the central pivot upon which the story turns." But he hastily reassures that "there is no necessity for our stories to feature solely men, monsters and mechanical marvels." But on the other hand: "To keep on the right side of the vagaries of the existing law, however, it is necessary to keep such controversial ideas [earlier exemplified as multiple marriage or its abolition, '[s]tate control of child-birth, voluntary euthanasia, artificial insemination, and numerous other social codes not in practice today'] sublimated to the plots and not dominating them."

How religion fits into this picture of risk of prosecution is never quite clear. The BBC reported in 2004: "The last man to be sent to prison for blasphemy was John William Gott. In 1922 he was sentenced to nine months hard labour for comparing Jesus with a circus clown. In Scotland, there has not been a public prosecution since 1843."[43]

Carnell's editorial reaped a harvest of high-profile commentary; "Postmortem" in **33** prints letters from Eric Frank Russell (suggesting to McIntosh that he take up the cudgels of satire against censorship); Robert Heinlein (commiserating and offering famous last words: "Censorship in re religion is not a problem here; our constitutional guarantees are such that we need not worry on that score."); Alfred Bester ("the important thing is to fight censorship, to air it, discuss it, beef about it—

43. "Q & A: Blasphemy law," news.bbc.co.uk/1/hi/uk/3753408.stm (Oct. 18, 2004) (visited 9/8/11).

not deny it"; SF's purpose is to reflect humanity; "Carnell, torn by the problems of censorship, is far more vivid and memorable than Robotmen, Starmen, or even Demolished Men."); and John Wyndham ("Where there is a clear intention to corrupt, or to exploit depraved taste, there can be no resentment of censorship"; but fortunately it seems "a more enlightened censorship is in the making.")

32's editorial gives a preliminary report on the reader survey conducted in **30**. They have received about 5% response, more than they expected—2% is normal in advertising research, Carnell says. The average age of readers is about 30, with a "fair percentage of technicians" and many "advanced educations up to and including College." More detailed, but still preliminary results (from the first 1000 responses) appear in **37**. Average age: M 31.7, F 28 years. 95% male. 47% of males single, 60% of females single. 26% have degrees (13% B.Sc.; 4% M.A.; 2% M.D.; 7% other). 35% have some technical employment; average number of other magazines read, 4. (Competence of editor in presenting survey research findings: minimal. Here's my favorite item: "Preference for books or magazines: 30% didn't mind; 47% No; 23% Yes." Best guess: this meant "Preference for books *rather than* magazines.")

In **32**, the 1954 International Fantasy Awards are announced—or rather, Carnell describes the actual presentation of the award for *More Than Human* to Theodore Sturgeon at the Brooklyn Public Library by Ian Ballantine, with speeches by Sturgeon, Frederik Pohl, and Henry Kuttner. (The IFA is discussed in more detail by Leslie Flood, as described below.) Carnell also mentions the Science Fiction Luncheon Club, which meets every other month at the Criterion Restaurant in Piccadilly, with such speakers as author Miss Clemence Dane, Alan Pryce-Jones, editor of the *Times Literary Supplement*, and Professor A.M. Low—not to mention Patricia Laffan, who played the female lead in *Devil Girl From Mars*, but prefers to be remembered for her role as Nero's wife in *Quo Vadis*.

The **33** editorial, "Graduation Day," is an SF Is Growing Up piece, which notes that British publishers are now emphasizing writers new to the field, and publishers who are only beginning to move into the field are focusing on high-quality material without disguising its genre identity. He mentions in particular the Michael Joseph "Novels of Tomorrow" program, edited by the above-mentioned Miss Dane, which published among others Harold Mead's *The Bright Phoenix*, John Christopher's *Year of the Comet*, Wyndham's *The Chrysalids*, and the UK editions of the first collections by Sheckley and Kornbluth. He also notes Faber & Faber's "most peculiar approach": Edmund Crispin's *Best S-F* anthology, which asks readers to pay money for stories that have already been anthologized!

In **38**, Carnell takes up the question of a definition of science fiction, fortunately dropping it almost immediately. But here's his manifesto, delivered almost in passing:

> Apart from its entertainment value (its main function) science fiction should be primarily concerned with reasoning out the possible advantages or disadvantages of a given set of theories based upon present day knowledge built on a matrix representing *Now*, whether it be Man against Nature or Man against Machine or a combination of any two of those against the remaining one. And to be popular with the general public the plots should be located within a Time ratio which could be conceivably *in their lifetime*. That will thrust home the reality of the plot situation if the author has handled his theme properly.

That is, it's all about us:

> It seems significant to me that the novels which are best remembered by readers and receive prominent reviews in the literary journals and newspapers are those where the science or fantasy part of the plot is sublimated to strong human characterization based

on *ourselves* in everyday life—given the variations of an indeterminate number of Tomorrows how would *we* react to the changes which would effect [sic] our lives?... The stumbling block to a general appreciation of science fiction is that word "science" which in most cases seldom applies.

In **42**, "Current Criticism," Carnell notes a change of policy in UK SF hardcover publishing: space opera has had its day and "the desire now is to find novels of a literary calibre that will stand up to the harshest scrutiny of the learned critics." He speculates that SF hardcover publishing was not as successful as desired, and notes that the trend is following a bit over a year behind similar developments in the US, where the supply of new and good novels has slowed drastically, leaving UK publishers to look for home-grown material, daring the pitfalls of writers of general fiction trying to navigate the "technical taboos" of the genre.

Carnell kept a weather eye on commentary on SF from outside the genre. In **26**, "Carping Critics," he complains about the ignorance of those who try to judge contemporaneous SF having read nothing more recent than Wells and Verne. His fuse was ignited by a BBC discussion which does sound inane, with one panelist suggesting that SF is "a debased lay version of God.... Clarke's Overlords were the personification of the Second Coming." (Still sore in **42**, he compares this panel unfavorably to a BBC teen-agers' panel taking on Wyndham's *The Kraken Wakes*.) In **35**, "Interpretation" comments favorably on an article by one John Wren-Lewis or Wynn-Lewis, depending on which paragraph you're reading, titled "Spaceships and Providence" and published in the *Church Of England Newspaper*, which proposes that SF "fulfils the religious needs of the new age," and isn't escapist at all: "On the contrary, the majority of science fiction stories show a very real awareness of our contemporary problems and more often than not express a gloomy view of them.... The introduction of the cosmic setting seems to heighten rather than detract from the significance attached to human affairs, *and it is precisely this effect which I believe to be essentially religious.*" Carnell says he doesn't propose to add to these remarks—"an editor's job is to carefully steer his stories through the narrow shoals of overlapping creeds and ensure that he does not unwittingly upset any one particular religious group, for while the acceptance of one God is acknowledged by all faiths the method of acceptance differs considerably."

Carnell also took more than a passing interest in SF conventions, and not just in the public-service-announcement form common in US magazines (though there were certainly a few of those). He seemed to see these as important public and community-building events in which he had a stake bigger than just having a good time with like-minded friends. The editorial in **25** is titled "What makes a Successful Convention?" (capitalization sic), and the answer is... parties. But the earnest Carnell still doesn't quite get it, since his idea of the significance of parties is which authors and editors were seen in conversation with one another. This editorial also clarifies one of the more trivial mysteries in the companion magazine, *Science Fantasy*: Gene Lees, author of the story "Stranger from Space," was identified as female in Carnell's blurb for the story, but as male in connection with an article he contributed some years later. It is revealed that at this convention in Manchester, Carnell was enlightened in the flesh as to Lees' gender; Lees, completely by chance, checked into the room across the hall from Carnell while stopping to see a local friend on his way from Canada to Europe on a journalistic assignment. In **36**, Carnell comments on plans to bid for the 1956 World Science Fiction Convention (Worldcon), and in **41**, he notes the withdrawal of London's bid in favor of New York and the announcement of Plan B for 1957, with some classic Carnellian advice: "see that every minute is planned carefully and of outstanding interest to everyone."

There are some merely miscellaneous efforts among the editorials as well. "Prediction" in **23** recounts the results of a poll of scientists and SF types on the future course of space travel. "Visiting Season" in **39** recounts the people who have dropped in on Carnell during the last week of July 1955: Wyndham, Bester, Tubb, Kippax, Bulmer, Bradshaw the artist, Pierre Lundborg from Sweden. "One prominent topic of discussion with most visitors is—Has the present magazine science fiction story gone too far into the realms of the abstract to be good entertainment?" In **40**, Carnell discusses rumors about the US satellite program and reminisces about the early days of the British Interplanetary Society.

"The Literary Line-Up," the story rating and "coming next issue" feature, appears regularly, presenting an occasionally amusing conflict between Carnell's promotional instincts and his fundamentally dour outlook (in **30**: "Next month's issue will be a fairly average one").

§

The letter column "Postmortem" is at first conspicuous by its absence during this period, appearing for one page in **25** and not again until **29**. Carnell responds in his editorial in **28** to "younger and more enthusiastic readers" who ask when there will be a permanent letter section.

> To that request I will state that "Postmortem" will be featured when space permits and when the subject matter of such letters available has something to contribute to science fiction in general and not this magazine in particular. I would rather publish fiction than spare space for arguments on the merits or de-merits of stories we publish, knowing that 90% of such arguments are based solely upon personal likes and dislikes.... It is not a policy of mine to publish eulogies by readers about this magazine—it is as one-sided an opinion as story preferences.

What he is eschewing is a large part of what comprised "Postmortem" in the pre-Maclaren's issues. But having said it, he proceeds to quote the eulogy he received from Alfred Bester about his magazines—"I must write to tell you how wonderful I think they are and to compliment you on a splendid job."

In any case, what there is of "Postmortem" is pretty serious and high-minded. In **25**, there is one letter from a John H. Wallbridge of the University of Southampton debating Carnell's editorial view of the reason for the decline in reading SF—he fingers television, the technical difficulty of good SF, and SF's taking itself too seriously. "Postmortem" appears again in **29**, and we start to see another theme: big names. This time there is another Bester letter, which I quote at length later on because of his general comments about British SF, and one from an Alan G. Dunn complaining about a "severe decline in the inventiveness of science-fiction writers," which he compares to popular song-writing, now consisting mainly of "old tunes which have been 'mucked about with.'" **31** features a letter from Sydney J. Bounds, suggesting that *New Worlds* initiate a "regular critical forum," and to that end commenting on Tucker's *Wild Talent*. In addition, J. T. McIntosh responds to Alfred Bester's letter in **29** (later for that one too).

In **34**, "Postmortem" consists of another J. T. McIntosh manifesto, which states a reasonably interesting view of the state of SF. "The successful novel of the nineteen-thirties was a tale of wonder. We read avidly, open-mouthed, credulously. We didn't much care about character in our light reading. We didn't get it, anyway."

> In the nineteen-forties the pattern was complication, tension, thrills and mental gymnastics.... Science fiction writers had to keep us jumping through hoops, never allowing an instant to settle, or they'd lost us. Characterization was better than before, but stories by this time were moving too fast to be able to take time out for character drawing.

In the nineteen-fifties the pendulum swung back, and among successful novels we began to find many that were relatively simple, slow-moving, reflective, and often so prosaic that an earlier generation might have said they weren't science fiction at all.

He calls these latter two phenomena Class I and Class II. Examples of Class I are van Vogt's novels, Williamson's *The Humanoids*, Russell's *Dreadful Sanctuary* and *Sinister Barrier*, Judd's *Gunner Cade*, Orwell's *1984* (!), and Bester's *The Demolished Man* ("perhaps the last of the great Class I novels").

In Class II novels, "the people are more important than the science *or the ideas.*" Examples: *The Day of the Triffids*, *Earth Abides*, Pangborn's *West of the Sun*, Tucker's *The Long Loud Silence*, Clarke's *Prelude to Space*.

Well, this is an interesting perspective. Do you agree that *1984* has more in common with *The World of Null-A* than with *The Day of the Triffids* or *The Long Loud Silence*? Show your work, neatness counts. But back to McIntosh: Many writers who prefer to write Class II novels, including himself, are writing Class I novelettes. "How many of the above Class II novels were serialized in science fiction magazines? How many of the Class I books weren't?" Almost all the successful new novels are Class II while almost all the serials are Class I. Something's got to happen with magazine serials, though he doesn't pinpoint what. He says he prefers to write Class II novels. "Science fiction grew out of imaginative people's capacity for wonder. Their other virtues apart, most Class II books fail to exercise this capacity to the full. Can anyone write adult science fiction which will be fast, clever, exciting, yet warm and human as well? Can we have our cake and eat it too?

"We must see the answer soon. The present position is essentially unstable."

"Postmortem" vanishes for several issues and reappears in **38**, on a slightly more plebeian basis, with one reader taking issue with the science of Philip Martyn's "Forgetfulness," and Martyn (Tubb) responding forcefully; other letters are by Richard Varne, who published a few stories around this time; K. Houston (i.e. John) Brunner, praising Kornbluth's "Gomez" and pointing out that Tubb's "School for Beginners" uses the same plot as a story by Frank Quattrocchi; and a couple of unfamiliar names with not much interesting to say. In **39** "Postmortem" is devoted exclusively to Eric Frank Russell's article "Asstronomy" (see later).

§

As noted, the book reviews are now consistently by Leslie Flood, whose byline appears on the contents page starting with **24** (June 1954). The column appears regularly; it is squeezed out of only two of these issues, **27** and **36**, and in **27** Carnell has what he calls "Book Review Editorial," which recommends several books including the first *Star Science Fiction* anthology, without mentioning that he has already reprinted two stories from the US edition. Carnell also occasionally has an addendum to the book column on nonfiction or children's books. In **33**, for example, he praises Heinlein's *Starman Jones* and dismisses Tom Corbett, and in **42** he recommends as a Christmas gift Lancelot Hogben's *Man Must Measure*, "wherein by beautifully presented pictures and diagrams and a fascinating text the magic of numbers is explained from the Dawn of Civilisation down through the ages to the era of our modern technological age. Few books could be more acceptable to the 8-year-old and upward." (Yes indeed; just what I wanted in my stocking at that age.)

But in general the book reviews are Flood's show, and very different from Carnell's, which were mainly an exercise in boosterism. Within his limited space, Flood actually tries to be a critic, and often an acerbic one. (F. Dubrez Fawcett's *Hole In Heaven* is taxed with "banality of dialogue and stupidity of characterisation"; Philip Wilding's *Space-Flight Venus* is "the sort of trivial nonsense which can have but limited appeal.") He has no hesitation about slagging *New Worlds*'s contributors, or damning them with faint praise. Jonathan Burke's *Pattern of Shadows* is "a most disappointing waste of this author's talents." Carnell's anthology *Gateway To The Stars* is dismissed as "very uneven," and in it, Peter Hawkins "flounders" in an "inept" story Carnell published in *Science Fantasy*. Tucker's *Wild Talent* is "a superficial novel of a telepath.... Ingeniously plotted and slickly written, it nevertheless barely touches on the human problems of normals in conflict with this wild talent." Credulity is strained, however, by his review of Tubb's *Alien Dust*, which fixes up his early *New Worlds* Mars stories with some new material: a "supremely effective science-fiction novel" in "a style no less striking than Hemingway in his field."

Flood is tough on some well-regarded books: *Childhood's End*, he says, "falls just short of the greatness which is yet to come" and lacks the "poetic beauty" of *Against the Fall of Night*; Kuttner's *Fury* is "a competent work, marred only by the somewhat unreality [sic] of characterisation." On the other hand, his praise is unqualified for Fredric Brown's *Project Jupiter* (*The Lights In The Sky Are Stars*), Pangborn's *West of the Sun*, Sturgeon's *More than Human*, Asimov's *The Caves of Steel*, Margo Bennett's *The Long Way Back*, Charles Eric Maine's *Timeliner*, Clarke's *Earthlight*, Pangborn's *A Mirror For Observers*, Ward Moore's *Bring The Jubilee*, Wyndham's *The Chrysalids*, and Kornbluth's *The Mindworm*, among others. Dick's *A Handful Of Darkness* gets a pretty good notice: "If you like the unusual in science-fantasy try this excellent collection." He is... balanced... in reviewing E.E. Smith's *Triplanetary* and Howard's *Conan The Conqueror*. He praises a few books I've never heard of, notably Peter Crowcroft's post-nuclear war novel *The Fallen Sky* (**33**) and Silas Waters' (pseudonym of Noel Loomis) *The Man With Absolute Motion* (**40**) (the latter review is qualified praise for an extravagant space opera), and excoriates one John Robert Haynes' *Scream from Outer Space*: "To what lower depths can such writing sink in the name of science-fiction?"

Flood often frames his reviews in general commentary on the SF field at large. In **34**, for example, he views with ambivalence the tide of anthologies: "The preponderance of anthologies on this month's review shelf serves once more to underline an important weakness in the field of science fiction. This is the inability of most writers in this *genre* to pursue successfully their efforts beyond the development of a single idea sufficient for a short story." Overall, except for those by James Blish and Damon Knight, I'd say this is as good a review column as appeared in the SF magazines during this period.

There are also film reviews, presented in various ways but all by Carnell. In **24**, under the rubric "Film Review," he gives qualified praise to *Riders To The Stars* (among the qualifications: "Then Gordon's rocket blows up–and across the airless void *you hear the explosion*.") This is followed by an unqualified bash to the Ballantine novelization by Curt Siodmak. Carnell notes Siodmak's previous *Donovan's Brain*, not to mention "his still-famous earlier book and film *F.P.I. Does Not Reply*"; he says Siodmak is working on "a new script entitled *Steel Atlantis* which is patterned after the latter." It never saw the light of day, I assume. In **34**, a review of *Conquest Of Space* occupies the editorial spot; here Carnell's praise is unqualified, though he makes it a point that he is focusing on the science (actually, on the F/X, but nobody saw it that way half a century ago) and not on the "human interest angle." In **40**, Carnell has a piece labeled "article" about *Timeslip*, scripted by Charles Eric Maine. He starts out chiding the Hollywood "B picture" approach to SF films, which he says has quickly led to their being classed "at the bottom of the social scale of entertainment." This one, he says, is different. It's based on a half-hour BBC play and the premise is a man whose consciousness is seven and a half seconds ahead of the rest of us in time. This does not purport to be an arms-length review; Carnell had watched parts of it being filmed in company with Maine.

The *New Worlds* Profiles continue to occupy the inside front cover of most issues. I've excerpted some of these below in connection with their authors' stories. The profile in **40** is of an author who hasn't yet appeared in the magazine, the above mentioned Charles Eric Maine, pseudonym of David McIlwain (1921-81)—in fact, he doesn't appear in *New Worlds* at all for almost four years, and then only once (his novel *Count-Down* was serialized in 1959). The profile notes that he has become prominent publishing novels and radio plays, in his spare time while he works as editor of "a national television trade magazine published in Fleet Street."

There is considerable other nonfiction in these issues. Most of the issues contain an article, and a couple have two of them. Articles are mostly brief and on scientific subjects, and the majority are by John Newman—whose prolific collaboration with Kenneth Bulmer as Kenneth Johns has not begun yet—on subjects such as "Solar Interference" and "Spaceship Diet" (canned goods no, dried foods yes, plus bread—baked en route—to help maintain morale as well as nutrition). Newman, according to his *New Worlds* Profile in **30**, is an old fan, who ran the library and helped publish the fanzine of the Cosmos Club of Teddington, before becoming an industrial research chemist. He left school at 16 and "continued his education and studies in his spare time. His present work is a magnetochemical study of the physical structure of solid solution catalysts." Ah, for the days before career paths ossified! Other articles are by Maurice Goldsmith ("Eclipse"), Laurence Sandfield ("Interplay"—about heredity and environment in evolution), and Roy Malcolm ("A Tenth Planet"). The highest-profile article is Eric Frank Russell's "Asstronomy" (not a typo) in **37**, which is Russell in his most tiresome iconoclastic vein. Here is a sample, after recounting observations of strange lights on the Moon:

> We issue a challenge to professional astronomers. We point to the Moon and say, "Refine us that!—never mind the rest!"
>
> They won't. Professionals rarely look at the sky. They are too busy writing books in which data selected

from a great quantity supplied by amateurs is drilled to conform to dogma, all the rest being excluded, and the whole fantastic flapdoodle is expressed in terms suitable for a public that breathes with its mouth open and talks with it shut.

"Postmortem" in **39** is devoted exclusively to comments on Russell's article. William F. Temple thought it a "humdinger," an opinion shared by John Kippax, but not by John Newman, who provides a calm disquisition in defense of science. Then there's I.V. Krantoch of the Institute (which institute? Carnell asks), who proposes that Russell has missed the main connection between Astronomy and relativity: "The second derivative of the field equations shows that an image can have a fixed shift in frequency." After several steps, the bottom line: "...[A]n interesting explanation of the Universe can be derived from the above remarks. We see now that this consists of only one star (Sol) and a series of images. These images represent different times in the life of the Sun and their apparent motions are due to disturbances in the space-time continuum."

There are no more convention reports, except for those in Carnell's editorials, but Leslie Flood provides articles on the 1954 and 1955 International Fantasy Awards. The first of these, in **27**, notes that the Adjudication Panel is now down to 13 people: Hugo Gernsback, P. Schuyler Miller, Forrest J. Ackerman, Donald A. Wollheim, Groff Conklin, Anthony Boucher and J. Francis McComas (sharing one vote), Robert Frazier (*Fantastic Universe* book reviewer and instructor at CCNY SF Workshop), August Derleth, Basil Davenport, Georges H. Gallet (French editor of *Le Rayon Fantastique*), Igor B. Maslowski (French critic for *Fiction*), Carnell of *New Worlds*, and UK bibliophile Fred C. Brown. Flood does not repeat the tedious exercise of a prior year by disclosing the votes of the individual judges.

He notes generally that about 80 new eligible titles (excluding anthologies and books published for the juvenile market) were published, 50 appearing first in the US, 21 of these later reprinted or announced for publication in the UK. Sturgeon's *More than Human* beat out Bester's *The Demolished Man* and Pohl and Kornbluth's *The Space Merchants*; also-rans included Clarke's *Childhood's End* and *Against the Fall of Night*, Bradbury's *Fahrenheit 451* and *The Golden Apples of The Sun*, Moore's *Bring The Jubilee*, David Karp's *One* and Vercors' *You Shall Know Them*. The non-fiction award has been abolished. In **39** he recounts the 1955 awards, which went to Pangborn's *A Mirror For Observers* over Clement's *Mission of Gravity*, McIntosh's *One in Three Hundred*, Asimov's *The Caves of Steel*, Sheckley's *Untouched by Human Hands*, Anderson's *Brain Wave*, and Shepherd Mead's *The Big Ball of Wax*. (Looking back from some six decades later, this is a really extraordinarily rich haul, with at least 13 future classic works as finalists.)

Advertising continues as before, with virtually all of it being from publishers or booksellers advertising their SF lines. There are a few ringers, such as the ad in **28** for the "'Mexicano' Throwing Knife" ("Why not take up knife throwing as a sport?"), and several ads for *Fate* ("The Science FACT Monthly... Reprints the best of the American material *Plus* new British investigations beyond the borderlands of Science"), the *RAF Flying Review*, and the Southport Interplanetary Society. Overall, the amount of advertising is diminishing. The first two of these issues, **22** and **23**, contain half a dozen ads for five hardcover publishers and for three magazines and two book-stores. There is *no* outside advertising in four of the last six issues during this period, and in the two exceptions (**40** and **41**), there are three book publishers' ads and nothing else. This in my recollection parallels the decline in advertising in the US magazines from the early to the middle 1950s.

One other aspect of the magazine's presentation must be mentioned again: the proofreading, or lack of it. A steady proces-sion of egregious typos suggests someone is not paying atten-tion or doesn't have much aptitude for the task. For example, in **35**, Carnell's editorial refers to a Mr. Wren-Lewis in one paragraph and Mr. Wynn-Lewis in the next two, and one of the stories begins with a reference to a character's "nicotine-stained angers"—possible, I suppose, even incisive in some contexts, but an unlikely usage in *New Worlds* in 1955.

§

Turning to the fiction, and looking first at the reprinted novels, their common characteristic is their near horizons. All take place in the relatively near future; nobody gets further than the Moon or Earth orbit. There are no aliens to speak of, except some extremely human-style ones in *The Time Masters*. Transcendence and sense of wonder are not on the bill. These are essentially thrillers, and their selection is consistent with Carnell's proclamation in his editorial in **38**, discussed above, that "to be popular with the general public the plots should be located within a Time ratio which could be conceivably in their lifetime."

Kornbluth's *Take-Off* (**22-24**) is one of the subgenre about determined men getting into space despite all the political obstacles erected by lesser breeds. It remains an entertainingly over-the-top period piece, fortunately brief, pushing all the right buttons and moving on fast, full of cod-insider US politics and the romance of engineering, the whole at the top of its lungs through hard-boiled clenched teeth. Here's Kornbluth describing the treasurer of the American Society for Space Flight: "Friml continued to be—Friml. Bloodless, righteous, dollar-honest, hired-hand, party-of-the-second-partish Friml. A reader of the fine print, a dweller in the Y.M.C.A., a martyr to constipation, a wearer of small-figured neckties which he tied in small, hard knots." And: "The place on Figueroa Street wasn't a fairy joint, as Novak had half expected it would be." When the (Danish) Mata Hari figure is unmasked (edited from a longer soliloquy): "She was disgusted. 'Communist, hell! I'm a European.... I been raped by Yerman soldiers and sedooced vit' Hershey bars by American soldiers....'"

This serialized version (129 46-line small-type digest pages, compared to 218 32-line large-type Doubleday pages) does not seem to have been significantly abridged based on my spot checks, though there is some mucking around with chapter numbering, and I found one telling edit. In the Doubleday edition, Mata Hari, out to humiliate the deeply confused Friml, says: "You know what happen in Europe when out came you' Kinsey report?... All the dumb squareheads and the dumb dagoes and the dumb frogs and krauts said we knew it all the time. American men are half pa-a-ansy and the rest they learn out of a marriage book on how to *zigzig*.... Go find you'self a nice boy, sugar." In *New Worlds*, the second sentence ends after "marriage book" and "a nice boy" becomes "a *nice* girl." So there's a handy delineation of how far you could go in UK popular magazines in 1954—further, probably, than in US magazines.

Wilson Tucker's *Wild Talent* (**26-28**) is about a kid who's telepathic and who as a young man makes himself known to the government so he can help out. Not surprisingly he is feared, isolated, exploited, and ultimately betrayed. The story is about his maturation, his developing understanding of his situation, and the development of his paranormal powers. This is a good piece of storytelling, fast-moving but understated. Scenes of the protagonist's early life (some of which Tucker has said are directly autobiographical[44]) are vivid. The portrayal of the government personnel's (double-)dealing with him is well done and not overly simple-minded. There is the usual quota of Tuckerizations, and Carnell writes in the editorial in **28**: "On the title page of the original book version as with the Contents Page of this magazine there is a statement 'All characters are fictitious and any resemblance to living persons is entirely coincidental.' I can only quote that expression in reply to the number of people who point out that most of the characters in Tucker's story appear to have the names of well-known science fiction personalities." Indeed, one reasonably significant character is

44. Paul Walker, *Speaking of Science Fiction: The Paul Walker Interviews* (Luna Publications, 1978), p. 346.

named Carnell—though the one who proves to be the world-scale villain of the piece is Walter Willis. A quick rummage disclosed no notable divergences between this text and the US edition. However, Carnell says in his editorial in **32** that the Michael Joseph British hardcover version is "somewhat altered from its original serial form in *New Worlds*."

Dye's *Prisoner in the Skull* (**30-32**), the furthest-fetched of the serials, is a van Vogt pastiche rendered in an often over-the-top hard-boiled style ("She radiated enough sex to shatter a glass eye at fifty paces"). A guy wakes up and doesn't know who he is; check. He's in danger from contending forces of mysterious identity and unknown purposes; check. He's forced into a desperate quest to save his life and discover his identity; check. "The face was his own." Well, yes and no, it's actually more complicated than that. It's readable enough, even if a bit reminiscent of a last holdout partying on after everybody else has left the building. This is the one where the characters reach the Moon; however, considerably more of it takes place in New Jersey. There's quite a poignant note in **31**, where Dye has his *New Worlds* Profile: "Unfortunately, during the time at our disposal, it was not possible to learn much concerning the author of our current serial. In fact, Mr. Dye has apparently disappeared from human ken.... Should Mr. Dye ever get in touch with us we shall be more than glad to fill in the gaps in his casebook." Since Dye, who legendarily drank himself to death, is listed in such sources as the *Encyclopedia of Science Fiction* as having lived from 1927 to 1955, one might think he had indeed "disappeared from human ken" when Carnell tried to contact him. But in fact he seems to have lived until 1960,[45]

---

45. This death date is given in the short biography of Florynce Kennedy, to whom he was briefly married, in the index to her papers at the Radcliffe Institute for Advanced Study, Harvard University. See http://oasis.lib. harvard.edu/oasis/deliver/~sch01221 (visited 9/13/11). Kennedy's memoirs do not give a death date, but state that she and Dye married in 1957, and recount several years of travail thereafter before Dye's death, so the 1960 date is probably correct. Flo Kennedy, *Color Me Flo: My Hard Life and Good Times* (Prentice-Hall, 1976), pp. 43-47.

though he published no new SF after 1953.

Tucker's *The Time Masters* (**39-41**) is much less substantial than *Wild Talent*, though it's entertaining enough. It has the only long vista of time in these novels—a backwards one. Gilbert Nash is the extremely long-lived survivor of an alien spaceship crash thousands of years ago, and may also have been Gilgamesh. He encounters another survivor, a woman determined to be on the first available spaceship from Earth so she can get home. FBI agents are trying to figure out who they are and what they are doing. This is the only one of the four to have had a US magazine publication: abridged, in the January 1954 *Startling Stories*.

The sole indigenous serial, E. C. Tubb's *Star Ship* (**34-36**), unlike the reprinted novels, is set several hundred years in the future and light-years away in space, but there's still no sense of wonder here—its horizons are actually even narrower than those of the other serials of this period. It's a fairly standard generation-ship story: the voyage has been under way for nearly 300 years. The regimented society is dominated by a repressive elite under the guise of Psycho, a computer system that determines when people die (usually by age 40) and of course has been gamed by those in charge. Outcasts and rebels have fled to the lightless No-Weight, unused space in the center of the ship.

The protagonist is an undercover cop who gets tired of the nasty business and blows the whistle, leading the motley No-Weight refugees to a rendezvous with the mysterious Captain. Then the whole thing is mooted by the revelation that the Ship has arrived. Everyone seems to have forgotten this prospect. This is not too plausible, and as more elements of the grand plan are revealed in the last few rather perfunctory pages, things become even less so. But up to that point it's a reasonably capable and entertaining story, economically told, with a bracingly jaundiced view of human nature. It shortly became an Ace Double, backed with Philip K. Dick's *The Man Who Japed*. The review in *Infinity*, April 1957, called it "a competent, thoroughly readable and thoroughly unexciting success" and "a perfectly well-made book on a stale theme." Carnell says in "The Literary Line-Up" in **33** that it is "already earmarked for future book publication" but was "specially written for this magazine and close collaboration has been entailed between author and editor."

§

Novels aside, the quality of the fiction in these issues is a pretty mixed picture. The Mystery Science Theatre candidates—the floridly pulpy and clichéd items like Sydney Bounds' "The Flame Gods"—are mostly gone. The really bad stories in these issues tend just to be lame. However, there is very little that is outstanding, other than a few reprinted classics. Much of the rest consists of routine changes rung on themes even then too familiar, and many of the stories suffer from lapses of logic and plausibility. Thematically, the shorter fiction, like the novels, cumulatively suffers from a sense of constricted horizons: even those that take place off Earth tend to be down-to-somewhere-or-other problem-solving exercises, without much sense of expanded possibility.

In this connection, there is a letter from Alfred Bester, then in London, in "Postmortem" in **29**, posing a question to Carnell:

> ...It's about a quality I discover not only in the stories you run but in many other British stories and novels. Apparently it is an English style of writing, and it confuses me a little. It is this: an author sets up a problem or question in the opening of his story—he also indicates the likely solution. Then he slowly and carefully works toward the identical solution at the end. There is no surprise, no fillip, nothing unexpected. Sometimes an author prepares for a final conflict and resolution—having established the ingredients which will make for the final conflict (which the reader easily anticipates), he then constructs and executes the identical conflict.

Since I was raised and trained in the American School of the Unexpected, I find this technique tending to make for dullness at times—also disappointment. Although I'm the last man in the world to pay homage to the Monster of the Big Twist, I do become impatient occasionally with this meticulous working out of the obvious; and I feel cheated when the author has not taken the trouble to outsmart me.

I know this is not ineptness. It must be deliberate or, perhaps, traditional style, but I cannot quite make out the purpose. Have I missed the point somewhere?

To which Carnell responds:

I feel certain that a lot of our readers will attempt to refute your statements, Alfred, but I am inclined to agree with your puzzlement. It is obvious to anyone who closely reads both British and American style literature that the former is more prosaic—we seem to work in the formula of one plot one story, whereas most American stories have a formula of one Major [sic] plot and numerous sub-plots, which makes for faster action and greater surprise in the ending.

The main reader who tries to refute Bester is J. T. McIntosh, with a letter in **31**. He agrees that British writers don't try too hard to supply surprise endings, for a reason: "Now, Alfred, do you think we could outsmart you?... It is a long time since any science fiction writer, British or American, outsmarted me either, fairly." There's no point in a "brilliant, highly devious story" that supplies all the clues yet has a successful surprise ending, if only the high-IQ can understand it. It's more of a challenge to write something obvious and keep the reader's interest, and the writer may produce something "really good" that way. Of course both of these viewpoints have some merit, but a touch more of the brilliant and devious might have been a considerable improvement in these issues of *New Worlds*. In any case, it is interesting that this is the first substantive discussion in the magazine of what Britishness in SF actually means, and it was commenced by an American—and that Bester started a similar discussion in *Science Fantasy* very shortly thereafter.[46]

The non-serialized fiction in these issues is mostly fairly short, which is not entirely surprising since most issues have a reasonably long serial installment in them. The novelettes tend to run not much over 20 pages. There are only three pieces as long as 40 pages. (A quick sample word count suggests that a full page of *New Worlds* text will run over 450 words.) The distinction between short stories and novelettes is pretty haphazard. Dan Morgan's "Life Agency" (**39**) runs 31 pages, Rayer's "The Voices Beyond" (**41**) 29 pages and White's "Outrider" 28 pages, though they are all labeled short stories, compared to White's "The Conspirators" (**24**) and "Starvation Orbit" (**25**), both 24 pages, and Anderson's "Butch" at 25, all labeled novelettes. Carnell says in **36** in "The Literary Line-Up" that he intends to publish more novelettes since his reader survey indicated that they were the most popular item in the magazine.

The anthology reprints are a moderately mixed bag, ranging from classics (Kornbluth's "Gomez" from *The Explorers*, Bester's "Disappearing Act" (**29**) from *Star Science Fiction Stories 2*) to capable journeyman work. Carnell clearly has favorites: there are three stories by C.M. Kornbluth—"Gomez," "Dominoes" (**28**, from *Star 1*), "The Remorseful" (**29**, from *Star 2*)—three by Sheckley—"The Odour of Thought" (**25**, from *Star 2*); "The Last Weapon" (**26**, from *Star 1*); "Paradise II" (**37**,

---

46. Bester, Guest Editorial, "What's the Difference," *Science Fantasy* 12. *New Worlds* 29, carrying his letter, is dated November 1954, and that issue of *Science Fantasy* is dated February 1955. Since *Science Fantasy* was bimonthly at that point, the editorial would likely have followed the letter into print by only two months. The editorial and responses to it are discussed in our companion volume on *Science Fantasy*, *Strange Highways*, chapter 4.

from Derleth's *Time to Come*)—and three by Lester del Rey ("Idealist" (**24**, from *Star 1*), "A Pound of Cure" (**27**, from *Star 2*), and "Alien" (**38**, from *Star 3*). Others include H.L. Gold's "Man of Parts" (**36**, from Healy's *Nine Tales of Space and Time*); Poul Anderson's "Butch" (**37**, from Derleth's *Time to Come*), and Chad Oliver's "Any More at Home Like You?" (**39**, from *Star 3*). The best of these, other than "Gomez" and "Disappearing Act," include del Rey's "Idealist," a sort of anti-"Thunder and Roses": a man wakes up amnesiac on a space station; everybody else is dead, there's been a nuclear war on Earth, everybody wants him to fire his missiles at their enemy; he fires them off randomly at Earth and heads off to the Moon to live out his days. Del Rey's "Alien" is similarly misanthropic: a man is shipwrecked on a desert island with a jerk of a hanger-on. There's an alien stranded there too; by the end of the story the protagonist is so fed up with humanity he leaves with the alien's rescuers. I think it's fair to say that not only is there no British fiction in these issues as good as "Gomez" or "Disappearing Act," there is little that displays the compactly capable professionalism or unpredictable development of the two del Rey stories, or of Sheckley's—though some of them have other virtues.

The Kornbluth stories, incidentally, provide Carnell with splendid opportunities for missing the point in his blurbs. In "Dominoes" (**28**), a stockbroker, who travels forward in time to find out when the big crash will happen, comes back and sells off just in time, only to learn that his sell-off has precipitated the crash and to be strangled to death by the inventor of the time machine, who has lost his shirt. Carnell's blurb says of this story that it "creates a most entertaining situation." He is even more tone-deaf introducing "The Remorseful" (**29**), about the last man on Earth, who has gone miserably and hysterically insane (as the author demonstrates in graphic detail), and the aliens who make a pit stop and quickly move on. This is in the running for Kornbluth's blackest work; Carnell describes it as a "typically delightful story."

Turning to the indigenous fiction, again the magazine is dominated by a core of regular contributors. Of the 106 items of fiction here, seven writers—E. C. Tubb, Francis G. Rayer, Alan Barclay, E. R. James, James White, Kenneth Bulmer, and Lan Wright—account for almost half (51) of them. There are more significant writers represented in these issues, but they are either just getting started (Aldiss, Brunner) or are withdrawing (Clarke, Wyndham, Christopher) and do not put much of a stamp on this period of the magazine.

The dominant figure by far during 1954-55 is E. C. Tubb, with 14 stories in addition to his serialized novel, and we can see him turning a corner as a writer. His stories start out in the same overwritten and melodramatic vein that we are familiar with from previous examples in *New Worlds*. For example, "Homecoming" (**28**), first published in *Universe*, May 1954, is another typically overwrought example of his preoccupation with the domestic lives of spacefarers: a man returns home expecting to be met by his wife and newborn child, but nobody's there. His home is in disarray, his wife dead drunk, there's no child. The child was a short-lived mutant, the protagonist can't have normal children because of his radiation exposure, his wife is wailing that he's not a real man, and he is broken up about losing his chance for a normal life. It is revealed that he is 45 inches tall—apparently only midgets can be space travelers. It is interesting that this story first ran in a magazine whose editor was similarly challenged; could that be why Tubb submitted it there? This is one of Tubb's first stories to sell in the US as well as the UK. (He had a couple of others in 1954, both published earlier in *New Worlds*. Then three in *Galaxy* in 1956, and a scattering in *Galaxy*, *If*, *Astounding* and *Satellite* from 1958 into the early 1960s. Otherwise he stuck to the British magazines and of course to his numerous book projects.)

"The Veterans" (**33**), under the byline Norman Dale ("Another new author makes his debut," fibs Carnell), is simultaneously maudlin and bitter. Aging veterans of the Martian war are parked away in an institution where they can look at their old spaceships ("The ships! The ships of space which, like those who stared with hungry eyes, had once been strong and virile, shouting with their thundering venturis, blasting the tepid air with their impatient challenge to the void."), reminiscing about the war, which we learn was vicious and genocidal. The veterans are regarded as war criminals. Too bad the enlightened sentiments are swathed in such purple prose. Carnell, who rarely misses a chance to miss the point, describes this story as "nostalgic." "No Place for Tears" (**34**), as by R.H Godfrey, is a several-handkerchief return to Tubb's concern with the incursion of space travel on domesticity. A mother attends the annual memorial service for her husband, lost in space, but her son sees nothing but the rocket and she knows she's lost him too.

There are also some specimens of talky sociologizing. "The Robbers" (**30**) proposes that in the future everybody lives a long time, there's no initiative, everything's stagnating, and the frustrated sign up for the widely despised Service where they are subjected to the most idiotic military discipline imaginable. Why? So anybody with a brain will rebel. They throw the rebels in prison, and after their terms are up turn them into interstellar colonists. "School for Beginners" (**32**) continues Tubb's preoccupation with the social problems of space travel. Spacemen are isolated from the world for training at age 12 and mustered out at age 32, so they have no idea how to use money, how to interact with other human beings, etc., and can't survive on their own without attending remedial finishing schools. The future the protagonist is released into is reminiscent of Kornbluth's "The Marching Morons" but the story is played earnestly and not farcically and falls flat.

But things are gradually looking up. "Into Thy Hands" (**29**) is a pleasant relief from the *sturm und* soapsuds, merely involving the sole conscious crew member of a spaceship full of colonists in suspended animation, and his grandiose thoughts, which include fantasies of the terrible things he could do to the colonists, the hydroponics, the machinery, etc., but doesn't. "I am God!" he says at one point. Here the story is, literally, that nothing happens (the watch position rotates, so the story ends with the protagonist going back into the deep-freeze) despite the extensive expression of anti-social attitudes. This one could have fit comfortably into Moorcock's version of the magazine a decade later. Anyway, there's a fit here between style and substance that is lacking in a lot of its predecessors.

"Forgetfulness" (34), as by Philip Martyn, is "Treasure of the Sierra Madre" in space. Two asteroid miners hit a big strike, one contrives to murder the other, and then gets his comeuppance because of what he's failed to remember about working in space. There's not much to it, but it's less overwritten than usual. In "Samson" (35), as by Alan Guthrie, the protagonist recruits space pilots, but this early stage of space flight consists essentially of using humans as experimental animals to see what terrible thing the conditions do to them (in this case, they use the wrong alloy and the resulting radiation blinds the poor sucker). In substance it's another space-tear-jerker, but this one is told in the first person, more quietly than usual for Tubb. "No Space for Me" (37), also under the Guthrie name, extends this theme: people can't travel in space, because even if they can be protected physically, they go nuts. This is another quiet first-person job (it's harder to shout in first person), mostly advanced through conversations with a wise-old-geek figure, a professor of psychology.

"Perac," in the same issue, is under Tubb's own name, and it's more overt melodrama, but with a difference. A ship's doctor, a 50-year-old bachelor, has finally fallen in love, with a passenger on the ship, and as soon as they hit Earth he's going to retire and they are going to get married. But she turns up with Perac, a mysterious, painful, invariably fatal degenerative disease which is so dangerous that anybody who has it is euthanized out of hand. So he kills her and himself too. Despite the potentially soap-operatic plot this one is done quietly and economically and is really the earliest glimpse in Tubb's *New Worlds* short stories of the controlled and efficient professionalism that became familiar, e.g., in his later stories in *Science Fantasy*.

"See No Evil" (**38**), under Tubb's own name, is another step forward, or at least half a step. It posits that the galaxy is full of worlds that look habitable, and the modus operandi of colonization is to dump a bunch of people on a planet without much legwork, and come back after a few centuries to see if anybody is alive. On this planet, the colonists survived, but they refuse to pay the slightest attention to the agents of the Bureau of Interstellar Colonisation even when agents walk around their town, talk to them, stand in their way, knock things out of their hands, etc. This one is terse and to the point and the growing annoyance of the characters and their willingness to perform outrageous acts is developed efficiently and cleverly without overwriting. The final revelation (the colonists are adherents of a religion that makes them unable to believe their perceptions of things they've never seen) is fairly lame, but the story is very readable to that point.

"Little Girl Lost" (**40**) is the best of these stories. The protagonist is assigned to shadow a middle-aged widowed nuclear scientist who has developed the delusion that his child, who was killed by a hit-and-run driver, is still alive. He talks to her, combs her hair, tucks her in, etc. The assignment: help keep him and his delusion going long enough to complete his essential weapons research. So the protagonist joins in the illusion. But then the scientist finishes his work, and suddenly he's no longer deluded, but he's talking about how people do terrible things, like the unknown hit-and-run driver—and what's going to happen when somebody tests his plans for the fission of non-radioactive materials? This story, and "Into Thy Hands," "Perac," and "Forgetfulness," are the only ones from this period that Tubb rescued for his collections, old or new: good taste on his part.

These improvements don't mean all of Tubb's stories are now good; he's just freed himself from particular faults. In the last of these issues (**42**), he has two stories. The shorter is "Prime

Essential" under the name Frank Weight (used for this story only). Here, the characters are in a satellite facility called the Hive, being conditioned to become colonists on the planet below, and also being exposed to persons of the opposite sex who are potential mates. There are three women in this group, named (honest) April, May, and June. After various unsatisfactory exchanges with them, the protagonist, whose conditioning seems to be complete, drifts off to the landing vehicles, where he is joined by a woman he doesn't know from one of the other groups, and he realizes (having lost his veneer of civilization during the conditioning, as well as his tobacco and caffeine addictions) that "basically, to a man any woman is as good as another and, to a woman, any man will serve to father her children." Forgive me if I am not convinced.

"Lawyer at Large" (**42**), nominally the cover story, is not very good, but, like the other recent ones, it is free of overdone sentimentality and other bloviating. It starts out with the protagonist, an unsuccessful lawyer, trying to defend some poor sucker, during which objections are made and sustained in the course of legal argument. (Tubb is wrong: that ritual is part of the presentation of evidence, not argument, which is unlikely to change.) The protagonist gets mixed up in a sleazy deal that culminates in his supposedly defending the accused murderer of a visiting alien, even though he was an eyewitness to the crime and is called as a witness by the prosecution. He achieves victory by pointing out that murder consists of killing a human being and the alien isn't human. Then he changes sides and demonstrates that the murderer *thought* of the alien as human and is therefore guilty.

Of course this, too, is all ridiculous, starting with the proposition that extraterrestrials are allowed to wander around loose in human society without their legal status having been defined for either civil or criminal purposes. Any sane government, and any sane alien who understood what a legal system was (as these clearly do) would insist on having its protection. But if you buy the assumption that they didn't, the idea that someone would be prosecuted for murdering an alien and no one would realize that its status was an issue until the defense lawyer pulled it out of his hat is equally ridiculous. That a lawyer who was also a witness to the crime (and whose fingerprints were on the gun) would be permitted to represent the defendant is completely contrary to any notion of legal ethics, since there is both a conflict of interest and the possibility (which is realized) of the lawyer's being called as a witness in the case. The latter could barely be justified by the proposition that in this future, fact-finding is being done by machines which could put aside the lawyer's dual role; but not the former, especially since the conflict is realized, by the lawyer's assuming the role of prosecutor. The icing on the cake is a conversation between the protagonist and the President of the Bar Commission, who suggests that he throw the case. This of course is completely unethical and implausible; people that corrupt don't last unless they cover their tracks better. It's not clear to me whether this last reflects the depth of Tubb's cynicism or the shallowness of his understanding of the legal system, or of anything that might plausibly be extrapolated from it.

§

James White is the best of the other regular contributors, with half a dozen stories. White is a writer who always reminds me of the protagonist in Algis Budrys's story "Nobody Bothers Gus"—admirable enough when I'm reading him, but often leaving no strong impression behind.

"The Conspirators" (24) comes with a big build-up. Carnell says in the previous month's "Literary Line-Up": "Every once in a while a story reaches us which seems to make an editor's life worth all the blood, sweat, and tears expended in producing this magazine. It doesn't happen often, but when it does we throw caution to the winds and bluntly state we have a smash-hit." It's about the experimental animals aboard a spaceship, plus Felix the ship's cat, who have undergone the Change, i.e., developed not only human-scale intelligence but telepathy, empathy, and high moral sensibilities (Felix has become a vegetarian), as a result of the prolonged absence of gravity or maybe the removal of some unknown solar radiation. These cute furry characters are scheming to hijack a lifeboat so they can make their own landing when a planet presents itself, thereby escaping their future of continued servitude and possible vivisection. It's less cloying than it could be, though ultimately inconclusive and undeveloped—it is revealed that humans undergo the Change too, though more slowly, but it's reversed on landing, which we learn only at the end. The readers liked it; it tied with the conclusion of *Take-Off* as most popular in the issue.

In "Starvation Orbit" (**25**), a spaceship accidentally slams into a space station orbiting Venus. The fuel stocks are lost and everybody's marooned, with no way to get to the planetary surface. The situation is well developed and described, but arbitrarily resolved when the ship's captain, who has been unable to communicate for medical reasons, manages to tell everybody that there's an extra space-drive tucked away in a safe place, so they can fly to the Moon.

"Suicide Mission" (**27**) winds up a complex plot about a man who goes back in time to kill one of his ancestors, having not much idea why, because he can't really think about it because he has to evade his conditioning not to kill anybody. He is being chased by other time travelers further and further into the past; but in the end it's revealed that this all has to do with *space* travel and the protagonist's guilt at having killed a lot of people with his experimental interstellar drive. Like the problems in the two preceding stories, this one just goes away: the protagonist recovers his memory and decides he doesn't want to kill anybody after all, himself included. En route White proposes a different metaphor for time: a fence with many strands, some much longer than others, but all gathered together at certain crucial points.

"The Star Walk" (**33**) is White's longest story yet, running some 42 pages rather than the usual 20-odd of *New Worlds* novelettes. The protagonist is a spaceman stuck on a singularly unpleasant colony planet. The C-man—i.e. Courier, analogized to the Pony Express—arrives injured and needing help. Our hero, who doubts he is a genuine C-man, sees his chance to grab the ship and get off-planet. But it turns out the C-man is genuine, has a secret of enormous value to humanity (a vastly improved space drive), and is being pursued by thugs working for a sort of interstellar gangster who wants the secret for himself. There's a lot going on here. The interstellar economy is based largely on information, and the C-men are working to keep it free. The protagonist, embittered by being marooned, has decided he'll be just as evil as he needs to be to get off-planet with his girl friend and grab some money in the bargain (but he's ambivalent at length about it). Meanwhile, his girlfriend is falling for the injured C-man for no discernible reason. They flee the planet one step ahead of the thugs and escape them only by diving so deep into the sun's gravitational field that they can't be traced through sub-space. (Their destination: the Sector Twelve Sorting Office.) His personal problems then vanish because he realizes that he's not really interested in his girlfriend any more, he just needed to get back into space.

In "Outrider" (35), a spaceship returning to Earth runs into a cargo net that strips all its radar and communications gear, leaving it blind and unable to land. The protagonist, who has a preternatural sense of velocity and distance, winds up guiding them down from a sort of foxhole in the damaged hull. This one is a techno-geek epic and not much else, though it's certainly well visualized and thought through for what it is.

"Boarding Party" (37) is particularly shapeless: the protagonist is a doctor aboard a space battleship that has just been savaged by the alien Raghma, who continue to attack. The survivors have to get a badly injured engineer through vacuum to the life-ship in order to be able to escape. The protagonist is dispatched to get him. The story is mostly about the physical difficulties of getting to the injured man and then rescuing him (meticulously visualized and frankly a bit tedious), until the last couple of pages, when it takes a right-angle turn and becomes a completely un-foreshadowed revelation about who the aliens are and why they are fighting a war against humanity.

There is an attractive and well-meaning quality to all these stories, but reading them in close succession helps explain why I have long found White enjoyable enough but rarely memorable: he has a problem maintaining narrative tension. His plots often don't so much resolve as dissipate, in a couple of cases ("The Star Walk" and "Suicide Mission") because their ill-motivated protagonists just have a change of mind or heart. I think part of his problem may be that he was just too nice a guy and didn't really believe that anybody could be bad and stay that way. In any case he is certainly one of the more capable and hard-working of *New Worlds*'s regular contributors.

§

Francis G. Rayer is the second most prolific writer in these issues, with seven stories. Unfortunately there is no visible improvement in his work, which remains mediocre though reasonably readable. And he has 23 more stories in *New Worlds* before he's done, under his name and George Longdon. His flagship piece (i.e., one of the longest, and the one given the lead spot) is "The Voices Beyond" (**41**), which might have been a winner in *Wonder Stories* two decades earlier. In fact, Carnell virtually cops a plea on this one; in the previous issue's "The Literary Line-Up," he says that Rayer "has created all the atmosphere and suspense which made science fiction so popular in the 1930's." Astronomers discover a formation of three 500-foot-diameter objects headed for Earth—at a constant speed of about 15 miles an hour, not accelerating a whit as they approach the Earth. Specifically, they are approaching London, Paris, and a patch of ocean near Liverpool. They are dubbed "electroids" for no reason I could glean. They don't communicate; nuclear missiles are harmless to them. But Frank has been contacted by the Telepathic Institute, which proffers their star attraction

Elizabeth (blonde and good-looking, of course). They go up in a plane, see markings on a sphere indicating intelligent design, and Elizabeth says she can't make herself heard, but she is over-hearing something about "infinite speed." Of course! That's the explanation! "Infinite speed! The speed of light. Mass increased with velocity. At infinite velocity it would be infinite mass. Abruptly it all fitted.... The electroids were travelling at infinite speed relative to the universe of their origin, remote beyond calculation. That their speed relative to earth was only the scant twenty-two feet per second... would affect matters not at all." A. E. van Vogt once made the same ridiculous discovery, which utterly misunderstands the point of relativity theory.

Anyway, these irresistible objects are about to plunge into the Earth, where they will of course not go straight through because of the Earth's rotation, but will go around like a bullet through butter, as the author puts it somewhere, and then emerge... well, one of them is going to emerge in about 11 days right through a nuclear power plant in Chicago. Nothing can be done, the continent will be rendered uninhabitable. So Frank and Elizabeth head for Chicago, where she still can't get through to the aliens. There's a drug, dio-hyptane, which soups up telepathy but is also sometimes fatal; she's willing to take it, but Frank steps in and takes it himself, thereby facilitating her telepathy. They establish contact. The aliens had no idea. They divert their sphere and merely graze the nuclear plant. Continent saved. Only trouble with this: the author says that on the way in, the passage of the spheres caused earthquakes and volcanoes. Somehow that doesn't happen on the way out.

"Kill Me This Man" (31) involves a member of the Underground detailed to assassinate the dictator Hartland Smith, whom no one has ever seen. Of course it turns out that he doesn't really exist; but the idea that this man with a handgun and a bag full of gadgets would ever get close enough to find out is thoroughly implausible. There is a detour into the Martian desert and a cameo appearance by a Martian (walnut-skinned, big-chested), one of the Wise Ones, who "smile[s] with infinite sadness." Speaking of plausibility, at the end of the story, the protagonist, escaped back to Earth after killing one of "Smith's" handlers, returns to his job at a newspaper, where the editor believes his unsupported claim that Smith and the handler are dead, and is getting ready to print a story to that effect. Some dictatorship!

"Ephemeral This City" (**33**) is if anything more exasperating. It's another in the series about Magnis Mensas, the world-dominating super-computer. Earth is in a pollution crisis and has five years to survive, but MM is supporting more polluting activities even as it eggs on the development of space travel. It also kidnaps the protagonist's wife. Why? To keep him moving on his space travel project, as MM eventually implausibly explains. Why push for space travel by making pollution worse? Because there are alien spaceships on the way. Why not say so? It might cause panic, which would reduce efficiency. This is efficiency? By the way, who was it who tried to stab the protagonist to death in the middle of all this? That would surely have increased his efficiency in developing space travel. There's no explanation. Not to mention the absurdity of the proposition that space travel would be a solution to pollution except for the handful of people who managed to escape it—and where would they go? MM doesn't say.

In "The Jakandi Moduli" (**42**), the protagonist is a space traffic controller, managing the landings of 80 or so spaceships at a time using the Kelsy Stack landing system, which has 100 fixed courses down, and 100 up, all to be used simultaneously if necessary. One of the spaceships disappears from the stack. The venerable Hillington Kelsey is baffled. Enter Jerry Jakandi, of the computer section and the female persuasion.

> Hillington Kelsey pursed his lips. "A girl—with that responsibility?"
> "But the grand-daughter of Ayres Jakandi, the mathematician!" Frazer put in. "That helps explain."

Jerry Jakandi says, "You're Mr. Spey, who was on duty?... Then I'd like to check figures with you later." She is, of course, a babe ("When he closed his eyes her laughing face danced behind rows of computations.") Another ship vanishes in the landing stack and Spey is suspended—but he is also dispatched to Mars, with Miss Jakandi, to expedite the departure of the alarmed and suspicious Centaurian envoys. Then the trip is cancelled and they return—finding themselves on the same course as the vanished ships. Everything goes gray. They've modulated out of space!—"just as a musician can modulate chords from one key to another." They're also now travelling faster than light (fortissimo?), a point that is not explained or returned to, but nonetheless they have no difficulty matching velocities with the other two disappeared ships. Miss Jakandi, however, calculates the way back to our continuum ("A fiend-ish cartwheel followed.... 'This isn't a course—it's insanity!'") Back home, everyone is bent out of shape because of the lost opportunity with the Centaurians, but who needs them? Now we can get to the stars on our own. Miss Jakandi, departing, smiles and says: "I shall need to see you later, Mr. Spey. A mat-ter of the practical application of theoretical considerations.'... Jerry Jakandi was trumps!"

Rayer's "Pipe Away, Stranger" (25) is a bad Bradbury imita-tion: men arrive on Mars, hear a strange piping sound, try to dismiss it as the wind in the cactus (!). They find a deserted fairy city over the hill, most of them get drunk and scared and run back to their spaceship, wrecking it on takeoff. "Come Away Home" (27) is even more perfunctory: alien infant girl is dropped on Earth and recovered by a shepherd, next thing you know she's all grown up and conducting an altruistic black bag job against traitorous elements in the intelligence services, who catch her and haff vays to make her talk, except that her people, to be precise a "golden-skinned man clad in white edged with blue," show up to return her to her destiny. In "Stormhead" (40), to coin a phrase, a wind is rising, and the explorers from Earth have five spaceships resting upright on their vanes at risk of being blown over; but if they try to take off, the ships will probably blow up because they all need their drive liners replaced. What to do? Trust the ancient wisdom of the primitive natives (though at least this lot doesn't smile with infinite sadness), which tells them that the storm will veer off in another direction (i.e. towards the binary companion of the planet, whose tidal effect is what's causing the problem in the first place).

§

E. R. James has half a dozen stories in 1954-55. "Space Capsule" (23) is the most enjoyable story I have read by this writer. The protagonist is bumming around the solar system minding a "drifter," a very slow space cargo vessel, when he is rear-ended by what proves to be a derelict alien ship. He can't resist exploring it, being very careful of course; but he discovers that his pushing and pulling have generated enough movement that the two vessels have drifted apart and snapped his safety line. He's a dead man. But he continues his exploration of the alien ship, and suddenly the lights come on in the control room, and there's a representative of the Galactic Federation of Carbon Based Life Forms talking to him long distance. "The humanoid beckoned. 'Step through to me, Earthman.'" Crude as it is, this one captures the "ask the next question" attitude that remains the enduring pure quill of SF, for me at least. (But the *New Worlds* readership put it last in the issue.)

"The Minus Men" (26) starts out sharp and vigorously indignant. The protagonist is a jumped-up petty bureaucrat whose job is to shut down the British moon rocket project, which just happens to be run by the professor whose mathematics class was the scene of his humiliation. Unfortunately the story turns into confusing hugger-mugger and the protagonist undergoes an unconvincing conversion. The early parts, however, reveal James as a livelier writer than previously suspected, at least when he's angry about something.

James has several more hard-working stories that don't quite gel. In "Rockfall" (29), the Three Worlds Space Force has had reports from asteroid miners of aliens about, goes to look. The protagonist has a brief exchange of fire with an alien ship, and puts down on (or hitches up to) an asteroid. It turns out the alien ship is there too, and there's something funny going on in a deserted mine shaft, so the protagonist goes down to look, and winds up having an exchange of fire with a centipedal alien that looks built for Jovian gravity. The shots precipitate a cave-in, which doesn't immediately crush the parties because of the low gravity, but blocks the exit and will shortly settle on them and kill them. The protagonist revives the alien by opening up his spare oxygen tank, and the super-strong alien tunnels out through the debris, the human following in his wake. Looks like the crisis is over. Of course it's pretty damned unclear why there was a crisis in the first place—shooting it out at the beginning of alien contact, then following an alien down a deserted mine shaft, don't really seem to belong in the playbook. But James does do a good job of evoking the physical setting and operational difficulties of the environment as well as the character's state of mind, i.e., close to petrified of the unknown he is facing.

In James's "Highwayman Green" (36), Constable (I guess) Stan Green, fresh from the Mind Training College, notices that there certainly are a lot more service interruptions on the moving roads these days, and telepaths are getting shot by people who have no reason to do it and don't understand what came over them. He grabs one of these mystery assailants and hustles her away to his hotel to try to find out what's going on. Then he gets a telepathic call for help, and discovers another TP cop at bay in a room with the hotel manager, who explains (rather than sensibly shooting them out of hand):

> "I am a test case. Because I have been successful, my kind are certainly going to invade your planet. I have shown that you humans can be made to wreck your own economy, so that the invasion will be easy. By means of simple drugs and hypnotic suggestion

while people sleep unsuspectingly, other of our agents will soon be turning thousands of travelers into perfect saboteurs. All the important people of the world pass through such hotels as this one. We can turn them into wreckers or murderers in a single night!"

"So that's it!" Stan reached for the gun in his shoulder holster. "You—you won't get away with it."

And he doesn't, because Stan outwits the invader wannabe when it tries to take him over and make him shoot the other cop. Meanwhile the young woman whom he has spirited away from the previous crime scene is standing there, and he has a fleeting thought of getting to know her better, but then changes his mind: "What ordinary girl would think of romance with a man who could always know what she was thinking about?" Well, one could make arguments on both sides of that question, but probably not in a family publication like *New Worlds* circa 1955.

James' "World Destroyer" (**37**) is prefaced by an unusual consumer warning from Carnell: "The story which follows is one that breaks one of our strongest editorial taboos—that of current world politics coupled with the threat of atomic war. But Mr. James has handled the theme in such a delicate manner that for the first time in some years we felt inclined to break with tradition." As one might suspect, the story is actually about as delicate as a cast-iron poker. One of several childhood friends—the one who could never bear to lose—becomes an atomic scientist; another becomes a telepath. (How one becomes a telepath is not described.) The scientist defects to Them, never named, and goes nuts and builds a doomsday machine, announcing that he's going to blow up the world because humanity is so contemptible. The telepath is dispatched to talk him out of it and winds up deflecting his finger half an inch from the button. The scientist, however, is carried out in a fugue, believing he actually has destroyed the world. The telepath realizes that it is telepathy that will become the foundation of world peace. Now there's a despairing conclusion. This one makes me anticipatorily nostalgic for Aldiss's cynical "Basis for Negotiation" (114).

The least of James' contributions is "Man on the Ceiling" (25), a sequel to "Where No Man Walks," the one about the man who's lost his limbs but plugs into machinery for extraterrestrial mining. This time he's rescuing somebody who thinks he's invented antigravity from falling into Saturn, with ambivalence—antigravity would put him out of a job.

Reading James and Rayer, I can't help thinking of the marsupials, who are said to have lost out to the mammals in South America because they were less efficient. They survived only in Australia, where they were protected from competition by their geographical isolation.

§

Kenneth Bulmer's half-dozen contributions mostly continue in his established unsatisfactory vein. "All Glory Forgotten" (24) is a piece of loud and undistinguished pulp about a man who contracts an incurable and fatal disease on Venus. He can't go back to Earth, so he agrees to go undercover on Pallas, where the bad guys are developing a secret weapon, and sacrifice himself to sabotage it. The Palladians cure him of his disease, but he blows himself and the secret weapon (a small maneuverable spaceship) up anyway.

This is followed by the equally overdone "Bitter the Path" (26), set on a colony planet where the most lucrative employment is shooting venomous cats, if you can get them before they get you, and where life is possible only through constant electrically-powered vigilance to repel an aggressive moss which enjoys sporulating in people's lungs. A doctor, in hiding having deserted the Terran Space Medical Service, is now employed carrying water, in which capacity he is addressed as "Gunga Din." But he redeems himself when his old flame shows up unexpectedly and needs help with a Caesarian (someone else's) in the midst of a moss emergency. Carnell's uncharacteristically truculent blurb, possibly reflecting the low rating the readers gave Bulmer's previous story, says: "Part of our editorial policy is to occasionally have a space opera story—an adventure which, but for its future setting, could well happen at any time. This is one such tale. Moral—if you don't like space opera, move on." Unfortunately, being space opera (if that's the proper designation) isn't really the problem with this story. The readers, unmoved by Carnell's adjuration, placed the story last.

Next up is the lame "The Black Spot" (**32**), which opens with space turret gunners Scrappy White and Basher Stokes complaining about the oppressive Lieutenant Purchison. We meet their superior, Turret Captain Droop-Eye Dexter. Shortly, Purchison is dead because somebody painted a black square at the nape of the neck of his spacesuit and he broiled to death during EVA. Captain Dexter contrives to identify the real killer and absolve the unjustly accused Scrappy. This isn't really space opera; it's more like a space 60-cycle hum. It is followed by "Asylum" (**34**), another in the Palladian war series, which is less overwritten than some of its predecessors but equally lame: Earth scientists on Plantin III have vital knowledge, but the Palladians are landing with their telepathic devices. What to do? Post-hypnotic suggestion to them all to go insane and then to recover when rescued and returned to Earth. Presto!

This Palladian war series, by the way, has no continuity or developed background to speak of, or any explanation of why the residents of an asteroid have taken up arms against Earth, or how they manage to mount a military campaign that is not only interplanetary but interstellar. We do learn, however, that they wear lots of make-up into battle. The Palladians' make-up plays a significant role in "Total Recall" (**38**), in which Turret Captain Dexter returns, shell-shocked from a space battle in which he played cat and mouse with a Palladian in a pitch-black wrecked spaceship and emerged with a message about the enemy's battle plans. En passant during this flashback, he tries to track the Palladian by the smell of his cosmetics, only to discover that the Palladian is one step ahead of him: he has smeared cosmetics over an empty spacesuit. All this is framed in the story of a ship's doctor trying to get past his trauma-based amnesia and find out what happened. This one, too, is less overwritten and more readable than its predecessors, if no more substantial.

The next, "Plaything" (**41**), is encouraging for what it attempts, though it doesn't succeed. An Earth military ship, under Commander Bryant, gets lost and damaged in a space storm ("born of clashing electro-magnetic fluctuations"), but miraculously comes upon a deserted alien spaceship which has an atmosphere and seems comprehensible. They try to steer it home but it keeps going in a different direction. There's something very crude about this ship. They eventually figure out that it's really a toy model controlled from elsewhere; the reader will have figured out something of the sort much earlier from the story's title. On the way to this gimmicky revelation, though, Bulmer tries to write a story about a man who is seriously uncomfortable with the responsibilities of command and who is trying to rise to a very difficult occasion. It doesn't come off, but this is the first real sign in Bulmer's work for *New Worlds* of intelligent life and an interest in something more than precessing the clichés.

§

Lan Wright has five stories here, one of them the longest non-serialized item in these issues, the 50-page "The Messengers" (**29**), straight out of the Maguffin factory. In the future, there is faster-than-light travel but no other FTL communication, so it's all hand delivery. Naturally, there is a sort of guild called the Messengers who are a law unto themselves, answer to nobody but their own leaders, have a rigorous code, etc.—you know, all the stuff that didn't happen in previous times when there was no communication faster than physical delivery, i.e. all of human history before Samuel Morse. (Heliograph, semaphore, and smoke signals were too cumbersome and public to be widely useful, I think.) But never mind, this is the Future, another country where they do things differently.

Messenger Slade has lost a hand, which is, er, handy, because his prosthetic provides him a place that's different from the usual Messenger container to hide a particularly important message given him by a particularly sleazy character under particularly peculiar circumstances. Soon enough he's being followed by some thugs, who drug and later torture and threaten him; by the Stellar Corps, which asks him cryptic questions; and by somebody else, identity unknown. During all of this, apparently it never occurs to anybody to see if he's hiding the message in his obviously prosthetic hand. Of course nobody's what they seem and after the wind-up thriller plot has worked itself out, the message Slade is carrying proves to be a secret so monumental that the enlightened Messengers have to keep it to themselves for the good of humanity. The whole thing is made from a kit, but it's well enough glued, and every now and then Wright displays a certain over-the-top flair:

> The purple shadows of the night were coming down over the city as he was whisked across to the less salubrious part of Garden City. His choice of destination had caused the cabby to leer and wink knowingly, but Slade ignored him.... A dozen kinds of dope were peddled openly in the streets and dens, and a thousand women of a score of different races flaunted their dubious charms in the bars and brothels. The seamy side of Garden City was a mile wide and two stories high.

Later, Slade reflects on various suspicious events: "these, and other clues were the telltale warning lights that danger lurked in every light year between him and Earth."

Unfortunately the rest of Wright's stories in these issues are pretty mediocre even by undemanding comparison with "The Messengers." "The Ethical Question" (25) is another piece of tiresome science fictional contrivance: the man in charge of a rocket project has murdered his wife and her lover and pled guilty, and is now sitting on death row. He tells his former colleagues that he's sabotaged the spaceship so it will blow up, and he'll only tell them how to avoid this upon receipt of a pardon. They can't wait him out or the Russians will beat them to the Moon. But the scheduled pilot breaks his wrist, so they tell the smart guy that *he's* piloting the rocket, and he's got 45 minutes or so to straighten things out or he'll be the one who is blown up. So he does, but it's a put-up job. They gas him rather than launching him and put him back on death row, where he undergoes an improbable epiphany about having been part of the program. To their credit the readers put this last in the issue.

"Strangers in the Town" (**27**) is even lamer and more mechanical. Aliens have landed, they want to look around, they tire of the cities and want to see a rural area. So the President of the World Council takes them to his small home town, where they encounter a simple-minded farmer, and then the President has them mowed down with machine guns. The simple-minded farmer is the President's telepathic brother and he has plucked the invasion plans from the aliens' minds. In this issue is Wright's *New Worlds* Profile: he works in a clerical office of British Railways and writes during the cold months, being occupied with cricket during the summer. Wright looks quite priggish in his overly formal photo.

"Fair Exchange" (**31**) is another piece of mechanical cleverness, in which Wright's series character Johnny Dawson, interstellar trouble-shooter, is dispatched to Elkan, which has been colonized simultaneously by humans and Lutherians. Now large deposits of Stalumin, essential for spaceship hulls, have been found on Elkan, and the Lutherians are refusing to provide their product Betromicitine, without which Venus will become uninhabitable because of Venusian Swamp Fever, unless humans depart Elkan. Dawson quickly discovers that the Lutherians say that Elkan is rightly theirs because they got there first and the Earth explorers falsified their records to make it look simultaneous, and further they are fed up with the imperial expansion of Earth (nice lecture on this). Here is where they will draw the line. So Dawson goes out and gets drunk for several weeks, then sobers up long enough to order large quantities of copper, all the while going on about what a rat he is. The copper—the basis of Luther's economy—is smuggled to Luther and destroys its economy, solving the short-term problem but, we are told, creating a longer-term hatred—after all, there are five more stories by Wright in this series.

There's more of the same mechanical cleverness in "The Con Game" (**40**), in which Dawson is summoned to another world contested by the Lutherians, in which a seemingly primitive race has developed matter transmitters, but nobody can communicate with them about how the booths work. Whoever gets their secret will rule. Dawson snoops around for a while, and offers to trade the Lutherians the secret of the transmitters for mineral rights on the planet. Turns out the secret is that there is no secret. The Lutherians teleport, and they use the booths so they will have agreed places to do it so they won't materialize inside each other, and nobody can communicate with them because they're telepathic.

§

Alan Barclay is, if anything, the most tiresome of the more prolific contributors. Most of his half-dozen stories here are about the Jackos, mysterious aliens who send scout ships into the solar system which, of course, must be destroyed. The first of these, "Only an Echo" (**22**), is a piece of space-war yard goods, which contains some *pro forma* questioning of whether a war is really necessary, but mainly it's about skulking and shooting. If it were written today it would be a video game. "The Real McCoy" (**34**) is another Jacko story, but less tedious than its predecessor. McCoy is a space pilot, who has survived for two and a half years of warfare where most pilots last no more than six months. He engages a Jacko, and both run out of fuel, winding up engaged in single combat on the asteroid. After a while they give that up, throw rocks at each other and end by tossing them back and forth. Rescue parties from both sides are converging, and McCoy draws a picture and leaves it for the Jacko, suggesting that Earth has a lot of ships and will defeat the Jackos. He gets refueled and leaves—disobeying the order to kill the Jacko.

"The Single Ship" (**39**), another Jacko story, reverts to tedium. Intrepid pilot volunteers for suicide mission to follow the Jackoes home in a fake Jacko ship; discovers that they come from... more ships, and then kills himself kamikaze-style, since in order to maintain his disguise he had to kill another Earth pilot in an encounter along the way. In "Rock 83" (**40**), the protagonist, fighting the Jackoes, tries to evacuate an outpost which proves to be commanded by a man who claims he's really an old Earth Navy man and has a bookcase full of the exploits of Lord Nelson and the like; he's a fraud but dies honorably acting out his fantasy.

Barclay's non-Jacko stories are no improvement. "Walk into My Parlour" (**23**) is a different kind of yard goods. Guy walks into Martian Internal Security because he knows they're looking for him; he was close to the place where some important documents were taken but he says he's not the culprit. He volunteers to help out interviewing people who might be. In the course of this activity he proves himself to be effortlessly multilingual and a devil with the ladies to boot. There's a complicated game of spy vs. spy going on, and we know who will win because he's just cooler than the Martian cops and bureaucrats. It's like Eric Frank Russell in pot-boiler mode minus the sense of humor— pointless indeed. "The Firebird" (**26**) is even more dreary. Earth ship lands, finds itself across town from five enemy ships, the captain contrives to mislead them about his ship's capabilities, wins the shootout with the aid of crack gunner and ostentatious drunkard Laszlo, a.k.a. the Firebird. Although it's labeled a short story, it goes on for 25 pages. Barclay had a couple of reasonably good stories in *Science Fantasy*, and there were about a dozen more *New Worlds* contributions before their abrupt cessation in 1961.

§

The big-name veterans of the first years of *New Worlds* are present in these 1954-55 issues, but not very much. Arthur C. Clarke has only one story, and that a reprint, "The Sentinel" (**22**). There is not a whole lot to this story, as I thought when I read it nearly 50 years ago in *Expedition to Earth*, and as the *New Worlds* readers seem to have agreed, placing it fourth in the issue. Its after-acquired fame as the seed for *2001: A Space Odyssey* is more that of a lottery winner than of a striver. But it does display Clarke's offhandedly graceful and vivid way of showing you what consumes him: "When life was beginning on Earth, it was already dying here: the waters were retreating down the flanks of those stupendous cliffs, retreating into the empty heart of the Moon. Over the land which we were crossing, the tideless ocean had once been half a mile deep—and now the only trace of moisture was the hoarfrost one could sometimes find in caves which the searing sunlight never penetrated." There's your sense of wonder in a nutshell, underscoring by contrast the relative drabness of most of the magazine's other contents, even worthy efforts like those of James White.

John Wyndham is present with two of his urbane and well-turned short pieces. "Opposite Numbers" (**22**) is a typically understated, smooth and clever time travel piece about people who married the wrong spouses and are set straight by their counterparts from different time-tracks. "Compassion Circuit" (**35**), which previously appeared in the December 1954 *Fantastic Universe*,[47] is a disengagedly macabre piece about household robots.

John Christopher has three stories. "Museum Piece" (**22**), which also appeared in the US in *Orbit* 2 the previous year, is a competent but forgettable story about space explorers finding a planet whose seemingly incurious and relatively primitive

---

47. And also, bibliographer Phil Stephensen-Payne reports, in the *Sunday Chronicle* (August 29, 1954), and between the two magazine appearances, in *World's News* (Australia), February 1955.

inhabitants have discovered the gateway to Paradise; but Earth folks are too crass and would ruin it, so the human who learns the secret decides he won't tell a soul. The more pointed "Escape Route" (**24**) posits that after a nuclear war, an elite group is about to escape to Mars, but the ordinary folk—"Indians" as the swells like to call them—outsmart them, get into their stockade and destroy the spaceship. Their program: you're the smart guys, you're going to stay here and apply your talents to making things better on Earth. "Manna" (**33**), too, is reasonably incisive: manna, literally, begins to fall; it soon becomes almost the exclusive foodstuff of humanity; what's the catch? But in the end it's no more than a well done gimmick story.

Finally, A. Bertram Chandler's "Zoological Specimen" (**23**) splits the difference between his urbane and fairly inconsequential tales of space-shipboard life and the pulp excesses of his lead novelettes of 1951-52. A zoological specimen is being returned from Mars to Earth, except it's really the body of an eccentric archaeologist, and it proves to be inhabited by improbably fearsome and powerful aliens, who are defeated in an equally improbable and flippant fashion, though not before utterance of the immortal line: "'You gave your word to a... a *prawn*!' spluttered the Second Pilot."

J. T. McIntosh is back as well, less often than before but at greater length, with three novelettes and a short story. "Relay Race" (**22**) is, I suppose, one of his better stories. My brief against McIntosh is lack of logic and plausibility.[48] This one is reasonably well worked out internally, however off the wall it may seem by any external standard. It also stands out in this crowd for its extravagance, a marked contrast with the relative mundanity of most of the other stories here. In the far future, humanity has been dominated for thousands of years by the

---

48. See the comments in Chapter 3 on his "The ESP Worlds," and on his stories in *Strange Highways*, the companion volume to this one on *Science Fantasy*. In fairness, McIntosh later contributed several worthy stories to which this complaint does not apply or does not loom large. These are discussed later in this volume.

Edril, who have reduced humans to servitude, albeit a reasonably prosperous variety. All humanity is divided between the Nith, who wear red and think there should be a rebellion right away, and the Enwyes, who wear green and think it's better to wait. (Nith means "now is the hour," Enwye "not yet." Honest.) The leaders of the factions meet secretly and plot under cover of large-scale rumbles between their followers, which generate a mind screen that the surveilling Edril can't penetrate. Finally, everybody agrees that now *is* the time. The factions' relationship is analogized to a relay race, the Enwye handing the baton off to the Nith. So Arthur and Lida and Joe and Crystal, after opening their minds to one another, take off in the ship. Ship? In a passage that must surely have inspired Lionel Fanthorpe, McIntosh tells us:

> Small and sleek, it was a marvel of theory. Terran science had passed far beyond the method of trial and error, for it had had to.... There was no need to test the ship, just as there was no need for a name for it. It was the only ship, the first ship, the first interplanetary ship, the first interstellar ship, the first intergalactic ship. If it had been necessary to test it, its manufacture would have been premature.

They trace the ship of the Edrin straw boss by traveling faster than light and seeing where it used to be (using "a telescope which was more than a telescope"). In fact, they trace its path through several planetary stops, finding the inhabitants similarly dominated by the Edril. The Nith/Enwye argument continues to erupt, albeit in new contexts. They begin to perceive that if they overthrow the Edril they may have to take over their role; exactly why is not explained. On one world they find dumped all the spaceships that Earth has been constructing under the thumb of the Eldril—it's all been makework, for Earth and for the other Edril-dominated worlds, to keep the conquered peoples too busy to rebel.

So they head on to Edris, where they are informed by a disembodied recorded voice that they have been under surveillance all along. They proceed, and find themselves in a place without sensation, but with comfort, warmth, light, air. "Not real, however; reality had no more place in this kind of existence than gravity." They are at the eighth level, though a couple of them are not really ready for it. The Edrin explains to Joe, who is having difficulty, that he hasn't quite passed the point where science and knowledge stop being destructive and cold.

> "When you have—and you will—you'll know that in the end beauty *is* truth, truth beauty, and that that is all you need to know. The scientist, the philosopher, the psychologist, the anthropologist, the mystic, the theologist, the biologist, the hedonist, all merely have to go far enough and they meet in the same place—the eighth level."

The Edril and humanity have been running a relay race too: the Edril took the baton from Earth a thousand years ago, since Earth folk were "rash and cruel and unstable and capricious," but now it's time for Earth to take the baton again. This is all unutterably silly to me, a sort of metaphysical cartooning, but it's well enough executed on its own terms. So I suppose this is a good J. T. McIntosh story.

Note that I didn't say "a good story by J. T. McIntosh." That is an important distinction, and to my surprise, the gulf is bridged in "Bluebird World" (**36**). In a utopian world of the future, where hardly anybody seems to need to work, Syl is unhappy, or at least less happy than everybody else. She's always wanted to have her own way, unlike the accommodating people around her. She commits some bad, or bad-looking, acts (a fake attempted killing, art theft) to see if somebody will stop her. Nobody does. She starts looking into history to see how things got this way. History is about a thousand years long, and what happened in the first 100 is a bit murky. There's precious little left of prehistory—fragments by Shakespeare, for example, but no complete works. Syl talks to learned people, discovers that there seems to have been mass censorship of prehistoric art and literature, and that people used to be a lot less cooperative and tranquil. Outraged at the apparent manipulation of all of humanity to narrow its emotional range, she learns that she's not the only throwback, and goes to visit one of the others, who knocks her around a bit. Uncooperative, Syl eventually gasses him unconscious, but her plane has been sabotaged and she is almost killed. Meh, enough, she decides, giving up on the principled pursuit of atavism and going back to her blandly devoted boyfriend, not reconciled but afraid to do otherwise. I am tempted to describe this as the staid UK counterpart of Knight's "The Country of the Kind." That's an overstatement, but this is a thoughtful and well constructed exploration of a significant theme. It's certainly the best McIntosh story I've seen, the first in which my enjoyment clearly outweighed my irritation. Never anthologized, of course.

Unfortunately, it's back to business as usual with McIntosh's "The Way Back" (**38**), in which seven intrepid space explorers wake to find they have been drugged unconscious by the Pinkies of Micla, who have taken their spaceship. Lifeboats remain, neatly lined up; but are they sabotaged? Well, yes, and the characters engage in a sort of eenie-meenie operation to decide who's going to try to find out how and test them. Three are left when they come up with an answer that has been (in broad outline) obvious since about halfway through this long (44-page) novelette.

It's readable enough, but so contrived as to be pointless. McIntosh posits an alien species that is nomadic but nonetheless has a highly developed miniaturized technology (guess they put their labs and clean rooms on wheels) allowing them, e.g., to turn an article of clothing into a surveillance device that won't be noticed. And why is this happening anyway? Why didn't the aliens just kill the humans outright? Maybe, it is suggested, because they wanted their bodies and the lifeboat wreckage to be found somewhere else, not realizing that their bombs would actually blow up the humans and all their works without a trace. The strained logic is now pureed. There is also the familiar McIntosh take on matters of gender. "'You men can work out what's happening and what to do about it,' said Doreen firmly, surveying her soaking, bedraggled frock in dismay. 'I wouldn't be able to think straight, knowing I looked like this.'" And later: "Joe did shut up for a moment, for the girls came out of the hut and rejoined them. By rushing off to make themselves look presentable they had shown that they were women above all." It's nice that McIntosh acknowledges that men and women aren't necessarily the same and sometimes they are interested in each other (and he probably has more foregrounded female characters per capita than any other SF writer of the time besides Judith Merril[49]), but this insistence on reproducing the stereotypes of his day gets tiresome fast, and is not enhanced by the notion that we (of any gender) will be exploring the distant stars in frocks.

"Hitch-Hikers" (**30**), under the name Gregory Francis, a pseudonym of McIntosh and Frank H. Parnell, is shorter and sharper. Interstellar explorers (male and female, seem to be on pretty good terms) land on an alien planet. Weird stuff starts happening. They head back towards their ship and it disappears and appears in the opposite direction; a walk around a wooded copse takes them twice as long in one direction as the other. They find a couple of cute dog-like animals who follow them home and jump into the airlock, so of course they take the animals in. They're very neat and they start having litters. When the explorers get to the next planet in the system, somehow the young are out the airlock. After a while they realize they've

---

49. On this subject, McIntosh said: "I always felt that if science fiction were to grow up the women in it had to grow up first. This was just as important as the total banishment of mad professors with beautiful daughters. And it was in the 1950s that women in science fiction began to become real rather than stock characters."—Interview conducted by Ian Covell, 1977, on file with interviewer.

been had, and the indigenes of the first world are using them to get a foothold elsewhere in their system. The dog-like animals suddenly are dead and look like the remains the explorers found on the first planet.

McIntosh gets the *New Worlds* Profile in **38**, written in the third person, but most likely by himself: "McIntosh has remained rather more popular with editors than with readers. Editors comment enthusiastically; readers grunt noncommittally. He concentrates on technique and character—he wouldn't cross the road for a good idea. Rewrites are numerous, done before the story is sent out. Many novelettes are rewritten a dozen times before being typed." Fortunately the passive voice is not as overworked in his stories.

Other familiar if less consequential names include Sydney J. Bounds—the new Sydney J. Bounds, that is. "Portrait of a Spaceman" (**28**) is the best Bounds story so far, a sort of inversion of "The Green Hills of Earth." A journalist is assigned to investigate the life of a hero spaceman who locked himself in a radioactive engine room, fixed the problem, and saved the ship while sacrificing his life. The truth proves to be much more sordid. While it's not great literature, this one is pointed and economical and avoids the clichéd pulp histrionics in which Bounds has been prone to wallow. In "Sole Survivor" (**32**), a man accidentally thrown from a spaceship happens upon a derelict alien spaceship and has to figure out how to get into it and then survive in it. This one, too, is economical and (for Bounds) effectively understated. "The Active Man" (**33**) is a step backwards, but still readable in its over-the-top (but commendably short) way. The janitor at a nuclear power plant overhears the owner scheming to nuke the capital in order to ramp up nuclear weapons development and increase his contracts. In the course of his eavesdropping he receives a lethal dose of radiation; so he runs around glowing (honest) and breaks up the plot, beating the truth with his radioactive hands out of the man with the (literal) suitcase bomb. It's "The Long Watch" gangster-style.

Peter Hawkins' "Ship from the Stars" (**25**) is another variation on the menace-in-space plot, familiar from his earlier *New Worlds* stories and pretty obviously owing a lot to van Vogt's *The Voyage of the Space Beagle*. His characters find a wrecked alien spaceship on the Moon, with a life form inside that looks odd (like a pool of spilled ink) and acts odder (disappearing periodically), proving even stranger and more dangerous when they start investigating closely. It's a capable and mildly ingenious piece, though in the end the alien is outsmarted a bit too easily. Hawkins gives the impression of a writer of modest talents who is working very hard to get it right—maybe too hard. This is his last story for almost three years.

Jonathan F. Burke contributes his last two *New Worlds* stories (almost all the rest of his output went to *Authentic*), neither amounting to much. "The Gamble" (**23**) posits a sort of draft lottery to colonize Venus, and you can never come back. The corrupt official protagonist contrives to get his daughter's unsuitable suitor drafted, except that she vows to go with him, so he unfixes the fix, and on the next run of the lottery he's drafted, and nobody is going to let him unfix this one, but daughter and husband (they've secretly married) decide they'll all go to Venus together, so this initially dark satire bashes itself to death on the rocks of Pollyanna. Burke's "The Perfect Secretary" (**27**) is quite lame. Things are sliding towards war between the Galactic Council, including Earth, and the Medeans. The protagonist, working on a contested world, gives a robot secretary scientific calculations to do, it says they're correct but the menacing Medeans have already figured it out, demonstrating development of independent intelligence and handing the Council the edge needed for victory.

§

Then there are the newcomers, the soon-to-be regulars. Brian Aldiss's "Outside" (**31**), his first *New Worlds* appearance, is one of his better early stories, about the house of people who never go out and prove to be captured shapeshifting aliens rendered amnesic and under observation—pretty implausible if you stop and think about it, but it's well enough written and visualized to minimize the temptation to do so. Carnell had said in "The Literary Line-Up" that it would "probably prove to be the gem of the issue." The readers put it second in the issue, after the second part of the serial, *Prisoner in the Skull*. "Our Kind of Knowledge" (**36**) is also good if a bit twee: the childlike inhabitants of a far-far future Earth find a loose spaceship lying around, ride it home to the embattled galactic empire that lost it thousands of years previously, effortlessly defeat the empire's techno-paranoid strategies and devices, and head home, after revealing that they are actually the descendants of humans who interbred with the empire's great enemy, and maybe that would be a better way to resolve their differences. This is Aldiss's take on the tradition of John W. Campbell's "Forgetfulness," Eric Frank Russell's "Metamorphosite," van Vogt's "The Monster," etc.

The standard drops a bit in "Panel Game" (**42**), a somewhat overdone satire of a TV- and advertising-dominated world, though done in what would prove to be typical Aldiss fashion. A man drops into the main characters' garden, announces he's an escaped prisoner (the former Prime Minister, who voted against perpetual entertainment), and cadges some food from them. They change channels on the TV and the upper-class channel is running a game show in which the same man turns out to have been a contestant in a scavenger hunt, showing off the food items he got from their lower-caste household. All three of these stories were in Aldiss's first collection *Space, Time, And Nathaniel*, but "Panel Game" was omitted from the first American collection, *No Time Like Tomorrow*.

Aldiss has his *New Worlds* Profile in **42**, typically flip: "Having just left the serious twenties behind, he is now beginning to feel young and frivolous. He fears, however, that he may be some sort of mental case, certifiable but unclassifiable, since his two main ambitions lie in diametrically opposed directions: to become a solemn, intense novelist and to write a really funny book." He expresses his admiration for Proust, Hardy, and Amis. "He is married and has one cherubic baby son, Clive. His interests include women and words. Tactfully announcing his favourite woman to be his wife, he says his favourite word is 'detergent.'"

John Brunner's *New Worlds* debut follows Aldiss's by a few months. For "Visitors' Book" (**34**), he's John on the contents page and K. Houston on the story itself. It's pretty routine: aliens arrive in the solar system, they're a nasty bunch, but they're outfoxed by the humans and flee in terror of fake technology. For "Fiery Pillar" (**38**) he's K. Houston everywhere. This one is a considerable improvement. The first interstellar spaceship has returned and materialized inside the Earth, causing an enormous and continuing explosion, for decades now (this is the pillar of the title). Not surprisingly, Earth has rejected further interstellar space travel. Meanwhile, they are beset by mutants caused by the explosion, who are universally hated and have to be saved from lynching in order to be executed properly. The protagonist is a police captain who investigates the apparent suicide of the one man who has kept pushing for more interstellar flight, and is himself revealed as a mutant in the process. The story is well constructed and not too long.

By "The Uneasy Head" (**41**) Brunner has resolved his identity crisis and is John, unqualified. This one is fairly trivial and obvious—interstellar rogue and smuggler evades the cops, sets down on an out-of-the way planet where the isolated colonists have backslid a bit, discovers that the locals are looking for a king and finding it hard to get a good candidate, so he takes the job, failing to ask how long it's for and what happens at the end. But it's smoothly and vividly done, surprisingly so for a writer this new (and he was perhaps not yet 21 when he wrote it). "Problem for Spacemen" (**42**) is a space detective story: a spaceship arrives at its destination with the air blown out and the pilot dead of explosive decompression. Suicide or murder? The reasonably clever mystery and solution are framed by the overly earnest back and forth between the man in charge of the space station construction site where the story takes place, and the investigator whose presence and activities are threatening his ability to get the job done. The ambition is nice but it doesn't quite come off. In this story and in "The Uneasy Head," by the way, Brunner does a very good job of visualizing the mundane physical details of space travel.

Dan Morgan, who had one story in *New Worlds* two years previously, is back and on his way to a more modest career in *New Worlds* than Aldiss or Brunner. "Jerry Built" (**24**), telegraphed by the title and Carnell's blurb, is about the first space pilot, who returns from his mission to be told that he's going to be kept under surveillance. However, for some unexplained reason he has become telepathic in space, and he quickly figures out things aren't what they seem. Turns out he is an android copy made for experimental purposes and destined for vivisection. He doesn't much care for this idea, and hijacks the spaceship to avoid it, only to be told he wasn't really well made and will shortly be disintegrating—*Bladerunner* a few decades too early.

Morgan collaborates with John Kippax, in the latter's second SF magazine appearance, in "Trojan Hearse" (**30**), a tiresome alien invasion story, in which the limp-wristed World President ("One pale hand fluttered lightly"; "The expressive hands fluttered again") refuses to let the solid military types take care of business, which they eventually do by attacking enemy ships while supposedly recovering the dead from the previous skirmish. Forgive me if I do not find this plot device compelling.

"Life Agency" (**39**) is Morgan's bid to Signify. This 31-page piece (oddly, labeled a short story), ostentatiously divided into 10 chapters, is about ETRA, the Extra Terrestrial Relations Agency, which has complete authority over all dealings with intelligent ETs, but doesn't have much to do because none have been found. Nevertheless, for some reason somebody seems to want to put it out of business. Could that have something to do with the first interstellar expedition, about to return? The well-stuffed plot is thoroughly hokey and the writing bounces off the ceiling periodically (e.g., the Senator's daughter has just died in childbirth secondary to the genetic damage sustained by her space-traveling husband: "Dead because she had married a space man who carried the poison of twisted genes in his loins"), but corporate chicanery is foiled, enlightenment triumphs, maybe the Centauran natives won't get exterminated or exploited too badly, and ETRA finally has something to do. "The task ahead was big... *as big as the universe*." Still, this is an energetic and reasonably enjoyable amateurish story by a writer who is clearly trying to become less amateurish. Morgan gets the *New Worlds* Profile this issue: he's a wholesome-looking apple-cheeked guy, 29 but looks 20, an "ex-professional guitarist" (doesn't say what his day job is now) who has moved to Spalding, "a small Lincolnshire market town," aspires to write the kind of SF story he likes to read, and has nothing much more interesting than that to say.

§

This brings us down to the Little Known Writers. The best of them is Arthur Coster, whose "The Other Door" (**34**) is a surprise; it's the sort of thing that was more characteristic of *Science Fantasy*. A man consults a psychiatrist because he thinks he sees the future, but gets a runaround. He says there is too a way he could know the future, if the psychiatrist had a time machine in his closet and had seen him before and sent him back in time. It only gets crazier. The author of this agreeable farce is really a pseudonym for Richard deMille, though why he needed a pseudonym is a mystery. The career of this Little Known Writer, said to be the son of Hollywood mogul Cecil B. deMille,[50] consisted of six stories, two under the Coster pseudonym, 1953-59, in as various a group of magazines as you could want: *Astounding*, *Science Fantasy*, *New Worlds*, *Authentic*, *Science Fiction Stories*, and *Fantastic*.

50. H. J. Campbell, Editorial, *Authentic Science Fiction Monthly* 41 (Jan. 1954), p. 3.

Next in line of merit is Richard Rowland, who contributes "Ferrymam" (sic) (**35**). He published two stories in *New Worlds* and two in *Science Fantasy* from 1954 to 1956, one of them, "Double Act," a bizarre piece of metaphysical slapstick in *Science Fantasy*, about the same time as this story under the pseudonym Howard Lee McCarey. (Why a pseudonym? Again, beats me.) This one is pretty bizarre too. The eponymous Ferrymam (plural: ferrymem) is a young woman who has taken a job as a relativistic interstellar space pilot, which means she takes trips that are subjectively about three years long but objectively take about a thousand years. So she arrives on Earth ready for some company, but the spaceport is deserted. Taking the automatic train into the city she finds only a few people, all of whom are extremely aged and act pretty strangely towards her. ("Tuanie found it almost impossible to restrain a shiver: these were not casual contacts but firm, deliberate and embarrassing grasps. For some reason they were interested in feeling her. They can't want to eat me, she thought, I wouldn't go around. Besides, most of them have no teeth.") Drugged and stripped to no obvious purpose, she's rescued by one Trad, a person nearer her own age, who explains that the planet has been beset by a sterility-causing disease so almost everybody has abandoned the cities and turned away from technology. She can't join them because she will be feared as a carrier, and she has to leave. As he doesn't quite say, their love can never be (but he shows up just before takeoff anyway).

Michael Harrison's "Getaway" (**42**) is an amateurish but engaging story about the prison break of a captured revolutionary, who is placed on an asteroid in a dome with all the comforts of home, rather than being locked in a cell under close surveillance. He contrives the appropriate technology and busts out, only to kill himself by not having thought everything quite through; but his escape becomes legendary and inspires a revolution which succeeds. According to Miller/Contento this Michael Harrison also had several stories in *London Mystery Magazine* in the 1950s and several in *Fantasy & Science Fiction* in 1969, making one wonder if it's really the same Harrison.

From here it's downhill fast. Gavin Neal's "Short Circuit" (**31**), the first of three stories under that byline, all in *New Worlds* and *Science Fantasy* in 1955, announces itself unequivocally: "Fred Lancing looked at the five determined faces before him and felt the heightened throb of his pulse and a quick stab of excitement that, through long practise, was instantly controlled. These then were the Brotherhood: these the men who, even in this hell of a penal settlement, still maintained the traditions of freedom and liberty which were ruthlessly stamped out in the Solar System." Right. They escape from the prison camp via a boring hardware gimmick and head for the other side of the galaxy. Ho hum. "Logical Deduction" (**33**) is about a murder on a spaceship, less overwritten but equally boring and gimmicky.

Richard Varne's "Regulations" (**28**) is about the wise old spacer who follows the regulations and the young bronco who doesn't. They find an alien artifact and the young guy, insisting on opening it up rather than reporting it as prescribed and getting the hell out, blows himself up because it's booby-trapped. At 16 digest pages, it's about three times too long. This is one of only two stories in the SF magazines by this Little Known Writer, the other being "In a Misty Light," an entertaining but nonsensical novella in *Science Fantasy* the following year.

P.W. Cutler's "Reconnaissance" (**30**) rehashes the familiar plot of alien invaders accidentally bamboozled by humans, in this case a kid who shows them his comic books and his older brother's copies of *New Worlds* and *The Conquest of Space*, so they flee in terror of this obviously superior civilization (serving them some of his father's whiskey helped too). It goes on for 18 pages; it might have been amusing at five. P(eter) W. Cutler seems to be a fan very briefly turned pro (total output, this story and one in *Science Fantasy* the same year); at least his name is familiar from the letters column of earlier issues of *New Worlds*. This story is notable for an early appearance outside fanzines of the term "zap gun," applied to the protagonist's de luxe water pistol.

In David Gardner's "Staying Guests" (**25**), a professional hypnotist discovers mutants among us, and now they're after him, except they're not really mutants but three brands of extra-terrestrials. When he brings in the proof to his journalist friend, he discovers that they've infiltrated further than he thought. This is an amateurish change on Henry Kuttner's "Don't Look Now." Gardner had three other stories in *Nebula* and an article on the Liverpool SF Society in *Authentic*.

Finally, and very much bringing up the rear, Burgess Brown's "Fire" (**24**) pointlessly relates an atomic bomb test which leaves behind an unstoppable nuclear reaction that takes a couple of days to consume the Earth. Brown had no other appearances in the SF magazines.

§

Setting aside the reprints, what's worth saving from these two years of *New Worlds*? For the ages, not a lot. Aldiss's "Outside" and "Our Kind of Knowledge," McIntosh's "Bluebird World," Tubb's "Into Thy Hands," Wyndham's "Opposite Numbers," Christopher's "Escape Route," and James' "Space Capsule" would go into my hypothetical anthology; and McIntosh's collaborative story "The Hitch-Hikers" is growing on me. Coster's "The Other Door" makes it on sheer eccentricity, with Rowland's "Ferrymam" just a bit behind. Honorable period-piece or nice-try mention go to Tubb's "Little Girl Lost," White's "Suicide Mission" and "The Star Walk," and Christopher's "Manna." Judith Merril gave Honorable Mention in her first annual best SF anthology (covering 1955) to "Our Kind of Knowledge" and "Manna."

5: CRUISING SPEED (1956-57)

New Worlds hits and keeps its stride in 1956 and 1957 (issues **43** through **66**), maintaining its monthly schedule, its size (128 pages exclusive of covers), and its 2/- price. There's a house ad in **61**: "Memo from Nova Publications Ltd. As from July 1ˢᵗ, 1957, our New Address will be Maclaren House, 131 Great Suffolk Street, London S.E. 1," etc. Presumably this means Carnell is moving into the headquarters of Maclaren's. There's still no comment on the relationship between Nova and Maclaren's.

But a stride can also be a rut, and by the end of 1957 it's fair to say the magazine is in one. It has banished the floridly inept fiction of earlier days and developed a stable of writers who can be relied on to maintain a base level of competence (though that proposition is tested at novel length). But there's little that is outstanding by any measure, and not much that is original or even interestingly eccentric in content or style. The overall interest and readability of the magazine was probably higher in 1954-55, with its heavy reliance on reprinted serials and stories selected from the US original anthologies. To his credit, Carnell more or less recognizes the problem and undertakes to do something about it starting in early 1958, as detailed in the next chapter.

The magazine's outward appearance stays mostly the same in 1956-57, though the band at the bottom of the cover featuring story title or authors' names appears on **52**, vanishes, reappears on **56** (February 1957), and stays there for the rest of 1957. The covers themselves continue uneven—sometimes impressive, sometimes pretty inane, almost never quite like anything you'd see on a US magazine during this period. The guard changes during this period. Quinn fades out in 1956, and appears to have lost interest in any case. Take a look at his covers for **46** and **47**, purporting to illustrate Lan Wright's "Who Speaks of Conquest?"[51] They are confusing and hackneyed respectively. (**46**, with spacecraft near Jupiter, probably portrays a space battle; it took me a while to figure it out.) Terry—actually F. J. Terence Maloney, of Surrey, per his *New Worlds* Profile in **53**—enjoys a brief ascendancy; a number of his covers are relatively pedestrian space-traveling scenes (see **48**, "Mars—A Plan for Better Living," for a representative one), though a couple of them—**62** and especially **53**, one of the more tasteful and attractive covers I've ever seen on an SF magazine—are quite striking. Towards the end of 1957, Terry too begins to fade out, and the long reign of Brian Lewis begins—not too auspiciously either. Lewis's work is colorful but stiff, especially the human faces and figures, some of which look like he used wax mannequins as models. The results can be a bit absurd, as in his cover for **66**, which manages to look simultaneously garish and stuffy.[52] Overall, it's fair to say that the covers have deteriorated both in imagination and in execution over this period.

Carnell is clearly aware of the problem: in his January 1958 editorial (**67**), he says "we have gradually been working up to the idea that abstract art is an expressionistic medium readily adaptable to stories of the future. I am of the opinion that science fiction magazines now need something more than the accepted form of spaceship cover or prosaic action-adventure illustration." Lewis apparently got his marching orders, or his freedom, pretty quickly. The first of his Richard Powers-influenced covers appears two issues later.

---

51. See these covers at http://www.sfcovers.net/mainnav.htm or http://www.philsp.com/mags/newworlds.html.

52. But delightfully enthralling to a 14-year-old boy, reports Damien Broderick.

Two of the artists get profiled. Terry, as noted, gets his in **53**. He is "well known in other circles—notably that of astronomy," has appeared in national weeklies, is about to publish a book on the solar system, makes telescopes and cameras in his optical workshop, and is presently modifying a Littrow type spectrograph—he doesn't say whether he does this for fun or profit. Terry had 15 covers from 1956 into 1958 in *New Worlds* and *Science Fantasy*, and then he was gone from the field. Gerard Quinn is profiled in **51** and talks mostly about interior illustration. His style has become simpler, with less shading and cross-hatching, and he explains why: "The most pointed reason for my own economy of line in recent months has been lack of time—and still is. Commissions for science fiction are few and my services are often better employed elsewhere although I would prefer to spend all my time working in our own specialized medium. Intricate line-work was once my pride and pleasure but for the time being I will have to continue my approach to fantasy work with the simpler style that has been evident of late...." Short version: he can't do his best work for what Carnell can pay. This factor might also account for his fading out as cover artist and the diminished quality of his last covers.

Quinn also says, "Editor Carnell has suggested that if fantasy art in this country deteriorates any further it will cease to grace the pages of this magazine at least—can you imagine *New Worlds* without interiors?" That is exactly what came to pass, and within six years, art disappeared from the covers as well. In his editorial "Traditions..." in **62** (August 1957), Carnell says he has gradually reduced the amount of interior illustration, and now it's gone—by popular demand, he claims; based on reader suggestions, he tried dropping it in *Science Fantasy* and didn't hear a peep.

> Art work in the digest-size magazines is as out-of-date as a coal fire... the trend is for the cameo-type illustration one sees in journals like the *Reader's Digest*. In particular, art work in science fiction magazines is a

hangover from the days of the large-size pulps, just the same as two columns of type is a hand-down from the old three columns of the large magazines. Both are traditions which are dying hard—but nevertheless dying.

Before, large-format magazines needed illustrations to break up the vast expanse of print. Also, the illustrations were "as much an introduction to science fiction as the stories themselves."

Carnell continues: "Following in the footsteps of tradition, *New Worlds* used interior art work (although I was never very happy about it, and, except when Gerard Quinn was at his peak, seldom satisfied)." He complains of "the standard of work produced by both professional and amateur British artists in general. I think an entire editorial could be devoted to the subject. Let's say after the World Convention in September, when I will have had an opportunity of talking to a number of artists and prevailed upon some of the visiting Americans to express an opinion." No such full-scale editorial on artwork appears, but Carnell does say in **67** (January 1958) that he got no storm of protest from its elimination, and the dissenting voices within the Commonwealth "have been so few as to be virtually non-existent." Americans are going ballistic, though, and Carnell quotes and dismisses an article in *Science Fiction Times* asserting that the "failure of modern science fiction magazines" is "the lack of art work, readers' columns and good fan departments." Carnell says these are economically unfeasible and let's move on.

For perspective on this, I looked again at the illustrations in four issues of *New Worlds* (**53-56**), and found them often poorly executed and mostly fairly unimaginative and uninteresting. By contrast, those in the contemporaneous issues of *Astounding* were lively and imaginative, in addition to being very well done (Freas and van Dongen were into their heyday by then), and the reproduction appeared higher quality. Several contemporaneous issues of *Infinity* split the difference (i.e., Emsh was nearly on a level with *Astounding,* and the other illustrators were more comparable to those in *New Worlds*). So on the whole, the end of interior illustration in *New Worlds* was no great loss.

There is an editorial in every issue but one (their contents will be discussed after the fiction), and at least one science article and sometimes two or three in all but one issue. "Kenneth Johns"—John Newman and Kenneth Bulmer—is by far the most frequent article by-line, followed by Newman solo. Typical titles include "Antarctica," "The Solar Atmosphere," and "Contra-Terrene Matter." "The Literary Line-Up," with story ratings and "coming next issue," appears in each issue. Most issues have a *New Worlds* Profile with author photo and brief text on the inside front cover—in some cases, two profiles, shrunk to fit the space. "Postmortem," the letter column, is conspicuous by its absence; it does not appear until issue **59**, and then vanishes again for the rest of the period.

Leslie Flood's book reviews are in most issues from **43** through **58**, then they abruptly disappear, though not without harbinger—the **58** review column is heavily leaded, to the point of looking like 1.5 line spacing. There is not a word of explanation for the absence until **65**, where the reviews reappear with this comment from Flood:

> This column's absence for several issues has been regretfully occasioned by the sharp decline in hardcover fantasy books published over several months. With the near cessation of reprints from America and stereotyped series from publishers who had jumped in with both feet and found the boom's-end too precarious for science-fictional adventuring, it remains for the more reputable houses—who shun the tag "science-fiction" for what must be depressing reasons for the enthusiast reader—to present occasional novels with a science-fictional content for their general lists.

This collapse seems to have been extremely abrupt. In the February 1957 *Astounding*, in a review column that would probably have been written in late-middle 1956, P. Schuyler Miller says: "From all reports, the hosts for the 1957 World Science-Fiction Convention now have the world's healthiest market for hard-cover SF." We'll return to Flood's column after the commentary on the fiction.

In addition to the book reviews, there are a couple of film reviews by Carnell, of *Forbidden Planet* (**48**) and *Man In Space* (**57**), and a one-off "SF on Television" listing in **45**.

The only other non-fiction is a peculiar item in **65** called "Quotations," by Iris Harvey (no other SF magazine credits), which looks more like a parlor game than anything else. For example: "'The new shells have proximity fuses that explode them as soon as they feel hardware ahead.'—*Nymphomaniacs.*"

Occasional filler items are stuck at the bottoms of pages, e.g., in **50**, reference to *Publishers' Weekly* sales figures on the paperback edition of *Forbidden Planet*, which Carnell warns is "pure corn." One in **51** is about Londoners planning to attend the New York Worldcon, in **54** about magazines on space-flight, and in **57** from one John F. Barrie, who wants to start a Cambridge SF club. (There is no evidence that he succeeded; these days, though, there is a well-established Cambridge University Science Fiction Society.) Barrie is also featured in the brief return of "Postmortem" in **59**, where appears his three-page letter comprising a philosophy and taxonomy of SF; my eyes glaze over.

Outside advertising falls to a low level during this period. The inside and outside back covers are devoted to house ads, usually for *Science Fantasy* and Nova Novels, though that moribund series is displaced in late 1957 by binders for *New Worlds*. Publishers' advertising disappears entirely—not surprisingly, if there was nothing published to be advertised—Sidgwick & Jackson in **49** being the last gasp. Except for that issue there is no outside advertising at all from **45** to **53** and again in **64** through **66**. What little advertising there is in the other issues is generally for booksellers (or -renters, i.e. the SF Postal Library): one-offs for the Fantasy Book Centre, Ken Chapman, Plus Books, A.M. Bain ("Science Fiction—Popular Astronomy—Astrology"). There are a few ads for the London Worldcon and the occasional ringer ("Solascope: The Giant Rotary Guide to the Solar System," 1000 facts, 12" square). The only ad of any entertainment value is the one in **57** for the SF Postal Library: "Know your SF authors? *Omavis * Retinsel * Turknet * Lunkthrob * Truesong * Hilennie * Berets * Barrybud.*"

§

Again, a small group of writers supplies a disproportionately large amount of the magazine's fiction contents. E. C. Tubb, the dominant contributor in 1954-55, has only four stories in 1956-57, all of them under the Alan Guthrie pseudonym, presumably because he became editor of *Authentic SF* early in 1956. The slack is taken up by Francis G. Rayer (10 stories, including three under the George Longdon pseudonym), James White (eight stories including a novel), John Brunner (eight stories including a novel), Kenneth Bulmer (seven stories including a novel), A. Bertram Chandler (seven stories), Alan Barclay (seven stories), Lan Wright (six stories including a novel), Dan Morgan (six stories including a novel) and Brian Aldiss (six stories). By my count, these eight authors account for more than half of the magazine's contents, 65 of the 125 pieces of fiction in these 24 issues, including all of the serialized novels.

The trend towards longer stories continues. Most issues contain a serial installment, and in those that don't, the lead novelette usually approaches or exceeds 40 of *New Worlds*'s 450-word-plus pages.

The use of reprints has slowed considerably. 13 stories in these 24 issues had some prior publication, compared to 19 in the 20 1954-55 issues, and only one is from an original anthology. The rest are from magazines, many with relatively recent prior publication, so they look like simultaneous submissions rather than cherry-picked items. And a number of stories were published in US magazines after they appeared here, including four by A. Bertram Chandler.

As to the quality of the fiction... overall, it's mediocre. There are some worthwhile stories but no forgotten classics—and only a couple of remembered ones, for that matter—and no idiosyncratic and off-trail gems (those are across the street at *Science Fantasy*). Some talented writers are working hard to improve, several of whom will eventually succeed remarkably well (Aldiss, Ballard, Brunner, James White); a few seasoned professionals are displaying various degrees of effort and success (McIntosh, Tubb, Chandler); and there are several regulars who seem to have reached their limits, their futures behind them (F. G. Rayer, E. R. James, Alan Barclay, Peter Hawkins). There's not much in the way of originality, and there's also not much facility. Reading Heinlein's reprinted "The Menace from Earth" in **64**, I was struck by how much more lively that irritatingly lightweight story is than what surrounds it, much of which is, relatively speaking, labored, clumsy, or just dull at the word-and-sentence level. There are exceptions, of course: Aldiss, Brunner, Ballard, McIntosh—but they are indeed exceptions.

The showpieces of these issues are the serials, all of them written by established contributors of short fiction, and probably all written by invitation from Carnell, as some of the authors make explicit. They're pretty lackluster, though all in different ways. The first is Lan Wright's "Who Speaks of Conquest?" (**46-49**), which is longer than its predecessors and runs four forty-plus-page installments rather than three. I observed in the previous chapter that *New Worlds*'s serials were notable for their near horizons. Apparently the readers made the same observation. The blurb to the first part says: "To date all our published serials have been popular but some readers have put forward the minor (!) complaint that we have never had one which really deals with the Galaxy. Those of you who are now enjoying the E.E. Smith 'Lensman' series being published by T.V. Boardman Ltd. will delight in Lan Wright's offering herewith, which is in the tradition of 'Doc' Smith with the vast sweep of the Galaxy as a background to Man's first interstellar adventures." Thus Carnell beats a strategic retreat from his earlier dictum that "to be popular with the general public the plots should be located within a Time ratio which could be conceivably in their life-time" (Editorial, **38**).

In fact, the novel is another of Wright's exercises in mechanical cleverness, scaled up from yard goods to light-year goods. The first interstellar expedition is returning home to report that not only is there sentient life out there, but they've got it all sewn up: there are civilizations everywhere and they all belong to the Rihnan Empire or else. How? The Rihnans have invincible weapons. They hand these out on a limited basis to the lesser breeds, who quickly learn not to fight wars because they just result in bankrupting stalemates. These races are of course incapable of figuring out how to make the weapons themselves and thereby threaten Rihnan hegemony. So how is Earth going to respond? The President of the World Senate decides we're going to fight, consulting with no one except the heads of the armed forces, certainly not the billions of people whose lives will be put at risk, and with no discernible consideration whether the benefits of joining the Empire might outweigh the costs of fighting it. (In fact, there doesn't seem to be any identifiable down side of joining the Empire.)

Earth cleverly captures one of the Rihnan ships, discovers that not only can humans (unlike those who have already knuckled under) figure out their weapons but they can improve on them. They hastily manufacture a fleet of high-tech warships, wipe out the Centauran fleet dispatched at the Rihnans' command, and get the Centaurans to join *our* newly declared Empire. There's a capture-and-rescue subplot followed by the expeditionary force careering across the galaxy to intercept and warn the main Earth fleet of the ambush awaiting it, followed in turn by a sequence of space battles which seems to owe equally to C. S. Forester and to a particularly elaborate pinball machine.

Victory is Earth's, except that there's a mysterious antennaed humanoid race skulking around in the margins. The whole thing—the Rihnan ascendancy and the human conquest—has been manipulated by these Alkoran with their higher mental powers. The protagonist slinks away: "He did not feel like the conqueror of the galaxy." And that's about all there is to this exercise in rug-pulling—a wrinkle in who's top dog, without any suggestion that that's not necessarily the right question, or that there might be a better way to do business than military conquest. The whole thing is cardboard—not just the characters, but also the plot, the settings, the motivations, and the thought. P. Schuyler Miller (*Astounding*, September 1957) said of the Ace Double version, "Doc Smith makes his unbelievable goings-on pretty nearly believable, and Lan Wright just fills in the formula." But the readers voted all four installments into first place.

Wright's *New Worlds* Profile in **46** says that he "has always felt that the main theme of science fiction will centre on good quality space stories. 'Every science fiction writer,' he says, 'has at some time or other written about a human-dominated Galaxy, but to my knowledge, no-one has ever tried to picture the actual overall accomplishment of that domination. It is a vast, fascinating theme and it filled most of a seven week period when I was laid up with pneumonia.... The story is also one good example of the co-operation and assistance afforded by the editor of *New Worlds*—John Carnell's guiding hand is strong in the background."

After Wright, James White's "Tourist Planet" (**52-54**) is a relief, at least for a while. Dr. Lockhart is helping his old friend Hedley of the intelligence services to find out what the deal is with a rash of old people with no discernible pasts who kill themselves with a mysterious poison if interrogated. As their investigation starts to get somewhere, their facilities are inexplicably bombed, so they flee to Ireland. In successive revelations, we learn that the old folks are extraterrestrial visitors who come to Earth because it's the only habitable planet in the galaxy with an axial tilt and interesting weather and scenery, and hence is an unparalleled tourist attraction to the galactics, who live a long time and are all bored to death. The Agency that manages the tourist trade, and which had a lot to do with World War II, is now fomenting a war that will exterminate humanity, leaving the Agency to take over and colonize. (Presumably the galactics have a high tolerance for radioactivity.)

Hedley, Lockhart and company make contact with dissidents, including the beautiful Kelly (not Miss Kelly, please—"Miss" sounds like a rude word in an extraterrestrial language), who don't care for this plan and are scheming to get to the Galactic Court with the damning truth. Off they go, with a white-space-filling pit stop on a planet where Dr. Lockhart figures out in about two hours how to save the life of an ailing *Grosni*, one of a species of gigantic telepathic amoebae who wear their spaceships—any part of their bulk that won't fit gets parked in the fourth dimension. At the Galactic Court, the Earth folks discover they have been subjected to chicanery in a manner too contrived to bother relating, and overcome it in an equally contrived fashion.

White clearly has no idea at this point how to plot and pace a novel, and the longer it goes on the more he flounders and the sillier it gets. (The readers were not impressed either. Part III came in at third place in "The Literary Line-Up," very unusually for a serial installment.) Still, I find White's amateurism more attractive than Lan Wright's professionalism; White makes a stab at actual characters (Lockhart is a man with a temper who tends to lose it when the situation gets hard to understand; Kelly works hard at being stiffly intense and businesslike about her cause, but is overcome by her greed for Earth landscape and music), and there is actually something worth caring about in this book (truth, justice, the avoidance of an exterminating nuclear war), as opposed to the empty who's-gonna-win maneuvers of "Who Speaks of Conquest?"

White says, in his *New Worlds* Profile in **52**, that "Tourist Planet" was inspired by watching a World War II movie with no redeeming features except the shots of palm trees against the sunset. "I thought then, and still do, that the wild and alien beauty of far-off planets will have a tough job competing with what we have right here on Earth." Other revelations: his day job is as assistant manager of a large Belfast tailoring firm; he recently got married to "a tall willowy blonde daughter of the Emerald Isle—so we can expect his writing technique to go on improving" (the connection is not explained); and he wrote part of the novel by candlelight during a power strike, resulting in a days-long headache from eyestrain. "Tourist Planet" subsequently appeared as half of an Ace Double under the title *The Secret Visitors*. SF critic Rich Horton says the book seems to be about 10,000 words shorter than the serial and has a "radically different" ending, without going into detail—but he too uses phrases like "extravagantly silly" and "absurd," so it can't have been too much improved.[53] Anthony Boucher said in *Fantasy & Science Fiction* that *The Secret Visitors* "makes no attempt at plausibility or even coherence" and is "composed in contented ignorance of the techniques of prose fiction."

Kenneth Bulmer's "Green Destiny" (**57-59**) is a command performance. Carnell says in **56** that Bulmer has "developed into one of the rising stars" of British SF so "we prevailed on him to write our next serial, which has more than come up to expectations." Bulmer confirms in his **57** *New Worlds* Profile that it was Carnell who "suggested it should be an undersea story," though he also says he had previously planned such a novel and then put it aside because of the large amount of research necessary for it. He declares, "The quicker the world wakes up to what will happen to the food situation the better. The hope of the world's stomach for the future is in the sea and its riches; unless we develop its resources and reap its bounty— we will starve." (Flash forward half a century, and we've reaped it all right, catastrophically depleting major food fish.) Bulmer also reveals that whenever he travels by water he gets seasick.

In the future, the oceans are the other final frontier, and the

---

53. http://www.sff.net/people/richard.horton/aced21.htm (visited 9/8/11).

story begins on a suitably portentous note:

Prologue

The water was deep and black and cold. Caught in the grip of crushing pressure, the molecules scarcely moved above the pelagic ooze, its profundity embalming reason, its bulk covering a vasty gloom, drowning a mysterious world of eternal night.

Unfortunately matters quickly segue into an all too familiar world of eternal plot devices. Captain Jeremy Dodge of the Space Force is on his way to meet a Mr. Grosvenor in an underwater hotel, escorted by the voluptuous Miss Tarrant, when he is kidnapped and pressed into manual labor (fish-herding) by one of the evil corporations that is exploiting the oceans, and then subjected to the ultimate horror: he is turned into a manfish, undergoing surgery to install gills and disable him from breathing air. (In compensation, he winds up with a pet pilot fish, called Sally.) There is intercorporate warfare undersea, drastically escalated with a barracuda onslaught; an underfunded and ineffectual United Nations regulatory effort; and something lurking in the Juliana Trench snatching an occasional submarine, which the United Nations decides to A-bomb.

Dodge of course eventually escapes and rescues Miss Tarrant from a corporate harem, and the subplots unconvincingly coalesce (the Trench-dwellers are—also of course—extraterrestrials, who never meant any harm), and the ultimate theme is exposed after Dodge is rescued and contact established with the aliens: "'But the real thing is this,' Dodge said with passionate conviction. 'Symbiosis. Ocean and Space. One and One makes the biggest number you can think of!... You can't conquer the stars until you've conquered the seas!" Etc. At the end, Dodge tells Miss Tarrant that he's getting the surgery so he can breathe air again, and she tells him she's getting gills installed; clearly made in heaven. This one became half of an Ace Double as *City*

Under the Sea, and P. Schuyler Miller (*Astounding*, July 1958) said "in spite of a wealth of detail and color, it never quite jells."

Dan Morgan's "The Uninhibited" (**62-64**) is a pleasant surprise, by comparison both to its predecessors and to Morgan's previous short fiction, which has been consistently inconsequential. Keenan, a supposed doctor, fires a tiny device into the head of a newborn infant—a telepathy suppressor. Keenan is really a Lessigian, a member of a telepathic extraterrestrial species that is trying to destroy human telepathy to save it, avoiding a pogrom until humans can be relied on not to conduct one. He is also in love with the sister of the telepathic child's mother.

Meanwhile, a surgeon comes across a peculiar needle in one of his patients' brains and removes it, and the patient is suddenly telepathic. The telepathic patient is kidnapped from the hospital. The Lessigians discover somebody powerfully telepathic is after them. The brain surgeon is recruited by a faction that knows about the Lessigians and is trying to uninhibit as many telepaths as they can find to resist the alien invasion. The thriller plot works itself out to a plausible if hardly revelatory resolution. The logic can be questioned at places but it holds up better than the preceding serials. The Lessigians are not particularly alien but for compensation are an interestingly motley crew of the weak, the ambivalent, and (it transpires) the megalomaniac. Oddly, this is the only one of the sequence that did not wind up as an Ace Double, or indeed have any US publication—the only book version I can track down is a 1961 UK paperback.

Morgan has the *New Worlds* Profile in **63**, talking entirely about the story with no biographical or other distractions (previously, he and Kippax were photographed with their guitars). He says it started with the complete and vivid visualization of the opening scene, then he discarded everything but that scene halfway through and started over. He says: "There's been a lot of argument about telepathy, one way or another. But anybody who has been married for any length of time will tell you that it is an established fact."

John Brunner's "Threshold of Eternity" (**66-68**) begins in December 1957 and has two further installments in 1958, but I'll deal with it here since it fits nicely into the sequence of serials. Like its four predecessors, it went straight to original paperback, and like three of them (and Tubb's "Star Ship," *New Worlds*' first indigenous novel-length serial) it became half of an Ace Double. Good place for it, too. Brunner never permitted it to be reprinted, or tried to expand it, as he routinely did with many later short novels.

Red, a sculptor, is minding his business in Northern California when there's a flash of light and suddenly there appear a young Frenchwoman, usually resident in London, and a man injured and unconscious. The latter, when he wakes up, persuades Red to handle a mysterious luminescent rod, and bingo! They're all in the future, 4070 to be precise. From this point, the story is so stuffed full of plot I can scarcely bear to retrace it. Here is a sample from the synopsis introducing part 3:

> Red and Chantal discover that the human race in this period are fighting a losing battle against an unde-fined enemy which is complicated by the presence at a number of points in the structure of the Universe by [sic] a Being of four dimensions. Warps in the Time continuum are breaking further and further back in history as the Being is affected by three-dimensional power surges from the opposing forces.... As Magwa-reet's anchor team approach the temporal surge indi-cated on the Time map where Wymarin is thought to have disappeared their ship is confronted by a gigan-tic Enemy spaceship, a huge black rod-like structure which could easily turn the Sun nova.... In the resultant battle another Time peak overlaps the 20th-century and transfers a war party of Croceraunian warriors from the 23rd-century into Russia.

Of course Red and Chantal prove to have a central role in all this hyper-brouhaha, and by the time he's through Brunner has not only saved the universe as we know it but has also accounted for the disappearance of Ambrose Bierce and the *Mary Celeste* as well as the appearance of Kaspar Hauser. It probably hangs together about as well as could be expected, but ultimately it's just Too Much. This one takes too closely to heart the readers' earlier complaints about near horizons. The inspiration is obvious and Brunner doesn't conceal it in his *New Worlds* Profile in **66**. He says

> all I've tried to do...is to write an adventure story which reflects in its development a few unprovable but to my mind stimulating speculations about the nature of the universe—particularly time—and the place of human thought in the whole scheme.... This undertaking is not a new idea. The grand master of the form used to be A. E. van Vogt.... He mingled philosophy and metaphysics with his science, and this seems to be a commendable practice within limits, for to declare that science is nothing but the truth and the key to the whole truth smacks unpleasantly of dogma.

§

As noted, there is less use of reprints than in the past, and in particular less use of reprints by marquee names. The most notable exception is Heinlein's "The Menace from Earth" (**64**), which Carnell notes was published in *Fantasy & Science Fiction* a few months earlier. This, in case you've repressed it, is about the 15-year-old girl on the Moon who is concerned that a visiting actress is going to steal her boyfriend, who she doesn't really acknowledge is her boyfriend. There is one interesting piece of usage, after our heroine has broken both arms and is in the hospital, and a nurse is feeding her: "Hush,' she said and gagged me with a spoon." Could this be Heinlein's greatest, though hitherto unheralded, contribution to the development of English, overshadowing "waldo" and "grok"?[54] Heinlein of course has the *New Worlds* Profile in this issue, with one of the more unflattering photos of him I have seen; he is holding a rather uncomfortable-looking cat, who allegedly is "Pete," of *The Door into Summer*. Otherwise, the profile says nothing interesting or novel.

Carnell completes the trinity of 1950s SF prestige with Arthur C. Clarke and Isaac Asimov, both with fairly trivial stories. Clarke's "Royal Prerogative" (**55**) is reprinted from the July 1955 *Fantasy & Science Fiction*, where it was titled "?"; it has also appeared as "This Earth of Majesty" and "Refugee."[55] In the story, the Prince of Wales, who has been kept by his handlers from going into space, stows away. Asimov's "The Message" (**54**), two pages from the February 1956 *Fantasy & Science Fiction*, explains Kilroy, and there's not too much more to be said about it.

There's also a Sturgeon story, "The Clinic" (**46**) from *Star Science Fiction Stories* 2, presented with some fanfare by Carnell: "There is always a first time for everything, but we didn't expect to wait so long for a Ted Sturgeon short story, especially after the success of his *The Dreaming Jewels* in Nova Novels." This is typical Sturgeon, simultaneously appealing

---

54. For anyone who has forgotten, "Gag me with a spoon" dominated slang discourse in the US for about 15 minutes around 1987. Heinlein's is the earliest use of the phrase I have seen.

55. *Fantasy & Science Fiction* held a contest to rename the story, and in the October 1955 issue, announced the name of the person who won, but not the winning title. The story appeared as "This Earth of Majesty" in *The Best from Fantasy and Science Fiction, Fifth Series* (edited by Anthony Boucher, Doubleday, 1956), suggesting that that title was the contest winner. In Clarke's next collection, *The Other Side of the Sky* (Harcourt, Brace & World, 1958), the story appeared as "Refugee," and a "Bibliographical Note" confirmed that editor Boucher found that title unsatisfactory, and settled on "This Earth of Majesty" after the contest. Presumably "Royal Prerogative" was Carnell's invention.

and frustrating, about a mysterious patient at an amnesia clinic which turns out to be where telepathic aliens send those who have lost their telepathy, since they have to start from scratch with language. The aliens start to figure out that they should stay on Earth where they are whole people rather than return to their home where they will at best be cripples. The question is posed what kind of human woman would be attracted to total amnesics, the answer being one whose own past is too painful to remember. It's the usual Sturgeon mix of brilliant, sentimental and didactic. The readers placed it fourth in the issue.

The best of the reprinted stories is probably Chad Oliver's "Artifact" (46), which first appeared in *Fantasy & Science Fiction*, June 1955. An archaeologist is summoned to Mars to investigate a find of primitive tools and discovers the surviving Martian culture, which is anything but primitive. Oliver's stories never quite achieved greatness but almost always had a quiet dignity and charm that were rare in magazine SF: gravitas without pomp.

The rest of the reprints are unremarkable either in content or authorship and we shall return to them later. For the most part, it appears that some writers simply submitted a number of stories both to US and British markets, as Carnell had said was the case in the early 1950s, rather than Carnell's cherry-picking his favorites from US sources—though in at least one case, Silverberg's, he invited the author to submit stories already sold in the US.

§

Of the indigenous fiction, to my surprise, one of the solidest overall contributions is that of J. T. McIntosh, whose four long stories collectively are a considerable improvement over most of his prior appearances in *New Worlds* and his earlier and later stories in *Science Fantasy*, though none of them is as impressive as "Bluebird World" from *New Worlds* in 1955. Had I started out reading these I might have had a considerably different and much more favorable impression of McIntosh's work.

"The Solomon Plan" (44) is quite reminiscent in plot of the second half of "The ESP Worlds" from 1952: find the dangerous secret of the seemingly innocuous colony planet. Welkin, historian and spy, arrives on Bynald to discover what's going on: the place has about half the population and considerably fewer riches than it ought to. Several previous Earth spies have disappeared. Everybody knows Welkin is a spy, and he knows the people he is dealing with know he's a spy and are engaged in counter-espionage. One of them is Ronnie, the daughter of one of the local counter-espionage guys, and not as patriotic as some think she ought to be. Apparently her father is perfectly content that she get killed in the course of (his) business. There is a passing reference to the Solomon Plan in his thoughts—he's glad he really doesn't know what it is. (George Solomon is the George Washington figure on this planet.)

Welkin snoops around, accompanied by Ronnie, who has become captivated by him and switches sides. He discovers a remarkable dearth of historical writing and research on the planet, learns that a lot of people seem to disappear on Bynald—but not the dissenters. The plan, he figures out, is that large numbers of fanatically loyal people are being stored in suspended animation. Several hundred years hence all will be awakened at once, creating the population base to start an economic explosion and then seek galactic domination militarily. Next task: escape with his skin, bargaining with the fact that his shirt buttons have been transmitting his conversations to waiting Earth ships, and Ronnie's too if possible—though the Bynald machers are extremely reluctant to let her go, for no particular reason I can see. The secret's already out, and she didn't have any inside knowledge anyway. Nonetheless they shoot her non-fatally as she and Bynald enter the rescue ship.

McIntosh works pretty hard at portraying the entirely chaste relationship between the older, married, and conflicted Welkin, and Ronnie, who is young and flirtatious and doesn't know her own mind too well. He is hampered as usual by his unquestioning adherence to the social attitudes of his day. For example, when Welkin wants to know something about local sexual customs, he asks: "How are morals on Bynald?" But overall the story is pleasant and entertaining, free of the (to my taste) gross affronts to logic and plausibility that often mar McIntosh's work. (The locals' refusal to let Ronnie go quietly is, in context, a relatively small affront to logic.) This story was reprinted without acknowledgment in the April 1959 *Satellite*.

McIntosh has half the *New Worlds* Profiles page, and he says:

> I have always preferred not to have the hero marry the heroine, if possible, and in "The Solomon Plan" I managed this by having her a little too young and him a little too old. I liked this story—I always like writing spy stories. I feel that detective stories cannot be done very successfully in science fiction, but spy stories are just right for the medium.
>
> With luck we shall all live to see the day when science fiction writers try to do as little as possible within the framework of their stories, instead of as much as possible. I think—and hope—the genre is coming to the end of the throw-everything-at-the-reader era.[56]
>
> "The Solomon Plan" is one story in which quite a lot of time is taken to say very little. You are simply invited to come by Bynald with Adrian Welkin and see why a world which should be rich is poor—and to meet a girl who wants to be a heroine.

McIntosh's "Empath" (**50**) is another fairly long novelette, quite readable if you don't think too much about it. Protagonist Betty Lincoln is snatched by thugs and framed for throwing a man off a high roof. The man was an empath. "It isn't telepathy. No one can pick words or ideas out of another person's brain—yet. It's a sensitivity to aura. To feelings. Mostly, the

---

56. McIntosh expressed similar sentiments in his letter in "Postmortem" in 34, discussed in chapter 4.

atmosphere created by a lot of people, close to you. Sometimes just the attitude of one person." That's what Tim, another empath, says later. Meanwhile, Tim sees immediately that Betty is innocent. The cops let her go, but the main thug is waiting for her in her apartment with a gun. She outwits him and beats the crap out of him, completely implausibly but at least it's a refreshing change, and calls the cops who have just let her go.

There are legit empaths and rogue empaths, and the latter—known as the Circle—are trying to kill the former. In an extrasensory cat-and-mouse game in a public park the Circle is vanquished, at least locally. Betty is revealed as an empath herself, and she gets her man, i.e. Tim. There is some basic implausibility; for starters, the proposition that anyone would care enough about this rather limited talent to engage in a murderous conspiracy over it, especially since empaths have only been around for about five years—that's a fast job of developing identity politics and organizing around it. Betty is an "angel"; after a limited nuclear exchange, the rich have all decided to live underground and the poor are consigned to vulnerable high-rises, hence moles and angels. This too seems pretty unlikely to me, though McIntosh's description of ostentatious subterranean mansions facing onto 24' x 24' corridors is amusing. But the story moves along quickly and economically and the viewpoint character is appealing, so none of these credulity-stretchers seriously impairs readability. Judith Merril gave it an Honorable Mention in her annual anthology.

Again McIntosh has half of the *New Worlds* Profiles on the inside front cover, and he says:

> "Empath" is one of those stories which some people consider new and original and others regard as the same old line merely given a new twist. What do you do with a new idea, anyway? Do you plug it until everybody is sick of it, or do you toss it out casually and be accused of wasting a good idea?

In this story I have gone back to one of the basic things in science fiction—the situation being that someone finds he can do something different. I believe that the idea of empathy has a firmer believe [sic] in common experience than telepathy or clairvoyance. We are all to some extent sensitive to atmosphere—we can all sense danger, and the more we have experienced danger the more we trust this instinct. Whether "Empath" is a good story or not, it is one that somebody had to write sooner or later.

McIntosh is back in the next issue with "Report on Earth" (**51**), which also has its problems of plausibility and logic but handily overcomes them. Wallin, a Quinnan, is mind-transmitted to Earth to hang out for 50 years or so and report back on whether there's any reason not to exterminate humanity and take over the planet. As genocidal monsters go, the Quinnans are highly moral: they only transmit their minds into young, physically healthy madmen. It is explained that Frank Connor, the former occupant of Frank Connor's body, is now entirely dead, except that his memories are readily available to Wallin (albeit distorted by Frank's insanity), except for a blank spot, "something dark and secret," that wasn't available to Frank either. "Though he used Connor's brain, his capacities in no way depended on its capacities. He was Wallin in every significant mental respect. He could have used the brain of a cat or a dog in the same way." Oh, and it turns out that Wallin's mind is about 50% slower than a human mind. This is all very dodgy as cognitive science, even of the speculative sort, but then cognitive science didn't really exist in 1956.

In any case it's all just stage-setting. The now-replaced Frank lives in a rooming house and is a remittance man. Another resident, Louise, for some mysterious reason goes around with him and puts him to bed at night, accompanies him on walks, and generally takes care of him. A second woman, Hari, works as a model. As Frank/Wallin figures out what he is going to do on

Earth, he is attracted to both. When Louise flees, he tracks her down, and she shows him the place at the center of his missing memory, tells him what it is that's missing. She knows he really isn't Frank any more, but she has come to love whomever he has become. As he has come to admire humanity, he has ceased to be a Quillan. So we're going to get a good report card and not be annihilated after all. It's an interestingly Sturgeonesque plot with no Sturgeonesque flavor at all—by comparison, it's dry and remote—but that isn't necessarily bad; it can be just as affecting to let the reader do the work as to tell the reader what it means.

"Unit" (**55**), one of the few McIntosh stories from Carnell's magazines to be anthologized (in Groff Conklin's *Five-Odd* (Pyramid, 1964)), takes the dodgy cognitive science to a new level. It's about people who are cleared—not in the Dianetics sense of supposedly removing obstacles to their buried memories, but having their memories stripped entirely so they can start over. It is posited that after this process, it takes three or four months to restore the person to full adult human functioning—plus. The "weeds" (neuroses and everything else, it seems) are cleared from the mind, and they take a long time to grow back; if you're already an adult, you can recognize them as they grow, and pull them. The cleared are (re) brought up in groups of five called Units, which "could do things no electronic brain could do and no group of a thousand individuals could do. You see, the Units never made mistakes."

Each has a Unit Father, a sort of team manager, to take care of the practical stuff like booking accommodations. The protagonist is a Unit Father, recruited by one of his old friends after being fired from his executive job, because the friend's daughter Lorraine is about to be cleared and he wants somebody to keep an eye on her. So she gets wiped and turned into a Unit with four others, and they and their Unit Father head off to another planet with an overt problem-solving assignment and a covert mission to track down the Traders, a conspiracy organized for the dastardly purpose of *evading export-import duties*. On this planet, speaking of identity politics, a great schism has developed between one hemisphere, which has decided to exalt all things of Earth, and the other, which eschews Earth and everything associated with it, including clothing styles:

> A child of five, sex unknown, went past wearing what looked like a model spaceship. A girl hobbled past in a dress shaped like a water-pipe. A man wore a box-shaped garment about his hips and a shirt in the shape of a sphere. The sphere idea was quite common. Apparently the perfect sphere was passed as non-Terran. The next man we saw wore what looked like a big cannon-ball about his middle and smaller cannon-balls everywhere else. A girl came along in the first skin-tight outfit we'd seen, with holes cut for her naked breasts to stick through.

McIntosh gets away with this essentially on style, and with plenty of other things that strain credulity. (Lorraine, after being cleared, observes that having lost her memory, she doesn't know whether she is a virgin or not. One would think she could find out, or at least make a pretty good guess, easily enough.) The story, with its reasonably fast-moving thriller plot, is told in a plain, stripped-down, first-person conversational fashion (the quote above is not the only use of the expository "you see"), so it all goes down very smoothly, and once you swallow the initial implausibility of the clearing process and the resulting Units, the subsequent whoppers are side issues. You don't have to believe six impossible things to go on with the story, you can just let them pass.

This contrasts sharply with his annoying *Science Fantasy* stories from this same time period or later (like "200 Years to Christmas" and "Planet on Probation" in 1959 and 1960), where the implausibilities are too central to ignore.[57] Maybe Carnell

57. See our companion volume, *Strange Highways*, concerning *Science Fantasy*.

decided that the McIntosh stories making the most sense should go in his pure SF magazine, while the rest went into the (partly) fantasy magazine? Seems unlikely. For whatever reason, "Unit" is McIntosh's last story in *New Worlds*. He had three more in *Science Fantasy* after this point. Apart from those, though he remained reasonably prolific into the mid-'60s, his SF stories appeared only in the US magazines.

§

The hardest-working contributor to these issues is probably James White, the house moralist—not in any priggish sense, but there's always a moral as well as a technical problem in his stories, and the main or viewpoint characters are not always on the right side of it. The last of his stories in these 1956-57 issues, "Sector General" (**65**)—which is also the first in the series that occupied White literally for the next 40 years—illustrates the point.

Conway, a fairly new doctor at a space-station hospital for all species, responds to one alien medical emergency, watches surgery on another alien, all the while seething at the Monitors, who have some vaguely described military role and some equally vaguely described position of authority in the hospital. Conway hates violence and all those who would perpetrate it. Then he responds to another emergency, consisting of a number of casualties of a *war*, and he gets a lecture/tongue-lashing *in medias res* from one Williamson, a Monitor, about how he lives a sheltered life and the Monitors give up their freedom to protect everybody else's, and arrange wars in a damage-limited sort of way whenever there are belligerents who just won't be dissuaded. We are asked to believe that Conway—presumably an educated and sophisticated member of his culture—has never heard any of this rationale before.

A ship with an apparently injured pilot smashes into the station, and its occupant, thrown free, is lashing about derangedly, destroying equipment and threatening everybody's safety. Conway is the only person who can get to the scene, and he is given a pistol; after considerable agonizing, he shoots the pilot (it is suggested that the pilot would want to die under these circumstances). Afterwards, as Conway is reviling himself because he has "violated the prime ethic of his profession and killed an intelligent being," it is revealed that what he killed was actually a pet, "the equivalent of a fear-maddened dog." So White pulls the rug out from under what was a contrived set-up to begin with. On the other hand, at least he is seriously trying to frame a substantial issue, and as a moral document it beats the hell out of *Starship Troopers*.

This sort of rug-pulling is characteristic of White's stories. In "Red Alert" (**43**), a fearsome alien invasion fleet comprised of many species enters the solar system apparently bent on conquest, telepathically stoking militarism and racial and ideological hostility, but tortured with guilt about the terrible things they are doing. They work up to the strategic moment when the world's leaders will simultaneously address their populations... and, telepathically compelled, announce that the aliens have come to rescue them from the imminent nova of their sun. 97% of the population is saved, since ramping up war fever has gotten everybody so organized they're ready to march into the spaceships right away. This one was voted first by the readers, over a pretty good John Brunner novelette.

It's followed in the next issue by "Question of Cruelty" (**44**), in which another crew of marauding aliens—dying of radiation poisoning but determined to carry out their mission before they die—blows up a spaceship in low orbit en route to exterminating all higher life on Earth. They retrieve what's left of its occupant and reconstitute him, telepathically finding him vicious and brutish. These aliens are the remnants of a highly civilized and pacifistic race, unique in a galaxy where every other known species is genocidally evil—so now their Execution Ships stamp out young intelligent species before they can grow up and attack. But wait! What they have seized is an experimental monkey. Even though the animal badly injured several people, the humans nonetheless sent him into space with a device to kill him painlessly when the experiment was finished, and with some cake to make life more pleasant in the interim. So here's a species that will become peaceful, but won't forget how to fight, without being needlessly cruel. We likes them! Execution cancelled.

Well, that's a whole lot of inference from mind-reading a chimpanzee, but in the *New Worlds* Profile we see that White is preaching to the converted, i.e., himself. The story "grew out of a Willy Ley article I read on orbital rockets—including the need for data on the effects of such orbiting on the flesh and blood component in such a rocket—and a personal aversion for the down-beat type of science fiction story which writes the human race off as a planetful of juvenile delinquents. On the whole I think that we are pretty nice people—this even includes myself sometimes—and we have a long and interesting future ahead of us."

"Patrol" (**55**) posits an invasion of Earth by extraterrestrial insects with guns—very small guns, to be sure, but there are a lot of them, and they can inflict pretty nasty wounds—and an expedition against them, in which the mysterious lieutenant who has been put in charge proves bent on making peace with them. The virtues of merciful forbearance are foregrounded by their failure in "To Kill or Cure" (**58**). An alien spaceship crashes in the Derryveagh Mountains. The military relief crew sent by helicopter, thinking they are looking for a downed plane, crash-lands in bad weather. They enter the ship, find repellent-looking aliens in various states of serious injury, and try to patch some of them up. When they try to stop the aliens from communi-cating with their compatriots, things go south fast and a pitched battle ensues. In the middle of it the alien mothership shows up and now it's the aliens who are patching up the humans, i.e. replacing the limbs they have burned off. This is a very well-drawn picture of people acting in fear and under pressure, ulti-mately resolved by White's seemingly unshakeable confidence that eventually good will and good sense will prevail.

In "False Alarm" (**61**) they prevail only by accident. Three men are exploring the base left behind by the aliens introduced in White's first story, "Assisted Passage" (**19**). They discover a communications device and activate it. Two of them decide they will ambush the alien rescue ship so humans will have the benefit of their technology. The protagonist objects but is overpowered. Turns out the communications device is actually a nova alarm, and the aliens show up as in "Red Alert" with enough ships to evacuate the whole solar system.

The most eccentric of these stories is "The Lights Outside the Windows" (**56**)—nominally a short story, but running some 28 magazine pages—which must set some sort of record for contrivance. Adult men can't tolerate space travel, because if they look at the stars, they go nuts. Women don't have that problem. However, women don't have all the necessary aptitudes to run spaceships. So the ships are captained by women and crewed by men who are conditioned temporarily to an emotional age of about 4, so the captains are also babysitters. Captain Miller has had to ship out with a crew including one conditioned man with whom she has a, er, close emotional relationship, and there's an emergency, and they have to go EVA, with her... husband? lover? (the point is to keep the reader guessing)... blindfolded so he won't see the stars and lose his mind. This is not necessarily a very good story, but it's certainly an interesting and clever one, with White attempting to invert some gender roles while he remains chained to them in other respects, and also slyly exploiting a slightly prurient ambiguity—just what male intimate of Captain Miller *is* this guy?

I think it's fair to say that all of White's stories here have something wrong with them, but in part that's because they are more ambitious in their unpretentious way than most of the other contents of the magazine. White's propensity to bite off more than he can chew seems much more admirable than the opposite propensity of some of the magazine's other writers.

§

E. C. Tubb, a dominant contributor in earlier years and one who was notably improving, has a much reduced presence during this period, all of it under the Alan Guthrie pseudonym—both circumstances undoubtedly the result of his becoming editor of *Authentic Science Fiction*. Carnell plays the pseudonym game—the blurb for Tubb's story in **56** says "Mr. Guthrie's literary efforts are none too frequent, but when they do appear they are usually worthwhile." In "The Pensioners" (**43**), some strange folks move into the neighborhood, don't get their electricity or phone hooked up, and prove upon investigation by the insurance salesman next door to be about 150 years old. The gimmick is the same as John R. Pierce's "Invariant" from *Astounding* 12 years earlier, and the story is (unusually for the new Tubb) much longer than its substance will support.

The equally lackluster "Emergency Call" (**44**) is a routine space-disaster story (meteor in the oxygen supply) with the melodrama pumped up by the fact that one of the crew members is unknowingly the son of the captain, who sacrifices himself so his son and the rest of the crew will survive.

"Thirty-Seven Times" (**55**) is an improvement, a tight and clever time travel story about a man who keeps coming back after death, except that for him, obviously, it's before his death. Improvement continues in "The Greater Ideal" (**56**), a lacerating piece of cynicism about a pair of spacemen, one idealistic and the other grasping and cynical, who encounter a disabled alien spaceship among the asteroids and debate how to deal with it, with consequences fatal both in the short term and the long.

§

Now to the up-and-comers, writers of promise who got a later start or developed more slowly than McIntosh and White. John Brunner's long novelette "Host Age" (**43**) proposes a new and mysterious plague that kills 10% of those infected and defies treatment because the microorganism constantly mutates. There's one antibiotic that seems to have promise, but whenever anyone tries to work with it, their lab burns down or blows up in seemingly impossible ways, with saboteurs getting past their airtight security. What's the answer? Time travelers! In the future, people have tuned up their immune systems to deal with almost anything known and medical science has fallen into desuetude. This new plague has been unleashed by enemy aliens and is killing 90% of those who contract it. They've come back to give it to us so we'll have to become selectively immune and figure out how to deal with it, thereby saving their bacon in the future. The logic sounds a bit strained in synopsis, but this is actually a pretty nifty story, the best of Brunner's *New Worlds* contributions so far, reminiscent (or should I say prescient?) in its nightmarish quality of "Some Lapse of Time" in *Science Fantasy* ten years later, though much more clumsily done. (For example, the protagonist is unmarried; it is revealed that this is because he's in love with his best friend's wife, or was, since she just died of the plague; but nothing turns on this, so it's just a distraction.)

Brunner's *New Worlds* Profile is in this issue. He would be 21 or 22; his photo looks about 17, hair slicked back, wispy moustache, head cocked, knowing look. There's nothing of substance in the text. In the next issue (**44**) he has "Thing Friday" (**44**), a simple and affecting story about a dying man who has been marooned on a distant planet for the last 30-plus years, and the beetle-like inhabitant who has taken care of him when he needed it for all that time. He overdoes things a bit in "Fair" (**45**), which goes in Kornbluthian mode for most of its length. A man in a xenophobic cold-war, balance-of-terror near future is walking through a large and meretricious "Marching Morons"-style carnival operation thinking "Altar at Midnight"-ish thoughts, since he had something unspecified to do with bringing the world to this pass, though now he's down and out because his mother was foreign born and no one will hire him. But Brunner is not one to keep this up: his protagonist goes into the newest attraction, a sort of virtual reality parlor, and discovers that it is really a device for promoting tolerance and reducing international tensions in its prurient way (e.g., the fare includes African and Russian Jewish weddings and their sequelae).

Those three stories, though flawed, paint an attractive picture of an ambitious young writer looking to get better in a variety of directions. Unfortunately things go downhill from there, in equally various ways. "Two by Two" (**47**) posits the end of the world: a man is exploring the Moon when the Sun goes nova during the lunar night and subsides in time for him to decide he'd rather head back and die on Earth rather than the Moon. When he gets there he discovers nothing is left alive except bacteria, so he realizes he's got to contribute himself to the cause, and marches out the airlock to Brunner's quote or paraphrase of the Old Testament re Noah. It's well enough done except for the small fact that, notwithstanding a different Biblical metaphor, it's a reprise of Bester's very well-known "Adam and No Eve," from 1941. Nonetheless it appeared in Brunner's first collection, *No Future In It* (1962), and was anthologized a couple of times, once by Brian Aldiss.

In "To Make a Man" (**48**), the protagonist, a brash young cyberneticist, rubs his elders the wrong way by questioning one of their number's denial that artificial intelligence will ever be developed. He's tossed out of his job and goes to work for industry, where he makes an intelligent robot. The key is to give them hunger (for energy) and the drive for self-preservation and let them develop on their own, rather than try to program them entirely. Unfortunately Brunner can't resist the cheap sentimentality; in the last line, one of the robots says "Da-da!" and it is not discussing art movements.

In the jokey "Out of Order" (**58**), the foundations of civilization are threatened when the worldwide computerized just-in-time ordering system fails to deliver the goods. After several labored pages of investigation, it is revealed that the purchaser said, "I want it yesterday!" so that's when the system delivered it, and that's why nobody could find it. "Eye of the Beholder" (**60**), previously in the January 1957 *Fantastic Universe*, is a heavy-handed morality play: people are stranded on a hot desert planet. They find a hut with a stack of splendid paintings; what could have happened to the artist? Suddenly a huge and fierce-looking beast shows up and they shoot it, figuring that earlier it got the artist; but we know all along that it *is* the artist, notwithstanding these crass humans' inability to see past its outward form.

§

Brian Aldiss's half-dozen stories here are a mixed lot, none quite his best, though all perfectly respectable in their company. There's nothing here quite as good as, say, "The Failed Men" in *Science Fantasy.* His breakthrough will come in 1958 with "Poor Little Warrior!" and "The New Father Christmas" in *Fantasy & Science Fiction,* among others.

The best of this lot is "Gesture of Farewell" (**61**), a harbinger of things to come, dense and knotty if not entirely successful. Lester Nixon has brought his family to Risim, where he is engaged in terraforming this planet, won in a war of interstellar extermination, that is most likely booby-trapped as all the rest of them have been. He's dedicated to his work but just doesn't seem to be able to get it right with his family, especially his uncomprehending wife, who hates the whole venture and is getting pretty fed up with him. He takes his daughter on an ocean-sowing voyage; she falls overboard and gets chewed up in the propeller. This makes two, since his son was killed in an earlier accident. He promises his distraught wife that they will return to Earth. Then the booby trap is found. Nixon heads there immediately; his wife shows up. They go into a little room in an alien artifact, and a recorded voice tells them there's a test. They have five seconds for someone to stick his head into an aperture to be annihilated, or the planet will blow up in 28 days. Nixon contributes his head, sacrificing himself for his cause and simultaneously expiating his guilt and escaping his failed marriage. It's completely contrived, but the set-up is well enough done and sufficiently anchored in sensory detail and in dialogue that it doesn't much matter. It's a worthy tune-up for Aldiss's best stories of the 1960s like "A Kind of Artistry" and "Man in His Time."

"There Is a Tide" (**44**) is Aldiss's familiar story about a future Africa. The Africans are moving right along building a prosperous civilization when Lake Victoria blows a gasket, sending a torrent of water to wreak havoc to the south, while millions are faced with death by drought as the Nile dries up. It is revealed in passing that the Plague that has been mentioned killed all the white people. "Now we negroes, in our turn, stood at the bar of history." I never quite got the point of this story. Premature post-colonial resentment? The Mau Mau uprising would have been going for three years or so when this was written. But like most of Aldiss, even this early, it's well enough done. "Psyclops" (**49**) is another near miss to my taste: it's about a telepathic fetus whom his father, approaching death, contacts telepathically in a doomed attempt to stave off disaster for him and his mother. The degree of communication that *is* achieved in the failed effort is far too much to swallow. Judith Merril gave this one an Honorable Mention in her annual anthology.

"Conviction" (**51**) is another misfire, but a revealing one. David Stevens, arbitrarily chosen while down at the reagent docks on Ganymede, has received a summons from the Supreme Ultralords of the Home Galaxy to be put on trial to determine the fate of humanity.

> Squaring his shoulders, Stevens walked between the massed shapes of the rulers of the Home Galaxy. Although it had been expressly stated before he left Earth that no powers, such as telepathy, which he did not possess would be used against him, he could feel a weight of mental power all around him. Strange faces watched him, some just remotely human, strange robes stirred as he brushed past them. The diversity! he thought. The astounding, teeming womb of the universe! [But later:] "Irritation means unbalance," said

Deln Phi J. Bunswacki. It was the only sentence he spoke throughout the interview. On his shoulders, a mighty brain syphoned its thoughts beneath a transparent skull-case; he wore what appeared to be a garishly cheap blue pin-stripe suit, but the stripes moved as symbiotic organisms plied up and down them ceaselessly, ingurgitating any microbes which might threaten the health of Deln Phi J. Bunswacki.

This is not a very good story (it was in Aldiss's first UK collection *Space, Time, And Nathaniel* but omitted from the US collection *No Time Like Tomorrow*), but, as the quoted passages show, it displays Aldiss's ambivalence toward the givens of SF, vacillating between homage and mockery. The story sums up his SF career in a nutshell. Of course Aldiss might say that mockery is the sincerest form of homage, a point with some merit.

"Oh, Ishrael!" (**58**) is a slightly overwrought item about a Berkshire farmer named David Dale who has found one Ishrail, who claims to be an extraterrestrial and bears tales of galactic war. Dale has foolishly brought him to a hospital. Now they have declared Ishrail insane and won't let him out or let David see him. As David argues against their dogmatic smugness it becomes pretty clear who's crazy. So why does the title say Ishrael and the story, Ishrail? Presumably more of Carnell's nonexistent proofreading. But I took a look at Aldiss's collection *The Airs of Earth* to see if Aldiss had straightened it out in later publications, and discovered he did more than that. The story is titled "O Ishrail!" and Toto, we're not in Berkshire any more, we've been press-ganged into Aldiss's future history. Or, as the Author's Note puts it, now the story is one of that book's "slices off the enormous carcass of the future": "The Mental Health Ship *Cyberqueen* lay quietly against a long wharf. Alone in one of its many cabins, Davi Dael sat waiting." The hospital waiting room's touch of chromium has become the ship's "faumium fittings." Etc. Aldiss's blurb in the book says 40 million years have passed. He should have stayed at home. The revision adds nothing but distraction.

Aldiss's last contribution in these issues is "The Ice Mass Cometh" (**66**), which posits that the Russians have discovered there's really no continent of Antarctica, it's just floating ice, and what will the Russians do? Tow it north into the Atlantic, ruining the climate and commerce of Europe and America? Silliness is redeemed only by brevity.

§

Kenneth Bulmer is often spoken of with Brunner as one of the mainstays of Carnell's magazines. To my taste he is not in the same league by a large margin, though there's no doubt he's striving to get better and to diversify his output. His novelette "The Smallest Ally" (**45**) is a considerable improvement for him. It's another unabashed space opera, except that this one, unlike some of its predecessors, has enough of a story to carry it along despite the relatively crude writing.

Earth has been contacted by the extraterrestrial humanoid Spaceborn and negotiations are commencing. Meanwhile, the aliens snatch an Earth spaceship into one of their five-mile-long ships in order to study us to see if they can get an edge. They manage to get the humans out of their ship and locked up, but in time-honored pulp fashion don't guard them very well, so the humans sneak back to their ship, get a culture of bacteria, and sneak it into the aliens' air plant (one of them knocks out and ties up a Spaceborn and takes his uniform, and there's not much security at the air plant). So now the air plant starts pumping out high-oxygen Earth-type air instead of low-oxygen alien air, discombobulating the Spaceborn long enough for the characters to escape. Spaceborn yesterday, anybody? This is a lot of implausibility to swallow, but enough happens and there is enough of an attempt at characterization other than with funny hats to make it reasonably entertaining. This one could have appeared in *Planet Stories* comfortably enough.

Bulmer gets his *New Worlds* Profile in this issue, first of several, in which it is revealed that since his photograph was taken he has grown a pointed beard and was mistaken for Fletcher Pratt in New York, where he was "official British representative" (i.e, winner of the poll of the Transatlantic Fan Fund, which paid for overseas travel to SF conventions by a popular SF fan each year) at the 1955 Worldcon. "His other hobbies include model ship construction, motor racing, and the study of the Napoleonic legend; psychiatrists are cordially invited to make the logical deduction." In the next issue he has "Sunk" (**46**), about double-dealing in a marine salvage operation that takes place on Venus but could just as well have been set in Florida or the Indies and published in a crime fiction magazine. It's unremarkably competent, which remains an improvement for Bulmer.

In "The City Calls" (**52**), he tries for more but doesn't make it, adopting an ostentatiously literary voice ("The orange sand that had slithered and whispered all day across the desert had grown by wind-driven stages into a ceaseless fretting torrent without demanding his attention: until now, standing awkwardly in the shadowed pit, Hunter brought his time-ensnared mind back to an annoyed understanding of the pressures of the present.") He seems to be trying to split the difference between Bradbury's Mars and E. C. Tubb's. Hunter works at a sort of terraforming station where no Terra seems to be forming, and in his spare time he and his buddy are excavating what they claim to be the site of an ancient Martian city, except that whenever anybody else comes to look, the shifting sand has covered the evidence again. They try to keep going by faking a Martian artifact, but the station gets shut down anyway. On the way out, as a big storm is brewing, Hunter breaks away and heads back to the site, which is now clearly revealed: it's where space travelers landed, set up shop, and died, thousands of years ago, as he is going to do shortly. At half the length and half the pretense it might have worked, but Bulmer doesn't have the stylistic chops to bring it off. It's a nice try, however, and provides more evidence of a writer with at least some ambition.

It's back to *Planet Stories* for the next one, "Defiance" (**61**), about which Carnell promised or warned: "Most outstanding stories, whether science fiction or in the general categories, are usually based on a simplified type of plot. From there on it is the author's skill that develops the magic to hold the reader." This one is *Fitzcarraldo* in space. Two scout ships, the *Outrider* and the *Courageous*, collide and crash ten miles apart on an inhospitable and rugged planet. The subspace radios are trashed. The front half of one ship and the rear half of the other are destroyed. The solution is obvious. So this one is a Sweat Opera or an Exertion Romance, engagingly enough written to be tolerable or even amusing. One guess as to the name of the cobbled-together ship.

"Native Law" (**62**) reads like an *Astounding* reject: Earth contacts aliens, one of them arrives and kills the customs agent he deems insolent, and by the way he's an alien aristocrat and can do anything he wants to with lesser breeds—that's what their law says, and their law applies everywhere, why it says so right in their law. So the choice is between putting the alien aristocrat on trial and inviting military intervention by the aliens, or letting him get away with it, in which case the government will fall in a tide of domestic outrage. So they take the murderer to his victim's funeral, showing him that on Earth (unlike his world) everybody has a soul, even the working stiffs, thereby persuading him that he's committed a crime even under his own world's law. He remorsefully submits to justice, but the authorities contrive an acquittal so everybody's happy. This is the kind of facile resolution of a completely contrived problem that the US magazines were full of back then.

Unfortunately it's back to cliché-land in "Mission One Hundred" (**63**). Flux Navigator Bradley has flown 99 bombing runs against the alien Octos, with whom humanity is contending for planets. One more mission and he's out of there (to "Earth—and Moira."). Things go badly wrong but of course are salvaged by the skin of Bradley's teeth, other characters being dispensable, teeth and all. The only thing interesting about it is Bulmer's self-conscious adoption of a terse tough-guyish style. E.g.: "The fluxwagons were the only concrete realities in the world. Forty foot long, with control compartments above and the sealed-off bomb bays beneath, they looked like ranks of eggs in a packing factory. Eggs laid by the base ship to go winging across interplanetary space in towards the sun and Octo strongholds and there to lay their own eggs of death upon some Octo fortress or citadel...."

§

At this point, Lan Wright is of comparable prominence to Bulmer in the magazine, if not in my estimation. Wright's "Time Will Tell" (51) is at least a slight relief after the empty longueurs of "Who Speaks of Conquest?" It's an unpretentious and mildly carbonated piece of thriller-product in which Romberg, an industrial psychologist, is asked by Calder, the leader of his post-nuclear domed city-state, to investigate the increasing rate of accidents in transportation, industry, etc., looking for patterns of sabotage. Almost immediately he is robbed of the precious files, then kidnapped, coming to consciousness a month later, drug-addicted and in rags, in another domed city on the other side of the world. He looks up an old friend there who helps him get home—in disguise, since he has become a public scapegoat since his disappearance—and then he is kidnapped again. This time when he wakes up he slugs the first person who enters his locked room, who proves to be (as the author puts it) "a chit of a girl," makes his escape, and finds himself, for the first time in his life, outside. They Have All Been Lied To—it *is* possible to live outdoors, grow one's own food, etc., but the rulers of the domed city-states don't want anybody to know that because it threatens their control. The story concludes with several pages of socio-dump on that subject, on the growing psychopathology that accounts for the disastrously increasing accident rate, and on who has really been manipulating whom for the preceding 40 pages. It's all clichés, but capably manipulated, and the scenes in the depths of poverty and degradation are a modest hoot.

"And Earthly Power" (55), unfortunately, is a big step backwards. Laraby has been dispatched by the Sector Chief to Xenon with orders to kill one Vincent Audus within three weeks. Why, and who is this Audus? "That's all I can tell you, Laraby." Wound up with this contrived set-up, Laraby finds V. Audus, who proves to be the Mayor, and is Victor rather than Vincent. A detective he hires to check the archive finds out that Victor has a twin named Vincent who hasn't been seen for 20 years, and then somebody kills the detective. So Laraby kills the Mayor's evil security chief, who is the only one who could have engineered the detective's murder, and persuades the Mayor to come out to the security chief's house and let Laraby tie him up.

As expected, a delegation shows up including the just-arrived Vincent Audus, and after a certain amount of back and forth Laraby shoots them all, though not before it is revealed that Vincent was proposing to replace Victor at an interstellar conference and stand up for throwing off the colonial yoke, a cause that includes repealing the Colonial Exploitation bill ("Eight hours work a day from every native Xenian could turn the mines of this world into an Aladdin's cave.") Exactly why the Sector Chief couldn't tell his designated assassin at the outset what was going on and why this man needed killing is not explained. The story ends with a stirring speech by Laraby, which does not appear to be satirical, in support of execution without trial: "Public trials and prison sentences accomplish nothing—they only give publicity to those [for] whom publicity and martyrdom mean ultimate success.... They make their own trial.... By their own actions they condemn themselves in the eyes of those that watch them. It is on their own actions that the troubleshooters report, and it is on those reports that the Board prescribes sentence." Dick Cheney couldn't have put it better.

"And Earthly Power" is singled out for scrutiny by Brian Aldiss in his long article "British Science Fiction Now," published in his and Harry Harrison's critical journal *SF Horizons* (**2**, 1965),

in the subsection titled "The Knitter of Socks: Lan Wright."
The reference is to Wright's *New Worlds* Profile in this issue of
New Worlds, in which he says that you can plan a story before-
hand, or you can just start writing, and this story is in the latter
category: "It started with one sentence and kept growing like a
person knitting a sock who cannot turn a heel." He continues:
"When in doubt I ended a chapter and started a fresh one with a
new character—and the result surprised me. I found that it was
fascinating to write this way and the end result was much more
satisfying than if it had all been planned at the start." Aldiss has
even more to say about "And Earthly Power" and its logic, or
lack of it, than I do, and he notes the amorality of the characters,
which "suffuses the whole text," e.g., in Mayor Audus's quick
rationalization of his brother's murder.

"All That Glitters" (**59**) is another in Wright's Johnny
Dawson series, and the most inane yet. Dawson is dispatched
to the home world of the Lutherians, which is in the grip of an
epidemic. Earth wants to help, but the Lutherians, of course,
suspect the worst, and as usual are right. What Earth wants in
return for its help against the disease (which turns out to have
been planted by Earth) is a planet that produces a super-special
metal. The Lutherians give in, but their leader says it's OK,
they're just giving up the planet, not the method of refining the
metal... which is iron ore. The Lutherians win one, pleasing the
protests-too-much Dawson.

This is followed by "Mate in One" (**64**), in which the
Lutherians are menaced by the Tallitians, who clearly have been
preparing for a long time to eat the Lutherians' lunch and who
win battle after battle in clockwork fashion. Dawson warns his
boss on Earth that we'd better do something or we'll be next,
and is told they want no part of the problem. Dawson figures out
that the Tallitians are being guided by... a computer, and a big
one: "a city in itself, with hundreds of scientists and thousands
of technicians" to feed it. He advises the Lutherians to fake
a top secret crash project (people go in but don't go out, etc.)
and start a rumor that they have their own giant computer. The

rumor gets fed into the Tallitians' computer; but the Lutherians fail to act according to prediction because they really don't have the computer, meaning the Tallitians' computer is no longer accurate, and they start losing and then give up. Carnell's blurb refers to "this final story" in the series, but no such luck. There are two more to come.

Matters improve marginally in "Conquest Deferred" (66), which rehearses a standard theme amusingly: aliens deciding whether to conquer Earth are bemused by linguistic and racial differences, so they grab a couple of samples, one from the US and one from the Soviet Union. Then they learn about ideological differences and gender differences, and the Yank guy decks one of the aliens when he tries to conduct a physical examination of the Russki (sic) woman without consent. Before long they are demanding a clergyman to marry them, and the united Earth governments, who are somehow on to the aliens, have demanded that they get out of Dodge on pain of nuclear war, notwithstanding that this will render the Earth at least partly uninhabitable for us as well as the aliens. The aliens decide Earth is more trouble than it's worth, though they leave with a nagging suspicion that this might give them even more trouble later.

§

Dan Morgan has several short stories, running the gamut from A to B, or maybe from B- to D+. None of them, as noted earlier, are nearly as good as his serial "The Uninhibited." "Wunkle" (46) is a jokey story about a space expedition that finds a precognitive bear-like animal. "Controlled Flight" (47) involves a couple of crooks fleeing from justice (specifically, from Walker, a Ganymede Conditioned agent of the Interstellar Police). They hide on a colony planet which proves to have been abandoned for no reason they can discern, until they run afoul of the native parasitic intelligences that like nothing better than to take over humans for joy-rides. It's not exactly a good story, but the author appears to be a bit more engaged than in some of his others, and enough happens to make the pages worth turning. The same cannot be said of "The Little Fleet" (**50**), about a nebbish who yearns to go into space and has the model collection to prove it, but when the opportunity actually presents itself, he chickens out. Yawn.

Equally lackluster is "The Whole Armour" (**54**), in which the characters crash-land on an inhabited planet and need to fix their spaceship, but the natives are shooting at them. Eccentric Maxwell tells them they can do what they want and he won't retaliate (and they do shoot and wound him), and then he does what's necessary without being further molested. It is then revealed he is a priest. Equally gimmicky but slightly more incisive is "The Humanitarian" (**58**), in which an alien crash-lands on Earth, his food animals are lost, he's in big trouble. He shape-shifts, walks into a restaurant, encounters a butcher who is militantly carnivorous with philosophy to match. Here's the perfect food animal, who helps the alien reconcile his needs with his squeamishness about eating something intelligent. One suspects Morgan might be a vegetarian.

§

A number of prolific *New Worlds* contributors make their debuts in these issues. The most notable ingénue is J. G. Ballard, whose *New Worlds* debut, "Escapement," appears in **54**, the December 1956 issue, more or less simultaneously with "Prima Belladonna" in *Science Fantasy* (though *Science Fantasy*, as a bimonthly, would have gone on sale first; "Prima Belladonna" is described as his debut in Ballard's *New Worlds* Profile in **54**).

"Escapement" is pretty inconsequential, both in itself and by comparison to the gaudier "Prima Belladonna." The protagonist is watching television and it starts repeating itself. This keeps happening, it affects all the channels, and he tells his wife: "For some reason, I don't know why, we seem to be in a sort of circular time trap, just going round and round. You're not aware of it, and I can't find anyone else who is either." She isn't impressed, and time pops back again so his effort is wasted. After a few more iterations, he snaps out of it and wakes up half an hour later with a headache. Then his wife starts complaining that the television is repeating itself. There's not much more to it than that; it slides by pleasantly, lubricated by smooth writing.

"Build-Up" (**55**) is quite different from either of its predecessors, though like "Prima Belladonna" it is cobbled together out of some pretty mismatched materials. Titled "The Concentration City" in some reprintings, it starts:

> Noon talk on Millionth Street:
> "Sorry, these are the West millions. You want 9775335d East."
> "Dollar five a cubic foot? Sell!"

So we start out slick and fast in *Galaxy* country, then meet a character named M. who is being interrogated by the police. On the blotter he's Franz M., but we quickly learn his name is Mattheson, and the Kafka homage is forgotten.[58] In the gargantuan enclosed city, Mattheson dreams of free space. He makes a model glider and dreams of flying are alluded to as he test-flies the model in an enclosed stadium. But that goes nowhere too, and eventually M. sets off on a Super-Sleeper train, looking to find free space at the end of the line. He travels west for days. Suddenly the train is moving east, and the crew says it's always been going east. So it's turned into an urban reprise of Clarke's Möbius-twist "Wall of Darkness" (which Ballard likely did not read in 1949 in *Super Science Stories* or in the subsequent Sam

---

58. Mattheson may be a homage to the SF and fantasy writer Richard Matheson, of whom Ballard said, "He was one of the sf writers I read when I was in Canada. One of the very few books that I brought back with me, if not the only one, was a collection of Richard Matheson's short stories...." (Quoted by David Pringle in "Interview Fragments" in his Ballard newsletter *News from the Sun* 17 (December 1987), available at http://www.jgballard. ca/pringle_news_from_the_sun/news_from_sun17.html (visited 10/26/11).

Moskowitz anthology where it was reprinted, *Editor's Choice in Science Fiction* (McBride, 1954)). At the end, Mattheson and the police psychiatrist are discussing whether and how there could be anything outside the City, and how the City could have come into being. It's held together by smooth writing and a sense of conviction, buttressed by good visualization—nothing as colorful as "Prima Belladonna," but, e.g., a striking scene of a three-mile-long construction site. Judith Merril gave it an Honorable Mention in her annual anthology.

As noted, Ballard has the *New Worlds* Profile in **54**, unusually for such a new writer. It says he "has spent most of his life travelling, with the exception of two and a half years in a Japanese internment camp.... From Cambridge he went into copywriting, then flying in the RAF, and now works as a script-writer for a scientific film company." His first novel was "a completely unreadable pastiche of *Finnegans Wake* and the *Adventures of Engelbrecht*." In SF

> he found a medium where he could exploit his imagination, being less concerned with the popular scientific approach than using it as a springboard into the surreal and fantastic. Most of his own ideas come, if anywhere, from visual sources: Chirico, the expressionist Robin Chand[59] and the surrealists, whose dreamscapes, manic fantasies and feedback from the Id are as near to the future, and the present, as any intrepid spaceman rocketting round the galactic centrifuge.

---

59. Internet research and the combined erudition of the members of the listserv where these comments were first aired did not uncover an Expressionist named Robin Chand. However, a recent biography of Ballard indicates that he befriended one Dhun Robin Chand, an Anglo-Indian student one form above him, at the Leys School. John Baxter, *The Inner Man: The Life of J. G. Ballard* (Weidenfeld & Nicolson, 2011), p. 31. If Mr. Chand became an Expressionist, it appears he made little impression.

So inner space puts in an early appearance, if not quite by name. "He admits that though she doesn't actually write his stories his wife has as much to do with their final production as he has himself. She hopes to have his novel *You and Me and the Continuum* finished by the end of this year." He purportedly says, "Writers who interest me are Poe, Wyndham, Lewis and Bernard Wolfe, whose *Limbo 90* I think the most interesting science fiction novel so far published." That misleading comma between Wyndham and Lewis is doubtless due to Carnell. (Ballard eventually published an essay on Wyndham Lewis's "Human Age" trilogy in the post-Carnell *New Worlds*, March 1966.)

Ballard's next *New Worlds* appearance is not until **65**—"Manhole 69"—though he has had another one in *Science Fantasy* ("Mobile") in the interim. "Manhole 69" is his most ambitious yet, though I don't think it quite comes off. Three people have volunteered for neurosurgery so they won't need sleep any more, at the hands of Dr. Neill, who says: "For the first time Man will be living a full twenty-four hour day, not spending a third of it as an invalid, snoring his way through an eight-hour peepshow of infantile erotica." They are under observation in a gymnasium (overlit, of course). Dr. Morley, Neill's colleague who is taking the night shift, leaves for ten minutes. The gymnasium shrinks and the walls close in. When Morley comes back the three subjects are in a deep fugue state. Why? Morley speculates: "Continual consciousness is more than the brain can stand. Any signal repeated often enough loses its meaning. Try saying the word 'sleep' fifty times. It's no longer able to grasp who or why it is, and it rides adrift." Then one of the subjects calls for Neill, who strokes his forehead and says, "Yes, Bobby.... I'm here, Bobby. You can come out now."

So what exactly is going on here? Withdrawal from continual consciousness turns into regression to childhood? That doesn't seem to follow. There was a lot of blather earlier on about the transference of the subjects towards Dr. Neill, but I'm not sure that accounts for anything either. To me, the point of the story is ultimately muddled. But getting there is pretty satisfying. The story is very crisply written and Ballard has gotten very good very fast at vivid visualization of people and physical settings. This story virtually acts itself out in the mind's eye as it is read. The *New Worlds* readers were apparently impressed too. The story was rated first in its issue.

§

Arthur Sellings, who makes his first *New Worlds* appearance in "The Masters" **(49)**, belongs in the company of Ballard (and Brunner and Aldiss) for the sharpness of his writing. Sellings at this point had already published 13 stories in the SF magazines, mostly in the US, about half of them in *Galaxy*. "The Masters" is the kind of thing we might have seen had acerbic playwright Edward Albee begun his career in *Planet Stories*. Hedley and his wife Elsa are heading back to Earth when the inter-transit field generator self-destructs, and he barely gets her into the lifeboat in time. They are not getting along too well because she has been having an affair with George Manders, who is coarse and stupid but has a way with women, and now she despises her husband. They land on an unknown planet, since that's the only one readily available, and shortly a procession of robots greets them and takes them into their city to a gala dinner, hosted entirely by the robots. Who's in charge? Just the robots, apparently. Pursuit of this question must, however, await exchanges like this:

> "There's no knowing what their system of etiquette might be. But the impression we make might be important. So don't let's have any scenes. I mean—" he felt suddenly conciliatory—"can't we forget our differences, just for the time being?"
>
> She looked at him with mild incredulity. "You mean—just to please a lot of—" She gestured with a scornful hand. Then a look of pained understanding

came into her eyes. "Any excuse, eh? You make me *sick.*"

He turned miserably away from her contempt, knowing that she was right, that she knew him too damn well....

Things go on in this vein, as it becomes clear that the robots' original masters have departed but they are happy to serve and obey their new ones with the super-technology they have inherited, up to and including making a replica of George Manders for Elsa, which provokes Hedley to murder and suicide. We then learn that the previous inhabitants didn't really emigrate, they killed themselves too; we're in the subgenre of *Forbidden Planet* and "With Folded Hands."

Sellings extends his theme of marital rancor in "The Warriors" (**50**), which has essentially the same plot as "The Masters" for most of its length, except this time the male lead is an overbearing jerk rather than a whining weakling. The narrator and his wife Linda are on a ten-year space mission to go boldly, etc., and by now they can't stand each other. As the story opens, he is refusing to attend to the hydroponics, so the ship stinks, and she refuses to deal with engine maintenance, so the lights keep going out. They arrive at a nice planet, and the obsequious and peaceable natives soon roll out the red carpet for them and make them at home. However, they continue fighting, and eventually wind up rolling around on the ground pummeling each other. Shortly, the native dances cease to be peaceable and begin to present stylized representation of the humans fighting. They realize that they are regarded as gods and the example they have set has changed the course of civilization on this planet. They (mainly he) realize the folly of their ways; exit, billing and cooing. So this one is as uplifting as "The Masters" was... not.

Sellings has the *New Worlds* Profile in **49**, and there seems to be a controversy about his birth date; Carnell and the *Encyclopedia of Science Fiction* say 1921, the Contento anthology index has it as 1911. Either way, he gives the canonical history: captivated by *Metropolis* and *The Girl In The Moon*, later by Wells and Frank R. Paul. He started writing in 1953, placed in the Sunday *Observer* contest, which got him a collection, *Time Transfer*, published by Michael Joseph. He doesn't like critics who say SF is humorless (see Kuttner, Brown, Sheckley, Wyndham—Wyndham? well, OK, sometimes) and fans who mourn the "sense of wonder." "Obviously, science fiction, like any other genuine literary form, must evolve. It was easier in the old days—easier to find ideas, to stop in the middle of everything for a dissertation on Jupiter's moons. The modern way, starting a story in the middle of a future- or other-world environment and taking it from there is a challenge to the writer. It isn't always easy, but it is fun." Sellings' day job is as an antiquarian bookseller. (And—though you won't find it in the magazine—his real name is Robert Arthur Gordon Ley.)

Sellings' next appearance is "Birthright" (**53**), forceful and clever but ultimately unconvincing. It starts with a barely articulate first person narrator ("As early I can speak I ask, where I come from?") who is apparently being educated remotely by TV and robots ("I anger and smash god's face with fist.... God mends his face on wall. Iron god rolls in and picks up broken face, rolls out.") When he learns enough to ask the right questions, he's told he's a member of an alien refugee race salvaged by humanity and soon to be repatriated to a world they can live on. Shortly, he sees through that and figures out he's actually a product of genetic engineering, a freak made to mine extraterrestrial uranium for Earth's enrichment, and he's not at all pleased. But then he learns that his human ancestors gave their lives (irradiated and subjected to surgery, commemorated with statues and a plaque) so humanity could Go To The Stars pantropically through him and his lab-littermates. Oh, never mind, that's all right then. Did I mention that this is unconvincing? Also unconvincing is how quickly he develops and how good his broken English is at the beginning.

"Fresh Start" (**61**) features a man who wakes up partly amnesic with his legs amputated after an automobile accident.

He goes home with his wife, whom he sort of remembers, and more things come back as time passes. He gets in practice with his new artificial legs. But they won't take him back at his job, and he can't find another one, and he's getting very frustrated and suspicious until one night he wakes up in the wee hours. His wife isn't around, so he takes a walk downtown and discovers the entire population of his small town is having a meeting... about him. He flees what is now obviously a fake set, they give chase, he runs off the road, and then he learns that he's in the hands of benevolent aliens who are just trying to make him feel at home after he crashed on their planet. But his fake wife tells him she wasn't faking, and he's ready to help tear down the fake scenery and hit the big time. This one is pretty well done, reminiscent in places of Philip K. Dick's *Time Out of Joint*, which was probably being written about the time this was published, though it's extremely unlikely Dick would have seen it.

§

Philip E. High, a mainstay through the Carnell years, makes his first *New Worlds* appearance with "Guess Who?" in **56**, though he'd already had several stories in *Authentic* and *Nebula*. *New Worlds*'s storied (by me at least) proofreading renders him as "Philip E. Hind" at the end of the piece. Carnell's blurb describes him as "a writer better known in contemporary magazines" without giving any details. This is a compact and enthusiastic "Who Goes There?"/"Impostor" variation, in which returning spaceships and their crew must be closely inspected for the presence of invisible shape-shifting mind-controlling aliens.

"Golden Age" (**60**) posits a future where there is plenty for everyone, consumption of intoxicants is encouraged, but there's nothing really to do; also, Africa seems to have vanished. Carmody is a former alcoholic who used to spout off against the regime while drunk, until its representatives beat him brutally and conditioned him to keep his mouth shut. So he is recruited by the underground, and pretty much becomes its leader almost immediately, and prevails against the regime—alien invaders— by, in effect, calling the interstellar cops. It doesn't make much sense but is told with utter conviction and is short enough to work, sort of.

In "Buried Talent" (**62**), an outpost on Ganymede comes under attack by aliens, who have devised a weapon of individualized distraction: it stimulates the brain "to emphasize or exploit, man's latent talents, real or imaginary, at the expense of other faculties." The Earth contingent wanders off into their hobbies and preoccupations, leaving their posts unguarded, except that luckily the latent talent of one of them is prowess at close combat, and he single-handedly cleans the aliens' clocks. This one is utterly trivial, but again gets by on van Vogtish enthusiasm and propulsive writing.

John Kippax makes his solo *New Worlds* debut (he previously had a collaborative story with Dan Morgan, and he has had ten or so stories in *Science Fantasy* and *Authentic*) with "We're Only Human" (**53**). All the kids have personal robots except little Billy, so Gramps says he'll whip one up in his workshop. The result, Jones, looks a bit strange and seems to have more initiative than usual. It's not really a hobby job, but an "imitation human" about a thousand years old that has gone to ground. The robot confides that he wants "...a son." No fear, Gramps is making up a new and more conventional robot body, but it will receive Jones's brain. Bit of a non sequitur there, one might say, but the whole thing is so silly that criticizing that piece of logic is beside the point.

Kippax is back in **58** with "Point of Contact," an inconsequential piece of filler about interstellar explorers who can't make contact with the primitive natives because they ignore the intruders. One of the Earthfolks is an inept amateur juggler, but the aliens are superlative at it, so contact is made easily once they learn there's something they can do and we can't. In "The Underlings" (**62**), aliens are much taken by the Earth folk who have come to visit them, but things aren't what they seem. This one manages to be both very dark and very trivial.

Kippax has the *New Worlds* Profile in **58**, photographed along with Dan Morgan, who also has a story in the issue, displaying their f-hole guitars: they play in the same dance band, it seems. Kippax is also an English master at a grammar school, who nonetheless writes a thousand words a day and has been published in magazines as varied as *Young Elizabethan* and *Melody Maker.* His first non-fantasy short story was published in 1954 in Putnam's *Pick Of Today's Short Stories.* He says, "I believe in the 'think piece' method of working out a story, which is to put a bare notion at the top of the page and pound the typewriter for as many thousand words as it takes for the story idea to emerge. This system does not often fail." Kippax's real name was John Hynam (1915-74), in which non-disguise he produced one story for *New Worlds* and several for *London Mystery Magazine.* Virtually his entire production under the Kippax name (38 stories) appeared in Carnell's magazines, *Nebula,* and *Authentic* from 1954 to 1961, with one outlier in *London Mystery* and one encore in the Moorcock *New Worlds.*

Donald Malcolm appears in **65** with "Defence Mechanism," his first story in *New Worlds* and in the genre, though he previously had a couple of articles in *New Worlds* ("Lunar Observatory" in **47** and "Halley—The Man and the Comet" in **55**), as well as one in *Nebula.* The story is pretty inconsequential and cookie-cutterish: explorers land on bucolic planet, except that the previous exploration team died; so what's the deadly secret? Why, the cuddly native critters defend themselves by suppressing predators' appetites, so the first Earth folks forgot to eat and were too weak to control their spaceship on takeoff.

This now-Little Known Writer (b. 1930 and alive at this writing) was once a *New Worlds* regular, publishing 16 stories there from 1957 to 1965, and almost nothing anywhere else—he had one story and a couple more articles in *Nebula.* He followed Carnell to *New Writings in SF,* with five stories, and that appears to have been it, except for a late story in a 1989 Duncan Lunan anthology. He did have a couple of novels published by Laser

Books in the US and Canada: *The Unknown Shore* and *The Iron Rain*, both in Canada in 1976 and both "routine" per John Clute in the *Encyclopedia of Science Fiction*. As far as I can tell he has never otherwise been published in the US except for a couple of stories in the US reprint edition of *New Worlds*. Outside SF, he recounts in a brief memoir,

> I had always published a variety of work, including science articles...and specialist features on aspects of philately, particularly aviation, such as pre-1914 air-meetings and events—I was pretty much *the* expert on that era—and research work on mail flown by various airlines. One monograph on the Lanark Aviation Meeting, 1910, gained four international aero-literature awards.[60]

The most conspicuous critical attention Malcolm attracted may well be the mild thrashing administered to him by Brian Aldiss in *SF Horizons* under the rubric "Donald Malcolm: Beyond the Reach of Criticism." Since the essay mostly deals with Malcolm's later story "Beyond the Reach of Storms," we'll come to it in the second volume.

A couple of American writers who appear in these issues became regular contributors, at least briefly, and mostly with reprinted stories. Robert Silverberg makes the first of his dozen or so *New Worlds* appearances with "Quick Freeze" (**59**), which also appeared in *Science Fiction Quarterly*, May 1957, the same date as this *New Worlds*. It's basically filler: a spacewrecked crew needs rescuing from an icy planet, their rescuers don't bother to think about what's involved in landing on a jet on an ice surface, and wind up frozen in the crater their exhaust melted. Solution: the to-be-rescued crew heats up their rescuers' insulated hull with electric current through a wire coil, and siphons

---

60. Donald Malcolm, "Reminiscences of a Science Fiction Writer, or, 'I Knew the Late, Great, Bob Shaw,'" *Relapse* 15 (Autumn 2009), p. 8 (http://www.efanzines.com/Prolapse/Relapse15.pdf) (visited 9/7/11).

off the meltwater so it doesn't refreeze. Then the rescuers blast off and place their ship in orbit, 30 feet off the ground, so the to-be-rescued can grab ropes and climb up. Orbit? Does not compute. Silverberg is featured in the *New Worlds* Profile, pre-beard and looking about 17. "Acclaimed the most promising writer of 1956," it says, "Bob Silverberg is one of those fabulous young Men [sic] who live in the steel and concrete jungle of New York City." He works eight hours a day five days a week, has sold 200 stories and five novels in three years, appearing in 18 different US SF magazines. (There's no mention that his first sale was to a UK competitor, *Nebula*.) *New Worlds* has been one of his favorites since he encountered it in 1949. He's "married to one of America's very few female electronics engineers," and they live with cat Antigone in a "large, book-filled apartment." He doesn't think that SF is a major art form or that Heinlein measures up to Thomas Mann, but he likes it. He also likes atonal music, *Finnegans Wake*, Cyril Tourneur and Olaf Stapledon.

Silverberg appears again in the next issue with "Sunrise on Mercury" (**60**), from Lowndes' *Science Fiction Stories* for May 1957 (the month before the *New Worlds* issue date). This is a considerably better story. A space crew lands on the twilight belt of Mercury (extravagant fiction yesterday, discredited science today), discovers the hard way that they are closer to the Sun side than they thought so the Sun makes its brief over-the-horizon appearance a week early. How could they make such a mistake, and what is it fogging their minds? Justly, in *To Be Continued*, the first volume of Silverberg's everything-worth-keeping *Collected Stories* (Subterranean Press 2006), "Sunrise on Mercury" appears and "Quick Freeze" does not.

"Critical Threshold" (**66**), which did not appear in the US magazines, is a paint-by-numbers *Astounding* story: Aherne of the UN is dispatched to Mars to report on the viability (and seal the fate one way or the other) of the colony. On arrival he finds there are now two colonies: one dome living at Earth normal atmospheric conditions, another inhabited by Peruvian high-altitude dwellers at much nearer Martian conditions. The latter was established by the man who lost out for UN sponsorship but who scrabbled around for private funding. Aherne is not about to rock the boat, given that he's acting under a UN resolution establishing the Earth normal colony. As he's about to leave, an earthquake devastates the population of the official colony, while the unofficial people are relatively unscathed and head over to rescue the others. The answer, obviously, is interbreeding: the story closes with a 9-year-old Peruvian boy and a 4-year-old blonde girl staring curiously at each other. It's well-meaning but lifeless, but the readers liked it: they voted it into first place ahead of the Brunner serial that begins in the issue.

Richard Wilson makes his first *New Worlds* appearance in "Press Conference" (**52**). Carnell's blurb says "Author Richard Wilson was recently in London and this particular story is a legacy from that visit." In fact, it was previously published in *Amazing*, Oct./Nov. 1953. This was the first of five Wilson stories in *New Worlds* and four in *Science Fantasy*, four and three of them respectively reprinted from US sources, and it makes one wonder whether personal contact was frequently a basis for the appearance of reprinted stories in Carnell's magazines. Robert Silverberg has said that when they met at a Worldcon, Carnell invited him to submit stories already sold in the US. In this Wilson story, the President's press secretary distributes a schedule that indicates a conference with Mr. Kjal, Mars, sending the journalists into a frenzy. The President doesn't really tell them much. As he doesn't say, Mr. Kjal was a really nice guy who just sort of materialized and suggested that Earth people needed to get mature before they went into space, and the President is going to be a much wiser man and work for good. There's not much to this except for the mild satire of journalists' mores at the beginning, unless Wilson also meant to satirize the widely perceived insipid character of then President Eisenhower (as Philip K. Dick was doing in "The Mold of Yancey" around the same time)—in which case there's still not much to it. To my taste much of Wilson's fiction is rather insipid, though there were exceptions, mostly much later.

Wilson's next appearance is one of the exceptions: "Double Take" (**54**), from the January 1954 *If*. Paul Asher finds himself in a fast car with a beautiful woman, evading roadblocks at her command, swerving into a barn which proves to be an extraterrestrial spaceship, and he's carrying something they want, etc., etc. Of course it's a virtual reality story, and the joker is when does the virtual reality end? It was no doubt original in 1954 and it's still readable, since it moves fast and wastes no words.

"*QRM*" (**61**), which Carnell acknowledges is reprinted from *Fantasy & Science Fiction* (April, 1957, only a few months earlier), is more mild whimsy, though less annoying in that regard than "Press Conference." A wire service starts receiving incomprehensible news from the future. Then it stops. Wilson has the *New Worlds* Profile in this issue, and says: "More than half the time I write on a salaried basis, for a global news agency which provided the background for my story 'QRM.' Nothing quite like the type of interplanetary conference therein described has happened to me as I sit in the New York office and edit the news for transmission to London, but as I handle factual stories about guided missiles and rockets and guarded forecasts about space travel I am convinced that the gap between my vocational fact-writing and my avocational fiction is gradually closing."

§

Now to the time-servers, the established contributors whose performance is mostly mediocre and who give no sign of getting any better at this point.

Alan Barclay's "The Hot Potato" (**43**) is another uninteresting Jacko story. In this one, the aliens have landed on Mars and the humans have got between them and their spaceship. But these ships are usually booby-trapped. What to do? The lower-rankers on the scene have whipped up a remote probe in their spare time, so they adapt it to this task, report their findings, and then a colonel shows up to try to take credit for everything, and gets his deserved comeuppance. This halfhearted satire on military life and bureaucracy, like some of Barclay's earlier stories, suggests Eric Frank Russell minus the sense of humor. It, and a couple of the earlier Jacko stories, also appeared in the US magazine *Saturn* in 1957, Barclay's only US SF magazine appearances after his 1952 story in *Astounding*.

"The Thing in Common" (**50**), thankfully, concludes the Jacko series, and is a considerable improvement. McCoy, who wrestled with the Jacko and ultimately spared its life in "The Real McCoy" a year earlier (**34**), is mustered out, and in his simple-minded way becomes a public figure questioning whether war with the Jackoes can ever be won. He winds up dispatched to the Jackoes as humanity's negotiator, and concludes that the answer is they just have to be accepted as citizens with equal rights in the solar system, since they have nowhere else to go and it would be too difficult to exterminate them. Barclay says in his *New Worlds* Profile that he knew this was the end since the first story, and in fact it was all set out ten years earlier in an unpublishable story which Carnell had the sense to reject.

"The Refugee" (**48**) is not part of the series and is much livelier. Lieutenant Anstar escapes in a scout ship from the final defeat of his planet's forces by the Troll-Angar (honest), who shoot everybody else after they surrender. 150 years later, it's 1963 and he is alive and well in London, living as a Trinidad-born engineer, but keeping his eye peeled for the Troll-Angar, who are beginning to infiltrate Earth. No one would believe him if he told them what was going on, but he dies contriving to outwit the Troll-Angar into revealing themselves so Earth will be ready when their main body arrives. This is a nice piece of straightforward storytelling by an author who seems briefly to have awakened. Unfortunately it is followed by the rather pointless "The Neutral" (**53**), about a major who is providing military space-piloting training to the froglike Pelleans, who are soon to be beset by the bellicose Hammerheads. Meanwhile he dreams about being reunited with his wife in a nice little place in Luna City. In the end he realizes that his wife is irredeemably worthless and throws in his lot and his life with the doomed Pelleans.

In "The Executioner" (54), a by-the-numbers colonel is ordered to test out a new model space fighter. He sends a bunch of test pilots to their deaths, then takes it up himself expecting to die, but of course masters the ship, and then everybody can do it. This time the point is clear enough. The question is why bother? "The Misfit" (60) is another lecture in military science, but a more engaging one. It, too, features a by-the-numbers guy, this one a general assigned to wipe out the insurgency among the Martian colonists, many of whom are exercised that colonization is wiping out the indigenes' Mars-adapted way of life (recruiting them for mining labor, etc.) in favor of an exploitative and ultimately unsustainable one that will last only as long as the colonizers' interest and capital. General Knowles believes that artillery conquers all. The rebel leader pronounces that "Mars itself is on our side." The point is that victory comes from knowing the territory (in all senses). This is not exactly original, but the story is well developed and readable and its didacticism is a bit more sophisticated than usual, even if it is ultimately resolved by a silly gimmick.

"To Percy" (65) begins as another tedious tale of the foibles of military life and personality—the protagonist is detailed to the pompous Major in charge of Stores and Equipment on the Moon, who has it in for the men working on the FTL drive— which morphs into a slightly less tedious tale about the FTL men, who figure out how to steer in hyperdrive (oscillate it on and off so they can see out the windows, and keep mass distribution in the ship absolutely under control), and drop the protagonist off on Mars so he can visit his girlfriend.

Francis G. Rayer—as noted, the most prolific contributor to these issues of *New Worlds*—starts off well with "The Falsifiers" (44), as by George Longdon. The blurb invokes the last Longdon story, the tense and compact "Of Those Who Came," and this story is a nice try in that direction. Cutler, a manager at Jupiter Messages, is getting phone calls from... himself. Somebody has been mucking around in his apartment. Then his new secretary is seen in duplicate. What's going on? They hear hushed-up stories from the Jupiter operation about rocks that weren't really rocks, especially when they were emulating packing crates. So it's "Who Goes There?" time, and when Cutler and Cutler finally confront each other in the office, Captain Millrow has the heuristic: he points guns at each of them to see which of them is selflessly devoted to Earth and which cuts and runs. "... *It was safe to be a desk*." Derivative as it is, it's an entertaining enough story. Rayer can be an adequate writer when he keeps it short and to the point.

This observation is unfortunately borne out in the breach in the next issue by "Hyperant" (**45**), a long and densely cluttered novelette. The star of a colony planet has unexpectedly gone nova. Film shows that somebody blew it up. An alien spaceship appears at a distance from the evacuation ships, and they can't shake it by "space shifts." Meanwhile, Walney, captain of an evacuation ship, is interested in the possible existence of a Hyperant. A what? Doesn't say, but there's a mysterious lieutenant, Pakes, who seems to be harboring a silver globe in a triangular red frame, and is reading a book titled *Whole Mind of Man*, apparently a turgid treatise on solipsism: "That matter still exists when no mind is present to observe it cannot be deduced."

The globe and frame appear briefly in Walney's cabin and he seems to be overhearing a telepathic conversation involving nonhuman participants. The aliens dispatch a missile that will clearly destroy the human ships, but an asteroid materializes in its path so no harm is done. Meanwhile Pakes has disappeared from the sealed spaceship, then returns, so they throw him in the brig, from which he promptly disappears again. It is suggested that he may be the first Hyperant, and now we have a clue: a Hyperant is someone who has no limitations (this is on page 18 of a story that began on page 4 and introduced the term on page 8).

Pakes reappears in a state of physical collapse. No limitations? More of *Whole Mind of Man* is revealed, such as: "For the observer, knowledge that a thing exists means that the state where it may have influence on him is reached.... The object that has become subject of his observation has not changed, but its effective relationship to himself has." Etc. "Heavy going," says Walney. And this (underlined): "The foregoing chapters suggest the effective presence of a thing depends upon knowledge of that presence. Without knowledge, effect is absent. Knowledge thus creates." "Pakes has gotten into this pretty deep," says Walney's sidekick Bell.

However, Pakes dies (no limitations?), but a tape of his deathbed maunderings (which Walney hears only after it is stolen by crew members who belong to the Pagans, an anti-space expansion group) reveals that he has "understood the deepest implications of the *Whole Mind of Man*," viz., "A Hyperant can make or destroy matter, atom beyond atom, universe beyond universe." So Walney catches on too—"The totality of all phenomena existed in the mind"—and he walks through the wall of the room he is locked into, along with the female crew member who has also been captured, steps over to the alien ship, which is some distance away in space, and discovers it crewed by sentient piezo-electric crystals, who hate organic life. Naturally, he "shred[s] their vessel to its last atom." Then he thinks a Sol-type star with habitable planets into being so the empire can continue to expand.

"Hyperant" is reasonably amusing but makes very little sense (why does Pakes, with "no limits," get sick and die, when Walney proves capable of creating stars and planets with a thought? What's this communication globe? Was it sent by the piezoelectric aliens who hate us? What for? Why does the Empire put known members of a subversive cabal on the crew of a military ship? And above all, why should we take seriously the notion that reading *Whole Mind of Man* confers omnipotence?). The story is also remarkably, pervasively, distractingly badly written. For example, it begins: "In V-formation over ten thousand miles of space, the fleet drifted like silver ghosts behind the flagship *Tetracil*." Apart from Tetracil sounding like something you'd take for a urinary infection, this visual image is completely self-defeating: if the formation is spread over ten thousand miles, it isn't going to look like silver ghosts, because you won't be able to see it. Later, the protagonist encounters the female lead, Unity Austin (!): "At near twenty-four she had quickly expressive features and a height and build he personally liked." Talk about a description that does not describe. The story is absolutely full of this sort of thing, to the point where I wonder if Rayer's more competent stories were substantially edited by Carnell but he didn't have time for this one.

Rayer's "Consolidation Area" (**46**) is another "Who Goes There?" variation. Albert Mademann is on a fishing vacation at a lake. Mysterious objects, which we know from the beginning are parasitic alien intelligences, have been falling from the sky. He encounters a wading bird that is acting funny and adopts it as a pet, then finds the bird dead and his cat starts acting funny, then a woman shows up whose car has broken down and soon enough *she* starts acting funny. When the alien entity tries to take over Mademann it discovers that he is indeed a made man, and not of the Mafia sort, and his artificial brain provides no foothold for the alien, who dies. One would not mistake this for good literature even in a very dim light, but it arranges its used furniture reasonably cleverly, and like "The Falsifiers" is short enough for Rayer to stay out of trouble.

That is not true of "Culture Pattern" (**47**), in which Earth explorers, on a world with no rain and tinderbox forests (as we are told repeatedly from the beginning of the story), eventually figure out that the strange and sometimes violent behavior of the locals is directed towards keeping them from starting forest fires; it takes 19 pages for this leadenly obvious penny to drop. "Error Potential" (**50**) is in a similar vein, a virtual Thought Variant Revenant. Interstellar explorers arrive at their destination and discover that they can't land, because their spaceship has built up such a static charge from the friction of its 30-times-light-speed passage. "The winds of the void that had screamed past her hull had left no mark." But: "Space isn't absolute vacuum.

You can rub electrons off ebonite with a flannel. The wind rubs plenty of thunderclouds, until the voltage breaks down the atmosphere's insulation. Our trip from Earth has had a similar result. Plenty of particles are scattered over twenty light-years of space, our speed was high, and the medium a perfect insulator. An ideal set of circumstances!" So they tie all their ropes and cables end to end and lower them towards the planet from orbit (what's wrong with this picture?) to dissipate the charge. "At last planet and ship would be equal, and Cenis no longer at impossible relative potential. There would be honour and glory, for both were inevitable."

"Period of Error" (52), as by George Longdon, is even lamer. The Distant Enemy Warning radar system keeps going off when there's nothing there, and young Jack Bennett is on the hook, especially when General Cornforth (honest), whose baby it is, gets killed, and the irascible General Farram sees his chance to kill a project he doesn't like anyway. But Bennett, with the help or at least the presence of General Cornforth's beautiful daughter, figures out that it's really a Distant Enemy *Very Early* Warning system: this predictive product of General Cornforth's genius sounds the alarm two hours *before* there is anything to detect. Farram is vanquished.

Rayer's second story in **52**, "Three-Day Tidal" under his own name, is a modest improvement as long as you don't think about it too much. Regulus I has nine moons, some of them quite large. The human characters are there to establish a tidal power station to serve the colony that they hope is coming. There is no large vegetation anywhere. Somehow nobody has thought about what the tides might be like if there were a nine-moon opposition. So we know right away we're in the territory of Asimov's "Nightfall," writ small and wet. When everything including the shellfish starts heading for high ground, they do start to think, and figure out that they are looking at three to four hundred feet worth of tide, and this happens every three thousand years.

Meanwhile, they have been trying to make contact with the natives, whose language they can speak, but who are unreasonably churlish, telling the Earth folks that they weren't invited and it would be nice if they left. None of the Earth folks can understand why they might feel this way. (Well, that's a problem other Earth folks have had, quite recently and currently in fact.) But the tides come, and the Earth folks are floating over their usual haunts in their barges, and the not-high-enough ground to which the natives fled turns out to be a floating mass of vegetation—except that a hole opens up in the seabed and the Earth party saves the natives' skins by towing them out of the danger zone. So the natives are now properly thankful to Bwana, and colonization can begin. Why anyone would want to colonize a planet that has four-hundred-foot tides, even at three thousand-year intervals, is not explained.

"Tree Dweller" (**53**), as by George Longdon, is meant literally: a two-foot spaceship slams into a tree and buries itself. An unspecified time later, the tree finds itself in a sawmill and shortly the spaceship is breaking the bandsaw. When the assembled Yahoos figure out what it is, and that its occupant has slipped out, they start hunting for the alien with whatever blunt instruments are handy, and chain down and booby-trap the spaceship. But young Jim sneaks back into the yard after hours and helps the alien escape, and since the aliens respect any species capable of doing good, now they won't pick our planet to invade and render uninhabitable. This one is pleasant and means well, though that's about all one can say for it.

"Stress Test" (**60**) reminds me a little of the joke about the man who hit himself over the head with a mallet because it felt so good when he stopped. Ruby Bond (male) is in charge of testing of a Mars rocket with an advanced propulsion system. Instead of steady thrust, they have discovered, violent detonations at regular intervals produce more thrust. After two sets of test pilots have become uncommunicative and crashed and been killed, Bond of course decides to take the next one up himself, where he discovers that the intermittent super-acceleration is psychologically intolerable, and also that his wife has sneaked aboard. He loses consciousness, but unlike his predecessors he wakes up, because the owner has unbeknownst to him installed remote control equipment for this eventuality. The explanation for why this wasn't done from the beginning is particularly unconvincing.

Rayer and E. R. James join forces in **48** for "Period of Quarantine," a reasonably readable story about space explorers. Those who go down to the planet's surface get sick, and Coyne—ship's doctor and second-in-command—enters their returning lander to try to help them. Meanwhile, aliens have shown up but quickly abandon communicating with humans. In the lander, the crew is sick and delirious, Coyne's getting sick too, but the "disease" is really parasites that can make people telepathic, which will solve the alien contact problem, and not a moment too soon—the aliens are about to push the EXTERMINATE button to rid themselves of these mute primitives. There's a subplot about the subordinates' wanting to take the main ship and flee. Overall it is reasonably well plotted and concise, and one is tempted to root for Rayer and James anyway (at least I am) just because they are trying so hard.

Of course the dinosaurs probably tried hard too. E. R. James is back in **51** with "Creep," a romance of metallurgy that would have fit comfortably into *Wonder Stories*. The good ship A.S.S. *Romulus* is passing Jupiter bearing Steve Tinder, ace metallurgist of the Queen Pyrometals Company, who has been rewarded for his labors with an interplanetary vacation. Also on board are the windbag Bellamy Mellard, a pompous and ignorant company official (he "puffed out his florid cheeks"), and the boss's daughter Anna Queen (with "dark aquiline face"—well, that's a novelty). Of course something breaks in the engine room ("*Ting-g!*") and it is up to Steve Tinder, the man with the know-how, to suit up and descend into the radioactive hell (to be fair, not James' phrase) and save everyone's bacon.

> As he struggled into the thick protective clothing, Steve's mind went over every detail of the stresses for which he had been called upon to provide suitable

alloys. The crewman helping him was lifting the helmet and he was absently ducking his head into it, when he became aware that everyone from the men at control panels to Anna herself was staring at him... although he was only doing his job.

Mellard seemed to choke. "Good luck, Steve!"

"Eh?" He lifted his heavily gloved hand and felt Bellamy Mellard grip it.

Then Anna had her arms around his neck, and her lips were firm against his.

The helmet came down and he peered at them through its hazy glass, feeling foolish.

The day is saved and rewards are distributed appropriately to the deserving. ("Just as he knew his metals... he realized that *she* knew her men.")

This is followed by "Beautiful Weed" (**57**), equally lame and less entertaining, this one a kudzu variation. A scientist on Mars discovers that the feeble flowers of that planet grow like hell if you cover them with water; some of the seeds get tracked in on Earth and start blooming everywhere there's water. It looks like curtains for us, but those in charge track down our hero, who tells them they'd better get some of the Martian grubs to Earth to control the flowers, and then they'd better get some Martian crustacea to control the grubs. Cane toads, anyone? That should be the end of the matter, since we've now run through the entire Martian ecosphere. But no, there's a sequel, "Fourth Species" (**59**), which proposes that the crustacea somehow metamorphose into venomous lizards, in a plot so dated one expects to find unwelcome life forms growing on it.

"Made on Mars" (**63**) is a bit livelier. Explorers on a Mars ravaged and depopulated by ancient wars find a strange machine, carefully investigate it, and discover that it seems to provide a traversable window into space. Further research suggests that it's also a time machine, reaching only into our past. It's the last gasp of the Martians, who have thrown this lifeline into their future, hoping somebody will open the door so they can pile through, escape their fate, and take over from us suckers. But it proves literally their last gasp, since Mars no longer has an atmosphere they can breathe.

Bertram Chandler may seem an odd choice for the time-server category, since he hasn't appeared in the magazine in almost three years, during which interim he has shed his initial A. and moved to Australia. But on his abrupt return, he contributes seven stories in 11 issues, consistent in their inconsequentiality and annoying for it, since he has produced better work. "Alone" (**56**) posits a lone space pilot who is driven crazy by isolation, kills a Martian, and is sent back having been integrated into the ship's computer, in an early rehearsal for the Singularity. Carnell describes this rather morbid item as a "zestful short story."

"Time to Change" (**57**, later in *Fantastic Universe*, January 1959) is a reasonably clever but heavy-handed time paradox story about a future dominated by the Boss, and the underground that is trying to overthrow him by going back in time and shooting the first occupant of his position. "The Book of Power" (**62**) has a couple of spacemen doing some amateur archaeology on Mars, as they discuss the significance of religious and ideological conflict in history. This good smooth build-up is wasted on a jokey ending. In "Sister Under the Skin" (**63**, also *If*, August 1958), a space captain brings home a souvenir alien animal skin as a gift to his sister, which proves to be an... absorbing gift. "Sense of Wonder" (**64**, also *Fantastic Universe*, January 1958) starts off with a discussion of SF between Crowell and Whiting, and the loss of the sense of wonder therefrom. Whiting heads home, is picked up by the crew of a flying saucer, taken for an off-Earth spin, but is unimpressed—he explains to the slightly miffed aliens that he's lost his own sense of wonder.

"The Half Pair" (**65**, and *Amazing*, July 1958), says Carnell's blurb, "continues his series of cameo stories," seeming to acknowledge their insubstantiality. This one features husband and wife space travelers. He drops one of his cufflinks (cufflinks in space? Oh, it's rationalized) down the drain and his wife empties the drain into space. He goes after it, but his life-line isn't fastened, so his spacesuit-phobic wife has to rescue him or *she'll* be a half pair. In "Swap Shop" (**66**), a spaceship sets down on a colony planet, the crew see a swap program on TV where a fabulously expensive exotic dress is offered in exchange for a dressed duck (which only a spaceship is likely to have on hand). Sue, the ship's cook, makes the swap. There's a gimmick, of course, but it's even less interesting than the set-up.

A few other long-time contributors are back with minor entries. Peter Hawkins returns after nearly three years' absence, which Carnell says is "mainly caused by settling down to married life," with "The Tools of Orlas Boyn" (**57**), a pleasant enough instance of SF by and for the hardcore SF reader. Matt Drecklan signs on as Third Engineer on the *Eldrake*, replacing a Salvernian. These aliens infect the tools they use with a sort of pseudo-life, so the screwdriver writhes in his grasp. The gloves cringe away from him when he tries to pick them up and inflict a powerful delirium on him when he does manage to get them on. Eventually it turns out he can use the tools when his own personality is not in the way (e.g. when he's distracted in some fashion), and eventually the tools get to know him. That's all there is to it, though Judith Merril was impressed or amused enough to give it an Honorable Mention.

Hawkins is back in **63** with "The Watcher on Sargan IV," in which interstellar explorer Henderson, freshly landed on the very unpleasant world of Sargan IV, starts off by killing his predecessor, who seems to be trying to blow up Henderson's ship. His companion, de Voile, encounters Ghensar, an immortal green mist who proves to be the last survivor of his race, which otherwise got wiped out millennia ago in a war of mutual destruction with humanity's predecessors. Ghensar is creating a new immortal race of humanoids on Sargan IV that he hopes will redeem human civilization. The existentially conflicted Henderson first reacts violently, but then, when Ghensar appears to him too, becomes a convert to Ghensar's selfless cause and blows up his own ship so he won't be tempted to change his mind. Unfortunately the story that clothes these admirable sentiments is a considerable regression for Hawkins, clumsily put together (e.g., the initial killing of the earlier explorer after his attempted sabotage—the dramatic kickoff of the story—takes place offstage before the story begins, robbing it of all impact) and amateurishly written ("The fact that the something on Sargan IV had made Patterson responsible for his attempt to destroy their scoutship, as he had his own and maroon them worried Henderson too, but again he consoled himself with the thought that he was doing what appeared to be his duty.") Perhaps Hawkins' other recent stories were heavily edited by Carnell—this one appears in the October 1957 issue, which would have been put together shortly before the Worldcon of which Carnell was chair, limiting his time. In any case, it's clear that this once mildly promising writer's future is behind him. After this brief burst of productivity in 1957 (one story in *Science Fantasy* as well as these two), Hawkins has one more in 1959 and two in 1961 and then hangs it up for good.

Sydney J. Bounds abides, with an acceptable quality of mid-level product and flashes of cleverness. In "First Lesson" (**49**), aliens arrive, immediately plunge to the bottom of the ocean, and don't come up. Investigated by bathysphere, the aliens prove to be making friends with the fish, flashing lights at them while the fish respond by swimming in formation. Take that, Mr. Wise Guy Homo Saps! "Mutation" (**51**) presents the lone-liest man in the Galaxy, isolated by his talent of always knowing what symbols (speech, writing, whatever) *really* mean. His fate seems a bit exaggerated; one would think that someone in that position would learn to dissemble pretty quickly, and be pretty good at it; but no. So he is dispatched to a far planet where relics of a lost alien civilization have been found, since his talent extends to the symbols of a nonhuman species that neither he nor anyone else has any experience with; he reads their records, discover that unlike humanity they really get it about saying what they mean, and he realizes epiphanically that humanity is evolving towards that condition even if he won't live to see it. In "We Call It Home" (**53**), the new order after the Revolution wonders what happened to all those colony planets the old regime started, and to find out sends Ross, who finds a colony of beleaguered humans struggling for survival under almost comically adverse circumstances. By the end, he has barely survived a sandstorm, and then helps deliver a child in the middle of an earthquake—the first live birth. Cue Man-Will-Prevail crescendo. Bounds will be back with a few more stories in 1958, and then nothing more until, surprisingly, he pops up a couple of times in the Moorcock *New Worlds*.

§

In addition to the émigré Chandler, there are a couple of Australian writers in these issues. Frank Bryning (1907-99), whom Carnell describes as "an Australian author whose popularity is steadily rising both in his own country and in America," had a dozen or so stories in *Fantastic Universe* in 1955-56—many of which were reprinted from *Australian Magazine* earlier in the 1950s—and a scattering of stories in other SF magazines during the 1950s, and a resurgence of seven stories (a couple reprinted) in the 1970s in the UK magazines *SF Monthly* and *Visions of Tomorrow* and the dire Australian magazine *Void*. He published three stories in *New Worlds*, the first of which is "Place of the Throwing Stick" (**45**), about an Aborigine who heads towards Woomera to kill the white man's biggest horned beast with his war boomerang and his own *woomera* (spear-thrower); it's obvious but readable. "On the Average" (**56**), reprinted from *The Forerunner* (Fall 1953) and also published in *Fantastic Universe* (April 1956), reads like an outtake from the Tremaine-edited *Astounding* of the mid-1930s. A space-procedural about a space station crew responding to a meteor strike, it features a rough-hewn space dog whose pet peeve is the proposition that "on the average" one will be hit by a meteor every umpty-ump years. Interestingly, this was voted first in the issue by the readers, over quite decent stories by James White and J. T. McIntosh.

A few issues later Bryning has "For Men Must Work" (**61**), in the same vein as "On the Average." A spaceman's wife has persuaded him to take a job on the ground, but he's so good that (even as, in alternating scenes, he's masterminding the rescue of a meteor-damaged craft) they're going to offer him instead a juicier position, in charge of maintenance on the space station rather than at Woomera. In the end she sucks it up. (The rest of the titular line from poet Charles Kingsley's *The Water Babies* is "And Women Must Weep.") This one was rated last in the issue by the readers, and that's it for Frank Bryning in *New Worlds*. Bryning has the *New Worlds* Profile in **61**, which describes him as "undoubtedly Australia's foremost science fiction author," an interesting proposition, since the same issue notes that A. Bertram Chandler is now living in Australia—but then, like other recent immigrants, he was likely regarded as a "Pommie bastard." Bryning is 45 (the profile says—this doesn't jibe with the above birth date from Miller/Contento), born in Melbourne but now living in Queensland, and works as a journalist, editing a monthly building trade journal as well as free-lancing; he was a founder of the Brisbane SF Group (started in his home) and guest of honor at the Fifth Australian SF Convention, just held. There's a great photo of him, with broad unpretentious face under a jaunty wide-brimmed hat. Australia should put it on a postage stamp.

N(orma) K(athleen) Hemming's "Dwellers in Silence" (**51**) is another living fossil recalling a simpler and less competitive age, and reminiscent of Kris Neville's 1951 tearjerker "Bettyann." Space ship cracks up on Earth, parents and child stumble outside, parents die, simple farmer grabs child, space ship blows up, he rears the child, who proves telepathic and grows up beautiful. Then he dies. She goes to an orphanage, which is hellish; gets sent out to work for men, differently hellish; and finally is sent to work for a woman, which is more tolerable, at least until her son and his jealous wife show up. Then she goes out and telepathically bellows her distress at the sky, and is answered, and her people are on their way to pick her up.

This Australian Little Known Writer had as marginal a career as you can imagine: stories in every issue from **16** to **23** (1951-52) of *Thrills, Inc.*, a dreadful Australian magazine for which "downmarket" would be a compliment; one in *Science Fantasy* (1951), but more in *Forerunner*, the Australian *Future* and *Popular Science Fiction* (1952-54), and finally she hit the big time: this one in *New Worlds*, one in *Nebula*, one in *Science Fiction Adventures*. Then she died in 1960, age 33. En route she was part of the Australian SF community. Carnell's editorial in **57** retails Frank Bryning's account of the 1956 "Olympicon" (i.e., it happened right after the Olympics), describing Hemming as a "Sydney authoress and playwright" and reporting that her three-act play "Balance of Power" was presented: "Axiomatic [sic] of the increasing interest now being taken by women in the lighter side of science fiction, Miss Hemming designed and made all the costumes and played one of the leading roles."[61]

§

Of the (other) false starts and dead ends, the most interesting is Leslie Perri"'s "The Untouchables" **(49)**, which also appeared a month earlier in the June 1956 *Infinity* as "Under the Skin." The author—real name Doris Baumgardt—may be a Little Known Writer but she was also a Big Name Fan, a Futurian who was allowed to remain at the 1939 NYCon, the early SF convention, but was later suspended by the Futurians, and also a wife of Frederik Pohl. She had two other stories in the SF magazines: a short in *Future* in 1941 (reprinted in the Gerald Swan *Space Fact And Fiction* in 1954) and a vignette in *If* in 1953. And here's a biblio-pedantic gem: Leslie Perri is listed as editor of *Movie Love Stories*, vol. 1, no. 1, June 1941, published

---

61. A detailed study of Hemming's brief life and work is David Medlen, " 'I Wasn't Expecting That': The Career of Norma Hemming," in Ikin and Broderick, eds., *Warriors of the Tao*, Borgo Press, 2011.

by Albing Publications, which was also responsible for *Stirring Science Stories.*

"The Untouchables" is an amusing relic with the air of a 1940s movie adapted from a pulp of the time. On Mars, where the indispensable fuel diranium is mined and nobody ever sees the Martian women, there's a power failure at a mining colony that threatens the lives of everyone there. A journalist sets off to cover it with staff photographer Deborah Wayne, who proves to have smuggled aboard a Martian woman—the Martian leader's wife, in fact—who is distraught about her children in the stricken colony, and destined to become a pariah as a result of her purdah-breaking. Deborah was recruited for this mission in canonical *Thrilling Wonder Stories* fashion:

> The man who had intercepted her appeared out of the night, without warning. Tall and slender in a cloak of soft furs, his feet in fine leather quilted boots, the tall glittering oxygen cone crested with the phoenix-like emblem of the ruling group—he was regal, and tragic with uncertainty. He had no taste for his mission but he was urgent.

After a certain amount of hugger-mugger, the Martian woman appears ("She was gold and violet and seemed to float in a cloud of silk. She was tiny and slender and her oblique dark eyes looked first at Vechi, and then at me. There was in her manner the shyness of deer and the brightness of birds.") and is revealed to be, not the leader's wife, but his concubine, who is running away with this Vechi, to Venus no less. Deborah, initially presented as indomitably independent and untouchable ("Deborah, her red hair half over her eyes as usual came in—a blazing little fireball of energy.") has acknowledged that she needs the male protagonist to save her bacon, and for other reasons as well ("'You damned little fake,' I said huskily. 'It took you the longest time to figure me out,' Deborah sighed."), so all ends happily, and later on, as a result of these events the

Martian women are able to appear in public, though the connection is not too clear. As hokey anachronisms go, this is actually quite well written. There's no apparent reason why Leslie Perri couldn't have been a mainstay of *Thrilling Wonder* back in the day, just as there is no apparent reason why she is publishing this in 1956.

Duncan Lamont's "Magic Touch" (**43**) is a supposedly humorous but pretty boring story about a new washing machine which is also an antigravity device. "The Unconventional Dustbin" (**45**) is an ostentatiously comic story about a researcher who discovers a way of projecting unwanted stuff, like nuclear waste, into the fourth dimension, except the fourth dimension proves to be time, and watch out, now it's all coming back. "Sun Cycle" (**48**) is an unfortunate attempt at poesy, about a man on a frozen planet whose atomic pile fails and who dies when his air runs out, though not before colorful spring arrives. "Time was leaking back into the little world. A star grew and bloomed into a pale yellow disc. Once in a revolution it shone weakly through the encrusted ports, stirring faint shapes into the blackness. Wan images looked inward on the main cabin, where the all-consuming vacuum had claimed its hostage." OK, it's not so bad, but pages of it and not much else wear out their welcome. These are it for Lamont's *New Worlds* contributions. This Little Known Writer had one earlier story in *Science Fantasy* in 1955 and two more in *Authentic* in 1957; Miller/Contento thinks he may have been a pseudonym but doesn't know whose.

John Boland has three facile but insubstantial stories here. "The Man from Toombla" (**59**) is a lame story about a crazy guy who thinks he's from the planet Toombla, so he is put in an institution, where he begs the psychiatrist to let him have his transmitter, which will return him home. Instead, the psychiatrist uses the transmitter, a small metal block which one holds against the forehead and twists, to show it doesn't work. The psychiatrist winds up in an institution on Toombla, obviously crazy, claiming he's from Earth. "Fabulous Photographer" (**60**), the best of the lot, is a pleasantly silly story about Professor Proni, a refugee from Pransland, who is recruited to return there and neutralize El Supremo Groppo by the expedient of setting up a photography shop with special equipment that generates photos which look enormously flattering to the subject, but reveal the subject's true character to everybody else. El Sup goes for it, and soon is distributing the photos, which make him seem like a clown to the people, who start liking him better, and he's in a better mood anyway, so now he's a man of peace and no further threat to the world.

Carnell calls Boland's "Manhunter" (**62**) a "scientific detective story." After a several-page false start, the author sends Captain Sneeth of the Inter-World Police to a posting on Pheeloparia, where for some reason the accident rate is extremely high, with large numbers failing to come back when they go alone into the countryside. The Captain notices that these disappearances come in threes or fours (or is told, depending on which paragraph you are reading). Turns out the local cops are stalking people for sport. (So why do they keep going into the countryside alone? "'Shut up,' he explained.")

Boland (1913-76) had a brief SF career: he published nine stories, 1956-58, all in *New Worlds* or *Science Fantasy* except for one each in *Galaxy* and *Fantastic*. Most likely, as the SF magazines died off, he saw that there wasn't much future in it and decided to return to greener pastures, with which—as his *New Worlds* Profile in **60** makes clear—he was familiar. He's had the typical writer's quota of miscellaneous jobs and been around North America and Europe, but didn't think of writing SF short stories until he met Carnell, though he had published 100 or so in other fields—presumably crime fiction, since he just organized the first annual conference of the Crime Writers' Association. He was also a five-time president of the Birmingham Writers Group.

Boland published two SF novels in the mid-1950s, *White August* and *No Refuge*, neither of which appeared in the US. Leslie Flood gave both of them decidedly mixed notices, saying some nice things about *White August* but ultimately comparing it unfavorably to Dennis Wheatley, and saying of *No Refuge* that it "adopts that hardy perennial among fantasy themes, the utopian satire, and with the same imaginative flair that characterised his *White August* (and also the same almost indefinable wrongness of character and plot which places his intended realism just beyond credence) succeeds in producing what is to my mind one of the most unpleasant fantasy novels ever to cross my desk." It "compels the reader with the fascination of a hooded cobra." (**57**) The *Encyclopedia of Science Fiction* says his 1959 novel *Operation Red Carpet* has "borderline SF elements" and he had one more SF novel, *Holocaust*, in 1974.

Nita Polinda's "Prodigy" (**55**) is a well-meaning but heavy-handed story about the post-nuclear future, in which the Eugenic Sanitary cops are on the job weeding out mutant kids. Here's one who is such a musical genius that, once revealed, he is offered surgery rather than euthanasia. Carnell notes the author's gender: "we are always more than pleased to welcome a new name to their exclusive ranks. Usually, too, they have a completely different approach to science fiction theme." (Sic) This is her only credit in the SF magazines.

D.M. Parks, of whom the Miller/Contento index says "pseudonym?", contributes "A Sudden Darkness" (**64**), a gimmicky story about an alien animal that telepathically affects mood, but it turns out that's not what's going on at all. Equally gimmicky, but pleasantly acerbic, is "A Sense of Value" (**66**), featuring an insurance company man who does the payouts to people who took out policies, went into suspended animation expecting to wake up rich per Wells' Sleeper, but learn that they have been pauperized by inflation. These are his only SF magazine credits.

Richard Rowland makes his last SF magazine appearance (of four) with "Sold" (**47**), a broadly satirical item about a man who has obtained a mind-manipulating device from some aliens, making him the world's greatest salesman, but the aliens had a longer game of salesmanship going.

§

Now to the real flashes in the pan, those authors with only one story in the genre per Miller/Contento, and that one not worth bothering with. Philip Carver's "Death of Glass" (**59**) scarcely rises to the level of filler: a meteorite lands in Hyde Park, a peculiar fluid is extracted from it, some of it gets loose, it makes people sneeze, two hours after exposure to it (or the sneezes), glass disappears. It seems intended to be funny, but it barely qualifies as a joke, much less a story. P. Quinn's "Unwelcome Stowaway" (**47**) is about a man doing EVA who discovers a housefly in his spacesuit. Assume the worst and you can figure it out. John R. Day's "Birthright" (**49**) is a reasonably competent but unmemorable alien contact story. Paul McClelland's "According to Hoyle" (**62**) rather pointlessly takes up Fred Hoyle's notion that the universe is big enough that we might find a duplicate Earth. A space scout finds the duplicate Earth, which is about 250 years behind the one he came from, proclaims space travel to be an utter bore, and sends his ship off automatically, stranding himself in a more pleasant age and avoiding any jump-start into space of the world he's decided to adopt.

§

So what's for the ages from this period? The best of *New Worlds* during 1956-57 consists largely of nice tries and near misses. About the only story that represents its author at the top of his form is the best of the McIntosh stories, "Report on Earth." Aldiss's "Gesture of Farewell," Ballard's "Build-Up" and "Manhole 69," Brunner's "Host Age," "Thing Friday," and "Fair," and most of Arthur Sellings' and James White's stories are impressive promissory notes, of interest as much for what came later than for themselves.

§

Carnell's editorials during these two years are less tendentious than their predecessors. He still comments on the overall direction of SF publishing, but has less to say about the menacing flood of cheap and bad SF, presumably because it had largely subsided by then—though, to some degree, it is replaced in his disaffections by bad SF films. He spends a lot of words on the 1957 London Worldcon, of which he was chairman, and the run-up to it including his trip to New York in 1956. Other editorials are just benign commentary on passing events (**43**, noting the 1955 International Fantasy Award presentation) or space-filling blather. "S-F and Education" (**56**) says SF doesn't make scientists, but readers are likely to learn a lot about science and technology; "science fiction may not be the keystone to scientific knowledge but at least it is the shop window of the world of To-morrow." "Space Age, Year One" (**65**) acknowledges the launch of Sputnik I. "Superman—What Now?" (**66**) is a confused mélange about immunity, better health care, the emergence of new diseases, lost work days because of minor ailments ("sleeplessness!"), fetching up at the rather unearned conclusion that there is "undoubtedly a world-wide change in the bodily structure of man."

Of more interest with respect to the magazine itself is the **44** editorial, "For Authors Only," which starts with the usual advice about manuscript preparation, but goes on to describe Carnell's requirements and policies pretty specifically. He is only interested in stories from 3,000 to 15,000 words from new contributors; he doesn't use shorter than 3,000, preferring articles.

> Writers with little experience are seldom likely to produce a good first novelette of more than 15,000 words. For similar reasons we are not interested in reading MSS of novel length with a view to possible serialization—if the novel is that good it will sell to a hard-cover publisher long before it reaches our editorial desk. Our serials will either be written specially for us or chosen from novels already accepted for book publication.

Specifically for *New Worlds* stories should be based preferably in the future, although present-day settings are permissible, but not in the *past*—we do not publish stories of Time Travellers who go back to the stone age and hold monosyllabic conversations with Ug and his wife and then present them with a gas lighter and a used bicycle wheel.

We have strong feelings against stories directly connected with current world politics, religion, power-blocks [sic] between leading nations, atomic wars, post-atomic war civilisations dragging their weary way upward again, mad scientists, bug-eyed monsters, visitors from flying saucers and those that commence 'You won't believe this, but...' or are written in diary form and found in a metal cylinder floating in the sea....

Stories need not necessarily have an all-male cast but such stories are preferable to those which introduce questionable romance or still more questionable sex. It is to be expected that women will continue to play as important a role in the future as they have done in the past—there is a place for them in our stories, but writers should make sure that such inclusions are in good taste.

In issue **50**, the editorial is titled "Anniversary," and Carnell rehashes the magazine's history. He notes that in January 1954 "the Company was reorganized and *New Worlds* became a regular monthly publication" but still says not a word about the relationship with Maclaren's. He notes with pride the number of stories that have been anthologized, and mentions plans for the future. The success of Lan Wright's serial "Who Speaks of Conquest?" has "given me some ideas for the future," but meanwhile James White has completed "Tourist Planet." He adds: "There is a two-part serial under construction for early next year [either it got longer, or it didn't appear] and several long novelettes have already been planned and are in embryo stages. The short stories seem to be taking care of themselves."

Carnell doesn't editorialize about the magazine again until **62** ("Traditions..."), where as described above he pronounces the epitaph of interior illustrations. He also notes they've changed the typeface in the last couple of months to make it more readable without loss of wordage (to Times New Roman! an idea whose time clearly had come). Carnell presents the end of illustrations as a rejection of received tradition, along with dropping the two columns of type to one easily readable width (similar to that used in book production) and having no lettering on the cover illustration. "Both were radical departures from the norm and in those days (back in 1949) we were told that we would never get away with it." But, he says, *New Worlds* continued to experiment. "For instance, we never had a *regular* section for readers' letters, but "Postmortem" was set up for anyone who had something really worthwhile to say about science fiction in general. It is still used occasionally but isn't available for bouquets or brickbats. These latter are taken to heart privately."

In other editorials, Carnell writes about the broader world of SF publishing. In **48**, "About Books and Authors," he says that UK publishers are cutting down their SF lists, following similar reductions in the US, but there's still good stuff coming. He praises Clarke's *The City and The Stars*, which neither UK nor US publishers are labeling SF. "It is certainly the first time in science fiction publishing that an already-published novel has been rewritten and published again, and that fact alone makes it an historic occasion."[62] He also praises Bester's *Tiger! Tiger!*— soon to be in *Fantasy & Science Fiction* as "The Burning Spear," he thinks—which he read in ms. and, he says, "at [Bester's] request suggested a number of changes which were eventually incorporated—but we never did agree about the ending. It is

---

62. This is not accurate. One counter-example is Eric Frank Russell's *Sinister Barrier*, revised between its initial UK book publication (Worlds Work, 1943) and its US publication (Fantasy Press, 1947). We suspect there are others.

interesting to note that Anthony Boucher in the June issue of *Fantasy & Science Fiction* states that 'Mr. Bester was attacked by some striking creative afterthoughts.'" Heinlein's *Double Star* is a "powerful new book"—as good as, if not better than, *The Puppet Masters*. John Mantley's *The Twenty-Seventh Day* is "piling up fame before publication," with movie rights and US book rights purchased, probably to appear in serial form in many parts of the world; Carnell avoids saying it's any good.

In **49**, "Greatest Short Stories—1955," he notes that more UK stories are being selected for US anthologies, and there are two possible reasons: UK magazines' quality has improved or US anthologists are trying to be more representative, and in any case there are now fewer magazines. He also notes the decline of the Bleiler/Dikty anthologies and the absence from them of Bleiler, but touts the first Judith Merril anthology—which includes Tubb's "The Last Day of Summer" from *Science Fantasy*—as "first-class." He's pleased that Merril says that the UK SF magazines have a much higher *average* quality than the US magazines.

In **55**, "Congratulations," he observes the fourth anniversary of the UK SF Book Club, but continues: "In general, 1957 is going to be a very poor year for new science fiction books." Few publishers are listing new titles, there is "considerable recession in progress which will tend to turn novelists away from the field to seek other more remunerative themes. Conversely, magazine sales are steadily rising and it would appear that science fiction is swinging back to its original medium.... Many book dealers in USA maintain that the Doubleday Science Fiction Book Club was responsible for killing the general science fiction book market in their country"—its books were often offered almost before they appeared through normal retail channels. This is debatable, says Carnell—maybe SF books just don't sell—but it can't happen in the UK "owing to the conditions laid down by the Publishers' Association in relation to Book Club editions," concerning which he does not elaborate.

In **59**, "European Science Fiction," Carnell notes the spread of SF publishing from Portugal to Finland; *New Worlds* has one subscriber in Moscow and another in the Ukraine. There are European editions of US SF magazines: France, *Fiction*; Italy, *Urania*; Sweden, *Hapna* (eclectic, but mostly from *Astounding*). He says European readers are leaning away from US SF because "so much is taken for granted" that American stories "are almost impossible to follow." They've lost their sense of wonder, which means they are too sophisticated. American SF "is in the doldrums, finally bogged down by its own inventiveness, with all the old plots being reworked by new writing techniques in an attempt to find the missing formula which disappeared when the sense of wonder died." (In another decade or sooner, much the same complaint would be leveled at the New Wave spearheaded by the post-Carnell New Worlds—with the additional grievance that many of them, like jagged atonal compositions or William Burroughs-style word salad cut-ups, disposed of plots almost entirely.)

So more British stories are getting translated while fewer British writers are appearing in American magazines. "With the exception of Arthur Clarke, one seldom sees the names of Wyndham, Christopher, McIntosh, Sellings and other leading British writers on the American contents pages, while our new writers cannot get in at all—in the case of newer writers they simply aren't producing the type of stories required by American editors. Their material is too *simple*."

Carnell's facts are a bit dodgy here. Wyndham and Christopher were publishing almost no short fiction anywhere in the period before this was published in mid-1957. McIntosh had been appearing very regularly in US magazines, though he had a brief falling off in early 1957. Most of Sellings' stories had been in US magazines. And of course Eric Frank Russell, the "other leading British writer" of the moment, was published almost entirely in the US. Carnell admits that by US standards British material is "slightly 'old hat,'" but he says the *New Worlds* serials "Who Speaks of Conquest?" and "Green Destiny" are "receiving considerable continental acclaim." (He doesn't quote any, and it seems unlikely.) He predicts that within seven years, British SF will predominate in the European market.

In **61**, "As Others See Us," Carnell takes an expedition in another direction. He notes the falling off of British SF book publishing in 1957, then quotes at length an editorial in *Science Fiction News* by Australian Graham B. Stone, who has a related complaint. Australians get too many elementary books by authors who don't know the field. His implausible solution: reprint earlier writers who wrote before there was an educated audience and therefore had to explain more—John Taine! A. Merritt! ("His neglect is inexplicable.... In America it would be hard to name another writer in the field who has had a comparable following.") "Similarly with Ray Cummings, Ralph Milne Farley, Victor Rousseau, S. Fowler Wright, Fred MacIsaac, George Allan England." (In fairness, he also complains they are not getting books by Asimov, Bond, Clement, Heinlein, Williamson, etc.) Carnell says: "Mr. Stone's comments are more than reasonable, although I would hate to see some of the earlier 'classics' published *in lieu* of new stories."

"Death of a Corpse" (**45**) is an exasperated rant about the reception of SF by outside critics. "For several years now leading British reviewers and critics of literature have been trying to find some reason for not accepting science fiction into the world of letters and through the medium of radio and the national press we have been treated to a number of face-saving movements which have left the intellectuals secure in their lofty paradise and the body of science fiction a corpse at their feet." This comment is directed towards a BBC "Books and Authors" program "with author-playwright J.B. Priestley in the role of the coroner and thriller-writer Edmund Crispin as the mortician, wherein they endeavored to find by way of assumption a pattern of behaviour for science fiction which would fit into the accepted framework of modern literature." However, they selected two books of short stories, and *American* short stories at that: Crispin's *Best SF* and William Sloane's *Stories for Tomorrow*. "Little wonder that Mr. Priestley complained rather bitterly that science fiction had a predominantly American flavour, which he deplored."

What's more, these hifalutin' mandarins proceeded to pontificate about the SF *novel* from this basis, without acknowledging that "the novel labeled 'science fiction' has only been with us for seven years and is still in its infancy," though a host of prominent writers—including Priestley—have "used science fiction or fantasy as the background to the modern novel." Priestley thought there was little science in SF and the name ought to be changed, and also that there was little satire or humor (to which Crispin cited *The Space Merchants* and *The Big Ball of Wax*). Crispin, according to Carnell, "thought that in many cases they took sin, vice, and political implication and showed them in their nastiness against a future possible background—what he didn't infer was that such stories point a moral to our present way of life." Priestley thought in general SF is badly written, even in Crispin's collection, and that "people shrink instinctively from science fiction... it shows something is wrong with Man who is not (in the stories) moving forward and widening his consciousness." Carnell suggests that Clemence Dane or Nigel Kneale (misspelled) would have been better choices than Priestley, since they actually know something about the subject. "But personally, I wish the intellectuals would leave science fiction alone while there is still time to revive the corpse."

The other subject that arouses Carnell's ire is the movies, which he seems to take very personally indeed. In **46**, "S-f—Hollywood Version," he denounces the current state of SF films, prompted by *Day The World Ended* and its "nauseating companion" *The Phantom From 10,000 Leagues*, "a duo of puerile rubbish it will be difficult to live down in a decade"; *Tarantula*, "in similar vein to the foregoing rubbish"; and *1984*, "which relies upon horror and sadism to hold its audience." He invokes the decline in US SF book publishing and says that "the Hollywood brand of science fiction... will effectively curtail the improvement of the genuine product for many years to come." (Twenty years later, he was right on the money; thirty years after that, it was a done deal, with sci-fi everywhere and real SF appealing to so narrow a slice of the cinema market that it was unprofitable to risk making it.)

He is equally vociferous on the upswing. In **48**, separate from his editorial, he has a film review, of *Forbidden Planet*: "I never thought that I would see the day when a truly first-class science fiction film would be presented on the screen—especially after the many abortive attempts from Hollywood in recent months.... The type of story you read in this or any other leading magazine which has devoted years to perfecting science fiction... so ably handled that the entire film never once enters the realm of pure corn.... *On no account miss this film.*" He returns to this theme—both ends of it—in his **51** editorial, "Horrors to Come?" He has more praise for *Forbidden Planet* ("It is the almost perfect translation into a two-dimensional moving image of magazine science fiction as read and enjoyed by so many thousands of readers for over two decades"), though now it's tempered a bit by the admission of some flaws: "let us at least be pleased that M-G-M didn't include a floor show, two name bands, performing seals and a gum-chewing space-hand from Brooklyn."). He seems to have been set off by Forrest J Ackerman's criticism of the film. An unnamed writer friend describes "the Hollywood treadmill" as "like a giant mincing machine where ideas, inspiration and individual personalities go in at one end, are prefabricated into robot-like components and shot out the other end labeled 'This Side Up—Made In Hollywood.'" In this vein, he bemoans *It Conquered Earth, The Beast With One Million Eyes, Creature From Green Hell*, and others of that ilk. More neutrally, he has a favorable half-page review of the Disney *Man In Space* in **57**.

No fewer than seven editorials are devoted to conventions, starting with the 1956 Eastercon and the announcement of London's Worldcon bid with Carnell as chairman (**47**), Characteristically, he describes conventions as "the finest way of bridging the barrier between professional and amateur and reader." In **52** ("It's London in '57," datelined the Biltmore

Hotel, NY, September 3), he breathlessly relates that "before the tense audience Chairman David A. Kyle of New York City has informed them that by the overwhelming majority of 203 votes to 65 London has outbidden [sic] Oakland, California for the honour of having next year's Convention." Anthony Boucher spoke for Oakland, E.E. Smith supported London. In **54**, "Back to Normal," Carnell is back in London, complaining of the New York heat and glad to be back to "cool air and grey skies, left-hand drive, football pools, warm beer, and no commercials on the BBC." In **57**, he detours to "Australia's 'Olympicon'" of December 1956 in Melbourne at the end of Olympic Games, relying on a report sent by Frank Bryning, which cites appearances by Eric North ("Bernard Cronin"), Norma Hemming, Mr. Wyn (sic) Whiteford, "a local Melbourne author currently selling to Australian publications," and Harvey Blanks, author of the Australian "Captain Miracle" radio serial.

In **58**, "15th World Convention—London," Carnell reports on progress. He's glad that it will be in a hotel that is somewhat isolated from main thoroughfares and "for the first time in the recorded history of Conventions delegates will dine together during off-business hours.... One of the biggest problems at most Conventions has been to find specific delegates or celebrities who are due to appear on a programme after they have gone out for a meal."... "One major difficulty at all Conventions is to get them to start on time." They're going to fix that by formally starting with a banquet luncheon introducing the Guest of Honor and other celebrities. **60**, "More Convention News," reports that John Brunner is hustling the film industry to arrange special theater showings during the Convention. The International Fantasy Award may be revived; a charter flight from New York is being arranged. In **63**, "Final Convention News" as of four weeks before the event, there's an "atmosphere of excitement and anticipation." "Delegates [that word again] are coming from a wide variety of places—the radius exceeds 9,000 miles!" (Apparently he means Clarke and Mike Wilson from Ceylon—otherwise, the most exotic source is Sweden.) He anticipates newspaper and BBC coverage—and "look for *Pathe Pictorial* movie magazine in colour after the Convention ends. Anything can happen!"

In **64**, "The Little 'Bigcon,'" tension is released. It was wonderful, there were 250 "delegates," even John W. Campbell thought it was great. There was lots of interest from the press, "although most of their copy was 'killed' at the editorial desk." Carnell catalogues the prominent attendees and the forgotten, e.g. "Rainer Eisfeld, a young student from Germany, whose brilliant speech brought thunderous applause." BBC interviews with Wyndham and Christopher were "linked with Mr. Campbell's talk and beamed to North America." There was an interesting talk about the new London Planetarium, a display of hypnotism, and Campbell "spoke at some length on the intensely interesting subject of 'psionics'." The inside front cover of **65** has photos of the three magazine Hugo winners (Carnell for best British magazine, Campbell for best American one, and John Victor Peterson picking up the fanzine award for the publishers of *Science Fiction Times*), and of Carnell receiving his from John Wyndham.

§

Leslie Flood, the regular book reviewer, appears in most issues up through **58**; he's not in **45**, which has instead a page on "S-F on Television," or in **48**, where Carnell's editorial is "About Books and Authors," and as noted the book column disappeared in **59-64**. Flood remains lucid and sensible in both praise and criticism, though most of his praise has become conventional wisdom in retrospect. For example (in **50**), he says Bester's *Tiger! Tiger!* is "a slightly tarnished masterpiece.... a furiously paced story which can bludgeon the unwary reader into accepting it on first impression as one of the most significant and spectacular novels ever written in the genre. When the first shock of wonder has worn off, and the pulse has quietened down, it might seem that Mr. Bester, perhaps with tongue in cheek, had resolved to write *the* science-fiction novel to end all such novels." But at the end, "somehow the author loses his grip on his creation.... It is as though Olaf Stapledon had finished a manuscript by Heinlein and Kornbluth and Spillane." But he relents: it "must surely take its place among the top ten science-fiction novels of all time"—a more plausible claim in 1956 than half a century later.

He expresses "jubilation" at Clarke's *The Deep Range* (**65**), and is "tempted to hail this new book as his best novel to date.... I cannot recall a story which has done more than mention in passing the possibilities of the vast undeveloped resources of our oceans being tapped for Man's larders." Either he has a short memory or he hasn't been reading the magazine he reviews for—see Bulmer's serial "Green Destiny," concluded six months previously.

Flood's bile is much more entertaining than his praise. Relish, for example, his comment in **44** on Jerry Sohl's *Costigan's Needle*: "The contribution to the American science-fiction book field by part-time journalist Jerry Sohl has been to date five original hard-cover novels of consistently mediocre stf.-suspense, of which the third and easily the worst, has unfortunately been chosen to mark his debut on the British book scene." On a roll, Flood proceeds to John Taine's *G.O.G. 666*: "science-fiction of the most boring and tasteless sort... incredibly banal ending...." He's a bit nicer to Charles Eric Maine: *Escapement* (*The Man Who Couldn't Sleep* in the US) is "heavily disguised science fiction for popular consumption.... As usual I found Maine's style to be an exasperating mixture of good, bad and indifferent, but with an undefinable attraction that holds the reader to find out how it all ends—something like experimenting with hashish." This is not an analogy I have encountered before in connection with Mr. Maine, whose work might more justly be compared to Nembutal.

John Boland's *No Refuge* (**57**), as noted above, is "one of the most unpleasant fantasy novels ever to cross my desk" and "compels the reader with the fascination of a hooded cobra."

Shute's *On The Beach* (**65**) is "tedious in the extreme."

Most interesting are his comments on books that are less well known. In **43**, for example, he has kind words for *The Demigods* by the erudite (it says here) Alfred Gordon Bennett, a "fairly distinguished literary figure," whose scientific romance about... wait for it... giant ants bent on world domination... missed its chance at immortality in 1939 when the print run was destroyed in the War. In **44**, Flood says of Reed R. DeRouen's *Split Image*, about a near-duplicate Earth, "I finished this profoundly interesting book completely baffled." In **46**, "When a writer of the calibre of Lance Sieveking turns his attention to science fiction one may confidently expect a high degree of literary and entertainment value." This Sieveking is Advisory Editor of "Modern Novels of Science and Imagination" for publisher Ward, Lock, and the first two selections are Conquest's *A World of Difference* ("I applaud Mr. Conquest for a sincere try at a superior s-f novel, and hope that his next book will be more readable") and Sieveking's own *A Private Volcano*, "a cracking adventure novel" involving the discovery of "volcanium"—it turns base metals into gold—on a Pacific island.

In **49**, he reviews S. Makepeace Lott's *Escape To Venus* decidedly mixedly. Citizens have Ability Level numbers and "Gamma nervous ratings," and the only freedom is a one-way trip to a Venus colony. This is an "exceedingly complex and thoughtful novel... another unsuccessful example of mainstreaming the science fiction novel by a competent writer whose approach to this medium is over-sophisticated...." In Claude Yelnick's *The Trembling Tower* (**56**), translated from the French, a body and a journal are found in a lighthouse; Flood says realism of style contrasts to "fantastic theories of vibrational, other-dimensional entities" and the "uneasy ending"—"very readable." Harold Mead's Orwellian *Mary's Country* (no US edition, little known in the UK) is "a very fine piece of story-telling indeed."

Flood gets his *New Worlds* Profile in **48** (an issue without reviews), his large and genial face accompanied by genial comments: 34 years old, 14 of them married, education interrupted by the war and service overseas with the R.A.F. "Science fiction was the beacon that brought me out of earning a living the dull way and finally into bookselling." He adds that reviewing comes naturally from his inability to write any original SF of his own. "I sincerely hope that I am succeeding in the impossible task of pleasing readers, authors, publishers—*and* my conscience."

6: UP A NOTCH (1958-59)

New Worlds entered 1958 as a smooth operation, maintaining a regular schedule, consistent in presentation and reasonably competent in substance—but, as suggested in the previous chapter, in a bit of a rut. Carnell himself implicitly acknowledges as much. His editorial in the first issue of 1958 promises that changes will be made, and they are. Whether and how they actually address the problem is a matter of debate, though in the end it seems indisputable that *New Worlds* becomes a better magazine in 1958-59 than during the previous two years.

First, the basics. The magazine remains digest sized, 128 pages exclusive of covers, priced at 2/-, monthly with one exception: it misses an issue, with **86** being dated August/September 1959 and running only 112 pages as a result of a printers' strike, as Carnell explains in his editorial in that issue. There are ads, first half-page and then full-page, usually on inside and outside back cover, for *New Worlds*'s companions *Science Fantasy* and *Science Fiction Adventures*, begun in 1958 (and we'll deal in detail with that magazine separately, in the second volume), and a scattering of smaller house ads for back issues and binders.

"The Literary Line-Up" appears in every issue. The *New Worlds* Profile of author or artist appears in all but one issue, on the inside front cover or occasionally the inside back cover. There is an editorial in every issue but one (in **76**, the space is used for a Solacon convention report by Ron Bennett). The book review column has become irregular, in four issues only (one of them in the form of a guest editorial), apparently because

UK SF books have slowed to a trickle. "Postmortem," the letter column, now appears in almost every issue, as discussed further below. There is an article on a scientific subject in nearly every issue, usually by Kenneth Johns.

So what changes? In Carnell's editorial in **67** (January 1958), titled "Happy New Year," he promises "many stories with a 'different' outlook," citing Brian Aldiss's "The Pit My Parish" and Peter Phillips' "Next Stop the Moon" in that issue. These are, he says, "completely different from the normal type of presentation, yet are still written around ideas which have been used many times before. John Brunner's serial [the recent "Threshold of Eternity"] is another case in point, only more so, as he has more than one idea running at a time." He announces a new serial next issue by Eric Frank Russell: "Russell has been tradition breaking for many years and this new story is no exception. It ties in well with our search for the 'new look' in science fiction."

As a package of innovations these stories don't much impress. Aldiss, yes: "The Pit My Parish" is solidly in the chilly and depressing vein—"The Stars My Detestation" as he titled a book chapter in *Trillion Year Spree*—that he made his own for the next several years. But Phillips' story, a space rescue in cheerleading mode written for a newspaper immediately after the first Sputnik, departs from the *New Worlds* mainstream only in being told in the form of journalistic dispatches and written in a glib and breezy Yank style (nothing new for Phillips). Russell's serialized novel *Wasp* is if anything a throwback, essentially a World War II behind-the-lines sabotage story with aliens instead of Germans or Japanese, written in *his* glib and breezy American-pastiche style, the one he'd been developing for going on 20 years. And Brunner acknowledged that his novel was inspired by A. E. van Vogt.

One thing that is different from the previous couple of years is that the novels are no longer all by Carnell's home-grown contributors. He has gone for some marquee names with track records of book publication. While there are serials by Lan

Wright, Kenneth Bulmer, and Brian Aldiss (all of which went straight to Ace Doubles), the others are by Russell (his first fiction appearance in *New Worlds*), Charles Eric Maine (his first and only appearance of any sort in *New Worlds*, but he'd had a number of novels in hardcover in the UK and the US by this time), and Philip K. Dick (whose *World Of Chance* and *A Handful of Darkness* had been well received in the UK, though none of his subsequent books had yet been published there).

In addition, John Wyndham appears with a near-serial, the four novelettes that were assembled and published as *The Outward Urge* and that Carnell refers to as a novel when he first announces it. They appear between the April and September 1958 issues (**70-75**). However, these big-name items (with the exception of *Time Out of Joint*, no doubt one of the half-dozen best pieces of fiction *New Worlds* ever published) are not necessarily their authors' best work or significantly better than the other contents of the magazine, though they are smoother and more professionally done than the preceding crop of serials by the *New Worlds* regulars.

But the *New Worlds* of these years is improved, and the changes are mainly at the middle and bottom. More capable, or at least livelier, new writers are starting to appear in the magazine; some of the familiar contributors are getting better. The more lackluster of the established contributors are appearing less frequently. In 1956-57, Francis G. Rayer, E. R. James, and Alan Barclay had 22 stories among them; in 1958-59, they have 11. Sydney J. Bounds has three stories in 1958, and then he's gone for the rest of Carnell's reign. But Colin Kapp and Robert Presslie appear with 11 stories between them, and Philip E. High has four. They are far from consistently excellent, but even their lesser productions are more readable than most of those of Rayer, James, Barclay and Bounds (though in fairness, even these writers—except for Bounds—are looking a little better by the end of 1959).

This improved home-grown material may be the reason the number of stories previously published in US magazines dropped from 12 in 1958 to 3 in 1959 (and to one each in 1960 and 1961, and to zero thereafter). Mike Ashley has said in the Tymn/Ashley reference volume that the "golden era" of *New Worlds* was from 1956 to 1961. By the end of 1959, I'd agree that *New Worlds* was quite competitive with most of the US magazines at the second tier and below—*If, Fantastic Universe*, the Ziff-Davis magazines, the Columbia magazines—and not far behind *Galaxy* and *Astounding*, which were then at a fairly low ebb. Carnell energetically agrees that his magazine is making great strides, saying in his editorial review in 1958 (**79**): "Despite the poor year universally, it seems that *New Worlds* has had one of the best since it was first published and we are looking forward to an equally good 1959." And in the next issue: "Undoubtedly... 1958 will turn out to be one of our most important literary years—a keystone in our future publishing programme—in view of the number of new writers it produced and the improvement in technique of writers who had already begun to establish themselves." Unfortunately, he then touts the forthcoming Charles Eric Maine serial—see below about that.

Another change promised by Carnell is in the magazine's visual presentation, and that promise is delivered on much more clearly and dramatically. The issue after next, he says in **67**, "will probably see something quite different in the way of cover pictures, too, as we have gradually been working up to the idea that abstract art is an expressionistic medium readily adaptable to stories of the future. I am of the opinion that science fiction magazines now need something more than the accepted form of spaceship cover or prosaic action-adventure illustration." The background here (as observed in the previous chapter) is that *New Worlds*'s covers had been becoming less and less interesting, dominated by conventional space scenes and cartoonish human figures, often quite cluttered, SF business as usual without any flair to speak of.[63] The cover of **69**, by the same Brian Lewis responsible for the rather dismal ones on **61** and

---

63. See these covers at http://www.sfcovers.net/mainnav.htm or http://www.philsp.com/mags/newworlds.html.

64-66, is a shocking departure of the most pleasant sort: cryptic machines on a desert surface against a scarlet sky, which after you look at it a bit resolves into a tethered airship or spaceship, maybe being refueled by the strange structure it is connected to. It appears that Lewis has gone to school on Richard Powers and then nudged things a few degrees back towards the illustrative. **70**'s cover is a bit of a misfire, too far back in the illustrative direction and not especially tasteful—woman seated in spacesuit, boots and helmet off, and a variety of other artifacts foregrounded, including a couple of copies of *New Worlds* (**64** and **66** to be precise), all against a garish yellow background.[64] Among the odd items in the foreground are what appear to be a lipstick and a compact. (Well, they could be a vibrator and a diaphragm case, but that seems unlikely.)

But Lewis is back on track in **71**: blue desert surface, less garish yellow sky, helmet and other small artifacts in the foreground and what looks like an alien city or other installation in the background, with aurora-like discharge over it. There are a number of these covers through 1959 (**74**, **76**, **83**, **88** particularly) in which Lewis to my taste improves on Powers, with results that are livelier and more vivid than Powers. At the other extreme, Lewis reverts to clumsy conventional illustration on several of the covers (notably **77**, with a cheesy dinosaur illustrating James White's "Trouble with Emily," and **81**, **82**, and **84**, back to the wax-model style of depicting people). In between, however, he does several other very fine illustrative covers, avoiding both the clichés and the clutter of his 1957 covers. See especially **78**, phallic spaceship with style; **79**, a distant view of spacesuited humans inspecting an ancient extraterrestrial building, one of the most pleasing covers I've seen on an SF magazine; **87**, illustrating Kapp's "The Railways Up on Cannis," with hyperreal railroading scene against volcanic background.[65] In all his styles, Lewis displays a startlingly distinctive color

---

64. Broderick, who finds this quite striking, disagrees.

65. An especially vivid and memorable image, reports Broderick.

sense compared to his competition at other SF magazines. After **69**, all the covers are by Lewis except for **80**, by one Edwards, who did not appear again and about whom the less said the better. Midway through 1958, the cover format changes, from full-page picture and band with titles or author names at the bottom, to side band and much narrower picture field (the look kept by the magazine until the beginning of 1962). This format actually frames Lewis's work to better advantage than the full page format, especially his more vividly colorful efforts. At this point, *New Worlds* is in the running for best-looking SF magazine anywhere.

There is a certain amount of comment on the new covers in "Postmortem," of which the liveliest is by Brian Aldiss, who says in **72** that the cover of **69** "raises my hopes again.... [Lewis] has the essential ingredient needed on the cover: style." In **76**, one A. Taylor of Surrey argues at length that the covers are not, as Carnell termed them, abstract, but rather surrealistic. In the next issue, Aldiss agrees that Lewis's covers are not abstract as the term is used in artistic circles, and adds:

> Nor are they strictly surrealist, though many of them remind me of Tanguy. You should invent a new term for them; how about "cosmic ghismics"? later to be known more simply as "ghosmics" or "chismix." Where your correspondent goes wrong is to suggest they aren't good covers. I don't think they're always good art, but by crikey they're always good *covers*! They give the whole thing style.

In **78**, Laurence Sandfield of London dissents: the new covers "are very effective as posters and that is about all one can say about them.... I never could stand purely symbolic art, or yellow skies, either." Carnell responds that he didn't intend to produce posters "although posters are usually designed to sell goods—and we have a magazine to sell," and that yellow cover on **71** was a good seller.

Lewis has the *New Worlds* Profile in **72**:

> Technical artist with a leading radar company, it has only been in recent years that Brian Lewis has become interested in science fiction art, most of his work having taken him through engineering draftsmanship. He feels, rightly, that this profession has given him a good grounding in mechanics and enables him to be technically accurate when illustrating spaceship scenes. In fact, he was recently consulted by Associated Rediffusion and had a credit line as Technical Adviser on a thirty minute TV play hammed-up as science fiction.

He went from technical school to the RAF for seven years, where he started reading SF, though he never expected to do anything other than read it. He admires Ed Emsh, "America's s-f artist," but doesn't intend to emulate him. He says:

> The new-style paintings requested by editor Carnell give tremendous scope to an artist with imagination and I hope to make every painting as radically different as possible. There is no limit to the colour combinations and abstract symbolisms that can be used and I feel that we are setting a new standard of cover illustration specifically suited to science fiction.

The other notable change does not get much discussion from Carnell: the return of "Postmortem" as a regular feature, and further, as a general forum for discussion of the magazine. Since the takeover by Maclaren's, Carnell has repeatedly denigrated that kind of letter column, which in his editorial in **28** he said was sought by "younger and more enthusiastic readers"; his policy statement was that "'Postmortem' will be featured when space permits and when the subject matter of such letters available has something to contribute to science fiction in general and not this magazine in particular. I would rather publish fiction than spare space for arguments on the merits or de-merits of stories we publish, knowing that 90% of such arguments are based solely upon personal likes and dislikes.... It is not a policy of mine to publish eulogies by readers about this magazine—it is as one-sided an opinion as story preferences."

As late as **67**, he disdains a review in *Science Fiction Times* that says the "failure of modern science fiction magazines" is "the lack of art work, readers' columns, and good fan departments." He ripostes: "Traditions die extremely hard—the last place these particular ones will perish is in the USA where they originated," but economics dooms them.

Nonetheless, having appeared only once in 1956-57, "Postmortem" appears in **68**, with one long letter consisting of the formerly condemned bouquets and brickbats, and in **69** it's six pages long, and it appears in all but five issues thereafter. In the editorial in **69**, Carnell says "we are receiving lots of interesting letters from readers all over the world. As long as these keep coming in we will devote space to them in the 'Postmortem' section—it's up to you." And in **74**, where it is absent, he says: "Sorry your letter section has been squeezed out this issue, but we will make up for it next month." There's no comment at all on the reasons for Carnell's drastic change of heart, or even the fact of it.

§

In **68**'s editorial, "Bridging the Gap," Carnell announces *Science Fiction Adventures*, to start bimonthly, alternating with *Science Fantasy*, "but I wouldn't be the least bit surprised to see it a monthly before the year is out." (It wasn't; it was monthly for a couple of months at the end of 1959, but that was it.) "Basically, the formula for all the stories will be action-adventure against a science fiction background, written by most of the leading American writers in the field." Carnell acknowledges the stories will be reprints from the American magazine of the same name, and says that Larry T. Shaw, its editor, is "one of the liveliest of live-wire editors to enter the publishing field in recent years," who has found the missing sense of wonder. The intent is to provide an "introductory medium," because SF in the long established magazines is often "incomprehensible to casual readers." In today's critical terms, newbies are as yet unacquainted with the SF *megatext* or immense backstory, created and sophisticated over decades in a thousand earlier stories and novels, with its long-established tropes, devices, ways of building worlds with words old and new.[66]

The magazine will be a *must*, Carnell assures us, because readers "already know the literary skill of such American authors as C.M. Kornbluth, Robert Silverberg, Jerry Sohl [!], Algis Budrys and others...." I can't imagine what he means with respect to Sohl, who had not previously appeared in any UK SF magazine—and here again is what Leslie Flood had to say in **44** about *Costigan's Needle*, Sohl's first UK book: "The contribution to the American science-fiction book field by part-time journalist Jerry Sohl has been to date five original hard-cover novels of consistently mediocre stf.-suspense, of which the third and easily the worst, has unfortunately been chosen to mark his debut on the British book scene."

Carnell concludes: "As a final testimonial, let me say that with over thirty years science fiction reading behind me, and despite many years professional experience, the stories in *Science Fiction Adventures* are once again giving me the same thrills I encountered a quarter of a century ago." Of course he had to change his plans less than a year later, but the news was not all bad. In **78**, he reports that the US magazine has folded, but the UK version has been successful and he has arranged to continue it with new material. We'll look in detail at *Science Fiction Adventures* in the next volume.

In his **84** editorial, "Science Fantasy," Carnell tries to give his other magazine a comparable boost. His reader survey shows that many *New Worlds* readers do not also read *Science Fantasy*,

66. See the discussion in Damien Broderick's *Reading by Starlight* (London: Routledge, 1995).

though he says it has nearly as high a circulation and "probably has a higher literary standard" based on anthologization and foreign publication. "There must be something psychological in the word 'fantasy' which puts many readers off." They've thought about changing the title, and certainly American magazines with "fantasy" in the title are mostly SF. This is Carnell's bid to reassure the *New Worlds* readers that they should try *Science Fantasy*, too, since it really has a lot of SF in it, especially stories too long for *New Worlds*, like Brunner's "Earth Is But a Star," McIntosh's "200 Years to Christmas," and Clarke's "The Songs of Distant Earth."

As usual, Carnell has a lot of color commentary on the state of SF. In **69** ("Phases of S-f"), published in March 1958, he reveals the secrets of circulation: "Year after year our sales graph follows a recognised pattern, increases and decreases being almost entirely governed by the vagaries of the weather— with bad weather (and a corresponding increase in illness) the more reading is done." So Sputnik doesn't account for the recent increase. Carnell notes reports that US SF magazine circulation has dropped slightly in recent months despite the huge publicity about Sputnik.

> In view of such wide publicity there must be a vast new potential readership which has hitherto been untouched by the American magazine publishers—if only a small percentage of this untapped source were to buy one magazine a month sales would double over night, yet if anything the response is lower than before last October.
>
> I think there is a simple enough reason for this— a factor I have pointed out in earlier editorials. The science fiction magazines are too specialised for the general market and rely almost entirely on their own "closed-shop" type of readership. Readers in this field are made, not born to it, and it takes several years for such a reader to graduate to the stage where he can

fully appreciate and understand most of the deeper complexities of plot and theory promulgated by most of the leading writers (who were, at one stage, just such readers themselves).

Carnell cites a letter in "Postmortem" from one Bryan Welham:

> He complains that the stories in this magazine are boring, gives his reasons and asks for more human interest. Basically I think that his complaint is one against magazine science fiction in general and not this magazine in particular as subsequent correspondence between us revealed that he and his friends are in the under-20's. He has now reached the stage where the short story no longer appeals because there is insufficient length for the author to develop both scientific context and characterisation. Only in the novel will he find the two combined in a satisfactory manner.
>
> Casual new readers to science fiction undoubtedly find the same dissatisfaction in the magazines although they probably cannot define the reason. Or don't bother.

Even regular readers have highs and lows of interest, sometimes stopping for years.

> These "low" periods always coincide with outside factors involving a change of job, moving to a new neighborhood, marriage, the arrival of a family, increased study—in fact, *any* change in the norm plays a prominent part in the temporary decline of a person's reading habits. Science fiction, however, has that elusive "something" which always draws a reader back again with renewed interest.

At the moment there is a greatly increased interest in science fiction—although an early Spring could well force a decline—and we are receiving lots of interesting letters from readers all over the world. As long as these keep coming in we will devote space to them in the "Postmortem" section—it's up to you.

In the next issue (**70**, "Phases of S-f (2))," Carnell recaps an article, "Science Fiction and the Space Era" by Robert Hale in *Publisher's Weekly*. An overall increase in the sales of existing SF paperbacks was seen after Sputnik, publishers predict increased print orders, but none of them expect to increase the number of SF titles for 1958. The sales of factual books, especially on satellites, has jumped tremendously. General bookstores in New York find a heavy demand for SF novels, yet specialized SF stores have had a big fall-off. Publishers predict a gradual long range increase in the SF readership. Carnell asks where the magazines fit in.

You have to remember that there is a wide difference between the appeal of the novel and that of the short story. In the novel the mechanics of the plot are not so exacting and the author has far greater room for movement of both characters and locale—in the greater length he can develop his theme slowly but at length using the subtleties of the written language to their best advantage; whereas in the short story the author is limited in his word-length and must place action and characterization above all else.

Therefore there are more readers for paperbacks than magazines, this borne out by a survey at Nycon, the last world SF convention, which allegedly showed that "on an average the same people bought *all* the magazines published—there were no different classes of readership for differing magazines—but that the proportion of sales for pocketbooks was higher than the magazine sales." It remains to be seen, he notes, how this will play out in the UK.

Carnell is back on the case in **74** ("Around the S-F World"). The US recession has hit SF magazines, industrial unrest has "played havoc with all fiction sales in Great Britain, but the wet June and July has apparently put a stop to falling sales." The British Science Fiction Association (BSFA) has been founded, and *New Worlds* has received a request from the Lenin State Library in Moscow for "copies regularly!" More portentously (**77**, "Is this the New Trend?"), he says 1958 has been a peak year for British writers selling to the US. More novels were reprinted in the US than in any year since 1948. On both sides of the Atlantic there is a sudden expansion of science fiction paperback titles. "The sudden increase in the British market is not a reflection of the American trend in this instance. Here we have seen the belated rise of all types of pocketbooks into a major form of publishing—certainly the popularity of the cheap mass market approach was a natural outcome of the high cost of bound books." He expects a larger number of SF titles in the UK. Already there are more titles in paperback than at the peak of the hardcover boom four years previously.

> A significant pointer to British sales potential is the fact that publishers are now offering four times as much for pocketbook Rights than they were five years ago. Most of our top writers are finding that one novel now sells in hard and soft-cover editions in Britain and America and produces a net return never before expected in this specialised medium. [This improvement is attracting more writers to the novel] but at present there is a controlling factor in the pocketbook field which does not offer a great deal of hope for the new-comer. Practically all pocketbook titles are taken from the lists of already published hardcover books, where at present there is a considerable backlog of good material by well-known authors. The few "original" titles

are *always* by established writers—no pocketbook publisher is going to risk his money on an unknown unless his name has at least been established in the s-f magazines.

Undoubtedly a compromise will materialise in the form of limited bound editions for sale to libraries and the connoisseur, followed by large printings of paper editions....

It looks, therefore, as though the novel-length s-f story will come into its own very shortly.

In **79** ("1958 in Retrospect"), Carnell notes the dearth of SF books in the UK and the recession in the US. He says the only notable books in the US were Clarke's *The Other Side Of The Sky,* Heinlein's *Have Spacesuit—Will Travel* and *Methuselah's Children,* Fadiman's *Fantasia Mathematica,* Merril's *SF: The Year's Best,* and Sturgeon's *A Touch Of Strange*—ignoring Blish's *A Case Of Conscience*, which went on to win the Hugo but was published in paperback only. In the UK, the two most outstanding books were Aldiss's *Non-Stop* and Crispin's *Best SF 3*. In films, there was "nothing above the moronic level." But: "Despite the poor year universally, it seems that *New Worlds* has had one of the best since it was first published and we are looking forward to an equally good 1959."

In **87** ("Comment from Australia"), Carnell cites the views of R.D. Nicholson in the Australian fanzine *Scansion*, denouncing the US SF magazines and stating that "at present only *New Worlds* holds any promise." (In 1953, he had published "Far From the Warming Sun" in *Galaxy*.) Nicholson also asks why the quality of stories falls off so much in the "lows" of SF publishing. Carnell replies that as markets narrow, the best professionals move to other fields and editors have to rely on second-string writers, and new writers are discouraged. During the past two years Heinlein, Bester, Bradbury, Asimov, Williamson, Clarke, Wyndham, Sturgeon, del Rey, Tucker, McIntosh, Christopher, Hamilton, and many others have nearly disappeared from SF short fiction. (This list is a trifle dodgy. In reality, Asimov had 13 stories in the SF magazines in 1958-59, though he did disappear thereafter; Bester had three, after having none in 1955-57; Sturgeon had 5; McIntosh had 7; Tucker disappeared after 1954 and reappeared in 1959.) Nicholson states that Carnell has not added anything distinctly new, and can't rely on getting the output of his most promising writers because they move on to the US magazines—what could he do if he could draw on a US budget? "One of the most discerning statements I have yet read!" Carnell laments. "I have often wondered myself!"

Carnell took another readers' survey in 1958, reporting that compared to 1955, the readership is slightly younger, slightly less male (90% vs. 95%), better educated but not more affluent on average (though the highest income bracket is much larger), more likely to have technical employment. 28% belong to the SF Book Club. The women are much like the men, except 24% of them are housewives with no income. They also seem to read more than the men. (**83**, "Survey Report 1958"; **85**, "1958 Survey... The Ladies").

Carnell continues his commentary on SF in the media, with "Bouquets for the BBC" (**81**), praise for "Quatermass and the Pit," and "And Brickbats to ITA" (**82**), about the TV play "Before the Sun Goes Down," which had a similar effect in the UK to that of the Welles "War of the Worlds" broadcast in the US. Carnell condemns its sensationalism and says it was a bad play anyway. There's a filler in **79** noting the forthcoming filming of Leonard Wibberley's *The Mouse That Roared*.

§

Leslie Flood's book reviews continue, much diminished. Review columns appear in **68**, **76**, and **84**, and he gets the editorial space for a "Guest Editorial About Books" in **73**. Why the shrinkage? No books. He says in **73**: "I have received, in the past six months, a grand total of *three* books submitted for review, of which two bear the same publisher's imprint." All are reprints from the US. "The cornucopia of English science fiction books, as we all know, blocked itself finally with its own squashy outpouring of perished fruit, and after its spring-clean, appeared to have dried up forever." Flood remains as concisely wise as ever about the few books that do find their way to him. Hoyle's *The Black Cloud* "suffers from a welter of scientific garrulity and a lack of smooth novelisation" (**68**). Heinlein's *Double Star* is "one of the more pleasurable pieces of escapist entertainment I have read for a long time," but "[t]he most rewarding buy of the month" is Jack Finney's *The Clock Of Time* (UK title of *The Third Level*) (**73**). Aldiss's *Non-Stop* is "a science-fiction adventure in the grand manner. Having nothing in common with the Aldiss of *Space, Time, and Nathaniel*, except satisfying storytelling.... Where Aldiss scores is in his uncomplicated action-filled development of the story which guarantees interest to the end." (**76**) Of Edmund Cooper's *That Uncertain Midnight* (a.k.a. *Deadly Image*), he writes: "Seemingly trite? Yes, but lifted out of the ordinary by the author's elegant prose and flair for the occasional polished phrase which delights enormously, particularly in the opening chapters." But then it "lapses into a hack battle between the androids and the rebels, whilst the emotional situation between hero and female android, always incredible, becomes slightly ludicrous."

He praises the early parts of Blish's *A Case Of Conscience*, complains that once back on Earth "the various sub-plots muddy the story to an extent that the original impact of the Jesuit's troubled conscience is nearly, but not quite, lost. Recommended." (**84**) Compton Mackenzie's *The Lunatic Republic* is a Swiftian satire about a Lunar society, which palls after a while (**84**). Tellingly, Flood admits in **76**, "Moreover a small but steady flow of science-fictional paperbacks, mentioned later, continues to represent the genre in this increasingly important book field." He lists them in a couple of paragraphs (nine such, seemingly all reprints). The writing is on the wall: sooner or later Flood and *New Worlds* will have to take paperbacks seriously.

There is relatively little advertising other than house ads. The publishers' advertising of prior years is gone (the only exception is in **68**, from Acorn Press, for *Other Worlds In Space* by Terry Maloney). The UK SF Book Club takes up a bit of the slack, with full-page ads in **71**, **78**, **81**, **84** and **86**. In **78**, they tout *The Blockhouse* by Jean-Paul Clebert, translated from the French: "A group of men suffer the nightmare of being entombed for six years. This is the fantastic story of how the lucky ones died and two monsters who survived." I think I'm glad I missed it. Blue Centaur Books in Sydney ("Australasian Readers: A science fiction service on your own continent") advertises in **72** through **77**, and the UK's Plus Books in **79**. The BSFA takes the bottom of a page in **80** and **83**.

On the inside front cover of **72**, there is "The Versatile R.F.T" —"Richest Field Telescope"—sold by Charles Frank: "With an RFT in your hands you are no longer earthbound." It says here it "will also reveal all the brighter asteroids." Also (smaller type, and hilarious, but deeply misleading to youthful or excessively hopeful readers): "The image is erect—making it no mean instrument for the observation of distant terrestrial life forms and for the identification of buoyant artifacts on the surface of the condensed portion of the planet's hydrosphere." They want 3 pounds 15 shillings, postage included. The inside front cover of **74** is taken by Planned Families Publications: "Worry and upsets between husbands and wives are so frequently caused because they lack knowledge of modern family planning.... Every married couple should have a copy. You can get yours now, absolutely free." Sent "UNDER PLAIN COVER." Small ads ("Sales and Wants") are in most issues starting with **75**.

In addition to the ads, there are several brief fillers endorsing worthy projects which appear to be in the nature of public service announcements, presumably by Carnell: half a page about the Detroit Worldcon (**80**), Eastercon (**81**), the forthcoming BSFA index to *New Worlds* (**82**), and the Donald Tuck *Handbook of Science Fiction and Fantasy* (**86**). In **78**, there is "Young Ideas for Christmas," endorsing the Rathbone edition of the Disney *World of Nature* book, as well as *Satellite Shoot*, a board game based on *Battleships*, with plot-tables for players to work out their moves, space satellites of different denominations to shoot at, and a scoring system for shots fired. Had he but known where that would end, in the dawning age of computers.

The new "Postmortem" is, in Carnell's former disparaging phrase, mostly brickbats and bouquets, few of which are very interesting at this late date. But there are exceptions. In **69**, a Bryan Welham of Clacton-on-Sea, Essex complains that "your science fiction stories are becoming boring in nature and monotonous by their constant similarity.... Almost every story is jam-packed with science and pseudo-science and become rather tedious as you read them. They are becoming this because they omit one thing—the human element.... [Characters] do not appear as people. They are robots, totally devoid of human emotion and instincts...." But in the next issue, Harry Harrison, in Napoli at the moment, says the difference between *New Worlds* and US magazines is elusive, but "I think perhaps that it is your policy of *people* in science fiction futures, not just science fiction stories."

Brian Aldiss in **72** says, "You may recall that Sir Thomas Beecham once described British music as 'a continuous series of promissory notes.' Sometimes I have wondered if he was not talking about British s-f. However, let's not raise that here: the point is, the scene has changed." He says that *New Worlds* now "looks a real professional job," praises Brian Lewis as quoted earlier, and says the best part of the magazine is the revitalized "Postmortem." Then he takes up the cudgels over Mr. Welham's complaint about characterization, surmising that what bothers him is really people doing unlikely things, like rebelling against an oppressive system. The "real story" would be one in which hypothetical protagonist Joe behaves "like most of today's heroes: loathing a lot of what he sees going on around him, but sweating it out and giving all those round him the best life possible in the circumstances."

This arouses John Boland (**75**) to ask "isn't it rather dangerous to allow him to air his subtle fun in the way he does in 'Postmortem'?" Boland takes issue with Aldiss's suggestion that we need fiction about the ordinary Joe. We need it about the "extra-ordinary Joe," and says it's a leg-pull that today's heroes are the ones who sit around and sweat it out. Oh dear, I thought that kerfuffle didn't start up until about 1965. J. Curzon (Mrs.), Marlborough, Wilts., provides Aldiss with the kind of support he probably would rather do without: "How I agree with Brian Aldiss about lack of characterization. I often feel I would like to tell the authors to go and read books by *real* authors."

In **78**, it's manifesto time again. Dan Morgan has 2 ½ pages about how he used to prefer American SF writers: "The one thing I loathed above all was the typically British science fiction with its pages of 'Lo and Behold!' descriptive matter.... Until I began to read an increasing number of stories in American mags which left me at the end with a feeling of: 'Yes, very clever, but *so what?*" He perorates briefly on Character and Suspense, then complains that the Americans

> are in the main writing in an efficiently professional manner for the pulp magazines of their own country which require fiction catering for a semi-juvenile level of intelligence.... Science fiction *is* a product to them, something turned out to order with an eye mainly on the average rate of around [ten pounds] a thousand.... For my part, I am trying to produce something which gives me the satisfaction of feeling that I am communicating something of value to human beings about the proper study of mankind. I make no claim to literary merit. I am just trying to do the job in the best way.

In the same issue is a bracing rant from F. Haller of Derby, prompted by the non-appearance from UK publishers of Frank Herbert's "Under Pressure" a.k.a. *The Dragon in the Sea*: "It is sad to think that the publishers at large have so debauched and finally reduced the science fiction buying public to such numbers that we are not given this novel as a matter of course.

It is maddening to know that that frantically lunatic story 'Recruiting Station' [a novella by A. E. van Vogt] has attained the dignity of hard covers while the 'Dragon' has not." He suggests that the Science Fiction Book Club produce its own anthologies, instead of "such unmitigated rubbish as *Moment Without Time* [a.k.a. *The Best From Startling Stories*] or *World Of Chance* [in the US, *Solar Lottery*, by Philip K. Dick]."

But the last word belongs to Lt. Col. O.R. Franklin, USAF, of Florida: "In all honesty, I must admit that the last few issues of *New Worlds* have been superior to all the rest, well edited and clearly printed in excellent type on rather good paper."

In **81**, Arthur Sellings has *his* manifesto, a long letter that purports to be a stock-taking of SF. Strong editors lead to a new conformism (mentions no names). SF is a literature of ideas, notwithstanding J. T. McIntosh to the contrary of several years previously. There are lots of ideas you can't write stories about. "For instance, two forms that are frowned on are the interior monologue and the episodic pattern which shows the impact of a central event on unconnected characters. Which is unfortunate, because both are obviously useful in science fiction." SF identifies too much with the mainstream. "Science fiction must be itself." In **88**, Mr. Haller of Derby is back, this time denouncing "childish wishful thinking on psi" and suggesting "more *Black Clouds* and *Preludes To Space* and few[er] *More Than Humans*."

It seems pretty clear that most of what goes on in "Postmortem" will have little or no effect on anything that happens in the rest of the magazine, but there's one exception. In **75**, an R. Critchley of Bournemouth, Hants., complains of the lack of articles on "historical, psychological scientific or sociological" subjects, and here in **78** is "Year 102 A.F."—i.e., after the birth of Freud—by Roger Critchley, a reasonably well done term paper about the basics of Freud's work and theory. He says: "Nowhere have Freud's theories been more readily used than in literature, and above all in science fiction. Perhaps the most complete application is in Alfred Bester's *The Demolished*

Man, where telepathy is the only psychological concept not descended, directly or indirectly, from Freud."

§

The serials and quasi-serials in these issues are, as suggested, a very mixed bag. Eric Frank Russell's "Wasp" (**69-71**), previously published by Avalon in the US and later to be published by Dobson, seemed tedious when I took it from the public library at age 10 and it hasn't improved since—essentially a mundane war story about a saboteur (or terrorist) behind enemy lines, told in Russell's cartoony and wisecracking style but without much actual humor. It is a smoother and more professional read than most of the preceding serials by Carnell's tyros, and apparently it was reasonably popular with the readers. Leslie Flood puts the best face on it in his review of the book version in **79**: after acknowledging its implausibility, he concludes: "Nevertheless, as a lively puppet show can be enjoyed by a tolerant audience, so it is possible to revel in Russell's smoothly styled action, sardonic eye for humourous details, and, let's face it, his gift for sheer readability." (**79**) So I was an intolerant child.

Brian W. Aldiss's two-part serial "Equator" (**75-76**) is a sort of thriller with benefits, some of them a trifle ostentatious. The alien Rosks have shown up on Earth claiming they thought it was uninhabited and they can't go back home, so they have been awarded a big chunk of Sumatra and part of the Moon—but it looks like they have more expansive plans. Tyne Leslie and companions are spying on their lunar installation, get caught and he's knocked unconscious. He wakes up on the way home with Mumford telling him that Cunliffe was killed. He's suspicious; on arrival at their Sumatra base, Mumford immediately disappears, so Leslie chases after him into Padang without bothering to talk to anybody, even though he's part of at least a quasi-military operation (there's reference to a Commander and a Squadron Office).

The usual moves follow: talking to Mumford's beautiful native girlfriend, being warned away by a dodgy character in a bar, being kidnapped and knocked unconscious again, and interrogated and threatened by a sadistic thug (the Rosk War Colonel Budda Buddo), escaping with the help of a beautiful Rosk renegade, being chased around and making various narrow escapes, and continuing to insist on acting on his own rather than high-tailing it to his superiors for succor at the first opportunity. At a certain point this all becomes a little reminiscent of Lan Wright's extruded-product novellas, an impression that is confirmed when it transpires that one reason everybody is so anxious to get hold of Leslie is that while he was unconscious on the Moon, a crucial piece of videotape was concealed in his artificial hand. This is the gimmick of Wright's "The Messengers" (*New Worlds* **29**), and it puts Aldiss's subsequent slagging of Wright in his *SF Horizons* article in a new light— anxiety of influence, anyone?

Still, no vigorous chase story is complete without rug-pulling revelations, and in addition to that one (hunter was unknowingly also quarry), we learn midway that the Rosks are clearly plotting an invasion of Earth. But this proves to be a red herring: at the end we learn that in fact the Rosk sun, Alpha Centauri, is about to go nova, and this lot are the only Rosk survivors and not much of a threat to anyone. En route there is a great deal of sharp and showy writing; sometimes it's a bit too much: "The starry void blossomed up again in Tyne's midriff. Action: this was what he feared and what he wanted." "The alien domes became visible as black breasts against sequin-studded silk." Aldiss wants to play the game but he also wants to—has to— tweak it (overturning the board will come later).

"Equator" (the title refers not just to the location of most of the action, but also to the speed at which things allegedly move there, rotationally speaking—not Aldiss's most successful metaphor) became, appropriately, an Ace Double, titled *Vanguard from Alpha*. Damon Knight reviewed it in *Fantasy & Science Fiction* and the review is reprinted in *In Search of Wonder*. I'm pleased to see that he agrees with me, or vice versa. He refers to parts of the plot as "comic-book sequence[s]" and says the whole "alternates more or less regularly between thoughtful analysis and pointless action." He concludes: "But even in his comic-book writing, Aldiss is more perceptive than most. The final solution of his puzzle is ingenious and reasonably satisfying; his future world has at least touches of reality, because it's as idiotically patched-together and complicated as our own. And at times Aldiss's gift for phrase-making triumphs over the plot.... If this writer ever does a novel with his right hand, it will be something worth waiting for." Just so, on all counts.

Lan Wright's "A Man Called Destiny" (**78-80**) reverts from the empty galactic grandiosity of "Who Speaks of Conquest?" to the more conventionally clichéd thriller plots of his novellas, though this one, too, gets fairly grandiose at the end. It takes place in a world of interstellar travel where psi talents seem to be emerging seriatim, though exactly why and whether this process is somehow being fostered are not discussed. Telepaths are well established and treasured. There is talk of pyrotics and prognosticators. Argyle (a fitting name from a writer who has compared his craft to knitting socks) suddenly is sought after by the head of a huge interstellar trading company, and just as suddenly becomes the object of attempts to kill him and frame him for various crimes, perpetrated by an individual who we learn is (a) a teleport, apparently the first known, and (b) the heir to the aforesaid interstellar trading company, after its principal is mysteriously murdered (one of the crimes for which Argyle is framed).

Argyle's cause is taken up by Judd, the President or whatever of Earth, and the reason anyone cares about Argyle begins to emerge in canonical hyper-Little Tailor fashion: "An obscure space engineer named Richard Argyle held the fate of the Universe in his blunt, strong hands." "[Judd's] eyes bored relentlessly into Argyle's. 'The history of the Universe will be shaped by your hands, and yours alone. Don't forget it, Argyle, don't forget it for a single instant.'" Argyle is the first of a new kind of mutant—he has a 300-year lifespan and within it, he can't be killed. Exactly how this works is not explained, but data points are that his nemesis missed shooting him at point blank range, and a slow and fatal poison simply stopped working after doing no more than making Argyle queasy. After a stylized confrontation among Argyle, Judd, the aforesaid nemesis, and the heads of all the other interstellar transportation companies, who are trying to seize power, it is revealed that Judd represents a secret organization of mutants who are getting organized to run things for everybody's benefit, and they want Argyle in charge.

This is more smoothly done and less gratingly meretricious than "Who Speaks of Conquest?" but that's about all one can say for it. P. Schuyler Miller described it as a "time-passer of the interstellar intrigue variety, satisfactory as entertainment but nothing to remember," when it was published as—of course— an Ace Double. Wright has the *New Worlds* Profile in **79**, where he says it's easier to write novels than short stories, and "once you have written a novel the limited scope of the short story seems cramped.... Graduating from short stories to novels is like changing from draughts to chess...."

Charles Eric Maine's "Count-Down" (**81-83**) also appeared as "The Big Count-Down" in the December 1958 *Amazing*, presumably abridged, and as *Fire Past the Future* in Ballantine paperback. I read the Ballantine edition when it was published; it's the only Maine novel I ever got through (I gave up early on *Spaceways Satellite* and *He Owned the World*), and the last one I tried. Maine himself describes it in his *New Worlds* Profile in **81** as "basically a suspense novel of the whodunit type, using a modernised 'Ten Little Nigger Boys' theme in a setting of anti-gravity research on a Pacific island, but departs from the classic whodunit pattern in its scientifictional content." It's a readable but cheesy thriller in which the suspense is largely contrived. When the countdown for the launch of the antigravity missile starts on the island, strict radio silence is imposed for safety, and the characters are therefore on their own as they start turning up dead—though common sense suggests that if anybody's listening in, the sudden silence would make them more suspicious and likely to intervene.

We are also asked to believe that folks from the future want to stop us from developing antigravity, which is also time travel, so we can't move in on them and ruin their neighborhood. So they use the same technology the development of which they are trying to thwart (suggesting that they've already failed) to send a device which will take over people's minds and cause them to kill each other over a period of several days. Why not just send a big bomb a few minutes before the experiment is supposed to take place? Of course, that would not have presented an opportunity for scenes such as the protagonist brutally beating the woman he loves (admittedly she is under the control of their malignant adversaries and has already shot him in the leg).

Apparently the readers shared these reservations or had others. They voted the first installment into first place in its issue, but the next two installments came in third, unusually for a serial. In "Postmortem" in **87**, one of the readers slags Maine for his dodgy physics, and Maine responds, half-heartedly arguing with him but then saying, in substance, that he doesn't care: "Candidly, I do think that the science fiction writer's job is to tell a story rather than wrap fictional candy-floss around accurate and verified (20ᵗʰ-century terms) scientific fact. The sugar-coated scientific pill is outmoded. 'Count-Down' was essentially a new look at the Ten Little Indians: why dig deeper?" Another reader (SF scholar Norman C. Metcalf) suggests Maine has little respect for his subject, pointing out a series of petty errors and lapses of logic (e.g., a Navy lieutenant supervising a sergeant—there are no sergeants in the Navy).

These comments are consistent with Maine's general reception. Though Maine was pretty successful in getting his books published from the 1950s into the '70s, and apparently had a substantial career writing for movies and TV, he didn't get much respect from the SF community itself, despite his distinguished pedigree (sharing a residence with Arthur C. Clarke and Sam Youd—there's a "Doc Youd" character in "Count-

Down"; publishing an early UK fanzine; serving in the military with Eric Frank Russell). Leslie Flood's reviews of his earlier books, some of which I quoted in earlier chapters, were mostly exasperated, and Damon Knight's discussion of his novel *High Vacuum* appears in a chapter titled "More Chuckleheads" in *In Search of Wonder*. James Blish selects him as evidence that bad British SF is worse than bad American SF. "When John Wyndham is good, he is very, very good, but when Charles Eric Maine is bad, he is horrid. (I should add here that I have never seen a Maine book that was better than bad.)"[67] Indeed, Blish tees off on this very story, in its Ballantine incarnation as *Fire Past the Future*, in *More Issues At Hand*, commencing: "let us consider an extended example of how *not* to do it, also by a British author," and continuing: "As usual, Maine's contempt for science fiction, its readers, and its writers is evident in elementary scientific errors, slipshod dialogue, and other forms of inattention." He does concede that it has "some shreds of merit"—"like the kid in *Peanuts* who jumped into a pile of dead leaves holding a wet lollipop, the reader emerges from the novel with quite a few fragments sticking to his memory."[68] In any case, Maine did not appear again in *New Worlds* even though he published several more novels during Carnell's editorship. (For that matter, he only had two more appearances in any of the SF magazines.)

Kenneth Bulmer's second *New Worlds* serial, "The Patient Dark" (**85-87**), is no better than his previous "Green Destiny." It's another tatty thriller plot, melodramatically overwritten at times, with Earth occupied by the exploitative Shangs. There's an underground, of course, with a mysterious symbol/slogan, "ZI." The plot bounces around energetically with a high body count, getting less and less plausible as it goes. In the final installment, Rupert Clinton and two Earthwomen who have

67. William Atheling, Jr. [James Blish], *The Issue at Hand* (Advent, 2d ed., 1973), p. 134.

68. William Atheling, Jr. [James Blish], *More Issues at Hand* (Advent, 1970), p. 108.

been shanghaied to the aliens' home planet and then escaped are living well enough from a life of crime to be able to mix unremarked with Shang high society. Not bloody likely, I'd say. The secret of ZI is thoroughly banal and its revelation has not much to do with the preceding chapters of hugger-mugger, except that Clinton survives to see it. This became half of an Ace Double titled (of course) *The Secret of ZI*. It looks good only by comparison with the other half of the book, an ancient novella by Ray Cummings. I am tempted to say that the most interesting thing about this novel is that "Rupert Clinton" was used as a pseudonym by Bulmer several years later for another *New Worlds* serial, "The Golden Age" **(112-13)**. Bulmer has the *New Worlds* Profile in **85**, which goes on at some length about the differences between serials and novels, and Bulmer expresses the hope that he has managed both.

Not much need be said about Philip K. Dick's formerly obscure but now celebrated "Time Out of Joint" **(89-91)**, which neatly exemplifies the difficulties of PKD's early career. It had been accepted for serialization in the US in *Infinity* and announced under Dick's original and much inferior title "Biography in Time," but the magazine folded. (The announcement appears in its last issue, November 1958.) The novel was published by Lippincott, PKD's first US hardcover, well reviewed but apparently poorly distributed. It had no paperback edition until the mid-1960s. So most of the US audience did not see one of Dick's better books—his next SF novel after the well-received *Eye in the Sky*—for years, and in fact the only Dick novels published in the US between *Eye in the Sky* and *The Man in the High Castle* were the widely-excoriated Ace Doubles *Dr. Futurity* and *Vulcan's Hammer*, salvaged from mediocre early magazine stories. I somehow obtained the *New Worlds* issues with the first two installments shortly after they were published—the famous "hot dog stand" scene stuck in my mind for years—but wasn't able to finish the book until it finally appeared in paperback years later. This *New Worlds* serialization, popular as it was among the readership, did not give Dick much of a career boost in the UK either. Six years later, John Brunner found it necessary to promote him, lamenting in the Moorcock *New Worlds* ("The Work of Philip K. Dick," **166**) how little of PKD's work had appeared in the UK even then.

Dick has the *New Worlds* Profile in **89**, with photograph portraying him, chin resting in hand, wearing jacket over turtleneck, as a very serious-looking young man indeed. The brief summary of his career notes that in between novels he wrote scripts for the Mutual Broadcasting Company. There are also a couple of quotes from Dick. He notes that his short story "Foster, You're Dead," first published in Pohl's *Star Science Fiction Stories 3*, was reprinted in *Ogonek*, the largest circulation magazine in the Soviet Union: "In the Soviet Union it reached an audience of millions, whereas in this country (USA), it had gone possibly into no more than a few tens of thousands of hands." Concerning SF, he says: "Without being art, it does what art does, since as Schopenhauer pointed out, art tends to break free of the reality around us and reach a new level of gestalting. The virtue of its approach, too, is that it can reach persons who do not have a developed esthetic sense, which means that it has a higher degree of sheer communicability than great art."

The other (short) novel-length work in these issues is the highly touted return of John Wyndham after four years' absence from the magazine. Carnell says in "The Literary Line-Up" in **69**: "Next month, all being well, we hope to offer you another great First in British science fiction.... *John Wyndham has just finished a new novel!*" This is the series of four novelettes fixed up in book form as *The Outward Urge*. Wyndham wrote a fifth story later which appeared in subsequent editions of the book. It is underwhelming.

The first story, "For All the Night" (**70**), is a bucket of clichés about "Ticker" Troon (so named because his initials are G.M.T.), whose grandfather died in air combat a week after he married Ticker's grandmother. The story begins with Flight Lieutenant Ticker summoned before Air Marshal Sir Godfrey Wilde (a.k.a.

"the old boy"); he tells Wilde he has "a kind of urge onwards and outwards." The old boy responds by quoting Rupert Brooke, whom Ticker's grandfather used to quote, revealing that granddad "had that feeling too." Ticker heads off to the secret British space station, after illicitly getting married, and shortly after *his* son is born he dies heroically defending the station against a smart missile aimed at it presumably by the Other Fellows (sic). These latter scenes in space are reasonably well visualized and might have made a big impression in *Tales of Wonder* twenty years earlier; here they just creak a bit.

"Idiot's Delight" (**72**) is more agreeable, with fewer overt clichés in one's face. Ticker's son, a starchy military type, is in charge of the British Moon base, which he has helped bring into being through devious PR and politics. Nuclear war has broken out on Earth. The base crew is restive that they haven't shot off all their missiles like the Americans and the Russians (who are actually named this time—no more of the "Other Fellows"). The woman base doctor advises Troon that he'd better provide some explanations or there will be a mutiny. He shows the senior officers message files indicating that he's received no orders to fire more missiles. About that time, the survivors of the Russian base show up with their tale of destruction by robot bomb-carriers. It is revealed that the British base *has* no missiles to speak of, and its importance is that it's there and points the way further into space. Exeunt, Troon going on about "the thin gnat-voices crying" (more Rupert Brooke). The entire story is told in conversations, with all the significant action taking place off-stage, and the low-key presentation makes it easier not to snort at the talk of gnat-voices. Judith Merril gave it an Honorable Mention.

The next of these stories is *called* "The Thin Gnat-Voices" (**73**), and I keep thinking of what I am usually tempted to do upon hearing a gnat. This one takes place on Mars, where Geoffrey Trunho, of the now-Brazilian branch of the Troons, reflects on the history of the world and his family since the nuclear destruction of most of the Northern Hemisphere, and recounts his journey to Mars, where he is now sitting waiting to die. The ship toppled over, one crew member was killed, and the other was rendered implausibly delusional by a blow to the head. Eventually the latter wrecked the ship conclusively, leaving our hero with three years' food but without three years' desire to survive alone and without hope of rescue. Unfortunately the idiosyncrasy and unlikelihood of the plot is at war with the overall theme both of the story and the series, Man's March Into Space. This pratfall doesn't advance anything.

The series limps to an apparent close (as noted, there was one other story a couple of years later, apparently an afterthought) with "Space Is a Province of Brazil" (**75**), in which Brazil has declared just that, and George Troon isn't having any. With his cohorts, he's set up shop covertly on Venus. The Brazilians catch on and send the cavalry. Troon's planned double-cross with a Trunho relative doesn't work, but there's another double-cross brewing in the space stations around Earth. Space will declare itself independent. Or, as another relative puts it to George Troon: "From today, your gnat-voices are just a little closer." Bzzzzzz!

One may wonder why Wyndham is producing this sort of elementary fare after the chilly, sophisticated, and *very successful* sequence of novels from *The Day of the Triffids* to *The Midwich Cuckoos*. In the *New Worlds* Profile in **70**, he says: "Sometimes, too, when I read the more erudite and advanced science fiction, I have paused to wonder whether anybody but the author really knows what the hell is going on, and why...[I]t seems to me that the real reason for these many reprintings [of H. G. Wells] is that they are stories that can be understood by everyone." Leslie Flood (**84**) says the book version "is the type of straight science-fiction that the author did so well in the old days under his other nom-de-plume John Beynon" (citing works of the 1930s), and "even if we cannot have the usual 'Wyndham' masterpiece, then this self-styled 'threshold of possibility' space-flight speculation, warmly and humanly characterized and plausibly detailed (Mr. Wyndham is no slouch at 'technicalities') will do very nicely indeed." Forgive me if none of this convinces. Most likely these are trunk stories that Wyndham exhumed in response to Carnell's importuning.[69] Curiously, the fixup novel *The Outward Urge* was credited jointly to Wyndham and a non-existent collaborator, Lucas Parkes. The names are two of John Wyndham Parkes Lucas Beynon Harris's own, and this device was requested by the book's US publisher Ballantine Books because the book's style was not "your usual Wyndham style."[70]

§

There is a little less concentration of authorship during these two years than in the past. I count a total of 38 writers in the 24 issues of 1956-57, and 41 in the 23 issues of 1958-59. In 1956-57, there were nine writers who had half a dozen pieces of fiction or more; in 1958-59, there were five. The dominant writers in 1958-59 were Brian Aldiss (8 stories including a short serial), Robert Silverberg (8), James White (7), Robert Presslie (6) and Francis G. Rayer (6). To account for roughly half of the magazine's contents, as done in previous chapters, it is

---

69. Wyndham bibliographer Phil Stephensen-Payne has surmised that these stories were written around 1950, given their similarity to other material Wyndham published in the early 1950s and their dissimilarity to his earlier SF. He has pointed out that they definitely were written well before their 1959 publication in *New Worlds*—the book that became *The Outward Urge* had been announced for publication in 1954 by Michael Joseph, but did not appear. (Personal communication).

70. Letter to Wyndham from Scott Meredith, September 29, 1958, quoted at http://archives.liv.ac.uk/ead/search?operation=full&recid=gbl41wyn dham-wyndham11 (visited 9/18/11). In at least some Penguin paperback editions, Lucas Parkes is characterized as "technical adviser" on the back cover, and the Wyndham biography in the book states that "Lucas Parkes has confined himself to supplying technical advice in connexion with space travel." (Personal communication from Phil Stephensen-Payne, referring to Penguin 1964 edition).

necessary to include three writers who contributed five stories each, and some who supplied only four.[71]

The brightest star among the short fiction contributors is Aldiss, who has seven stories in addition to the serialized "Equator." 1958 was Aldiss's breakout year, when he began to appear in the US magazines with what are now some of his best-remembered stories ("Poor Little Warrior!" and "The New Father Christmas" in *Fantasy & Science Fiction*, "But Who Can Replace a Man?" in *Infinity*, and "Judas Danced" in *Star SF* as well as *Science Fantasy*), and the expanded *Non-Stop* was published in UK hardcover. None of his contributions to *New Worlds* in 1958 and 1959 are quite on that level, but most of them are sharply written and several rattle the cages of the genre in one way or another.

In "The Pit My Parish" (**67**), England is again at conventional war, and the Pit—a gigantic concatenation of bomb craters—has become a sort of free zone for juvenile delinquents, some of whom have fallen under the sway of Ed, formerly known as Father Edward, who has devised a deranged scheme to take some of his charges for a new start on Venus via an improvised rocket. It is played grimly and grittily rather than farcically, and just misses being one of Aldiss's best stories of this period. As a black deconstruction of the reigning To The Stars iconography of '50s SF, it foreshadows a lot of what annoyed the hell out of much of the SF readership during the New Wave years. Tellingly, it has only been reprinted by Michael Moorcock in his first *Best of New Worlds* anthology, back in 1965.

Aldiss kicks at a different set of traces in "Segregation" (**73**), which later appeared as "Planet of Death" in the US reprint edition of *New Worlds* and as "The Game of God" in Aldiss's collections. Aldiss says in the introduction to *The Airs of Earth* (1963) that it is "an attempt—an attempt I make too seldom—to

---

71. There were 113 pieces of fiction published in these 23 issues. The writers with 6 or more stories provided 35. Three writers with 5 each (Malcolm, Kapp, and Bulmer) brings the total to 50; those with 4 each (Wyndham, Sellings, High) bring it to 62.

write 'proper sf,' with a problem that introduces parasitology, or in this case para-parasitology." But Aldiss can't or won't play it straight. The planet the intrepid space explorers land on is called Kakakakaxo, they are members of the Planetary Ecological Survey Team, or PEST, and consistently with these signposts, Aldiss does everything he can in the course of a densely clotted plot to subvert the glorious adventure.

There's a sentient alien species on Kakakakaxo, comprising small upright crocodilians, but they are dim, ugly, and treacherous. There's a mystery—each of the natives keeps an animal the PEST folks refer to as a bear and another one they call a peke because of their resemblance to Earth animals. The revelation? They're the genders of another sentient species, this one decadent, which the crocodilians are trying to exterminate by capturing and separating the sexes, tethering them outside their hovels. The humans figure this out in part by studying their intestinal parasites and figuring out which are the longest-adapted to their hosts. One human, Dangerfield, has been living on the planet for 20 years, supposedly learning the secrets of the natives. In fact, he proves to be a pathetic figure, an ignorant and fearful fool. The crocodilians, every day, bring him two bowls of guts from disemboweled pekes and bears. Why? No apparent reason, though they do seem to infect him with the natives' parasites. And what does he do with all these guts? Tries to figure out how to get rid of them without being seen.

At the end of the story, the PEST guys go through the crocodilians' village and cut the tethers of all the pekes and bears (the crocodilians being down at the river chasing fish), but this liberating gesture is immediately undermined by the prediction that the pekes and bears will be gone in two generations at the hands of the human colonists to come. On the way out, one of them says, "'It must be odd to play God to a world about which you really know or care so little.'" "'It must be indeed,' Craig [the leader] agreed, but he was not thinking of Dangerfield." So despite the "proper sf" plot, every element of this story is turned against its ostensible theme of the conquest of the universe, proving ultimately futile or disgusting or both; plot a line from "The Failed Men" to *The Dark Light-Years* and this one would be right on it.

Aldiss gets his second *New Worlds* Profile in this issue. Since the last one, "much has been happening to this typical English gentleman with the penchant for explosive mirth and gagsterisms." He's now Literary Editor of the Oxford *Mail*, his first novel *Non-Stop* is out, he's been appearing in the US magazines, and he has two non-sf novels in the works and has just finished a serial for *New Worlds*. He says of "Segregation":

> The scientific ingredient consists of a few speculations which have grown out of an amazed, admiring, horrified, fascinated reading of books on parasitology, and parasites in relation to evolution. I could not help seeing how shallowly s-f has dipped into the range of scientific studies; parasitology, for instance, is a world of mindless monsters—but I want to do more fishing in these waters in future.

Perhaps this ambition was achieved in his enormous ecological *Helliconia* trilogy, some two decades later.

"Incentive" (**78**) is an ambitious near miss, beginning with a description of lemmings heading into the sea, then panning to Westerby of the Isolation League, who is trying to persuade Galactic Minister Jandanagger Laterobinson that Earth should not join the Galactic Federation, since consorting with superior civilizations will destroy our initiative. The Minister says Earth will need an incentive, and tries to give Westerby one by subjecting him to a sort of evolutionary diorama, with intelligence rising through the ages, and a hideous monster beyond the galaxy waiting to pounce. But the Minister goes further and informs Westerby that he needs to get the point of Galingua, which is more than a language, it's a vocal representation of the flux of the universe of which humanity is part—and the monster beyond the galaxy is the residue of evolution from which intelligent life must escape. That's the incentive. This is too much for Westerby, who dies in a tattoo of bursting blood vessels. Flash back to the lemmings, who are starting to drown. This downbeat visionary mini-epic is sort of a cautionary counterpart to Ballard's wider-eyed (!) "The Waiting Grounds," discussed below. The readers put it in a tie for last place, well behind Lan Wright's "A Man Called Destiny." The last word is that of Sven Hanson of Hastorp, Sweden, in **80**'s "Postmortem," who says, "Let me tell you something shocking—there is no annual suicidal pact among the lemmings!" Or maybe the last word should be Aldiss's, from the story itself: "The senior races of the Galaxy, having lost the taste for the spectacle of mental suffering, would be unlikely to find much attraction in your literatures."

From these it's downhill, though not too fast. "The Unbeaten Track" (**79**), which became "Three's a Cloud" in *The Canopy of Time* (1959), is pretty explicitly a Sturgeon pastiche, or critique, suggesting there's a down side to syzygy. Clemperer, an alienated drunk, meets Alice and Spring and they all realize they are part of a whole—a gestalt, as Clemperer puts it. But Spring, who has just met Alice on a yacht, is married, and his wife is out on the yacht in the harbor. There is talk of how their relationship is a "force beyond good or evil," beyond all the rules, "...supernatural." After they've gone back to the yacht, a storm comes up, the yacht sinks, Clemperer knows they are gone. But then he goes into the bar where he met them, and there they are—"wetter than he was, but they were smiling." And, presumably, Spring's wife is drowned. The gestalt's all right, to hell with you.

"The Other One" (**82**), never reprinted as far as I can tell, is a clever amalgam of "They," "Dreams Are Sacred," and Aldiss's own "Outside." Lazenby is vexed by the Other, which seems to inhabit his mind. Hospitalized, he finds himself in a place where he's the only patient and the rooms constantly shift in relationship to one another, and he schemes to escape. Point of view switches to the doctors: it's all metaphorical, Lazenby is actually on a hospital gurney and his tormentor is a cyst full of brain tissue. For the treatment, one doctor's mind is projected into Lazenby's and seems to defeat the Other; but there's another twist. It's about as subtle as a mallet over the head, which is probably why it hasn't been reprinted, but is vigorous and well paced.

77 has another PEST story, "Carrion Country," this one considerably less knotty and correspondingly less interesting than "Segregation." An untouched planet is inhabited by herds of herbivores who appear to drop dead and instantly rot whenever danger appears. This turns out to be camouflage. They have one good side and one rotted-looking side, and the predators have no sense of smell and can't tell the latter from real inedible decay. There is a perfunctory parasitology routine, and also the ruins of a primitive sentient civilization which wiped itself out through mass suicide, but nothing much is done with either of these devices. Aldiss gives the impression here of a kid kept after school to do boring homework—"proper sf" indeed.

The only complete misfire here is "The Towers of San Ampa" (**80**), a leaden satire about a man who comes back from years of hard work on Venus, his pennies saved to buy a job in a lampooned Cold War America, security-obsessed and economically ruined by military spending—but you'd better not say anything about it. Even from the perspective of post-9/11 Patriot Act America, this one is too extreme to be serious and too heavy-handed to be funny.

§

J. G. Ballard has only two stories in these issues, but one of them is probably the best piece of short fiction present. Ridiculous first, sublime later. "Track 12" (**70**) is an unattractive and gimmicky piece of Hitchcockery. Maxted is cuckolding the eccentric Sheringham, who has invited Maxted to his apartment and is playing him "microsonic" recordings—amplified versions of sounds too faint to be heard normally, like a pin dropping *before* it lands. He puts on another sound; Maxted realizes he's been poisoned, and Sheringham obligingly explains that it's chromium cyanate, which will drown him. The sound he dies to is the hyper-amplified sound of his kissing Sheringham's wife. Ho hum. So too said the readers of *New Worlds*, who rated this story fourth out of five in the issue. It did have one defender. John Hynam of Peterborough, Northants—better known to the readership as John Kippax—says in **72**'s "Postmortem" that "I think he has a new basis for a sure-fire standard plot." In the event, fortunately, not.

"Track 12," which appeared in April 1958, was the last story of the first phase of Ballard's writing, and he published nothing more until the end of 1959, following his traumatic encounter with an SF convention. As Ballard said in a 1975 interview with David Pringle and James Goddard: "I had this gap after I went to the SF convention in '57. Don't take this personally or anything—I think times have changed—but it put me off. I didn't do any writing for about a year and a half, so there was a sort of gap."[72]

Ballard returned to *New Worlds* in **88** (November 1959) with "The Waiting Grounds," on another level entirely from "Track 12." It is an uncharacteristic Ballard story. For starters, it is one of only a handful that take place off Earth. Quaine arrives on Murak, a desert planet whose temperature ranges daily from fatally hot to fatally cold, to spend two years in near-total isolation tending a radio observatory, and discovers a hidden basin

---

72. James Goddard and David Pringle, "4th January 1975: An Interview with J. G. Ballard," in Goddard & Pringle (eds.), *J. G. Ballard: The First Twenty Years* (Bran's Head Books Ltd. 1976), p. 20. Brian Aldiss recalled: "Was that nondescript year really 1957, and not 1947? The convention was held in a terrible hotel in the Queensway district. A distinctly post-war feeling lingered. Bomb damage was still apparent... I went to the bar and bought a drink. Standing next to me was a slim young man who told me that there were some extraordinary types at the convention, and that he was thinking of leaving pretty smartly. He introduced himself as J. G. Ballard." Brian W. Aldiss, "An SF Convention of the Fifties," in *The Shape of Further Things: Speculations on Change* (Faber & Faber, 1970), p. 103.

with stone megaliths bearing inscriptions in several languages (including "Earth's"). He loses consciousness and has a vision of beings who have slowed their metabolisms to virtually zero and have become a "great vibrating mantle of ideation," which eventually swallows the cosmos and blows up, starting the next cosmos. At the end of it a voice informs him:

> "Meanwhile we wait here, at the threshold of time and space, celebrating the identity and kinship of the particles within our bodies with those of the sun and the stars, of our brief private times with the vast periods of the galaxies, with the total unifying time of the cosmos."

So what exactly are they waiting for, these species whose names are carved like interstellar Kilroys' on the megaliths, complete with translation into "Earth's" language? Says Quaine, who now plans to stay on Murak, in the last line: "Whatever it is, it must be worth waiting for." (And "I am certain that whatever we are waiting for will soon arrive.") The more questions you ask, the more the story looks like a protracted shaggy God story.

On the other hand, it's a pretty effective read, a sort of Stapledonian fast package tour wrapped in a surprisingly standard mystery/adventure plot. Quaine arrives, there's clearly something his departing predecessor isn't telling him. A couple of geologists died in the field a few years previously; it looks as if maybe they weren't really geologists. Quaine finds the megaliths while trying to trace this mystery. When he takes his friend the mining metallurgist to see them, the friend becomes enraged and attacks Quaine when he learns that the megaliths are made of all the precious material he has been failing to find. Quaine shoots him with a flare gun and sets his vehicle on fire, marooning him in heat that will kill him. But these standard elements are well deployed to set the stage for the final revelation. What is most uncharacteristic about "The Waiting

Grounds" is the absence of the irony and distance that characterize most of Ballard. This one is as sincere as *Childhood's End*. It was popular in its time (and still has its advocates, who see it as an early Singularity story), and was voted the best in its issue by the readers.

The *New Worlds* Profile in **88** is Ballard's, complete with photo of the lean and hungry 29-year-old author looking intensely into the camera. He says:

> "What particularly interests me about science fiction... is the opportunity it gives for experimenting with scientific or psycho-literary ideas which have little or no connection with the world of fiction, such as, say, coded sleep or the time zone. But just as psychologists are now building models of anxiety neuroses and withdrawal states in the form of verbal diagrams—translating scientific hypothesis into literary construction—so I see a good science fiction story of [as?] a model of some psychic image, the truth of which gives the story its merit. Examples are *The Incredible Shrinking Man*, *Limbo '90*, and Henry Kuttner's 'Dream's End.'
>
> "In general stories with interplanetary backgrounds show too little originality, too much self-imitation. More important, the characters seem to lack any sense of cosmic awe—spanning the whole of space and time without a glimmer of responsibility.... It's just this sense of cosmic responsibility, the attempt to grasp the moral dimensions of the universe, that I've tried to describe in 'The Waiting Grounds.' Seen as a psycho-literary model, perhaps it represents the old conundrum of the ant searching hopelessly for the end of the infinite pathway around the surface of a sphere. 'The Waiting Grounds' offers it a solution, implies that instead of crawling on and on it will find the pathway's end if it just sits still."

This suggests an interesting view of responsibility, cosmic or otherwise, and the "moral dimensions of the universe," since after his revelation Quaine apparently doesn't tell anybody else about it, or intend to—just like his predecessor.

Finally, here's editor Carnell's blurb, demonstrating once more his ability to miss the point comprehensively: "Not for a long time have readers seen a story quite like this one. Those with extensive collections or good memories will remember the impact H.P. Lovecraft made in the middle 30's with his all-too-few science fiction stories, particularly 'At the Mountains of Madness.' Undoubtedly author Ballard has a touch of that same genius which eventually made Lovecraft great." Well, I guess "The Waiting Grounds" *does* feature some Great Old Ones, in a manner of speaking....

§

If Aldiss is the most mercurial of the *New Worlds* regulars, James White remains the solidest, contributing seven industrious if very uneven novelettes during these two years. "Tableau" (**71**) is the most impressive in its quiet way. There's a space war going on and Captain MacEwan is in the thick of it. After ramming a ship of the alien Orligs, he finds himself crash-landed and injured with the injured Orlig pilot. The Orligs prove to be telepathic, and he "hears" the Orlig view of how the war started and over what. This being White, it's all a misunderstanding. They would like peace too. Then the Orligian rescuers arrive, and they point their dread secret weapon at him. Betrayed! No, the weapon is a time stasis field, and they are freezing MacEwan until they are confident medical science can save him from his terrible injuries, and the Orligian pilot has insisted on going into the field with his new friend so he can see MacEwan cured. Until then, they become the Orligians' war memorial. This is probably White's best story to date in *New Worlds*. Judith Merril gave it an Honorable Mention, and John W. Campbell rejected it for its anti-war views, according to White's rather informal account.[73]

"The Ideal Captain" (**74**), on the other hand, gets high marks for sentiments (basically the same sentiments as "Tableau") but not much else. Surgenor is First Lieutenant on a spaceship. He's also a psychologist piloting (as it were) his big idea: since dissatisfaction on long voyages with the decisiveness of a ship's captain breeds "space neurosis" and indecisiveness on the part of everybody else, let's do away with captains entirely, and condition the crew to believe there's a captain whom each crew member thinks is just dandy and who will interact with that crew member in just the way he would like. This poses some technical problems, such as keeping the captain out of sight entirely (not hard, captains often like to be aloof) and having the internal communications set up so only one person can talk to the captain at once. Highly plausible, right? Midway through the voyage Surgenor overhears conversations among the crew that suggest treasonous intent—and of course when they talk to the captain, they hear just what they want from him, since they are in effect providing both sides of the conversation. They make an unauthorized stop on Deimos and find themselves in the midst of a shootout between the crews of two Russian ships. When it's all sorted out, a treasonous conspiracy is indeed revealed. All experienced spacemen are part of it, and the object is to abandon national allegiances and avoid wars, and everybody to whom it is revealed joins up because it just makes so much sense. The belligerent Russian crew was inexperienced and wasn't part of the act. Surgenor joins up and discloses the "ideal captain" scheme to the psychologist of the other Russian ship. Contrivance here is compounded and undermines White's admirable message.

The blurb to "Dogfight" (**81**) invokes "Tableau," and with reason. There's another interstellar war going on. Henson, a high official in the Earth military, is in fact a spy for the alien

---

73. Graham Andrews, "Dr. Kilcasey in Space: A Bio-bibliography of James White," http://www.sectorgeneral.com/biobiblio.html (visited 9/9/11) (quoting a conversation in the Blackthorn bar).

Semrans, who are slowly losing the war, outthought by Earth's supercomputer, which has been dictating strategy for decades. One of its decisions, we learn along the way, is that Semran prisoners are not kept in prisons or camps. They are dropped on a planet, given the wherewithal to survive, and left alone as long as they don't try to get off it. (This was an idea White would pursue at length, years later, in his *New Worlds* serial "Open Prison.") It turns out that the supercomputer is getting a little flaky, being based on a dog brain. The dog couldn't bear mistreating the captured Semrans, because they are too much like people. Now she's getting senile ("she has started to chase imaginary rabbits"). Should the plug be pulled? In a slightly confused (and arguably absurdly naïve) end section, the General seems to say no, they should stick with her after all the terrible things they've done to her. Hearing this, Henson decides he can't report this information back to Semra, and he's changing sides: "Semra could never win, never finally and unquestionably win, against a race that could spend countless millions on men and material movements out of kindness to a doting old dog. Nobody could win against a race which could be both so ruthless and so kind as that."

"The High Road" (**87**) might have been written to counter any accusation that White's stories are too staid, with enough U-turns to inflict whiplash. Stevenson is security officer of the British space program, and the rockets keep crashing. He is certain there is sabotage and suspects Miss Johns, the base psychologist. Yet he sort of has the hots for her, even though she's rather unattractive—he's unattractive too, he thinks, half of his face (and, it appears, a bit of his mind) having been messed up flying bombing runs in World War II. After a series of plot convolutions worthy of Harry Stephen Keeler, he is vindicated—Miss Johns is indeed at the head of a sabotage ring, but they're not Russian sympathizers—they are trying to thwart Western technological development so the West will turn to psionics!

And they have work to do, right now—the Russians have just

landed on Deimos, but they're not going to have enough fuel to get back, so the conspirators and Stevenson are going to fly, psi-powered, to Deimos in the base's mock-up spacecraft, and by the way, Stevenson is going to have to provide the juice—Miss Johns has figured out that the reason he can't remember what happened in that fateful ten minutes over Dusseldorf is that he teleported and time-traveled out of the plane to a moment in his childhood, then returned to the disabled plane and mind-hustled it safely back to base.[74] Oh, also by the way, Miss Johns is an extraterrestrial, and the reason she doesn't look so great is that she isn't quite mature yet, so can he wait a while? This synopsis is, of course, a gross oversimplification. Unfortunately the readers were not as taken as I am by this solemnly nutty extravaganza, voting it third of the four stories in the issue.

"Grapeliner" (**88**) also has a certain kitchen-sink quality to it, starting out as a sober projection of the difficulties of space travel. Because of the danger of radiation (van Allen belts, cosmic radiation, etc.), spacegoing personnel are all old, past reproductive age. And some of the most dangerous radiation is secondary radiation emitted from metal objects, so passengers can't be carried in metal spaceships—they have to be ferried in plastic capsules (grapes) suspended at a distance from circular frames. So off the unlikely craft goes, only to be confronted by an alien spaceship and rear-ended by it. The crew desperately try to save the passengers and defend themselves from this inexplicable menace. The menace fights back, and it becomes clear the aliens are telepathic. But the quick-thinking human captain devises a strategy, and—this being a James White story—it turns out it was all a misunderstanding, and the story ends with peace about to break out. Though the telepathy angle is a rather jarring intrusion in a story that started out with nuts and bolts, the story is fast-paced and well-constructed and overall works pretty well.

---

74. A device rather similar to Gully Foyle's spacetime peregrinations in Alfred Bester's *The Stars My Destination*, although less flamboyant in the telling.

The second and third of White's Sector General stories appear in these issues, and well-meaning as they are, they illustrate what have always seemed to me to be the problems with this series. "Trouble with Emily" (**77**), second in the series, like "The Ideal Captain" suffers from extreme contrivance. Conway is assigned to deal with a new patient, who is introduced as a dinosaur, and her doctor, Arretapec, a telepath who looks like a withered prune and lives in a transparent globe, and whom Conway must wear strapped to his shoulder. No one will tell him what the purpose is, and Arretapec is irritatingly arrogant, but Conway is game. He first figures out how to make the neo-brontosaurus's environment (a gigantic hold full of water, mud, and vegetation) more congenial, and then how (with the aid of tractor and pressor beams—quote unquote) to pet it and romp with it as one would a dog (in fact he borrows a dog to practice). Shortly thereafter it begins levitating and teleporting on its own.

Arretapec and his kind, it turns out, are not only telepathic but precognitive—but only demographically, able to foresee the future of species, not individuals. They have seen that these dinosaurs are threatened by climate change which they cannot escape, and if they die out no intelligent species will arise on their planet. But if they are taught to fly psionically, they will be able to head for the equatorial regions when it starts getting cold, and eventually will build their civilization. So add it up: telepathy, carefully limited precognition, artificial gravity that permits the creation of tractor and pressor beams, levitation and teleportation teachable between species. Of course there is plenty of SF that pours on the marvels and glories in them. But that is not what White is about. Ultimately he is telling simple morality tales (the moral here being that intelligent life is the highest value and imperfect sophonts like us and Arretapec should be devoted to its furtherance and preservation), and all this promiscuous and arbitrary invention simply doesn't fit.

"Visitor at Large" (**84**) is a bit more pedestrian but also looks pretty formulaic. As in "Sector General," a shape-shifting alien runs loose in the hospital, behaving irrationally and destructively, and is impossible to communicate with. The alien is a kid, come to visit its dying parent, and the solution is to scare it into silence and then get its parent to scold it via the intercom. The story is dense and frankly tedious, full of great blocks of exposition. White shoots himself in the foot in his presentation of the basic idea of the series, an institution that undertakes to treat all of an endless variety of sentient life. The various life forms are categorized with alphabetical codes, to which the reader is only fragmentarily privy, leading to such locutions as:

> The pseudo-Illensan shape of the SRTT lay plastered against the floor. It was twitching slightly, and already one of the larger FROB infants was coming pounding up to investigate this odd-looking object. One of the great, spatulate feet must have trod on the recumbent SRTT, because it jerked away and began rapidly and incredibly to *change*. The weak, membranous appendages of the PVSJ seemed to dissolve into the main body....

White has slumped here from worthiness into dullness and turgidity.

§

Arthur Sellings is back after a year's absence with "The Shadow People" (**73**), in which the protagonist and his wife rent out their spare room to some very pale-looking people who turn out to be refugees from the future, except they're really not entirely alive ("'there's a—a dilution, of impact, of sensibility, of—' He broke off, as if explaining the measure of that loss was beyond him—or beyond my understanding."), and they can't go back because they were fleeing the end of the world. Now they've admitted all this they can't stay in the protagonist's spare room any more, because he and his wife are young and in love and that would remind them too much of what they've lost.

It's well done but a mite precious, and it's not clear to me what this story is doing in *New Worlds* rather than *Science Fantasy.*

In the gimmicky but sharp and well-turned "Flatiron" (**77**), the protagonist shelters a telepathic shapeshifting dimension-traveling alien, who in gratitude gives humanity the gift that will end war and the abuse of power—he shapeshifts everybody to look like the protagonist and his wife.

"For the Colour of His Hair" (**79**) starts off a bit like "Flowers for Algernon," with seemingly somewhat impaired, headache-cursed Ernie an object of mockery at work and obloquy at home. But isn't the bearded caretaker of his building actually Hoskins, his probation officer from his family's previous town of residence? A Sturgeonesque green monkey detested by the normals, Ernie must flee. He heads off to hit the rails, but the probation officer catches up with him and reveals that he's followed Ernie because the youth is special, the first achieved step in our next evolution, intermediate between humans and the sublime entities up ahead in the future who are somehow calling him into being. The special poignancy of the story is Hoskins' self-awareness of his own status as an unfinished early model, gifted with some gappy telepathic or hyper-empathic sense, a "fairy godmother" to Ernie but lacking his own magic, delving into a critique of Darwinism for a teleological explanation for himself and his charge. This is actually a pretty well done minor story, with the character and his misery and fear and the dreary details of his life very well rendered.

Similarly, "The Outstretched Hand" (**83**) is a well assembled story about a man sent to a psychiatrist after a suicide attempt. He's a frustrated artist who feels that he betrayed his talent by succumbing to mundane pressures and going into business, so the psychiatrist prescribes... time travel. The protagonist goes back, buys a bag of candy, meets his child self, and tells himself that he must stick with the painting. When he returns to the psychiatrist's office he now has memories of trying to stick with it but finding that he didn't really have much talent. He's in the same place as before. Sellings then lays it on a bit too thick:

the psychiatrist reveals that he's done time travel therapy on himself, and he used to dream of being a concert pianist.

§

The most significant of a couple of auspicious debuts in these issues is Colin Kapp's. His first story, "Life Plan," appears in **77**. Kapp has the *New Worlds* Profile in **82**, looking out from his photo complete with writerly pipe and with a jaunty demeanor suggesting a Monty Python character who is about to be revealed as a complete lunatic. He also sports a very large pompadour which from appearances must be shellacked in place. Details: 30 years old, a technical assistant on electrochemical work in a leading electronics research laboratory, says that's what he would prefer to do as a hobby, so to keep things in balance he writes as a hobby since he wanted to do that for a living. His wife does the typing and is his severest critic. He's read SF as long as he can remember, graduating from the American pulps "up to the present standards of the 'Nova' magazines." He plans a lot more stories, "with some experiments in style and theme," and possibly a play for television.

Kapp (1928-2007) was a *New Worlds*-only writer until Carnell's departure, with 11 stories including a serial, and then followed Carnell to *New Writings in SF*, where he published another 11 stories (the last couple in Bulmer's volumes of that series). He also published a dozen or so stories, including several serials, in the US magazines from the late 1960s through 1977; he reappeared a couple of times in *Analog* in the 1980s; and that was it for his short fiction. He published about a dozen books, including one collection, but that was done by the early 1980s too.

"Life Plan" is a refreshingly vigorous piece of hokum which starts with Colonel Stormhaven of the Security Service bringing Professor Barr and Dr. Napier to a consultation with Serioa Passover, Consultant Philosopher, about their problem. Dr. Napier has resurrected and improved Life Plan, an old mind training program, to help sate the national laboratories' appetite for geniuses. It works up to a point—that is, the selected candidates get smart enough, but then they become sociopathic, and before long kill themselves, after passing what Napier has dubbed the *Mx* point.

Passover does his own run-through with Honeywell, his own candidate, a "third-year trainee philosopher." Honeywell soon becomes an amoral and manic-depressive superman who escapes (or seems to) and then reappears, announces his discovery of the irredeemable depravity of humanity, and demands answers from Passover, who provides them: yeah, it's all true, but mankind is immature and this is "the adolescent turmoil of a very young race." Passover reveals himself as the first (mutant) superman, who has passed through the *Mx* point by virtue of lacking "the Freudian censor mechanism." Now there are two of them and they can use Life Plan to "short circuit half a million years of evolution"—exactly how, Passover doesn't say.

This van Vogtian plot is moved along quickly by punchy and cadenced writing, most of the work done by dialogue. Much of the story is a bit reminiscent in tone of a good Dr. Who episode, and sometimes a bit like late Jack Vance, with a nice deadpan sense of the absurd, as in this exchange between Napier and Passover:

> "You must excuse my directness, but I cannot see how you are in any way qualified to take charge of this investigation. I do not believe there can be any such thing as a consultant philosopher."
>
> "Why not? You have consultants in most other fields of human endeavor."
>
> "True, but they are men with specialist knowledge for practical application. I can see I might consult you if I were doing some research on Kant or Diogenes, but I fail to see the practical application of philosophy in this day and age."

"Then," said Passover, "you make the mistake of confusing philosophy with the history of philosophy. Our humble art is now an exact science, and we are a specialist organisation dispensing services of an extremely practical nature."

"I stand rebuked but unconvinced," said Napier with courteous humour.

This entertaining story, which the readers voted into first place, has apparently never been reprinted.

In "Survival Problem" (**82**), the consultant philosophers are back in the person of Conyers, a "survival specialist" in the Philosophical Bureau, "a private organisation which does research work on semantics and paraphysics for the government. They have plenty of influence higher up so they do pretty much as they please." It is of course directed by our old friend Seroia Passover. Conyers is assigned to supervise an experiment involving the Housemann-Crane Discontinuity Theorem, "a curious little hole in the structure of numbers"—except they have discovered that "the flaw is not in the system but in the nature of things themselves." So they've set up an experiment to "stress a flaw in the fabric of the universe as we know it" and create a hole "which leads right out of our notions of time and space."

And why a consultant philosopher for this task? In Kapp's world or mind, philosophers live a more strenuous life than most of us realize: "As a philosopher his department was the technique of human survival under all forms of stress and danger. This was a rugged and practical field involving not only actual and simulated contra-survival problems but also scientific liaison on projects where the hazards were yet unknown. His unparalleled knowledge of the strengths and weaknesses of man made him a handy person to have around when potential danger loomed ahead." It's very reminiscent of van Vogt's Nexialism, deployed in the fix-up novel *The Voyage of the Space Beagle*. This set-up leads directly (albeit by way of various amusing hugger-mugger, concealed motives, etc.) to the immortal line, uttered by a character who has a revolver pointed at Conyers' heart: "One move, philosopher, and I'll drop you where you stand."

Luckily, Conyers has brought a missile warhead in his suitcase to stop this experiment into what Man Was Not Meant To Know Because He'll Blow Himself Up With It, and he doesn't hesitate to detonate it. The experiment, however, creates a passageway into another universe, apparently to a habitable planet, so most likely Conyers et al. went through it to safety. Seroia directs his own technicians to start working on a new gateway, like the one they have just blown up in a nuclear explosion. Why? So if Conyers has survived, Serioa can give him a new assignment: "Setting up the nucleus of a new civilisation based on sound philosophical tenets." It's reminiscent this time of van Vogt's Null-A supermen philosophers. Whatever happened to Life Plan? Doesn't say.

Kapp's next contribution, "Calling Mr. Francis" (**84**), bears considerably less freight. It's an amusing story about an industrial plant which accidentally produces "collapsed nickel" (incredibly dense and strong) in a routine plating operation, and about the resulting pandemonium. By the end, they're trying to reproduce the effect using the only clues they have, that half a cheese sandwich and a cigarette butt might have gotten into the vat.

"The Railways Up on Cannis" (**87**) introduces the Unorthodox Engineers, a crew of misfits and sociopaths who are dispatched to make the railways work on a planet with extreme vulcanism. The solution—put the trestles on volcanic cones and create new volcanoes as needed, since on this planet, unlike ours, they never form at the same place—is not very interesting, but the story is told in an amusing Eric Frank Russellesque up-the-bureaucracy style. The readers voted it first in the issue. Some years later, after Carnell's departure from *New Worlds*, Kapp wrote several sequels, which were published in *New Writings in SF* and eventually collected in *The Unorthodox Engineers* (Dobson 1979), now an extremely rare book.

Kapp closes out the year with "Breaking Point" (**89**), demonstrating once again his gift for lively and propulsive writing. It begins: "Hardinge was dead before they arrived. With injuries such as his it was the wisest thing to be." Society is falling apart into senseless mob violence. Why? Says one of the characters, a member of a military garrison, "We're at war with a far more dangerous and insidious enemy—a beat philosophy." Does he really mean that the spirit of Kerouac and Ginsberg is bringing civilization to its knees? It seems unlikely, but the term is never explicated. However, in the town where the story is set, the only one who can stop the violence even temporarily is the glib and charismatic Pandi. The military leader has him brought in for interrogation; after a few pages of snappy dialogue the leader orders him drugged and Captain Penny, the protagonist, has had enough—he smashes the drug vials and helps Pandi escape. There is a *sauve qui peut* underground of sane people; Pandi is part of it, and the whole business has been a set-up to recruit Penny, who, with others of his kind, will be dispatched to an island to ride out the coming dark age. The story is immensely readable and told with great conviction, as long as you don't think too much about it. Judith Merril gave it an Honorable Mention.

§

Robert Presslie's "The 40th of December" (**68**), his first story in *New Worlds* but his 18th in the genre magazines, is an inauspicious beginning. A soap opera of Martian colonization, it treads in the dusty bootprints of Tubb's Mars series of several years previously. The first women arrive at the all-male colony, various uninteresting problems arise, the stiff-necked commander winds up slated to head back to Earth to rendezvous with the de facto leader of the women, an over-the-hill actress who's returning too. It's dated and turgid.

"Next of Kin" (**69**) is a considerable improvement, actually containing some surprises. The narrator returns from Mars to

Scotland to spend his leave with his old grandfather, stereo-typically mourning the passing of their old world ("What with the forests being cut and the atomic factories everywhere, the hills are not what they used to be," says Gramp). Except that the protagonist has brought grandfather a present consisting of a gem rescued from the ruins of the ancient Martian civiliza-tion—but grandfather has one too. The gems store personali-ties of the ancient Martians, and both these men are harboring Martian symbionts, and they're ready to continue the ages-long job of saving civilizations from themselves.

"One for the Road" (**72**) is entirely conversation-driven, about a bunch of bums congregating under a bridge, drinking, and discussing the possibility (based on a newspaper clipping) that there is an alien walking around, indeed that one of their group might be the alien; and there is other business being done as well. It reads a bit like an exercise written for a drama class, but it's ingenious and very well done. "Sendoff" (**77**) presents the last day of Willy in his village, as he walks down the street from top to bottom saying goodbye to everybody and mentally noting the help he has given to all of them, for which most of them are not particularly grateful. He's the resident android, and people have been told that his lifespan is limited and he's shuffling off to die. In fact androids are immortal, but people mustn't know that, so he's heading off to another village to pretend to be 20 again. "Confession Is Good" (**82**) is a nicely turned story about an android trying to figure out the world and getting some fatal (to them) misapprehensions from his creators' dysfunctional interactions.

"Another Word for Man" (**78**) efficiently precesses the conventional sentiments: Pierre Medoc, fishing off the Gaspe Peninsula, pulls in an extraterrestrial in or on one of his lobster pots and hands it over to the deeply conservative and suspicious Father St. Emilion, who in turn hands it over to Drs. Meursalt and Chablis (Old Doc and Young Doc). H'rola, as he is known, is telepathic and also is a doctor, or trained as one, but the Docs won't let him treat patients, perhaps because he is bell-shaped and the color of pink dental plastic and people would talk. H'rola also has unorthodox views, regarding surgery as a betrayal of life. Father St. Emilion turns up riddled with cancer and insists that the alien be kept away from him. But when they make the incision they see it's hopeless so they turn H'rola loose anyway (these were the days before informed consent). H'rola extrudes his mass of cilia, eats or absorbs all the multitudinous metastases, withdraws, closes the incision, and conveniently drops dead, leaving Father St. E. as good as new. The Father wakes up, sits up, and confesses the error of his prejudiced ways and allows that H'rola was one of God's creatures.

Mock it as I will for its *bien pensant* piety, "Another Word for Man" is well written and developed. Judith Merril gave it an Honorable Mention, and even Michael Moorcock fell for it—he put it in the 1965 *The Best Of New Worlds*, along with Ballard's "The Terminal Beach" and Keith Roberts's "I Remember, Anita." However, reader G.B. Tait of Stockport, Cheshire— better known to *New Worlds* readers as Alan Barclay—gave it a raspberry in "Postmortem" in **80**: "Robert Presslie really is relying too heavily on other people's ignorance.... Medoc, Chablis, and St. Emilion are French wines. St. Emilion is, as a matter of fact, my favorite. These three coming together in the same story rather spoil it."

Presslie (b. 1920) has the *New Worlds* Profile in **77**, which notes that his first stories appeared in the now-defunct *Authentic*. Though his photograph would suit a funeral director, he is now employed as a "pharmacy manager for a firm of multiple chemists." (Charles Stross, a former pharmacist, says that this is a firm operating a chain of pharmacies in the UK with a dispensing pharmacist or "chemist" in each, under the supervision of a superintendent pharmacist.[75]) If Presslie could choose when to live, it would be now: "This must be the only age in which dreams come true while you wait." This is not a reassuring thing to hear from a pharmacy manager. He expects to

---

75. Personal communication to Broderick.

see a "drastic and dramatic change" in SF away from things like moon flights. "The change is going to call for a vast unfolding of the imagination by readers and writers alike. I hope to be able to contribute to that change." He did, but not for long. Presslie continued prolific into 1959, disappeared until mid-1962, then contributed eight more stories in a year and a half, hit *New Writings in SF* in 1965 and 1966, and that was it.

Philip E. High contributes four lively stories. "The Guardian" (**76**) is another of his exercises in compression. Aliens are loose on the planet, so the authorities (Barton and Marsh, apparently officials of some un-named security agency) call in the mysterious Lessiter, a brilliant "psycho-criminologist" and author of several "Physical Recognition Texts," to help catch them. The aliens prove instantly lethal to anyone who identifies and moves in on them, but Lessiter figures out their secret (supernally acute hearing) in jig time, only to be confronted by Barton and accused of being an alien himself, of a different and competing sort; Barton himself is a Guardian ("Wherever there is a Class Five culture, there is the Guardian Corps.") So he disposes of Lessiter and wipes Marsh's memory. All this takes 13 pages and is sharp and engaging; a lot of writers would have stretched it to 40 and made it boring and routine.

"Squeeze Box" (**81**) tests the power of sharp and economical style virtually to destruction. Marion has been sentenced to Lethal Deportation because he hit some jerk too hard and killed him. Now he's informed what L.D. really means: he's going to the planet Leinster, which is populated by the super-dangerous zipcats. If he kills one, he's reprieved, but they're invulnerable, seemingly invisible sometimes. Flash back to Earth where Arkroyd, world leader, has just been informed by the aliens who have cleaned Earth's clock that they need more room and the population of Earth is going to have to evacuate another thousand square miles right away—but the refugees in the dormitories are already sleeping in hammocks an inch apart. Back on Leinster, Marion is out on patrol, finds his way blocked by a tree that has just fallen, sees movement in the bushes. It's a small animal, trapped by the fall of the tree. He releases it, and suddenly the grove is full of zipcats, looking at him. He's just saved one of their young. Back on Earth, a bit later it seems, the alien boss stalks into Arkroyd's office demanding to know why the humans aren't packing up as ordered. Arkroyd tells him to go to hell, we don't have to listen to you any more, and he displays a zipcat: they're on our side now, and right about now a population of them is being released on your home planet, so your friends will be busy for a while. And by the way, the zipcats are so dangerous because they move faster than anyone can see, faster than sound in fact, like the Road Runner I suppose. (No sonic booms are reported, however.) Need I say this is ridiculous? It is reminiscent of some of the more embarrassing items in the *New Worlds* of 1946-52 or so, but is well written enough and short enough to be readable.

"Project—Stall" (**83**) is about Mars explorers who have found inexplicable remnants of a vast civilization, but they can't figure out how it worked. The artifacts they find include, e.g., a jar of blue goo with a label that translates "To Clean and Repair— For Interior Use Only." The breakthrough comes when some of the characters *really wish* that the mess that they have made by spilling stuff on the floor was cleaned up—so it gets cleaned up. Later, another jar of the blue goo, responding to a different wish, separates out the components of a dangerous accidental chemical spill. This is the plot of *Forbidden Planet*, with one small modification: the monsters seem to be from the Superego, rather than the Id.

"Pseudopath" (**86**) is an engagingly gonzo piece of nonsense. There's a war going on but nobody knows it. Organized crime has infiltrated government and taken it over, meeting only a small resistance within the armed forces. The theaters of battle are places like pubs. One Lott is detailed to protagonist Welling's operation, with instructions that he should be treated as a telepath even though he isn't one; nonetheless, he displays an uncanny talent for identifying enemies for his companions to shoot. The plot meanders off into a successful putsch against the underworld leader, and it is revealed that Lott's talent is lip-reading and the interpretation of gestures. Again, lively writing makes a readable story out of a pretty lame and silly set-up and plot. Judith Merril gave it an Honorable Mention.

§

Several other relatively undistinguished contributors show improvement in these issues. Dan Morgan's "The Unwanted" (**68**) is considerably more incisive than his previous short fiction. Space travelers returning to Earth after 500 years (much less for them, relativistically speaking) are instructed to dock at an unmanned space station, which is set up to kill them with cyanogen gas and finish the job if needed with a thermonuclear explosion. After evading this trap they demand an explanation from Earth and learn that the last space travelers returning after centuries brought home long-forgotten diseases and destroyed civilization. The locals are reluctant to have that happen again, so the travelers head back out, with food for ten years. So much for advanced medicine in the future, never mind the Singularity.

"The Star Game" (**72**) is an ambitiously well-meaning novel-ette, with chapter numbers no less, which begins: "Bradlaugh, the Astrogator's mother, was a big, balding man with gentle, brown eyes who moved like a worried grey bear in his sloppy cover-alls." This is not an early gender-bending effort. In hyper-drive, "men found themselves worse than blind, in a seething chaos of flame, all known points of reference gone and the usual naviga-tional aids useless." The nearest thing anyone knows of to this is the intense aurorae of Venus. Conveniently, the Venusians' idea of child-rearing is to abandon their kids in the swamp. The next generation is whoever survives. Earth rescues a few of these kids and trains them to be astrogators. They remain child-like and develop great loyalty to their psychologist rescuers, their only social contacts. Mostly they now live longer (approaching 20 years) than they would if left in the swamps, but never know their own culture. Thinking their job a game, they don't understand how crucial they are to the safety of space travel. Heilbron the researcher is assigned to study Bradlaugh and his Venusian astrogator Gareg and moves into their quarters, precipitating conflict and misunderstanding that lead Gareg to flee outside in his spacesuit where no one will hurt his feelings. Bradlaugh has to brave the sensory bombardment of hyper-space and talk him back in. Heilbron and Bradlaugh agree that this exploitation has to stop and some other way of astrogating must be found.

"Insecurity Risk" (**79**) is a moderately capable puzzle story. A robot, allegedly programmed with the Asimovian Three Laws, has beaten a worker to death, stopping only when his co-worker lunged for the big red "off" button on the robot's chest, which erases its memory as well as stopping the action. How could this happen? Of course, it didn't. Interestingly, the protagonist is a union leader who seems mainly concerned with keeping the lid on things rather than speaking up against this apparent deadly menace to his members.

Donald Malcolm improves too, if you can wait long enough. "The Long Ellipse" (**67**) is an inane bag of stale sentimentality about a cardboard general whose son was lost on a space venture years previously, killing his wife (through grief, one presumes). Then the son's spaceship, having assumed a long orbit rather than being destroyed or keeping going, is sighted. The crisis is, will the general get to go along to see his son's body? Of course he does and of course the son is alive, since they had experimental suspended animation equipment aboard but somehow nobody knew about this.

"The House of Lights" (**70**) swaps inanity for incoherence in a story that has its moments, if only they were connected sensibly. The protagonist is an Operator. That is, he watches a board of colored lights that reflect the emotional state of an Agent who is off spying on aliens (instantaneous transmission, forget light speed). Operators have been subjected to psychosurgery to eliminate their own emotions, all except 3% of them. The "sexual emotions" are retained because they are difficult to restore later. ("Nature could be tampered with only so far.")

But huge numbers of agents are being lost; it looks as if there's a spy in their midst.

The protagonist's old flame Carol is an agent who suddenly shows up at their base on a secret asteroid. When he sees her carried away, apparently suspected as the alien, he follows her to the interrogation chamber, knocking out two people along the way, sees her being tortured, and walks away. He is congratulated on passing his empath test, displaying zero emotional response. So why did he knock two people out to get to her? No questions please. Shortly thereafter it is revealed that she is back at her post light-years away. Was she ever really here? I said no questions. A bit later the protagonist discovers he has become telepathic. How and why? Doesn't say, but it's just in time for him to beat off a telepathic attack by the colleague who proves to be a spy and who is reduced to a mindless idiot in the conflict. The writing is as incoherent as the plot. Malcolm says of this story:

> One title, "The House of Lights," I'd had in my notebook for about five years before I wrote the story, and how John [Carnell] persevered with me over that one. I sweated blood over two re-writes and from him I learned what it meant to be a pro. He told me that he took two out of every hundred submissions. Every British writer, and a few Americans, too, owed him a great deal.[76]

But things start to get better. The blurb for Malcolm's "The Stuff of Dreams" (**80**) says he "has done considerable research into dreams and our dream-worlds," and he shows his work. "From a study of eye movements, the research group at Chicago had gradually been able to tell when a subject was dreaming and whether the dream was of an active or a passive

---

76. Malcolm, "Reminiscences of a Science Fiction Writer, Or 'I knew the Late, Great, Bob Shaw,'" *Relapse* 15 (Autumn 2009), p. 9 (http://www.efanzines.com/Prolapse/Relapse15.pdf) (visited 9/7/11).

nature. The eye movements were a reflection of what happened in dreams." One of the subjects of a dream researcher starts having extremely vivid and colorful dreams about a spaceship operated by blobs, and it seems to be coming closer. The plot is ultimately Hal Clement's *Needle* told from a different point of view, and reasonably capably.

Speaking of dreams, "Complex" (**86**) presents a pretty good one. Humans get into space to discover there's a whole fellowship of sophonts out there, and they don't fight wars. Nor do they have any geniuses—all their great accomplishments are group efforts. Why? As explained by Elis A'Kren, of the touristically beautiful planet Marella, to Roos of Earth, individual greatness stems from feelings of inferiority. The galactics have all had their complexes removed; and hey! we'll do it for you too. Roos reports back to his superior, General Haymire, reminding the General that he was once a picked-upon weakling who swore he would show everybody, and now that won't have to happen any more. General Haymire falls right into line. Wouldn't it be nice. This is actually a very pleasant piece of didactic wish-fulfillment, with the lecture interrupted by colorful descriptions of the scenery of Marella and salted with amusing one-liners. E.g., when the Earth military realized it was superfluous and had to come up with something to do, "Some units spent their time giving military tattoos, unheard of in the Galaxy." In case you're wondering, tattoos are formal marching displays with lots of drumming and bugling, nothing to do with needles and ink.

"Almost Obsolete" (**88**) is a piece of gender paranoia, but kinder and gentler than the usual. Kemp, a male medical statistician, starts to notice some funny stuff going on: higher rates of male sterility, lower male/female birth ratios, declining male life expectancy, etc. He contacts the World Health Organization, and the trends are confirmed, along with an increasing number of reports of virgin births. Kemp pronounces, "I think we are witnessing the beginning of the bifurcation of the human race. Men are in the process of becoming aliens on their own planet.

Mother Nature feels it is time for a change....Women have always been the more dominant species [sic], longer lived, more durable, less prone to killer diseases and worries. Now she is coming into her own. Some time in the future, a woman will not need a man." Tell the government? Why bother? "Governments can do many things, but they can't stop evolution." Is this the end of man (sic)? No! "The race of man is only *beginning*, my friend. Nature would not spend a million years shaping an intellect only to throw it away carelessly.... Man's destiny is among the stars.... Anyway, hasn't the woman always stayed at home while the man roved? Only, he has the Universe at his disposal, now." This is the sort of nonsense that is all too prevalent in older SF and that drives me up the wall. But the story is very readable, smoothly told and well developed.

Even Alan Barclay cranks it up a notch, returning after more than a year's absence (from fiction, anyway—he had an article in **67**) with "The Silver Moons" (**82**), a pleasant enough word from our sponsor, the conventional sentiments of SF. Morrison is going to Mars and paying his own fare, which boggles everyone's mind; he's sold everything up and cashed in his pension to fund it. Once in orbit, he takes passage on a solo freighter piloted by the eccentric Captain Jago, who plays a lot of grandiose recorded music and has a fantasy of chucking it and heading for Jupiter to see its moons. Jago is separated from his wife; Morrison's wife has died; what the hell. They decide to go for it, cutting loose their cargo, and using the fuel and food for the return trip to get to Jupiter where they can starve or asphyxiate. It's a welcome relief from Barclay's tedious string of stories about military life and personalities.

So is "Nearly Extinct" (**89**), which matter-of-factly depicts the remnants of humanity, harried and driven into the hills by the Frogs, alien invaders who hunt them for sport. But the humans have learned, or mutated, to teleport, which evens the odds a bit and will stave off doom a little longer–but no more than that, and everybody knows it. Judith Merril gave it an Honorable Mention.

Francis G. Rayer and E. R. James—collectively, the Christopher Anvil of *New Worlds*—are present as usual, but fortunately not as often. And towards the end of these two years, they both actually produce some work above their usual standard. Rayer appears in **69** with "Painters of Narve," and Carnell is pleased: "It is nine months since we published a story by Mr. Rayer and we freely admit that we have missed his refreshing style and plot twists. As a technical radio man, however, he has been writing countless technical articles and fiction has had to wait its turn." This one is a drab fairy tale. Chris Batley and his thuggish partner Emerald have come to Narve to pursue the legend of splendid native paintings, and steal them. They find them and the Painters in a remote desert, Emerald starts shooting the Painters, Batley shoots him, and gets turned into a painting.

Rayer then disappears for over a year, returning with "Searchpoint" (**83**), a well-meaning but incompetently written story about an alien spaceship that lands on a human colony planet, and the judgment that the invisible alien explorer makes on humanity based on our mostly paranoid reaction to its landing. In "Sands Our Abode" (**84**), Captain Bob resists the pressure of Major Ruffel to sign off on the habitability of a new grass-covered colony planet after only 24 hours, and is vindicated when it transpires that the grass shifts the sand to bury anything that sits still, including the explorers' spaceship. "Alien" (**85**) is livelier, if only because its idea is more bizarre. An alien spaceship lands in a meadow, but it proves to be two-dimensional: it has length and height but no width. It is unresponsive to communication attempts. Meanwhile, the denizens of the spaceship are appalled by the uncontrolled flow of time on this strange planet. Obviously there is no life here, so they may as well irradiate and colonize the planet, but they'll all need individual time-locks to live there. Earth's bacon is saved by one character's faithful dog Trotter, who sticks his nose into a mysterious circle that has emerged from the ship, and grabs a hitherto invisible two-dimensional disk with ideograms, displaying sufficiently purposive action that the aliens realize they shouldn't be irradiating us.

Rayer winds up 1959 with two stories. "Continuity Man" (**87**), under the George Longdon pseudonym, is uncharacteristically affecting, about the last two children on a generation-starship and their relationship with their foster parents, who aren't what they seem. This is followed by "I Like You" (**88**), also as by Longdon, an equally uncharacteristically effective horror story about a shape-changing alien whose *modus vivendi* is to imitate other life forms and stick to them, and the misery it brings to the ordinary man who has the misfortune to be selected for imitation.

E. R. James' "Routine Observations" (**71**) has a certain geekishly ingenious charm. A newly minted Ecologist is on his way from the Centauri system to get some experience as an assistant, all the while dreaming of having his *own* planet, meanwhile passing the time observing the diurnal cycles of the creatures in his aquarium. His spaceship stops by an uncolonized planet only to find that there's an unauthorized ship in orbit. This proves to have been launched from the surface so it can't be spotted on the ground and give away the locations of the escaped convicts who hijacked it and are hiding out on the planet. But the Ecologist and an officer go aboard the ship, which improbably has its own aquarium, and back on board their own ship, the Ecologist figures out the bad guys' location from the diurnal cycle of the bacteria in the water he has gotten on his pants cuffs. At the end, after the bad guys are in custody, he's the only civilian on the planet, so he claims it for his own.

"Sprinkler System" (**85**) is similar if duller: the protagonist goes to a newly discovered planet to figure out why the resident scientist's research assistants keep disappearing, taken by the sea, it seems. It turns out the island they are working on is alive, with a veneer of dirt, and whenever there's a fire (even a discarded lit cigarette), it shrugs, so the offending area is deluged with water, which threatens to carry off anyone in the vicinity.

"Beyond Surrealism" (**86**)[77] is livelier and more imaginative, if hokey. Gerard Avon is back from three years in space to visit his brother Mel. On the bus, he sees an eye-catching abstract poster that makes him feel like he's back in space. These Guided Auto Suggestion Pictures, a.k.a. Dreamies, prove to be the work of brother Mel, now in jail because he has confessed to killing the man who stabbed his wife, by means of one of his pictures. Gerard doesn't believe it for a minute and cracks the case— killing somebody else with Mel's picture and thereby demonstrating Mel's innocence.

§

A number of the outstanding names from earlier years appear during these two years, but to little effect. Arthur C. Clarke is here with his first original piece for *New Worlds* in some years, "Who's There?" (**77**): a man doing EVA discovers he's not alone in his spacesuit—well written but annoyingly trivial.

John Brunner has only two stories in these issues of *New Worlds* aside from the conclusion of "Threshold of Eternity," discussed in the previous chapter, though that's because he's writing longer stories. During these two years he has four novelets and novellas in *Science Fantasy*, and Carnell explains in "Postmortem" in **78**, in response to one Mike Moorcock's praise for "Earth Is But a Star," that it appeared in *Science Fantasy* only because of its length. Presumably the same is true of "Echo in the Skull" and the two long stories ("City of the Tiger" and "The Whole Man"), also in *Science Fantasy*, that were later developed into *Telepathist/The Whole Man*. All these stories would have fit comfortably into *New Worlds* in terms of theme, and considerably enlivened it in terms of style and storytelling.

In any case, Brunner returns to *New Worlds* after a year's

---

77. In another of the proofreading gaffes that dogged the Carnell magazines, the title is rendered "Beyond Realism" on the cover and contents page and "Beyond Surrealism" on the story's title page and the running headers. Take your pick.

absence with "The Trouble I've Seen" (**81**), a slick and efficient picture of a kid from the slums with a sort of precognition—he knows if something's going to turn sour so he can stay out of it—who uses the talent in a completely amoral and self-seeking fashion. He comes to a bad end as a result of the talent, but not as a result of his misuse of it, which vitiates the story's force. "Round Trip" (**85**) is an overwritten cosmology opera,[78] in the form of a letter to the protagonist's wife—the ultimate "Babe, I'm gonna leave you." People have traced the paths of all the particles in the universe (!) to determine where it all started. When they get there, they find a giant spherical spaceship, obviously made by people of earlier cosmic cycles to survive the re-coalescence of all matter and the next Big Bang—though by doing this, they have subtracted a certain amount of matter, which causes a minor modification in the next Bang. Our hero decides he will go into the inner core of the spaceship, and remain there, while his self from the previous cycle will emerge and return to take up his life, with the protagonist's wife; and the protagonist will likewise emerge during the next universe.

Kenneth Bulmer contributes four stories in addition to his serial, but they don't add up to a lot. The best of them is "Never Trust a Robot" (**67**), an energetic if gimmicky novelette about men who remotely control mining machinery on an uninhabitable planet, working under exploitative contracts and afraid that they are going to be displaced by robots. ("The food's disgusting, and such small portions.") The robots do appear, and display their heart by rescuing a man who has gone down to the surface physically, but then reveal to the protagonist that it was really all calculation ("We do not have emotions, but we use our brains.") They expect that the protagonist will keep quiet about this—why, they don't explain. The underlying labor-management conflict seems to be forgotten. Nonetheless the story moves along quickly and is one of Bulmer's better written pieces.

---

78. Broderick disagrees, finding this a poignant if scientifically absurd tale, elegantly framed and written, one of Brunner's best.

Unfortunately it is immediately followed by "The Unreluctant Tread" (**68**), a tiresome bag of clichés about a man who has just barely passed the Space Naval Academy, which he did only to please his father the Admiral. Now he's given an undeserved command with orders to crash his destroyer into a battleship and permit Earth to install a banned superweapon under cover of the confusion. After his contrived court-martial and discharge, he changes his name and (T.E. Lawrence-like) *signs up as an enlisted man*, since the service is really in his blood, as he tells his father the Admiral.

"Space Command" (**74**) is in the same vein, but more admirable and more exasperating; it represents a lot of work and skill devoted to the effective presentation of an irredeemably hackneyed plot. The narrator is a journalist/historian who has concerned himself for some years with the burning question why Rear Admiral Fairlee never got promoted to Vice Admiral and then Admiral. After the big interstellar war, in which he just missed getting his own ship to command, Fairlee is assigned to the planet holding the Academy for Children of Veterans of one of the former enemies. He thinks he's a failure and his life has been for nothing, which seems a bit extreme for a man who's had an honorable career and served capably in wartime. A deadly disease afflicts the planet. There's no way to get the kids evacuated in time. Wait, there's a grounded space ship that will be a death trap to fly for long but will get them off the planetary surface, if only someone will risk his life to take it up; guess who? Fairlee saves the kids, delivers them to a safe place, then heads off in the death ship and blows himself up. It's an extremely well written and constructed story, but all the effort Bulmer has put into it can't redeem this chestnut.

"The Gentle Approach" (**84**) is another variation on a standard theme, and not a very interesting one. Space explorers have found a planet inhabited by sentient humanoids, and the alien culture experts are hard at work. Their *modus operandi* is to bring representatives of Earth's variety of cultures—including, e.g., Australian Aborigines with Ph.D.'s—so they can use whatever Earth culture is closest to the aliens' as a basis for communication. The aliens are having none of it. So some of the crew go off on their own to get drunk and party with the aliens, and that's the ticket: it seems that the aliens are hypersensitive to insincerity, and an Aborigine with a Ph.D. going naked with his boomerang doesn't meet their authenticity standards.

E. C. Tubb's "Requiem for a Harvey," the lead story in **68**, is about Judd, a sociopathic spaceman due to be cashiered who develops a plan to smuggle the elderly Easton—a harvey—back to Earth from Mars in return for half the money the man has coming to him on Earth. A harvey is somebody who can't go home again for one reason or another. In this case, the doctors won't let him make the flight. How do you conceal an extra person on a space flight? "Compensating the load for [Easton's] added weight had been harder, and [Judd] wasn't certain that he had managed it, but he had done his best." Tubb posits that absolute privacy is observed in space, so Judd stashes Easton in his cabin. It all comes to a bad end as Easton becomes more querulous and demanding and Judd finally suffocates him with a pillow and throws him out the airlock—but not until the captain has decided that Judd has learned his lesson about his earlier transgressions and has made him the heir to his command, in an amusingly cynical inversion of Character is Fate.

Tubb's *New Worlds* Profile says his two-year absence from *New Worlds* was occasioned by his job as an editor (of, it doesn't say, the now defunct *Authentic Science Fiction*), ignoring his pseudonymous *New Worlds* stories in the interim. His message: "as John Wyndham has said, 'Stories are about people, not about things.'" This story is not, however, the beginning of a Tubb resurgence. After this one, he's gone again for another couple of years, returning in early 1960 as a regular contributor and staying that way, surprisingly, well into the Moorcock years.

Bertram Chandler (still no A.) reappears with several lightweight items, starting with the utterly trivial "In the Box" (**71**), in which the crew telepaths of the *Eupeptic Dragon* try to cheat and win on a game show on the planet they've stopped at. In

76's "Dreamboat" (also published in *Science Fiction Stories*, February 1959), crew and passengers celebrating the midpoint of their interstellar voyage are accidentally fed hallucinogenic fungi ("They're off things, those Mexican mushrooms") with their steaks, and the Chief Officer and one of the passengers experience ecstatic togetherness on an unspoiled Eden, at the end of which she has disappeared from the spaceship. Now he's got a handful of mushrooms and he's going to try to join her at the appropriate point on the return trip. This one is amusingly quaint in retrospect, but Chandler seems to have been paying more attention than usual while writing it: the characters are not ciphers and the plot that gets them to the denouement is actually moderately interesting.

Three issues later, under the George Whitley pseudonym, Chandler provides *another* psychedelic mushroom story, "The Right Ingredients" (**79**). A man gets a bit of the right, or wrong, stuff in his dried mushrooms while grocery shopping. He and his wife and dinner guests start to feel funny post-prandially, and start fooling around with a Möbius strip. When the protagonist takes off his left shoe, it has turned into a right shoe, folded through a higher spatial dimension. This is one of Chandler's purposely insubstantial stories, but one still has to give him credit for pioneering, whether at the library or by participant observation. It was not until 1960 that Timothy Leary first encountered these substances. (Maybe Chandler just read "Hallucinogens" by George C. Duncan, an article in *Authentic Science Fiction* #51, November 1954.)

"Chance Encounter" (**81**) carries a bit more historical weight—it's the first of the Grimes stories—but not much more of any other kind of weight, being a display of conventional sentiments. Peter the telepath is pining for a suitable mate but female telepaths are mostly stupid and unattractive. Along comes Grimes with a proposal to rummage round the Rim looking for the source of alien artifacts that keep turning up. So they head out, eventually meet up with an alien ship, and their telepath is a babe! Peter goes off to meet her and fireworks ensue—real ones, since the aliens are made of antimatter. But the narrator remembers Peter's premonitory dream, which ended in "utter and absolute oneness," and wonders "if he was the unluckiest, or the luckiest of men."

Chandler has the *New Worlds* Profile in **71**, looking sharp-eyed and intrepid in his photo. Of "Jack," it says, "Born in 1912, he went to sea at the age of sixteen and served in tramp steamers for eight years, then switched to liners and worked his way to Chief Officer before quitting and emigrating to Australia in 1955." As Second Mate of a coaster, he has more writing time than before, though he'll be Chief again shortly. He recounts visiting New York after Pearl Harbor and being invited to contribute by John Campbell. He says, "At present the main snag is shortage of ideas. Should this deplorable state of affairs continue I may have to make an honest living writing crime or sea stories (I know that I have been accused of doing the latter for years!)" Affirmative on both counts.

John Kippax's "Tower for One" (**73**) presents Margesson, an artist who feels underappreciated on Earth, so he takes one-way passage to Krios, where the photos he has seen show colors he would like to paint. Nobody is much impressed on Krios. Eventually he sees that the local artists are all far better than he is, although they only work in black and white, sepia, and the like. The Kriosians suggest that what they really need is a good water engineer, which Margesson was trained to be, and by the way they're all color blind because of the radiation of Krios's sun, as Margesson will be before long. He decides that they've shown him the way to live (besides, this way he gets the girl). The story's pious didacticism is made tolerable by smooth and unpretentious writing.

In "The Dusty Death" (**77**) (merely "Dusty Death" on the cover), Lunar explorers fall into a dust pit and one of them proves to be claustrophobic but to have concealed that fact in training. They get out anyway. Again, competent writing keeps one going through a fundamentally creaky and uninteresting story. Ditto "Friday" (**80**): space explorers discover somebody forgot to refuel their ship, the planet's Heaviside layer is too thick for their radio to penetrate, but they find the skeleton of another castaway from centuries before, and his faithful robot who helps them with the old ship's radio equipment before its last circuits expire.

Lan Wright returns in **85** with another dreary Johnny Dawson story, "Joker's Trick," which might as well have been called "Idiot's Plot." Dawson is summoned from retirement to help find out why five Terran agents have vanished or been killed on Mylon. Wright makes a big point of the backwardness, laziness, and dishonesty of the Mylonians. When Dawson finds the bad guys, instead of shooting him out of hand, they explain their diabolical scheme (to end Earth's colonial rights on Mylon by trumping up evidence of exploitation), and their explanation is transmitted to Galactic headquarters or wherever by the camera around Wright's neck. (Sixty years later, the same method has been used by protestors against school bullying or police misbehavior, using cell phones, so maybe Wright gets a few points for prescience.)

Peter Hawkins' "The Birdcage" (**86**) is a vague and turgid near-miss of a story in which, on Mars, a huge structure suddenly comes into being: "Birdcage was a misnomer; it was more like a coral yet something like an oaktree the way its branches grew, except that it was bushy and tight, roughly cubic and with roughly straight bars, which gave it its nickname enclosing the branches." How could this be? The Martians don't have a mechanical civilization. Turns out a Martian did do it, then killed himself because it was against the rules of Martian philosophical culture. And look, Earth folks can do it too, creating small Birdcage-like structure from rocks by mental power. It is asserted—based on what is not clear—that "In the Birdcage you [the Martians] found all the great discoveries we have made without developing them—fire, the wheel, electricity, $e=mc^2$ and then the Birdcage, as a discovery in itself, the first step to understanding exactly what a creative mind is." One of the Martians reveals the Birdcage ruined their world in antiquity, but maybe it will do great things for the humans. The protagonist says it might be "like giving a lunatic child a machine gun"—pretty close to a phrase we've heard before in SF (see Fredric Brown's "The Weapon").

William F. Temple's "The Different Complexion" (76) is ambitious but labored and ultimately pointless. Burns, having been dismissed by his gold-digging fiancée on Earth, is laboring and drinking on Mars. His boozing buddy Dodge advises him to take up with a Martian, but Burns finds them repellent. When he collapses, he is taken in and nursed back to health by Burns's Martian girlfriend Rowena, who decides she prefers him to Dodge because he has blue eyes, trumps in the Martians' elaborate code of snobbery based on physical characteristics. That's fine with Burns, because it turns out Martians are beautiful for three months of the year. Temple presents all this in a very positive light, with implicit comparison to the scheming ways of Earth women (or at least one of them). It doesn't seem like much of an improvement to me.

Temple has the *New Worlds* Profile, which notes that with Russell and Wyndham he is one of the contributors with the longest service to UK SF, was editor of the British Interplanetary Society's *Journal*, and contributed to the first issue of *New Worlds*. Since then he's written a thriller, a book on space travel illustrated by Gerard Quinn, and short stories, and more recently the juvenile Martin Magnus SF series, and edited the *Dan Dare Annual*.

Sydney J. Bounds' *New Worlds* career grinds to a halt (though not quite a permanent one) in these issues. "The Wayward Ship" (72) is introduced by Carnell: "It is a recognized fact that ocean-going vessels have personalities of their own, from the dirtiest tramp steamer to the largest liner. It is also logical to assume that spaceships will one day develop similar characteristics." The story is about as bad as you would expect. The ship is called Kate (short for Katherine of Padua), she hates planets, and the new skipper has to be stern indeed to master her. There's also a Scottish engineer named Mac who says things like, "Mon, those are hard words! Sure, she's a perverse female with her tail squatting on the ground... but take her up where the sky is black and the stars like fairy lights and she's as sweet a craft you'll ever find. A perfect little lady!"

"Outside" (**73**) is not as bad, but that's the best one can say for it. A man has to go outside the spaceship to fix something and experiences fear: "The fear of space, the fear of... *Outside*." "The Mules" (**74**) consists entirely of a gimmick too dismally tedious to bother repeating. And that's it for Sydney J. Bounds in *New Worlds* until 1964 (Bounds later sold a couple of stories to Moorcock), and just as well to my taste. He achieved competence on several occasions, but overall, he was a dire and dreary writer who was better left behind.

Peter Phillips' "Next Stop the Moon" (**67**), reprinted from the London *Daily Herald*, October 14-17, 1957—i.e., written immediately after the Sputnik launch—is a feel-good piece redeemed by Phillips' fairly lively writing and the telling of the story through excerpted news stories and interviews. Russia sends up some astronauts, their fuel tank is holed by a meteor, they can't get down. The US adapts one of its military missiles to get up there with fuel, but the weight constraints are severe, so it's piloted by Professor Oldcastle's 16-year-old son. The Cold War national stereotypes are rotated in gently satirical fashion, and it is suggested that the Cold War may now be eased. (It's mildly amusing to reflect, more than half a century later, the Cold War having not just eased but shut down, that it is the Russians who are ferrying the Americans up and down.) Judith Merril gave this one an Honorable Mention for its newspaper appearance.

Phillips has the *New Worlds* Profile this issue, which begins, "Born on the Isle of Dogs thirty-five years ago," and recounts his abandonment of his parents' chosen scientific career for journalism, first in the West Country and then to London, where he is now "chief sub-editor of the features section on the *Daily Herald*." It notes his burst of productivity from 1948 to 1952 and subsequent falling off in production, and expresses hope that he'll produce more. In fact, this is his last appearance in the SF magazines.

John Brody's cheery "Ring-Side Seat" (**72**) (or "Ringside Seat" if you look at the Table of Contents or running heads) proposes that Earth has been taken over by telepathic mutant supermen who are conducting a sterilization program (or "Pogram" as it is consistently labeled; whether pun or misspelling is impossible to tell in a Carnell magazine) of normals, with the cooperation of many of the normals, who have been thoroughly defeated. But one day somewhere in Africa, one of the black fellows (as Brody puts it, consistently with other casually racist usage throughout) sees through the game as his people are being marched past the sterilizing device; he's subdued with difficulty. He's one of *another* kind of mutant, and his kindred come to rescue him with impressive military force, and the story ends with the normal protagonist making his escape from the carnage, carrying hope—that the two varieties of mutant will kill each other off and the normals will survive.

John Boland's "Secret Weapon" (**69**) is an overlong joke (14 pages) about Melton and the Professor, career crooks who go to far Plooda to undergo the process that will allow them to teleport at will, which to them means stealing at will and always escaping; but to their horror they learn that the process also makes them incapable of dishonesty. At a third the length it might have been amusing.

There are a few more debuts in these two years, none of them amounting to as much as those of Presslie and Kapp. John W. Ashton's first story, "Companion" (**71**), is an inane gimmick story. Space explorers find a monstrous alien in suspended animation, then it's revealed the explorers have tentacles and antennae, so presumably the monster is a human. That's it. Carnell says this Ashton is "not to be confused with the 'John Ashton' who appeared in *Science Fantasy* several years ago." However, there was no prior John Ashton; he apparently means John Ashcroft. "Signora Porfiria" (**78**) is considerably better, a smoothly developed story about a man on vacation in Italy, who by the way does physics experiments in his basement, and who meets a mysterious woman who seems to have access to his mind. She turns out to have been waiting for him with extreme prejudice but lacks the courage of her time-traveling mission. Carnell described it in the preceding issue's "Literary Lineup" as a "piece of poetic nostalgia," which quite misses the point of this well-oiled machine.

Ashton has the *New Worlds* Profile in this issue, leaning into his photograph at about 30 degrees and looking like a minor bad guy in a James Bond movie. He had an English mother and a Hungarian father, served in the US Army, went to school in five European countries, and was a correspondent for newspapers all over the place until he opened his own public relations firm in Brussels. "Concerning future stories he says, 'Don't be surprised if next year's crop are sometimes datelined from the oddest places—I expect my movements to become rather hectic.'" Apparently they were more hectic than he expected—this was his last story in the genre magazines (of three—these two and one in *Science Fantasy* also in 1958), and his only other appearance was a guest editorial five years later, "Satellite Hunters" in **136**, at which point he is working in "the Rome bureau of London's largest daily."

Clive Jackson's "Death on the Wheel" (**74**) is a mystery set on a space station, as much a howdunit as a whodunit, where the murder proves to have been racially motivated—in this future there's a CLAN, the Caucasian League of Anti-Negroes, with ancestry in North America, and the Afro-Asian Federation of Free Peoples, and a couple of men get into a fistfight over whether the Americans should have rescued the French at Dienbienphu. At one tense moment the Captain snaps: "Now hear this! In Watchdog there are no Limeys, Yanks, Krauts, Nips, niggers or wops—there are World Security personnel! I will not, repeat not, have either personal quarrels or racial prejudices interfering with the efficiency of my command.'" It's a nice try, capably written.

Carnell describes Jackson as "another new British writer," which is true in a sense—although Jackson has credits in

Miller/Contento going back to 1949, they are all in fan or semi-pro sources like *Slant, Nekromantikon,* and *Fantastic Worlds* (though one of them, "The Swordsman of Varnis," wound up anthologized in Fredric Brown and Mack Reynolds' *Science Fiction Carnival*, and anticipated a famous comic killing in *Raiders of the Lost Ark*). Carnell congratulates Jackson on "selling another story to the highly competitive American market," but Miller/Contento doesn't list any such publication, and Jackson's only entry after this one is in the UK *SF Adventures* in 1959.

Clifford C. Reed makes his first *New Worlds* appearance (he's previously been in *Authentic, Nebula,* and *Science Fantasy*) with the dreadful "Morgan's Galatea" (**75**), about a man disappointed in love who bails a prostitute out of jail to serve as a model for the artificial woman he is building. His agenda: to make something that looks like a woman but is honest, kind, and true, unlike real women, so men won't be fooled by the latter. This purpose is ultimately discredited in pious and tiresome fashion. Reed (b. 1911) has the *New Worlds* Profile in this issue: moved from South Africa in 1950 when 39, works for an engineering firm. "His interests are in social work (his wife is Warden of an old peoples' home), walking, and drawing." Influences are the usual, except that he mentions Dornford Yates' *The Stolen March* as "the finest fantasy novel written."[79] Reed published another dozen stories in *New Worlds* and its companions (including a couple in the Moorcock-Bonfiglioli era), assembled three novellas from *Science Fiction Adventures* into the stuffily titled fix-up *Martian Enterprise* (Digit 1962), and that was it for him. Reed's fiction is mostly some combination of labored and boring, as is this one, and written largely in irritatingly fragmented sentences.

E. Henley contributes "Strange Menhir" (**84**), about a group of space colonists who arrive on a strange planet where the fertile area is dotted with menhirs (upright standing stones).

---

79. Yates (1885-1960), a bestseller between the Wars, is now largely forgotten. See http://en.wikipedia.org/wiki/Dornford_Yates (visited 9/9/11).

The sensitive women (Rozanne especially) are full of nameless forebodings, and the earlier expedition appears to have been killed. At the end Rozanne is drawn to one of the menhirs, which splits open, revealing a "spire of transcendent beauty," and covers her in some red stuff that seems good to eat. So now they know "that Man would not be master, but a vital part of something they could scarcely understand, which could live and grow again, and be food and drink for their children." The story doesn't make a whole lot of sense but is well written and carries a certain power, and it's certainly a welcome relief from the usual *New Worlds* fare. Henley appeared only one other time in the SF magazines, with "The Temporal Paradox" in the February 1957 *Fantastic Universe*.

§

As usual, there are a number of stories by US writers previously published in US sources, though as noted they diminish drastically from 1958 to 1959, and before long they vanish. The use of reprints is also a bit different from earlier years, when Carnell brought marquee names into the magazine (Heinlein, Asimov, Clarke, Sturgeon in 1956-57). In these issues, most of the previously published stories are journeyman work by competent professionals of the time.

Robert Silverberg contributes seven stories ranging from mediocre to clever and capable. "The Lonely One" (**69**), from the July 1956 *Science Fiction Stories*, is a fairly dull and obvious piece of product. Star travelers come to Earth to rescue the remnants of humanity who are freezing their buns in a new Ice Age; but the remnants say they can't leave, Earth won't let them, and when their benefactors try to leave they can't do it either—their fingers freeze above the buttons. "The Macauley Circuit" (**70**) (*Fantastic Universe* August 1956) is an improvement, a reasonably clever story about the invention of a device that can compose music and the realization that "We've synthesized our successor. Gentlemen, we are all obsolete." (In **72**,

John Hynam of Peterborough, Northants—better known as John Kippax—says in "Postmortem": "You have to hand it to young Silverberg.") "Absolutely Inflexible" (**72**, from *Fantastic Universe*, July 1956) is a glib circular time paradox story (as they pretty much have to be). Mahler is in charge of sending time travelers from the past off for life imprisonment in an isolated location, since they bear diseases for which future humanity has no resistance. Today's time traveler, unlike the rest, says he has a two-way time machine, but they pack him off like the rest, confiscating his machine. However, Mahler can't resist the temptation and finds that the machine will indeed take him into the past. He goes, comes back, gets picked up and brought before himself, who dispatches him to the isolated prison despite his protestations. It's almost glib enough to keep one from noticing that the central dramatic device of the story makes no sense— that time travelers carrying dreadful diseases would first be brought before a bureaucrat for a face-to-face interview and scolding rather than being taken directly to isolation (or, more logically still, shot on sight and their bodies burned).

"Slice of Life" (**74**), under the Calvin M. Knox pseudonym, from the April 1958 *Infinity*, is a bit more ambitious. Onslow is a psychiatrist in a world of telepaths, Danny an 11-year-old boy crippled in a fall who now spends his time in bed daydreaming. When Onslow discovers that the kid has daydreamed a whole complex world, he refuses to destroy it by restoring the boy's telepathy, and tells the parents he has failed, because Danny is showing signs of artistic genius. This one got an Honorable Mention from Judith Merril (for the *Infinity* appearance).

"In Gratitude" (**79**, from *Infinity*, November 1958, as "There Was an Old Woman—") concerns a former Professor of Biochemistry who has 31 cloned sons produced from her own eggs, fertilized from a sperm bank, all to test her environment/ heredity theories by rearing each for a different chosen occupation, and what happens when most of them decide they don't really like her choices. It's done in a solemn, almost pompous voice, given away only by passages like: "Only one of us was not sent to any accredited institution. He was Richard, who was to be our criminal. Already he had made several sallies into the surrounding towns and cities, returning a few days or weeks later with money or jewels and with a guilty grin on his face." (Pamela Sargent would develop the same theme, raised to a higher power, in her 1976 novel *Cloned Lives*.)

"Earthman's Burden" (**80**, from *Infinity*, March 1958 as "The Overlord's Thumb") is a pleasant piece about a military expedition from Earth, one of whose members transgresses in the sacred courtyard of the local humanoids and then kills the one who comes after him. His commanding officer turns him over to the aliens for trial, which fortunately he survives (it's trial by ordeal). This sets the precedent, and shows that humans don't want to be overlords. "Malnutrition" (**85**), first published in *Saturn*, March 1958, as "Alaree," posits an alien member of a gestalt mind who develops individuality through associating with humans, is cast out by the gestalt, and begs to go back to Earth with the humans. He dies en route, having been unable to establish a similar relationship with the humans.

Lester del Rey has three reprinted stories, all displaying his middle-of-the-road professionalism. Carnell reprinted five del Rey items in 1958—these three, plus "Little Jimmy" and "No Strings Attached" in *Science Fantasy* **30** and **31** respectively. They have in common, among del Rey's numerous stories of the mid-1950s, that all were reprinted in his 1957 Ballantine collection *Robots And Changelings*. "Keepers of the House" (**73**) is an agreeably done story about a dog surviving after some kind of unspecified disaster seems to have destroyed humanity, missing its master, and finding and leaving his body, reprinted from the January 1956 *Fantastic Universe*. "Stability" (**74**) is a competent performance from the legendary *Vortex 1* (1953), in which space explorers on Venus find out that the native life consists of shapeshifters who are trying to duplicate them, and then that they are in fact duplicates—but who cares, if they are really duplicates, and if, once changed to Earth life, they become as stable as Earth life?

"The Still Waters" (**78**, from *Fantastic Universe*, June 1955) is about an old spacer and his wife and their beat-up old nuclear-reactor-powered spaceship, which needs repairs they can't pay for and anyway it's an obsolete technology. They're thinking about just heading out to die of old age, but at the last minute they discover the Ceres colony is in deep trouble because of high energy costs, so they donate their reactor to keep the colony going, and Pop's got a job teaching the younkers how to run fusion. It's better than it sounds. The overt bathos is kept to a dull murmur.

Harry Harrison has three bi-continental stories, one of which appeared in *New Worlds* before its US appearance. The first two are about par for this writer's journeyman course. "Captain Bedlam" (**69**), reprinted from the December 1957 US *Science Fiction Adventures*, proposes that humans can't stand up to the stress of space flight, and the only way to get around the problem is to induce a second personality to pilot the spaceships. The main personality never sees space and experiences only periods of amnesia. But the protagonist gets into real trouble, and his main personality wakes up just long enough to see the stars, before the *third* personality is invoked to deal with the emergency at the cost of considerable injury. In "Trainee for Mars" (**75**), from *Fantastic Universe*, June 1958, prospective areonauts are training in an elaborate mock-up, but they keep screwing up and would die if they were really on Mars. Only four remain who haven't washed, or deaded, out. Headquarters announces that this time they won't save the trainees from their mistakes. They make it through, only to learn that the joke's on them and this time they are really on Mars.

"I See You" (**83**), which appeared two months later in the July 1959 *Fantastic Universe* as "Robot Justice," is a bit better, about a man sentenced to 20 years of drudgery by an automated judicial system, with his sentence lengthened or shortened as the system observes his behavior. Eventually he loses it, starts smashing everything in sight in the courtroom including the robot judge, and discovers he can live free of surveillance within the center of the system itself—except he isn't the first to have had that idea. It's a pretty good museum exhibit of the 1950s' SF preoccupation with a regimented and depersonalized future. Merril gave Honorable Mentions to both of these latter stories.

Richard Wilson's "Deny the Slake" (**76**, from the April 1957 *Infinity*) at first reads like one of his usual lightweight insipidly comic space-fillers, but this one has a sting. Explorers from Earth find a planetoid where all the inhabitants have turned to dust. Their main mode of expression was doggerel couplets. Two survivors are found, bearing the nasty revelation of who they are and why they've almost all died; pity and terror in a teacup.

Harlan Ellison makes his first appearance in *New Worlds* (he's been in *Science Fantasy*) with "Life Hutch" (**75**), from the April 1956 *If*, one of his better early stories, almost Campbellian. A space pilot with damaged ship makes it to a life-saving installation, but the robot assistant, controlled by a computer inside the hutch's walls, has gone berserk and lashes out at anything that moves, including the protagonist. How not to get killed?

Damon Knight appears in **84** with "Idiot Stick," reprinted from *Star Science Fiction Stories 4*, published the previous year in the U.S. As usual for Knight it's very readable, but it's not one of his better stories. Aliens arrive on Earth, eager to build some stuff, and buy a labor force with little bubble-like capsules that make people happy. But an alien gets drunk on aspirin and reveals that they are building a doomsday machine to blow the planet up. Earthfolks take the marvelous tools they are given to work with, figure out how to make weapons of them, and kick alien butt in the best Eric Frank Russell style. Unaccountably, Judith Merril gave this an Honorable Mention. Knight has the *New Worlds* Profile, sans photograph but with cartoony sketch by Knight (or knight) himself. The text is equally cartoony ("Knight...has since been instrumental in bringing to the science fiction public such now-famous institutions as the NFFF,[80]

---

80. I.e., National Fantasy Fan Federation.

Famous Fantastic Mysteries, Sam Moskowitz and the Milford Science Fiction Writers' Conference.") and there's nothing in it worth recounting.

§

To the dregs. "Aberration" by Roy Robinson and J.A. Sones **(88)** is a peculiarly clumsy story in which, at great length, the leaders of a post-nuclear computer-regimented society discover that their economic statistics deviate a bit from the supposed norm, showing that somebody is engaged in illicit manipulation of some sort. But that's impossible, because they'd have to know all the data that is closely held by the leaders and that almost nobody has access to in its entirety. Obviously there's a telepath in their midst! There ensues an elaborate scheme to catch the hypothetical telepath without the telepath's knowing what the scheme is, culminating in the telepath's falling off a building as they close in on him. The whole thing makes little sense and has the creaky and amateurish quality that marked *New Worlds* in earlier years but had mostly been banished by this point. Robinson had one more story in *New Worlds* in 1963. Apart from that, neither byline appeared in the SF magazines again.

"Peace on Earth" by Michael Barrington **(89)** opens with Bulik and Fra-Thala arriving on an Earth deserted and uninhabitable, at the direction of the Book, which says the Meaning of Life will be found there. Like everybody else in this far future, they are immortal. Roaming around, they find the body of a man who they realize is *dead*. They realize they've used up their air supply and will shortly join him. Hey, that's it! "[T]he intervening few seconds of his life were charged with meaning." Michael Barrington, according to Miller/Contento, was Michael Moorcock and Barrington Bayley in collaboration. So maybe it's a put-on. I was briefly afraid it would be a Christmas story.

§

So what are the best achievements of this period? Dick's *Time Out of Joint*, obviously. Of the short fiction, the outstanding items are Aldiss's "The Pit My Parish," Ballard's "The Waiting Grounds," and White's "Tableau," with respectable runners-up in Aldiss's "Incentive" and "Segregation," Kapp's "Breaking Point," Presslie's "Another Word for Man," and—dare I say it—Rayer's "Continuity Man." What's striking is how many stories fall short of this level by only a little: White's "Grapeliner," Kapp's "Life Plan" and "Survival Problem," Presslie's "One for the Road," High's "The Guardian," Rayer's "I Like You," Harrison's "I See You," Sellings' "The Shadow People" and "For the Colour of His Hair," and Barclay's "Nearly Extinct." A fat and respectable anthology could be put together from these years, perfectly competitive with, say, *The Fifth* (or *Sixth*) *Galaxy Reader*, which drew on multiple years from around the same time. This is the first period for which that could be said of *New Worlds*.

§

Carnell's long ascent had taken him and his magazine from the primitive early post-war issues of 1946 through the grim, shortage-ravaged opening years of the 1950s and then, step by grueling step, to the solid accomplishment of the closing years of that decade. Meanwhile, he'd expanded the range of his offerings into the quirky and usually better written work of Aldiss, Ballard, Brunner, and newcomers such as Michael Moorcock and Thomas Burnett Swann, in *Science Fantasy*, and a revival of more traditional space frolics in *Science Fiction Adventures*.

In the 1960s, as we'll see in the next volume, Carnell published another 54 substantial issues, struggling for air against the pressure of paperback competition and changes in public taste as a generation that would remake Britain and then the world was crystallizing "the Sixties." In his magazine's first decade and a half, the world had morphed to a striking degree, had become in some measure a genuinely new world, and *New*

Worlds had to change to keep up, let alone ahead. In the erroneous Lamarckism favored by so many of Carnell's writers, it was a hopeful monster striving to evolve into the future while clinging desperately with its hind claws to the eroding past.

Yet however far the post-Carnell *New Worlds* eventually veered from the magazine's prior trajectory—when it became, under Moorcock, Bailey, Ballard, Disch, Platt, Sladek, Spinrad, Zoline and others, the harbinger and flagship of the much reviled, much admired "New Wave"—it was the name, the reputation, and the market niche established under Carnell that made the ground-breaking magazine of the mid and late 1960s possible.

ABOUT THE AUTHORS

JOHN BOSTON is Director of the Prisoners' Rights Project of the New York City Legal Aid Society, where he has worked for many years, and is co-author of the *Prisoners' Self-Help Litigation Manual*.

DAMIEN BRODERICK is an Australian science fiction writer, editor and critical theorist, with a Ph.D. from Deakin University. Formerly a senior fellow in the School of Culture and Communication at the University of Melbourne, he currently lives in San Antonio, Texas. He has written or edited some 60 books, including *Reading by Starlight*, *x, y, z, t: Dimensions of Science Fiction*, and *Unleashing the Strange*. *The Spike* was the first full-length treatment of the technological Singularity, and *Outside the Gates of Science* is a study of parapsychology. His 1980 novel *The Dreaming Dragons* (revised in 2009 as *The Dreaming*) is listed in David Pringle's *Science Fiction: The 100 Best Novels*—and with Paul Di Filippo, he has written a sequel to Pringle's book, *Science Fiction: The 101 Best Novels, 1985-2010*. His recent short story collections are *Uncle Bones*, *The Qualia Engine*, and *Adrift in the Noösphere*.

INDEX OF NAMES

Bryning, Frank, 254-56, 270

Budrys, Algis, 155, 283

Bull, Reina, 63-64, 115

Bulmer, Kenneth, 75, 121, 133, 139, 150, 165-67, 191, 193, 198, 221-22, 224, 272, 277, 300-01, 306, 321, 338-39

Burke, J(onathan) F., 70, 79, 113-14, 137, 179

Burks, Arthur J., 36, 79-80, 116

Burroughs, William, 266

Caesari, Victor, 19

Campbell, H. J., 66, 77

Campbell, John W., Jr., 21, 23, 44, 71, 80, 92, 180, 271, 314, 342

Carnell, Edward John (Ted, or John), *passim.*

Carr, John Dickson, 76

Carver, Philip, 261

Chand, Dhun Robin, 230

Chandler, A. Bertram, 34, 38, 48-49, 78, 99, 101, 107, 173, 193-94, 251, 254-55, 340-42

Chapman, G. Ken, 63, 75, 77, 193

Christopher, John (Sam Youd), 79, 106-07, 113, 116, 130, 150, 172, 186, 266, 288

Clarke, Arthur C., 12-13, 30-31, 34-35, 38, 44-45, 57, 59, 66, 69, 72, 74, 76-77, 106, 118, 120, 131, 135, 137, 141, 150, 172, 203, 229, 264, 266, 270, 272, 284, 288, 299, 337, 349

Clebert, Jean-Paul, 291

Clement, Hal, 141, 267, 333

Clinton, Rupert (Kenneth Bulmer), 300, 301

Clothier (artist), 33-34, 63-65

Clute, John, 17, 238

Cockcroft, W. P., 27

Cole, Les, 36

Collier, John, 76

Conklin, Groff, 76, 122, 140, 209

Conquest, Robert, 273

Contento, William G., 17

Cooper, Edmund, 290

Cooper, Frank, 75

Maslowski, Igor B., 76, 140

Mason, Jeff, 94

Matheson, Richard, 229

McCarey, Howard Lee (Richard Rowland), 184

McClelland, Paul, 261

McComas, J. Francis, 76, 140

McIntosh, J. T. (James Murdoch McGregor), 79, 81, 88-93, 96, 118-28, 134-35, 141, 147, 173-78, 186, 194, 204-11, 215, 255, 261, 266, 284, 288-89, 294

McPhail, Dan, 74

Mead, Harold, 130, 273

Mead, Shepherd, 141

Medlen, David, 256

Mercer, Archie, 74

Merril, Judith, 76, 120, 177, 186, 207, 219, 230, 252, 265, 288, 303, 314, 325, 327, 330, 334, 345, 350, 353

Merritt, A., 267

Metcalf, Norman C., 299

Miller, Walter M., Jr., 96

Miller, P. Schuyler, 140, 192, 196, 200, 298

Miller, Stephen T., 17

Moorcock, Michael, 9-10, 21, 31, 94, 152, 237, 254, 302, 306, 327, 337, 340, 345, 348, 354-56

Moore, W., 60

Moore, Ward, 60, 137, 141

Mordecai, Lew, 66

Morgan, Dan, 79, 81, 112, 116, 121, 148, 182-83, 193, 200, 227-28, 236-37, 293, 330, 348

Moskowitz, Sam, 230, 354

Neal, Gavin, 185

Newman, John, 75, 77, 139-40, 191

Nicholls, Peter, 17

Nicholson, R. D., 288

Norton, Andre, 51, 103

Oliver, Chad, 120, 149, 204

Ostlund, Sigvard, 76

INDEX OF TITLES

Lightning Source UK Ltd.
Milton Keynes UK
UKOW03f1032140414

229923UK00001B/161/P

9 781434 445872